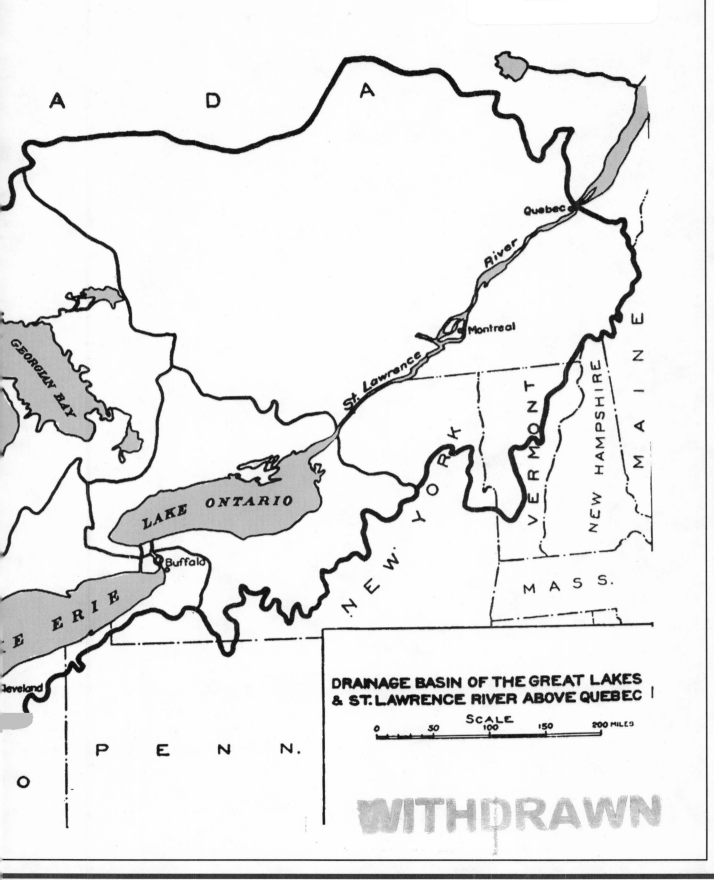

DRAINAGE BASIN OF THE GREAT LAKES
& ST. LAWRENCE RIVER ABOVE QUEBEC

SCALE

0   50   100   150   200 MILES

SHIPPING LITERATURE OF THE GREAT LAKES

A CATALOG OF COMPANY PUBLICATIONS

1852-1990

SHIPPING LITERATURE OF THE GREAT LAKES

A CATALOG OF COMPANY PUBLICATIONS

1852-1990

Compiled by
Le Roy Barnett

Michigan State University Press
East Lansing
1992

Copyright © 1992 Le Roy Barnett

All Michigan State University Press books are produced on paper which meets the requirements of American National Standard of Information Sciences—Permanence of paper for printed materials ANSI Z39.48-1984

Michigan State University Press
East Lansing, MI 48823-5202

Printed in the United States of America

00   99   98   97   96   95   94   93   92   1   2   3   4   5   6   7   8   9   10

Library of Congress Cataloging-in-Publication Data
Barnett, Le Roy
    Shipping Literature of the Great Lakes: a catalog of company publications, 1852-1990
edited [i.e. compiled] by Le Roy Barnett.
       p.   cm.
    Includes index.
    ISBN 0-87013-317-9 (alk. paper)
    1. Shipping—Great Lakes—Bibliography—Union Lists.
2. Advertising—Shipping—Great Lakes—Bibliography—Union Lists.
3. Catalogs, Union—United States. 4. Catalogs, Union—Canada.
I. Title.
Z7164.S55B37   1992
[HE398]
016.386'5'0977—dc20

Maps and graphs designed by Sherman Hollander

CONTENTS

ILLUSTRATIONS

TABLES

v

ACKNOWLEDGMENTS

Though an author, like a woman giving birth, gets credit for the new creation, there are usually a number of other people involved in the process who helped to make the blessed event possible. The genesis of this volume comes not from one individual—as the main entry implies—but is to some extent the product of a group effort. The supporting cast for this book is too large to cite individually, but a few persons do merit special mention.

Under the heading of foreign aid, I am pleased to recognize the assistance of John Burtniak (Special Collections at Brock University), Berthe LeSage (Canada Steamship Lines), Dawn Monroe (Public Archives of Canada), and Diane Thompson (National Library of Canada).

On the domestic scene, I must single out for attention and gratitude individuals like Ken Pott, of the Lake Michigan Maritime Museum; Jay Martin, formerly at the Institute for Great Lakes Research; the Crossman family; Martin McLaughlin of the State Archives of Michigan; Caroline Schofield of the Library of Michigan; Bob Coren and his staff at the National Archives; Sterling Berry of Grosse Pointe; and especially John Polacsek, of the Dossin Great Lakes Museum, who did more to support this enterprise than any other public servant with whom I worked.

At the institutional level, appreciation is due the Bureau of History (Department of State) for the support that it gave this undertaking, especially the Archives Unit. And recognition is in order for Fred Bohm, of the MSU Press, who made it possible for this bibliography to be shared with the general public. I also wish to acknowledge the contributions of the staff at the MSU Press, whose sharp eyes and sound advice enabled me to avoid making a number of grammatical and stylistic mistakes. Any errors found in this text—be they of fact or format—are those of the author.

Finally, like any other proud parent, I must thank my spouse for helping to bring this project to fruition. Without her patience and encouragement, this checklist would never have survived its long gestation period. It is to her, its foster mother, that this book is dedicated.

FOREWORD

During the last century and a half, the Great Lakes shipping companies have printed a substantial amount of material relating to their operations. These publications are mainly sailing schedules, tourist promotional pieces, annual reports, and so forth, primarily issued in the form of pamphlets and brochures. This literature is scattered all across North America in scores of public repositories, quite often uncataloged in ephemera collections. This situation makes it very difficult for someone to find Great Lakes navigation paper, particularly if they are looking for a spcific item.

As reference archivist for the State of Michigan, this problem has long been apparent to me. Quite often I was called upon to advise or help people who were seeking information on a particular fleet or ship. Since no access tool had been prepared that aided research in this area, I could only suggest that the person in need contact some of the larger maritime museums or collections in the United States and Canada. This response, dictated by circumstances, troubled me because of its inadequacy. Even the national data bases like OCLC and RLIN were of little help, since few institutions will take the time to catalog navigation company literature due to its specialized nature and unconventional format. Something had to be done, I felt, to correct this situation.

Seeing no evidence that a solution to the problem was forthcoming, I decided to attempt a remedy on my own. Consequently, I resolved to try to track down and catalog all of the substantive printed items that were ever issued by shipping companies operating on the Great Lakes. The information acquired about each published piece would be recorded in a standard library format, with the resulting list arranged alphabetically by name of firm and then chronologically by item. Excluded from the scope of this enterprise were paper things of marginal informational value like tickets, menus, wine cards, napkins, posters, handbills, playing cards, post cards, window cards, counter cards, matchbooks, fans, calendars, stationery, envelopes, mailing labels, luggage tags, identification tags, certificates, ink blotters, place mats, bookmarks, passes, and minor give-away items that were little more than insignificant promotional trimmings.

The product of this exercise you now hold in your hands. It does not, as I wished, account for every publication issued by Great Lakes navigation firms, because not all printed items still survive or have been deposited with public research facilities. This book does, however, identify about 80 percent of all literature ever issued by the shipping companies that plied our inland seas, and this sample should prove adequate to serve most users. So, historians, librarians, business scholars, book dealers, maritime enthusiasts, travel specialists, collectors, and the general inquisitive public will find herein a source of data that will help them with their respective endeavors.

By creating this reference tool, it is my desire to benefit more than just the individual researcher. Ideally, the existence of this checklist will encourage further study into the history of Great Lakes freight and passenger transportation, with the resulting books and articles serving to enlighten us all. Such an inventory will also, I hope, alert public institutions to the need for additional collecting in this area, and prompt them to fill in some of the voids revealed by this union list. Finally, I would like to think that this compilation would have a positive impact on the business community. When the staff of shipping firms examine this work and see how little evidence remains of some enterprises, perhaps they will be inclined to donate their corporate records to archival institutions for preservation and public access. Only in this way will we be able to substantially increase the volume of material upon which Great Lakes maritime research is based.

There are 3,042 entries in this catalog of navigation literature. Of this number, 1,540 items (or 50 percent) are represented by just one copy known to exist in a public facility. This fact is significant because it

1. shows how rare most of these publications are;

2. indicates a need for institutional buying in this neglected subject area; and

3. may help to alert holding repositories to the importance of protecting these scarce materials from possible theft.

If the history of the Great Lakes shipping industry is to be properly documented, the kinds of printed records described in this book will have to be more vigorously pursued and more widely collected than is presently the case with libraries, archives, and museums.

INTRODUCTION

Vacation, excursion, recreational, or pleasure cruising on the Great Lakes goes back nearly 200 years. For the first half century of this business, advertising was mainly limited to black and white posters, handbills, fliers, newspapers, and so forth. Starting about 1850, promotional notices began appearing with regularity in guidebooks, city directories, gazetteers, and other kinds of volumes. These announcements were usually devoid of pictures except for the possible inclusion of a standardized image of a ship. By around 1880 this means of communication was no longer capable of permitting steamship companies to compete effectively for tourists and travellers. A new form of media was needed to attract more customers, so the illustrated brochure or pamphlet was increasingly employed by the industry to announce its services.

This literature, though rather simple at first, soon became quite elaborate and decorative. The stimulus for this trend was the perceived public belief that the more sophisticated the handout, the more superior the shipping line. By approximately 1890 the ornate style of navigation printing was coupled with Art Nouveau color to dramatically increase the visual impact of promotional releases. This advertising trend was continued and accelerated when Art Deco productions became popular about 1925. By the time this form of expression had run its course around 1940, shipping enterprises had already started to abandon the fashion for simpler designs. Due to hard economic times, shipping firms became conservative in their spending to save money. Their publications became smaller and less artistic, eventually returning to the basic styles more characteristic of former years. Currently the industry seems to be leaning toward larger and flashier announcements, but there are so few active firms left that for all practical purposes Great Lakes navigation literature can be considered a genre of the past.

The publications of the shipping industry evolved not just artistically, but informationally as well. Initially these printed works were little more than sailing schedules with, perhaps, rates or fares included. Eventually a map of the route was added along with a picture of a vessel or the fleet emblem. This ensemble continued to develop over time, with some literature containing cruise itineraries, brief descriptions of the places to be visited, and details on the connections possible to other destinations with a list of the agents to see for reservations. The most complete productions might also describe the various tours offered by the line, the kinds of service available on board ship, plans and/or profiles of the vessel, plus general information about maritime travel and nautical matters.

Though some Great Lakes tourist promotional literature has been found dating as early as 1852, steamship and navigation companies did not begin to extensively issue advertising booklets and folders until the 1880s. The graph that follows shows that reliance upon this means of communication remained rather limited and stable through 1892. The following year saw the Columbian Exposition in Chicago, and many transportation companies plying Lake Michigan offered to carry passengers to and from this grand function by announcing their services in brochures and handouts (see figure 1).

This use of promotional material proved effective, prompting an overall increase in reliance upon this medium to stimulate Great Lakes travel. With the exception of a slight decline during World War I, the employment of paper to attract cruise business stayed rather constant until the mid-1930s. Then, in 1936, the amount of advertising literature in circulation increased again as America began to slowly emerge from the Great Depression and its citizens were more inclined to vacation afloat. Soon after, World War II brought gas rationing and large paychecks for defense workers, a combination that made Great Lakes voyages even more heavily promoted and popular. Though the post-war period saw a decline in the number of publications issued by the Midwest's freshwater fleet, the total amount of copy distributed remained historically high.

The level of printed navigation advertising after World War II stayed fairly stable until the middle 1960s, when the annual amount declined by more than half. The reason for this was largely attributable to the decommissioning or reassignment of many ships involved in the recreational trade. In 1965, for example, Canadian Pacific Railway and the Canada Steamship Lines both discontinued carrying passengers on the Great Lakes. Two years later, in 1967, the Chicago, Duluth & Georgian Bay Transit Company followed suit and ceased operating its steamers. The

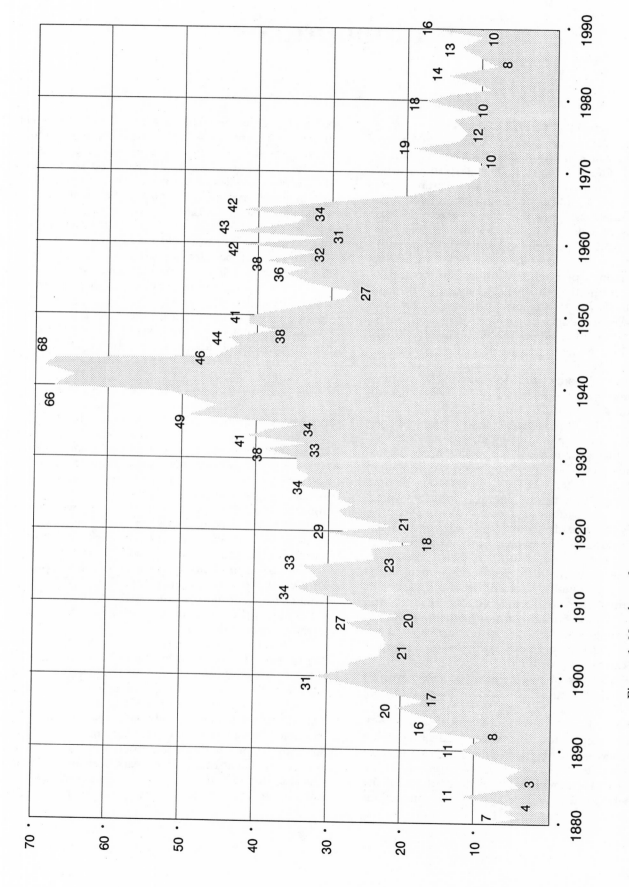

Figure 1. Number of printed materials from Great Lakes navigation companies, 1880-1990

result of this withdrawal from the tourist industry was a significant and permanent drop in the amount of Great Lakes navigation literature being generated.

The abbreviated trend established two and a half decades ago was not the only change in the industry. The nature of the publications being crafted began to differ from most of those produced prior to the late 1960s. Earlier, much of the literature being issued by Great Lakes shipping firms was designed to promote fairly lengthy recreational travel. Generally offered were tours lasting from three to fourteen days, the type of vacation that called for a descriptive brochure of some size and substance. Over the past 25 years, however, nearly all of the advertising pieces that have appeared are for the purpose of publicizing short ferryboat rides to island destinations. It is doubtful if we will ever see again the type of elaborate production that was once representative of the Great Lakes passenger business.

Because of their historical, informational, and artistic value, the publications of shipping companies are highly sought after by collectors. The number of items available to this fraternity are quite limited, however, for a couple of reasons. First, the industry tried to print just what the market called for and no more. This meant that there was a limited production to begin with, with more editions circulated only if demand was underestimated.

Navigation paper was treated like most other ephemera and simply discarded when it was out of date. The genre was created as cheaply as possible for immediate use or to serve a short-term purpose. When its limited period of validity had expired, the item was thrown away or even intentionally destroyed and replaced by a newer version.

Finally, the rate schedules, holiday guides, and informational leaflets produced by the navigation industry were usually small in size. This design enabled interested individuals to pick up the promotional pieces and carry them in a pocket. Advertising paper of a diminutive nature was often damaged in the course of such handling or was treated with less respect than was the case with larger or more substantial productions. These factors combine to make scarce a resource that is today in great demand by individuals and institutions.

Museums, for example, seek these brochures and pamphlets for use as popular exhibit pieces. Libraries and archives, looking for windows to the past, acquire shipping literature for its informational value. And boat buffs, wishing to possess interesting remnants of a lost era, search out these publications as romantic souvenirs of certain ships or fleets. Because of this strong competition for a relatively rare commodity, it is not uncommon to see navigation items from even the twentieth century selling for $50 to $100. At these prices, no person or repository can afford to assemble a large amount of this paper. Therefore, most of this material is scattered about North America in rather small collections, many of them uncataloged or poorly identified.

The dispersed nature of shipping company publications, and their tendency to be relegated to vertical files or low priority handling, means that it is impossible to know what has been saved by publically accessible establishments. Few libraries, archives, museums, or historical societies will take time to fully catalog these materials or enter them into the national data bases. Consequently, anyone wishing to track down a particular navigation item must telephone, write, or visit a long list of possible holding repositories to see if one of them has the desired piece. By using this union list, one can see at a glance if the sought after article exists and which institutions own it. It is hoped that, by taking the arduous effort out of research, this book will stimulate people to study, learn about, and write accounts of Great Lakes navigation and the firms involved in its development.

GUIDE TO USING THIS UNION LIST

Represented in this compilation are publications issued by 230 different shipping firms that operated on the Great Lakes. In every case, the corporation is listed as the author of the work, even if a person is cited as having contributed to the piece. The most productive concern was Canada Steamship Lines, which has 373 releases to its credit (446 entries if its Northern Navigation Division is included). The next most fruitful business is the Chicago, Duluth & Georgian Bay Transit Company at 317 entries, and the Detroit & Cleveland Company comes in third with a 210 count. Together, these three transportation concerns account for nearly a third of all the publications issued by the Great Lakes navigation industry.

Following the business name and the firm's city of residence, there is a brief history of the enterprise. Since much of this information was obtained from governmental sources, the dates given are often filing dates with a state or provincial office and not necessarily the actual dates of incorporation. However, any time differences between these acts should amount to no more than a few days.

In other matters of corporate history, one often encounters a dearth of information or even conflicting accounts about a shipping company's past. When evaluating these data, the author has used those descriptions of a business's evolution that best squared with the facts as he knew them. It is quite possible that, in the process of weighing different versions of a navigation firm's development, an incorrect choice was made. Errors of this nature, if any, are regretted and are solely the responsibility of the author.

Most of the literature included in this work are folders and brochures. Since these formats seldom have title pages like books, the descriptive information for each piece was usually taken from the covers. With each piece the title was recorded as it appeared on the printed item, with the Anglo-American Cataloging Rules being followed for style and format. When deemed necessary, words have been supplied [in square brackets] to make the title statement read smoother or more intelligibly. Most abbreviations have been fully spelled out to eliminate any chance of confusion on the part of the reader.

Often displayed in small type near the back of the pamphlet is the name of the company that did the printing. When this information was not disclosed in the publication, an effort was made to contact the issuing corporation or its former employees to garner these facts. The places of publication for materials included in this book, and the number of items produced in each city, are listed below. When the place of publication is not known, the code "N.p." is entered (No place). Similarly, when the date of publication is not known, the code "N.d." is used (No date).

Table 1. Places of publication for items cited in this work (total 983).

Chicago, IL	317	Petoskey, MI	9
Detroit, MI	148	Cheboygan, MI	8
Buffalo, NY	84	Midland, ONT	8
Sandusky, OH	57	Philadelphia, PA	7
Montreal, QUE	54	Put-in-Bay, OH	7
Cleveland, OH	32	Ludington, MI	6
Toronto, ONT	29	Eau Claire, WI	5
Lansing, MI	21	Green Bay, WI	5
New York, NY	21	Lockport, NY	5
Milwaukee, WI	20	Port Huron, MI	5
Boston, MA	16	Sarnia, ONT	5
Saint Joseph, MI	14	Battle Creek, MI	4
Rochester, NY	12	Watertown, NY	4
Ashland, WI	11	Kenton, OH	3
Grand Rapids, MI	11	Saint Catharines, ONT	3
Owen Sound, ONT	11	Sault Sainte Marie, MI	3

continued on next page

Table 1 continued

Toledo, OH	3	Kingston, ONT	1
Boyne City, MI	2	London, England	1
Clayton, NY	2	Madison, WI	1
Collingwood, ONT	2	Meaford, ONT	1
Duluth, MN	2	Netherlands	1
Hamilton, ONT	2	North Bay, ONT	1
Saint Paul, MN	2	Pittsburgh, PA	1
Virginia, MN	2	Pontiac, MI	1
Benton, Harbor MI	1	Rockford, IL	1
Cincinnati, OH	1	Saint Ignace, MI	1
Elyria, OH	1	Sturgeon Bay, WI	1
Findlay, OH	1	Traverse City, MI	1
Grand Marais, MI	1	Warrington, England	1
Grand Rapids, MI	1	West Nyack, NY	1
Kalamazoo, MI	1	Weston, ONT	1

There were a few firms in the Midwest that specialized in publishing promotional literature for Great Lakes steamship and navigation companies, a phenomenon indicated by the fact that 56% of the traceable printed items were produced in just three cities. Paramount among the custom presses was Poole Brothers, of Chicago, who accounted for nearly a third of all the material that had an imprint. Ranking second in activity was John Bornman & Son, of Detroit, with the Matthews-Northrup firm, of Buffalo, coming in third.

Following each imprint in this book are statements about the physical characteristics of each item. Since many of the things circulated by navigation companies were variously sized sheets of paper folded in small compass, the number of pages may on occasion also be interpreted to mean number of panels. Noting the presence of an illustration means that the item has pictures, deck plans, or ship profiles. Signifying the existence of a map indicates that the work includes a cartographic expression of some type.

The final statement for each entry is the symbol for the holding repository. Standard Library of Congress codes are used, and a complete listing of these abbreviations begins on the next page. All citations are taken from Symbols of American Libraries, the standard manual for such information. The most extensive holdings of shipping company literature will be found at CSmH, CU-SB, MSaP, MdBUS, MiD-D, OBgU, and ViNeM.

KEY TO LIBRARY SYMBOLS

CLU	Main Library, University of California, 405 Hilgard Avenue, Los Angeles, CA 90024
CSFMM	National Maritime Museum, Foot of Polk Street, San Francisco, CA 94109
CSmH	John H. Kemble Collection, Huntington Library, 1151 Oxford Road, San Marino, CA 91108
CSt	Hopkins Transportation Library, Stanford University, Stanford, CA 94305
CU-BANC	Bancroft Library, University of California, Berkeley, CA 94720
CU-SB	Romaine Collection, Special Collections Department, University of California, Santa Barbara, CA 93106
CaACG	Glenbow Alberta Institute, 9th Avenue & 1st Street SE, Calgary, Alberta, Canada T2G 0P3
CaBVaMM	Maritime Museum of British Columbia, 28 Bastion Square, Victoria, British Columbia, Canada V8W 1H9
CaBVaU	University of British Columbia, 2075 Westbrook Mall, Vancouver, British Columbia, Canada V6T 1W5
CaBViP	Legislative Library, Parliament Buildings, Victoria, British Columbia, Canada V8V 1X4
CaBViPA	Provincial Archives, 655 Belleville Street, Victoria, British Columbia, Canada V8V 1X4
CaMWU	DaFoe Library, University of Manitoba, Winnipeg, Manitoba, Canada R3T 2N2
CaNBFU	University of New Brunswick, Fredericton, New Brunswick, Canada E3B 5A3
CaNBSM	New Brunswick Museum, 277 Douglas Avenue, St. John, New Brunswick, Canada E2K 1E5
CaNSHPL	Nova Scotia Provincial Library, 6955 Bayers Road, Halifax, Nova Scotia, Canada B3L 4S4
CaOColM	Collingwood Museum, Memorial Park, St. Paul Street, Collingwood, Ontario, Canada L9Y 4B2
CaOH	Hamilton Public Library, 55 York Boulevard, Hamilton, Ontario, Canada L8R 3K1
CaOHM	Wills Memorial Library, McMaster University, 1280 Main Street West, Hamilton, Ontario, Canada L8S 4L6
CaOKMM	Marine Museum of the Great Lakes, 55 Ontario Street, Kingston, Ontario, Canada K7L 2Y2
CaOKQ	Rare Book Room, Queens University, Kingston, Ontario, Canada K7L 3N6
CaOKQAR	Archives & Historical Collections, Queens University, Kingston, Ontario, Canada K7L 3N6
CaOLU	Regional History Collection, University of Western Ontario, London, Ontario, Canada N6A 3K7
CaOMM	Moore Museum, 94 William Street, Mooretown, Ontario, Canada N0N 1M0
CaOOA	Public Archives of Canada, 395 Wellington Street, Ottawa, Ontario, Canada K1A 0N3
CaOOCC	Carleton University, Colonel By Drive, Ottawa, Ontario, Canada K1S 5J7
CaOOG	Geological Survey of Canada, 601 Booth Street, Ottawa, Ontario, Canada K1A 0E8
CaOOND	Canada Department of National Defense, 101 Colonel By Drive, Ottawa, Ontario, Canada K1A 0K2
CaOONG	National Gallery of Canada, 380 Sussex Drive, Ottawa, Ontario, Canada K1A 9N4
CaOONL	National Library of Canada, 395 Wellington Street, Ottawa, Ontario, Canada K1A 0N3
CaOOP	Library of Parliament, Parliament Buildings, Ottawa, Ontario, Canada K1A 0A9
CaOORD	Department of Indian Affairs and Northern Development, Ottawa, Ontario, Canada K1A 0H4
CaOOT	Canada Ministry of Transport, Place de Ville, Tower C, Ottawa, Ontario, Canada K1A 0N5
CaOOU	University of Ottawa, 65 University, Ottawa, Ontario, Canada K1A 9A5
CaOOwCG	Owen Sound Museum, 975 Sixth Street East, Owen Sound, Ontario, Canada N4K 1G9
CaOOwM	Marine-Rail Museum, 1165 First Avenue West, Owen Sound, Ontario, Canada N4K 4K8
CaOPeT	Bata Library, Trent University, Peterborough, Ontario, Canada K9J 7B8
CaOPoCM	Historical & Marine Museum, 280 King Street, Port Colborne, Ontario, Canada L3K 5X8
CaOPsM	West Parry Sound District Museum, Parry Sound, Ontario, Canada P2A 2X4
CaOStC	St. Catharines Public Library, 54 Church Street, St. Catharines, Ontario, Canada L2R 7K2
CaOStCB	Special Collections, Brock University, St. Catharines, Ontario, Canada L2S 3A1
CaOTAG	Art Gallery of Ontario, 317 Dundas Street West, Toronto, Ontario, Canada M5T 1G4
CaOTAr	Public Archives of Ontario, 77 Grenville Street, Toronto, Ontario, Canada M7A 2R9
CaOTHCA	Toronto Harbour Commission Archives, 60 Harbour Street, Toronto, Ontario, Canada M5J 1B7
CaOTMMUC	Marine Museum of Upper Canada, Exhibition Place, Toronto, Ontario, Canada M6K 3C3
CaOTP	Toronto Public Library, 789 Yonge Street, Toronto, Ontario, Canada M4W 2G8
CaOTPB	Baldwin Room, Toronto Public Library, 789 Yonge Street, Toronto, Ontario, Canada M4W 2G8
CaOTRM	Royal Ontario Museum, 100 Queen's Park, Toronto, Ontario, Canada M5S 2C6
CaOTY	York University, 4700 Keele Street, North York, Ontario, Canada M3J 1P3
CaOWA	Leddy Library, University of Windsor, Windsor, Ontario, Canada N9B 3P4
CaQMBM	Bibliotheque Municipale de Montreal, 1210 Sherbrooke East, Montreal, Quebec, Canada H2G 2H3

CaQMBN	Bibliotheque Nationale du Quebec, 1700 rue St. Denis, Montreal, Quebec, Canada H2X 3K6
CaQMCCA	Canadian Centre for Architecture, 1920 rue Baile, Montreal, Quebec, Canada H3H 2S6
CaQMFA	Montreal Museum of Fine Arts, 3400 Avenue du Musee, Montreal, Quebec, Canada H3G 1K3
CaQMG	Concordia University, 1455 de Maisonneuve Boulevard West, Montreal, Quebec, Canada H3G 1M8
CaQMHE	Ecole des Hautes Etudes Commerciales, 5255 Decelles Avenue, Montreal, Quebec, Canada H3T 1V6
CaQMM	McLennan Library, McGill University, 3459 McTavish Street, Montreal, Quebec, Canada H3A 1Y1
CaQMMRB	Rare Book Collection, McGill University, Montreal, Quebec, Canada H3A 1Y1
CaQMU	University de Montreal, 2900 Boulevard Edouard-Montpetit, Montreal, Quebec, Canada H3C 3J7
CaQQL	Bibliotheque de la Legislature de la Province de Quebec, Quebec, Quebec, Canada G1A 1A5
CaQQS	Seminaire de Quebec, 9 rue de l'Universite, Quebec, Quebec, Canada G1R 4R7
CaSRU	University of Regina Library, Regina, Saskatchewan, Canada S4S 0A2
CaSSU	University of Saskatchewan, Saskatoon, Saskatchewan, Canada S7N 0W0
CtMyMHi	G.W. Blunt White Library, Mystic Seaport Museum, Mystic, CT 06355
CtY	Sterling Memorial Library, Yale University, New Haven, CT 06520
DLC	Library of Congress, 10 First Street SE, Washington, DC 20540
DPU	Organization of American States, 17th Street & Constitution Avenue NW, Washington, DC 20006
DSI	Smithsonian Institution, Museum of American History, 12th Street & Constitution Avenue, Washington, DC 20560
DeU	Morris Library, University of Delaware, Newark, DE 19717-5267
ICF	Field Museum of Natural History, Roosevelt Road & Lake Shore Drive, Chicago, IL 60605
ICHi	Chicago Historical Society, Clark Street at North Avenue, Chicago, IL 60614
ICU	Regenstein Library, University of Chicago, 1100 East 57th Street, Chicago, IL 60637
ICF	Field Museum of Natural History, Roosevelt Road & Lake Shore Drive, Chicago, IL 60605
IEN-T	Transportation Library, Northwestern University, Evanston, IL 60208
IHi	Illinois State Historical Library, Old State Capitol, Springfield, IL 62706
IU	University of Illinois Library, 1408 West Gregory Drive, Urbana, IL 61801
KyLoU	Ekstrom Library, University of Louisville, Louisville, KY 40292
MB	Boston Public Library, Copley Square, Boston, MA 02117-0286
MH	Widener Memorial Library, Harvard University, Cambridge, MA 02138
MH-BA	Baker Library, Harvard University, Soldiers Field Road, Boston, MA 02163
MHi	Massachusetts Historical Society, 1154 Boylston Street, Boston, MA 02215
MSaP	Phillips Library, Peabody Maritime Museum, East India Square, Salem, MA 01970
MWA	American Antiquarian Society, 185 Salisbury Street, Worcester, MA 01609
MdBUS	Steamship Historical Society, University of Baltimore Library, 1420 Maryland Avenue, Baltimore, MD 21201
MeCasM	Nutting Memorial Library, Maine Maritime Academy, Castine, ME 04421
Mi	Library of Michigan, 717 West Allegan Street, Lansing, MI 48909
Mi-MISPC	Mackinac Island State Park Commission, Department of Natural Resources, Lansing, MI 48909
MiBayHi	Bay County Historical Museum, 1700 Center Avenue, Bay City, MI 48708
MiD-B	Burton Historical Collection, Detroit Public Library, 5201 Woodward Avenue, Detroit, MI 48202
MiD-D	Dossin Great Lakes Museum, 100 Strand Drive, Belle Isle, Detroit, MI 48207
MiDA	Detroit Institute of Arts, 5200 Woodward Avenue, Detroit, MI 48202
MiDbEI	Edison Institute, Henry Ford Museum, 20900 Oakwood Boulevard, Dearborn, MI 48121
MiGr	Michigan Room, Grand Rapids Public Library, 60 Library Plaza NE, Grand Rapids, MI 49503
MiGrH	Loutit Public Library, 407 Columbus Street, Grand Haven, MI 49417
MiGrM	Public Museum of Grand Rapids, 54 Jefferson Avenue SE, Grand Rapids, MI 49503
MiHC	State Archives of Michigan, Michigan Bureau of History, 717 West Allegan, Lansing, MI 48918
MiHM	Archives & Historical Collections, Michigan Technological University, Houghton, MI 49931
MiHolJA	Joint Archives of Holland, Van Wylen Library, Hope College, Holland, MI 49423
MiKW	Archives & Historical Collections, Western Michigan University, Kalamazoo, MI 49008
MiLuRH	Rose Hawley Museum, 115 West Loomis Street, Ludington, MI 49431
MiManiHi	Manistee County Historical Museum, 425 River Street, Manistee, MI 49660
MiMarqHi	Marquette County Historical Society, 213 North Front Street, Marquette, MI 49855
MiMtpC	Clarke Historical Library, Central Michigan University, Mount Pleasant, MI 48858
MiPh	Local History Room, St. Clair County Public Library, 210 McMorran Boulevard, Port Huron, MI 48060
MiPhM	Museum of Arts & History, 1115 Sixth Street, Port Huron, MI 48060
MiShM	Canonie Library, Lake Michigan Maritime Museum, South Haven, MI 49090

MiStj	Palenske Memorial Library, 500 Market Street, St. Joseph, MI 49085
MiU	Harlan Hatcher Graduate Library, University of Michigan, Ann Arbor, MI 48109
MiU-C	William L. Clements Library, 909 South University Avenue, Ann Arbor, MI 48109
MiU-H	Bentley Historical Library, 1150 Beal Avenue, Ann Arbor, MI 48105
MiU-RBSC	Rare Books and Special Collections, Harlan Hatcher Library, University of Michigan, Ann Arbor MI, 48109
MiU-T	Transportation Collection, Undergraduate Library, University of Michigan, Ann Arbor, MI 48109
MnDuC	Canal Park Marine Museum, Corps of Engineers Area Office, 600 Lake Avenue South, Duluth, MN 55802
MnDuI	William A. Irvin Museum, 350 South 5th Avenue West, Duluth, MN 55802
MnDuLS	Lake Superior Museum of Transportation, 506 West Michigan Street, Duluth, MN 55802
MnDuU	Northeast Minnesota Historical Center, University of Minnesota, Duluth, MN 55812
MnHi	Minnesota Historical Society, 690 Cedar Street, Saint Paul, MN 55101
MoKU	University of Missouri Library, Rockhill Road, Kansas City, MO 64110
MoSHi	Missouri Historical Society, Jefferson Memorial Building, St. Louis, MO 63112
MoSMB	Barriger Collection, Saint Louis Mercantile Library, 510 Locust Street, Saint Louis, MO 63101
N	New York State Library, Empire State Plaza, Albany, NY 12230
NBu	Buffalo & Erie County Public Library, Lafayette Square, Buffalo, NY 14203-1887
NBuU	Main Library, State University of New York at Buffalo, Buffalo, NY 14206
NBuHi	Buffalo & Erie County Historical Society, 25 Nottingham Court, Buffalo, NY 14216
NN	New York Public Library, Fifth Avenue & 42nd Street, New York, NY 10018
NNC	Marvyn Scudder Collection, Thomas Watson Library, Columbia University, New York, NY 10027
NNH	Hispanic Society of America, 613 West 155th Street, New York, NY 10032
NPlaU	Benjamin F. Feinberg Library, Draper Avenue, State University of New York, Plattsburgh, NY 12901
NR	Rochester Public Library, 115 South Avenue, Rochester, NY 14604
NRU	Rush Rhees Library, University of Rochester, Rochester, NY 14627
NcD	William R. Perkins Library, Duke University, Durham, NC 27706
NjP	Firestone Library, Princeton University, Princeton, NJ 08544
OBgU	Institute for Great Lakes Research, Bowling Green State University, 12764 Levis Parkway, Perrysburg, OH 43551
OCl	Cleveland Public Library, 325 Superior Avenue, Cleveland, OH 44114
OClWHi	Western Reserve Historical Society, 10825 East Boulevard, Cleveland, OH 44106
OFH	Rutherford B Hayes Library, 1337 Hayes Avenue, Fremont, OH 43420
OHi	Ohio Historical Society, I-71 and 17th Avenue, Columbus, OH 43211
OKentU	Main Library Building, Kent State University, Kent, OH 44242-0001
OLaK	Lakewood Public Library, 15425 Detroit Avenue, Lakewood, OH 44107
OLimaACH	Allen County Museum, Library Unit, 620 West Market Street, Lima, OH 45801
OO	Mudd Library Center, 148 West College Street, Oberlin College, Oberlin, OH 44074
OSandF	Oran Follett House Museum, 404 Wayne Street, Sandusky, OH 44870
OV	Great Lakes Historical Society, 480 Main Street, Vermilion, OH 44089
PHi	Historical Society of Pennsylvania, 1300 Locust Street, Philadelphia, PA 19107
PP	Free Library of Philadelphia, Logan Square, Philadelphia, PA 19103
PPPMM	Philadelphia Maritime Museum, 321 Chestnut Street,Philadelphia, PA 19106
RPB	John D. Rockefeller Library, Brown University, Providence, RI 02912
TxU	Perry-Castaneda Library, University of Texas, Austin, TX 78713
ViCFC	Chesapeake & Ohio Historical Society, 312 East Ridgeway Street, Clifton Forge, VA 24422
ViN	Norfolk Public Library, 301 East City Hall Avenue, Norfolk, VA 23510
ViNeM	Mariners' Museum Library, 100 Museum Drive, Newport News, VA 23606
VtU	Bailey-Howe Memorial Library, University of Vermont, Burlington, VT 05405
WGrM	Neville Public Museum, 210 Museum Place, Green Bay, WI 54303-2780
WHi	State Historical Society of Wisconsin, 816 State Street, Madison, WI 53706
WLacU	Special Collections Center, Murphy Library, University of Wisconsin, LaCrosse, WI 54601
WM	Marine Room, Milwaukee Public Library, 814 West Wisconsin Avenue, Milwaukee, WI 53233
WMCHi	Milwaukee County Historical Society, 910 North Third Street, Milwaukee, WI 53203
WManiM	Manitowoc Maritime Museum, 75 Maritime Drive, Manitowoc, WI 54220
WaSp	Spokane Public Library, Comstock Building, 906 West Main Avenue, Spokane, WA 99201
WaT	Tacoma Public Library, 1102 Tacoma Avenue South, Tacoma, WA 98402
WaU	Suzzallo Library, University of Washington, Seattle, WA 98195-0001

SHIPPING COMPANIES

ALGOMA CENTRAL & HUDSON BAY RAILWAY COMPANY, MARINE DEPARTMENT, SAULT STE. MARIE ONT

Established in July of 1900, when the firm was known as the Algoma Central Railway Company. Acquired corporate name shown above on 23 May 1901. Ceased passenger service in 1917. Name changed to Algoma Central Railway on 30 June 1965.

Algoma Central steamship line [serving] Sandusky, Toledo, Georgian Bay and Lake Superior, 1907. [N.p., 1907]. 30 [i.e. 16] p. Illus., map. MSaP, ViNeM.

ALGOMA CENTRAL RAILWAY, MARINE DIVISION, SAULT STE. MARIE, ONT

Established on 30 June 1965. Purchased Nipigon Transport, Limited, on 27 March 1986. On 30 April 1990 it became the Algoma Central Corporation. The tradition of beginning all ship names with "Algo" dates from the 1930s.

Christening of the M[otor] V[essel] "Roy A[delbert] Jodrey" ceremony performed at Collingwood, Ontario, by Mrs. Roy A[delbert] Jodrey [on] Tuesday, Nov. 9th, 1965. [N.p., 1965]. 1 sheet folded to [6] p. Illus. MiD-D.

Sir Denys Lowson on steady progress [with] good shipping developments. London, ENG: Times Newspapers, Limited, [1969]. [8] p. (3 blank). "Reprinted from the [London] Times Company meetings, Saturday, May 3, 1969." OBgU.

M[otor] V[essel] Algosea, self unloading bulk carrier for Great Lakes and ocean service. [N.p., 1976]. 1 sheet folded to [4] p. Illus. OBgU.

Ceremony performed at Collingwood, Ontario, by Mrs. W[illia]m G[renville] Davis of Brampton, Ontario, Wednesday, April 6, 1977, [at the christening of the Motor Vessel Algolake]. [N.p., 1977]. [8] p. Illus. MiD-D.

Ceremony performed at Collingwood, Ontario, by Mrs. C[edric] E[lmer] Ritchie of Toronto, Ontario, Monday, June 19, 1978, [at the christening of the Motor Vessel Algobay]. [N.p., 1978]. [8] p. Illus. MiD-D.

Ceremony performed at Collingwood, Ontario, by Mrs. H[enry] R[owell] Jackman of Toronto, Ontario, Monday, May 7, 1979, [at the christening of the Motor Vessel Algoport]. [N.p., 1979]. [8] p. Illus. MiD-D.

Christening ceremony performed at Collingwood, Ontario, by Mrs. D[ouglas] A[lbert] Berlis [on] Tuesday, October 7, 1980, [for the] M[otor] V[essel] Algowood. [N.p., 1980]. [4] p. Illus. MiD-D.

Algoma Central Railway Marine Division. [N.p., 1981]. 32 p. Illus., map. OBgU.

Algoma Central, Marine Division [fleet list]. [N.p., 1987]. [38 whole, 36 half] p. Illus., map. CaOKMM.

AMERICAN-CANADIAN LINE, INCORPORATED, WARREN, RI

Incorporated on 7 April 1980. Name changed to American-Canadian-Caribbean Line, Incorporated, on 18 January 1989

Discover the wild beauty of Georgian Bay/Great Lakes/Saguenay River aboard the new "Caribbean Prince" Canadian & Northern cruises, 1984. [N.p., 1984]. 1 sheet folded to [8] p. Illus., map. MiD-D, OBgU.

AMERICAN OIL COMPANY, MARINE DEPARTMENT, WHITING, IL

Established about 1962 as a name change to Standard Oil Company's operations. Title ends around 1972 with another change to Amoco Oil Company.

Safety manual [for] lake tanker and towboat operations. [N.p., 1969?]. [3], 89, [4] leaves. Contained in a 3-ring binder, pagination may vary. MiD-D.

AMERICAN STEAMSHIP COMPANY, BUFFALO, NY

Established in March of 1907 as a New York firm. Operated by Boland & Cornelius, Incorporated, until 1980. Acquired a half interest in the Amersand Steamship Corporation around 1952. Merged with the Oswego Shipping Corporation on 1 March 1967. Took over the Reiss Steamship Company in 1969. Became a part of GATX Corporation (General American Transportation) on 1 July 1973. Acquired the Gartland Steamship Company on 28 July 1986. Still active in 1990.

Statement of American Steamship Company, season 1940. [N.p., 1941]. [4] p. CtY.

Launching & christening [of the] St[eame]r John J[onathan] Boland, Manitowoc, Wisconsin, May 9, 1953. [N.p., 1953]. 1 sheet folded to [12] p. Illus. MiD-D, NBuHi, WManiM.

Launching & christening [of the] St[eame]r Detroit Edison, Manitowoc, Wisconsin, September 9, 1954. [N.p., 1954]. [10] p. Illus. MiD-D, WManiM.

Group insurance for our employees, unlicensed personnel of the American Steamship Company [and the] Amersand Steamship Corporation. [N.p., 1956]. 21, [1] p. OBgU.

Agreement between [the] American Steamship Company, the Amersand Steamship Company, and the Brotherhood of Licensed Personnel and Stewards of the Great Lakes, July, 1960. [Detroit, 1960]. 22 p. OBgU.

Group insurance program, licensed personnel [of the] American Steamship Co. and [the] Amersand Steamship Corp., as amended, effective June 17, 1960. [N.p., 1960]. 20 p. OBgU.

American Steamship Company 1965 annual report. [N.p., 1966]. [12] p. Illus. OV.

Navigation and piloting primer. [Buffalo?, 1976]. iii, 70 leaves. Illus. MeCasM.

Safety manual. [Buffalo?, 1976]. 40 leaves. MeCasM.

Agreement between [the] American Steamship Company and Amersand Steamship Corporation and District 2 [of the] Marine Engineers Beneficial Association, A[merican] F[ederation] [of] L[abor]-C[ongress] [of] I[ndustrial] O[rganizations], and Associated Maritime Officers (a division of District 2 Marine Engineers Beneficial Association) covering licensed officers and stewards, August 1, 1977. [N.p., 1977]. 67, [1] p. MeCasM.

Always be safety conscious. [Buffalo?, 1978]. 46 p. MeCasM.

1978-1981 freighter agreement between [the] Seafarers International Union—Atlantic, Gulf, Lakes and Inland Waters District, A[merican] F[ederation] [of] L[abor]-C[ongress] [of] I[ndustrial] O[rganizations]—and Great Lakes Association of Marine Operators, representing American Steamship Company and Amersand Steamship Corporation, Cement Transit Company, Erie Sand Steamship Company, Erie Navigation Company, the Cement Division (Huron) of National Gypsum Company, Litton Great Lakes Corporation, [and] Pringle Transit Company. [N.p., 1978]. 21, [1] p. MeCasM.

Soundings. — Vol. 1, no. 1 (March 1981)-present. — Buffalo, 1981-present. Illus. Irregular. MiD-D, MnDuC, OBgU, WM, WManiM.

How to make a steamship float and other Great Lakes recipes. Boyne City, MI: Harbor House Publishers, c1984. 135, [1] p. Illus. MiD-D, MnDuC, OBgU.

How to make a steamship float and other Great Lakes recipes. Boyne City, MI: Harbor House Publishers, c1985. 135, [1] p. Illus. MiMtpC, N, OCl.

AMERICAN TRANSPORTATION COMPANY, BUFFALO, NY

Organized on 24 January 1854. Date of dissolution unknown.

Articles of association of the American Transportation Company, the by-laws of the company, and the rules of order of the directors thereof, with the act under which such company is incorporated and that part of the revised statutes referred to therein. Buffalo: Democracy Association Print, 1855. 32 p. NBuHi.

Articles of association of the American Transportation Company, the by-laws of the company, and the rules of order of the directors thereof, with the act under which such company is incorporated and those parts of the revised statutes referred to therein, &c. Buffalo: Seaver's Steam Printing Establishment, 1856. 36 p. NBuHi.

Rules, directions and orders of the American Transportation Company to the agents, masters and employees. Buffalo: Thomas & Lathrops, [1856?]. 27, [1] p. NBuHi.

ANN ARBOR RAILROAD COMPANY, TOLEDO, OH

Organized on 21 September 1895, inheriting a lake car-ferry service that had started on 24 November 1892. Ferry operations were technically controlled by a proprietary firm, the Ann Arbor Boat Company, until 1943, when the parent company took over. Abandoned its route from Frankfort to Manistique on 5 August 1968, and its link from Frankfort to Menominee in January of 1970. The railroad stopped scheduled passenger service in 1971 and declared bankruptcy on 15 October 1973. The operation of the ferries was reactivated by the Consolidated Rail Corporation under state subsidy in 1976. The ferries were taken over on 1 October 1977 by the Michigan Interstate Railway Company.

Ann Arbor Railroad and Steamship Lines. Chicago: Poole Bros., [1911]. 38 [i.e. 20] p. Illus., map. WM.

Ann Arbor Railroad and Steamship Lines. Cincinnati: Spencer & Craig Printing Works, [1923]. 14 [i.e. 8] p. Illus., map. Effective June 16, 1923. MiHC

Ann Arbor Railroad and Steamship Lines local time tables. [N.p., 1927]. 1 sheet folded to [8] p. Map. Corrected to Nov. 1st, 1927. MiU-RBSC.

Ann Arbor Railroad [operating] six large modern steel steamships carrying automobiles & tourists. [N.p., 1930?]. 1 sheet folded to [8] p. Illus., map. WManiM.

Ann Arbor Railroad [operating] six large modern steel steamships carrying automobiles & tourists, 1931. [N.p., 1931]. 1 sheet folded to [8] p. Illus., map. WM.

Auto ferry across Lake Michigan via [the] Ann Arbor Railroad, six large modern steel steamships carrying automobiles & tourists, 1932. [N.p., 1932]. 1 sheet folded to [8] p. Illus, map. WM.

Auto ferry across Lake Michigan via [the] Ann Arbor Railroad, six large modern steel steamships carrying automobiles & tourists, season 1934. [N.p., 1934]. 1 sheet folded to [12] p. Illus., map. ViNeM, WM.

Auto ferry across Lake Michigan via [the] Ann Arbor Railroad, six large modern steel steamships carrying automobiles & tourists, season 1935. [N.p., 1935]. 1 sheet folded to [12] p. Illus., map. ViNeM.

Auto ferry across Lake Michigan via [the] Ann Arbor Railroad, six large modern steel steamships carrying automobiles & tourists, season 1936. [N.p., 1936]. 1 sheet folded to [12] p. Illus., map. MdBUS, MiD-D.

Auto ferry across Lake Michigan via [the] Ann Arbor Railroad, six large modern steel steamships carrying automobiles & tourists, season 1937. [N.p., 1937]. 1 sheet folded to [12] p. Illus., map. OBgU, WM.

Auto ferry across Lake Michigan via [the] Ann Arbor Railroad, modern steel steamships carrying automobiles & tourists, season 1938. [N.p., 1938]. 1 sheet folded to [12] p. Illus., map. WM.

Auto ferry across Lake Michigan via [the] Ann Arbor Railroad, modern steel steamships carrying automobiles & tourists, June 9th, 1939. [N.p., 1939]. 1 sheet folded to [12] p. Illus., map. CSmH, MiD-D.

Auto ferry across Lake Michigan via [the] Ann Arbor Railroad, modern steel steamships carrying automobiles & tourists, season 1939. [N.p., 1939]. 1 sheet folded to [12] p. Illus., map. MiD-D, MiShM.

Ann Arbor Railroad auto ferry across Lake Michigan, the shortest auto route across Lake Michigan, June, 1940. [N.p., 1940]. 1 sheet folded to [12] p. Illus, map. CSmH, MiD-D, MiShM, OBgU, OFH.

Ann Arbor Railroad auto ferry across Lake Michigan, modern steel steamships carrying automobiles & tourists, May, 1941. [N.p., 1941]. 1 sheet folded to [12] p. Illus., map. CSmH, MiD-D, OBgU, WM, WManiM.

Ann Arbor Railroad auto ferry across Lake Michigan, modern steel steamships carrying automobiles & tourists, May, 1942. [N.p., 1942]. 1 sheet folded to [12] p. Illus., map. CSmH, CU-SB, MiD-D, MnDuC, WM.

Ann Arbor Railroad auto ferry across Lake Michigan, modern steel steamships carrying automobiles & tourists, May, 1943. [N.p., 1943]. 1 sheet folded to [12] p. Illus., map. CU-SB, MiD-D, MiGr, MnDuC, OFH, WM.

Time tables [for] train and steamship, effective April 15, 1943. [N.p., 1943]. 1 sheet folded to [4] p. MiManiHi.

Ann Arbor Railroad auto ferry across Lake Michigan, modern steel steamships carrying automobiles & tourists, May, 1944. [N.p., 1944]. 1 sheet folded to [12] p. Illus., map. MdBUS, MiD-D, WMCHi.

Ann Arbor Railroad auto ferry across Lake Michigan, modern steel steamships carrying automobiles & tourists, May, 1945. [N.p., 1945]. 1 sheet folded to [12] p. Illus., map. CU-SB, MiD-D, OBgU, WM.

Ann Arbor Railroad auto ferry across Lake Michigan, modern steel steamships carrying automobiles & tourists, season 1946. [N.p., 1946]. 1 sheet folded to [8] p. Illus., map. CSmH, CU-SB, MiD-D, MiGr, WM.

Ann Arbor Railroad auto ferry across Lake Michigan, modern steel steamships carrying automobiles & tourists, season 1947. [N.p., 1947]. 1 sheet folded to [8] p. Illus., map. CU-SB, MiD-D, MiMtpC, MiShM, OBgU.

Ann Arbor Railroad auto ferry across Lake Michigan, modern steel steamships carrying automobiles & tourists, season 1948. [N.p., 1948]. 1 sheet folded to [8] p. Illus., map. CU-SB, MiD-D.

Ann Arbor Railroad auto ferry across Lake Michigan, modern steel steamships carrying automobiles & tourists, season 1949. [N.p., 1949]. 1 sheet folded to [8] p. Illus., map. CSmH, CU-SB, MiD-D, MiShM, WManiM.

Ann Arbor Railroad auto ferry across Lake Michigan, modern steel steamships carrying automobiles & tourist [sic], season 1950. [N.p., 1950]. 1 sheet folded to [8] p. Illus., map. MiD-D.

Ann Arbor Railroad auto ferry across Lake Michigan, [the] short auto route across Lake Michigan, season 1951. [N.p., 1951]. 1 sheet folded to [8] p. Map. MiD-D, MnDuC.

Ann Arbor Railroad auto ferry across Lake Michigan, modern steel steamships carrying automobiles & tourist [sic], season 1952. [N.p., 1952]. 1 sheet folded to [8] p. Illus., map. MiD-D.

Ann Arbor Railroad auto ferry across Lake Michigan, modern steel steamships carrying automobiles & tourist [sic], season 1953. [N.p., 1953]. 1 sheet folded to [8] p. Illus., map. CSmH.

Ann Arbor Railroad auto ferry across Lake Michigan, modern steel steamships carrying automobiles & tourist [sic], season 1954. [N.p., 1954]. 1 sheet folded to [8] p. Illus, map. WM.

Ann Arbor Railroad auto ferry across Lake Michigan, modern steel steamships carrying automobiles & tourist [sic], season 1955. [N.p., 1955]. 1 sheet folded to [6] p. Illus., map. WManiM.

Ann Arbor Railroad auto ferry across Lake Michigan, modern steel steamships carrying automobiles & tourist [sic], season 1956. [N.p., 1956]. 1 sheet folded to [6] p. Illus., map. OBgU, WM.

Ann Arbor Railroad auto ferry across Lake Michigan, modern steel steamships carrying automobiles & tourist [sic], season 1957. [N.p., 1957]. 1 sheet folded to [6] p. Illus, map. CSmH, MdBUS, MiD-D, WM, WManiM.

Ann Arbor Railroad auto ferry across Lake Michigan, modern steel steamships carrying automobiles & tourist [sic], season 1958. [N.p., 1958]. 1 sheet folded to [6] p. Illus., map. MiD-D.

Ann Arbor Railroad auto ferry across Lake Michigan, season 1959. [N.p., 1959]. 1 sheet folded to [6] p. Illus., map. MoSMB, WM, WManiM.

Ann Arbor Railroad auto ferry across Lake Michigan, season 1960. [N.p., 1960]. 1 sheet folded to [6] p. Illus., map. MiMtpC, MiShM, MoSMB, WM, WManiM.

Ann Arbor Railroad carferry schedule. [N.p., 1964]. 1 sheet folded to [6] p. Maps. Summer schedule. MiD-D.

Ann Arbor Railroad carferry schedule. [N.p., 1964]. 1 sheet folded to [6] p. Maps. Fall schedule. MiD-D, MiU-H, OFH, ViNeM, WManiM.

Ann Arbor Railroad carferry schedule, Frankfort, Mich., to Kewaunee, Wisc., Manitowoc, Wisc., Menominee, Mich., [and] Manistique, Mich., 1965 summer schedule effective June 12 thru September 12, 1965. [N.p., 1965]. 1 sheet folded to [6] p. Maps. MiD-D, MiMtpC, MiShM, OBgU, OFH, WM, WManiM.

Ann Arbor Railroad carferry schedule, Frankfort, Mich., to Kewaunee, Wisc., Manitowoc, Wisc., Menominee, Mich., [and] Manistique, Mich., 1966 summer schedule effective June 12 thru September 12, 1966. [N.p., 1966]. 1 sheet folded to [6] p. Maps. MiD-D, MiMtpC, MiShM, OBgU, WM, WManiM.

Ann Arbor Railroad carferry schedule, Frankfort, Mich., to Kewaunee, Wisc., Manitowoc, Wisc., Menominee, Mich., [and] Manistique, Mich., 1967 summer schedule effective June 11 thru September 11, 1967. [N.p., 1967]. 1 sheet folded to [6] p. Maps. MdBUS, Mi, MiD-D, MiShM, MnDuC, OBgU, WM, WManiM.

Ann Arbor Railroad carferry schedule, Frankfort, Mich., to Manitowoc, Wisc., Kewaunee, Wisc., [and] Menominee, Mich., 1968 summer schedule effective June 8 thru September 8, 1968. [N.p., 1968]. 1 sheet folded to [8] p. Maps. MiShM, WM, WManiM.

Ann Arbor Railroad carferry schedule, 1969 summer schedule effective June 14 thru September 7, 1969. [N.p., 1969]. 1 sheet folded to [8] p. Maps. CSmH, Mi, MiD-D, OBgU, OFH, WManiM.

Ann Arbor Railroad carferry schedule, Frankfort, Mich., to Manitowoc, Wisc. [and] Kewaunee, Wisc., 1970 summer schedule effective June 20 thru September 13, 1970. [N.p., 1970]. 1 sheet folded to [8] p. Illus., maps. CSmH, WManiM.

Ann Arbor Railroad carferry schedule, Frankfort, Mich., to Manitowoc, Wisc. [and] Kewaunee, Wisc., 1971 summer schedule effective May 28 thru September 12, 1971. [N.p., 1971]. 1 sheet folded to [8] p. Illus., maps. MiD-D, MiMtpC, MiShM, OBgU, OFH, ViNeM, WManiM.

ANONYMOUS

Under this heading are listed those pieces of literature for which no corporate author can be found.

Three grand excursions on the steamers W[illiam] R[ouse] Clinton and J[ames] W[ynward] Steinhoff to Lakes Erie and St. Clair. [Detroit]: Free Press Print, [1875]. 1 sheet folded to [4] p. Illus. MiD-D.

APOSTLE ISLANDS CRUISE SERVICE, LIMITED, WASHBURN, WI

Incorporated on 14 April 1987 as successor to Apostle Islands Outfitters, Incorporated. Still active as of 1990.

Cruise Lake Superior's Apostle Islands National Lakeshore. [Ashland, WI, 1987]. 1 sheet folded to [6] p. Illus. MnDuC, WM.

Cruise Lake Superior's Apostle Islands National Lakeshore [revised schedule]. [Ashland, WI, 1987]. 1 sheet folded to [6] p. Illus., maps. WM.

Cruise Lake Superior's Apostle Islands National Lakeshore [on] Apostle Islands excursions. [Ashland, WI, 1989]. 1 sheet folded to [6] p. Illus., map. MiD-D.

Cruise Lake Superior's Apostle Islands National Lakeshore [on] Apostle Islands excursions. [Ashland, WI, 1990]. 1 sheet folded to [6] p. Illus., map. MiD-D.

APOSTLE ISLANDS OUTFITTERS, INCORPORATED, BAYFIELD, WI

Incorporated on 13 May 1974. Succeeded by Apostle Islands Cruise Service, Limited. Dissolved on 29 June 1989.

Apostle Islands excursions, Bayfield, Wisconsin, 1977. [Ashland, WI, 1977]. 1 sheet folded to [6] p. Illus., maps. WM.

Cruise Lake Superior's Apostle Islands National Lakeshore, Bayfield, Wisconsin. [Ashland, WI, 1978]. 1 sheet folded to [6] p. Illus., maps. WM.

Apostle Islands cruises, cruise Lake Superior and scenic Apostle Islands National Lakeshore. [Ashland, WI, 1979]. 1 sheet folded to [6] p. Illus., maps. WM.

Apostle Islands cruises, cruise the Apostle Islands National Lakeshore on scenic Lake Superior. [Ashland, WI, 1981]. 1 sheet folded to [8] p. Illus., maps. WM.

Apostle Islands cruises, you'll find forests, sea caves, trout, sandy coves, sea gulls, fresh air, sunsets, on the largest body of fresh water in the world, Lake Superior. [Ashland, WI, 1983]. 1 sheet folded to [8] p. Illus., maps. WM.

Apostle Islands cruises, you'll find forests, sea caves, trout, sandy coves, sea gulls, fresh air [and] sunsets on the largest body of fresh water in the world, Lake Superior. [Ashland, WI, 1985]. 1 sheet folded to [8] p. Illus., maps. WM.

Apostle Islands cruises, you'll find forests, sea caves, trout, sandy coves, sea gulls, fresh air [and] sunsets...on the largest body of fresh water in the world!, Lake Superior. [Ashland, WI, 1986]. 1 sheet folded to [6] p. Illus., maps. OBgU.

APOSTLE ISLANDS TRANSPORTATION COMPANY, BAYFIELD, WI

Incorporated on 11 September 1926. Charter forfeited on 1 January 1938. Involuntarily dissolved on 2 January 1979.

To the Apostle Islands via the steamer Madeline. [N.p., 193?]. 1 sheet folded to [6] p. Illus., map. MiD-D.

ARNOLD TRANSIT COMPANY, MACKINAC ISLAND, MI

Incorporated 23 February 1900. Absorbed the Island Transportation Co. in May of 1946. Acquired the Straits Transit Co. in April of 1977. Still active as of 1990.

The Arnold Line steamers [offer] side trips from Mackinac. [Grand Rapids, MI: Dean Print, 1898]. [6] p. One folded map. WM.

Arnold Transit Company, the "Soo" route. [N.p., 1908]. 1 sheet folded to [12] p. Illus., map. WM.

Map of Les Cheneaux Islands reached by the Arnold Line steamers. St. Ignace, MI: Jones' Enterprise Press, [1909?]. 1 sheet folded to [24] p. with 8 panels blank. Illus., map. Mi-MISPC.

Bird's eye view of Les Cheneaux Islands. [N.p.], c1910. 1 sheet folded in covers. OBgU.

Bird's eye view of Michigan looking south from Sault S[ain]te. Marie. [N.p.], c1910. 1 sheet folded in covers. Illus., map. Text on verso. OBgU.

Arnold Transit Company, the "Soo" route, the "Western Hudson," the "Snows" route, [and] the "fishing grounds," 1911. Detroit: Stubbs-Esterling Printing Co., [1911]. [24] p. Illus., maps. MiD-B.

Arnold Transit Company, the "Snows" route, the "fishing grounds," the "Soo" route, [and] the "Western Hudson." [Chicago: Poole Bros., 1914]. [16] p. Illus., maps. WM.

Arnold Transit Company trips [to the] Straits of Mackinac and through [the] beautiful Les Cheneaux Islands.

Chicago: Poole Bros., [1924]. 1 sheet folded to [8] p. Illus. MiD-D.

Trips [to the] Straits of Mackinac and through beautiful Les Cheneaux Islands. Chicago: Poole Bros., [1925]. 1 sheet folded to [8] p. Illus. CSmH, MiD-D.

Mackinac Island, Les Cheneaux Islands, and St. Ignace-Cheboygan services. [Sault Sainte Marie, MI]: Sault News Printing Co., [1932]. 1 sheet folded to [8] p. Illus. MiD-D, WM.

Mackinac Island, Les Cheneaux Islands, and St. Ignace-Cheboygan services. [Sault Sainte Marie, MI]: Sault News Printing Co., [1933]. 1 sheet folded to [8] p. Illus. MiD-D, WM.

Mackinac, the island of romance, summer schedules via steamboats and speed cruisers. [N.p., 1935]. 1 sheet folded to [12] p. Illus., map. MiD-D.

Mackinac, the island of romance, departures from [the] St. Ignace state ferry dock, advance summer & fall season schedule. [N.p., 1936?]. 1 sheet folded to [4] p. Map. MiD-D.

Mackinac, the island of romance, summer schedules via steamboats and speed cruisers. [N.p., 1936]. 1 sheet folded to [12] p. Illus., map. OBgU.

"Arnold Line" service schedules [for] Mackinac Island, St. Ignace, Cheboygan, and through beautiful Les Cheneaux Islands, July 1, 1940. [N.p., 1940]. 1 sheet folded to [4] p. Illus., map. CSmH, MiD-D.

"Arnold Line" service schedules [for] Mackinac Island, St. Ignace, Cheboygan, and through beautiful Les Cheneaux Islands, July 1, 1941. [N.p., 1941]. 1 sheet folded to [4] p. Illus., maps. CSmH, WM.

"Arnold Line" service schedules [for] Mackinac Island, St. Ignace [and] Cheboygan, July 1, 1942. [N.p., 1942]. 1 sheet folded to [4] p. Illus., maps. CU-SB.

"Arnold Line" service schedules [for] Mackinac Island, St. Ignace [and] Mackinaw City, June 16, 1944. [N.p., 1944]. 1 sheet folded to [4] p. Illus., maps. CU-SB, MiD-D.

"Arnold Line" service schedules [for] Mackinac Island, St. Ignace, Cheboygan, and through [the] beautiful Les Cheneaux Islands, July 1, 1945. [N.p., 1945]. 1 sheet folded to [4] p. Illus., maps. CSmH, CU-SB, MiD-D.

Mackinac Island, St. Ignace, Mackinaw City, and through [the] beautiful Les Cheneaux Islands, June 16, 1946. [N.p., 1946]. 1 sheet folded to [4] p. Illus., maps. CU-SB, MiD-D.

Mackinac Island, St. Ignace, Mackinaw City, and through [the] beautiful Les Cheneaux Islands, May 30, 1947. [N.p., 1947]. 1 sheet folded to [4] p. Illus., maps. MiD-D.

Les Cheneaux, [a] vacation paradise [reached by] daily excursion [on the] M[otor] S[hip] Ottawa. [N.p., 1948?]. 1 sheet. Illus., map. MiD-D.

Mackinac Island, St. Ignace, Mackinaw City, and through [the] beautiful Les Cheneaux Islands, June 15, 1948. [N.p., 1948]. 1 sheet folded to [4] p. Illus., maps. CU-SB, MiD-D.

Mackinac Island, St. Ignace, Mackinaw City, and through [the] beautiful Les Cheneaux Islands, May 20, 1949. [N.p., 1949]. 1 sheet folded to [4] p. Illus., maps. CSmH, MiD-D, MiShM, WManiM.

Mackinac Island, St. Ignace, Mackinaw City, and through [the] beautiful Les Cheneaux Islands, May 20, 1950. [N.p., 1950]. 1 sheet folded to [4] p. Illus., maps. MiD-D, OBgU, OFH.

Mackinac Island, St. Ignace, Mackinaw City, and through [the] beautiful Les Cheneaux Islands, June 21, 1952. [N.p., 1952]. 1 sheet folded to [4] p. Illus., maps. MiD-D.

Mackinac Island, St. Ignace, Mackinaw City, and through [the] beautiful Les Cheneaux Islands, June 21, 1953. [N.p., 1953]. 1 sheet folded to [4] p. Illus., maps. OBgU.

Mackinac Island, St. Ignace, Mackinaw City, and through [the] beautiful Les Cheneaux Islands, July 1, 1954. [N.p., 1954]. 1 sheet folded to [4] p. Illus., maps. MiD-D.

Mackinac Island, St. Ignace, Mackinaw City, and through [the] beautiful Les Cheneaux Islands, March 11, 1955. [N.p., 1955]. 1 sheet folded to [4] p. Illus., maps. MiD-D.

Mackinac Island, St. Ignace, Mackinaw City, and through [the] beautiful Les Cheneaux Islands, June 20, 1955. [N.p., 1955]. 1 sheet folded to [4] p. Illus., maps. CSmH, MiD-D, MiMtpC, OFH.

Mackinac Island, St. Ignace, Mackinaw City and through [the] beautiful Les Cheneaux Islands, April 14, 1956. [N.p., 1956]. 1 sheet folded to [4] p. Illus., map. ViNeM.

Mackinac Island, St. Ignace, Mackinaw City, and through [the] beautiful Les Cheneaux Islands, April 23, 1956. [N.p., 1956]. 1 sheet folded to [4] p. Illus., maps. MiD-D.

Mackinac Island, St. Ignace, Mackinaw City, and through [the] beautiful Les Cheneaux Islands, April 2, 1957. [N.p., 1957]. 1 sheet folded to [4] p. Illus., maps. MiD-D.

Mackinac Island, St. Ignace, Mackinaw City, and through [the] beautiful Les Cheneaux Islands, June 6, 1957. [N.p., 1957]. 1 sheet folded to [4] p. Illus., maps. CSmH, MiD-D.

Mackinac Island, St. Ignace, Mackinaw City, and through [the] beautiful Les Cheneaux Islands, July 1, 1958. [N.p., 1958]. 1 sheet folded to [4] p. Illus., map. MiD-D, WManiM.

Mackinac Island, St. Ignace, Mackinaw City, and through [the] beautiful Les Cheneaux Islands, Oct. 15, 1958. [N.p., 1958]. 1 sheet folded to [4] p. Illus., map. MiD-D.

Mackinac Island, St. Ignace, Mackinaw City, and through [the] beautiful Les Cheneaux Islands, June 17,

1959. [N.p., 1959]. 1 sheet folded to [4] p. Illus., maps. CSmH.

Mackinac Island service schedules and speed cruiser services. [N.p., 1960]. 1 sheet folded to [4] p. Illus., maps. OFH.

Mackinac Island [via] safe, fast motorships, February, 1961. [N.p., 1961]. 1 sheet folded to [4] p. Illus., map. CSmH.

Mackinac Island [via] safe, fast motorships, July 1, 1963. [N.p., 1963]. 1 sheet folded to [4] p. Illus., map. MiD-D, MiShM.

Mackinac Island [via] safe, fast motorships, May 20, 1964. [N.p., 1964]. 1 sheet folded to [4] p. Illus., map. MiD-D.

Mackinac Island [via] safe, fast motorships, July 25, 1964. [N.p., 1964]. 1 sheet folded to [4] p. Illus., map. CSmH, OFH.

Mackinac Island [via] safe, fast motorships, July 25, 1965. [N.p., 1965]. 1 sheet folded to [4] p. Illus., map. MiMtpC.

Mackinac Island [via] safe, fast motorships, May 6, 1966. [N.p., 1966]. 1 sheet folded to [4] p. Illus., map. OBgU.

Mackinac Island [via] safe, fast motorships, June 26, 1967. [N.p., 1967]. 1 sheet folded to [4] p. Illus., map. MnDuC, OBgU.

Ferry schedule [to] Mackinac Island, March 1, 1968. [N.p., 1968]. 1 sheet folded to [4] p. Illus., map. MiD-D, OFH.

Ferry schedule [to] Mackinac Island, January 1, 1969. [N.p., 1969?]. 1 sheet folded to [4] p. Illus., map. OBgU, OFH.

100 years of passenger travel, the Mackinac Island boat book. Grand Marais, MI: Voyager Press, c1978. 28 p. Illus. Mi, MiD-D, MiU-H.

Arnold Mackinac Island ferry schedule, 1983. [Petoskey, MI: Little Traverse Printing, 1983]. 1 sheet folded to [4] p. Illus., map. OBgU.

Arnold Mackinac Island ferry schedule, 1984. [Petoskey, MI: Little Traverse Printing, 1984]. 1 sheet folded to [4] p. Illus., maps. CSmH, MiD-D, MiShM, OBgU.

Arnold Mackinac Island ferry schedule, 1986. [Petoskey, MI: Little Traverse Printing, 1986]. 1 sheet folded to [4] p. Illus., map. OBgU, WM.

Arnold Mackinac Island ferry schedule, 1987. [Petoskey, MI: Little Traverse Printing, 1987]. 1 sheet folded to [6] p. Illus., maps. MiD-D, WM.

Arnold Mackinac Island schedule, 1988. [Petoskey, MI: Little Traverse Printing, 1988]. 1 sheet folded to [6] p. Illus., map. MiD-D, WM.

Arnold Mackinac Island catamarans ferry schedule, 1989. [Petoskey, MI: Little Traverse Printing, 1989]. 1 sheet folded to [6] p. Illus., maps. MiD-D, Mi-MISPC.

Arnold Mackinac Island catamarans 1990 ferry schedule. [Petoskey, MI: Little Traverse Printing, 1990]. 1 sheet folded to [6] p. Illus., maps. MiD-D, MiMtpC, MiShM, OBgU.

ASHLEY & DUSTIN STEAMER LINE, DETROIT, MI

Formerly Ashley & Mitchell, the firm was established in 1887. Incorporated 6 March 1911. Dissolved in 1953.

The islands route daily between Sandusky, Kelley's Island, Middle Bass, Put-in-Bay, and Toledo and Cleveland via Put-in-Bay, 1896. Sandusky, OH: Register Press, [1896]. 1 sheet folded to [8] p. Illus., map. MSaP.

Put-in-Bay route [operating] daily between Detroit, Sandusky, Toledo [and] Cleveland via Put-in-Bay. Detroit: John Bornman & Son, [1899]. 1 sheet folded to [8] p. Illus., map. MiD-D.

Put-in-Bay route [operating] daily between Detroit, Sandusky, Toledo [and] Cleveland via Put-in-Bay. [Detroit?, 1902?]. 1 sheet folded to [8] p. Illus., map. MiD-D.

Put-in-Bay route [operating] daily between Detroit, Sandusky, Toledo, Cleveland, [and] Cedar Point via Put-in-Bay. [Detroit?, 1907?]. 1 sheet folded to [8] p. Illus., map. OFH.

Put-in-Bay route [operating] daily between Detroit, Sandusky, Toledo, Cleveland [and] Cedar Point via Put-in-Bay. [Detroit?, 1910]. 1 sheet folded to [8] p. Illus., map. Date from annotation. MiD-D.

Ashley & Dustin Steamer Line, [the] Put-in-Bay route [operating] daily between Detroit, Sandusky, Toledo, Cleveland, Cedar Point [and] Lakeside via Put-in-Bay. [Detroit?, 1911]. 1 sheet folded to [8] p. Illus., map. Effective June 25 to Sept. 10. Date from annotation. MiD-D.

Ashley & Dustin Steamer Line, [the] Put-in-Bay route [operating] daily between Detroit, Sandusky, Toledo, Cleveland, Cedar Point [and] Lakeside via Put-in-Bay. [Detroit?, 1912]. 1 sheet folded to [12] p. Illus., map. Effective June 20 to Sept. 10. Date from annotation. MiD-D.

Ashley & Dustin Steamer Line, [the] Put-in-Bay route [operating] daily between Detroit, Sandusky, Toledo, Cleveland, Cedar Point [and] Lakeside via Put-in-Bay. [Detroit?, 1913]. 1 sheet folded to [12] p. Illus., map. MSaP, MiD-D, OBgU, WHi.

Ashley & Dustin Steamer Line, [the] Put-in-Bay route [operating] daily between Detroit, Sandusky, Toledo, Cleveland, Cedar Point [and] Lakeside via Put-in-Bay. Detroit: John Bornman & Son, [1914?]. 1 sheet folded to [12] p. Illus., map. MdBUS.

Ashley & Dustin Steamer Line, [the] Put-in-Bay route [operating] daily between Detroit, Sandusky, Toledo,

Cleveland, Cedar Point [and] Lakeside via Put-in-Bay. [Detroit?, 1915]. 1 sheet folded to [12] p. Illus., map. Date from annotation. MiD-D.

Ashley & Dustin Steamer Line, [the] Put-in-Bay route [operating] daily between Detroit, Sandusky, Toledo, Cleveland, Cedar Point [and] Lakeside via Put-in-Bay. [Detroit?, 1917]. 1 sheet folded to [12] p. Illus., map. Date from annotation. MiD-D.

Put-in-Bay, now is the time to book your excursion to Put-in-Bay or a moonlight ride next summer. [Detroit?, 1918]. 1 sheet folded to [4] p. Illus., map. MiD-D.

Ashley & Dustin Steamer Line, [the] Put-in-Bay route [operating] daily between Detroit, Sandusky, Toledo, Cleveland, Cedar Point [and] Lakeside via Put-in-Bay. [Detroit?, 1920?]. 1 sheet folded to [12] p. Illus., map. MiD-D.

Ashley & Dustin Steamer Line, [the] Put-in-Bay route [operating] daily between Detroit, Sandusky, Toledo, Cleveland, Cedar Point [and] Lakeside via Put-in-Bay. [Detroit?, 1921?]. 1 sheet folded to [12] p. Illus., map. Mi, MiMtpC.

Ashley & Dustin Steamer Line, [the] Put-in-Bay route [operating] daily between Detroit, Sandusky, Toledo, Cleveland, Cedar Point [and] Lakeside via Put-in-Bay. [Detroit?, 1924]. 1 sheet folded to [12] p. Illus., map. MiD-D.

Ashley & Dustin Steamer Line, [the] Put-in-Bay route [operating] daily between Detroit, Sandusky, Toledo, Cleveland, Cedar Point [and] Lakeside via Put-in-Bay. [Detroit?, 1928]. 1 sheet folded to [12] p. Illus., map. MiD-D.

Ashley & Dustin Steamer Line, [the] Put-in-Bay route [operating] daily between Detroit, Sandusky, Toledo, Cleveland, Cedar Point [and] Lakeside via Put-in-Bay. [Detroit?, 1931]. 1 sheet folded to [12] p. Illus., map. OBgU, ViNeM.

Ashley & Dustin Steamer Line, [the] Put-in-Bay route [operating] daily between Detroit, Sandusky, Toledo, Cleveland, Cedar Point [and] Lakeside via Put-in-Bay. [Detroit?, 1932]. 1 sheet folded to [12] p. Illus., map. MiD-D.

Ashley & Dustin Steamer Line, [the] Put-in-Bay route [operating] between Detroit, Sandusky, Toledo, Cleveland, Cedar Point [and] Lakeside via Put-in-Bay. [Detroit?, 1933]. 1 sheet folded to [12] p. Illus., map. WM.

Ashley & Dustin Steamer Line, [the] Put-in-Bay route [operating] between Detroit, Sandusky, Toledo, Cleveland, Cedar Point [and] Lakeside via Put-in-Bay. [Detroit?, 1934]. 1 sheet folded to [12] p. Illus., map. MiD-D.

Ashley & Dustin Steamer Line, [the] Put-in-Bay route [operating] between Detroit, Sandusky, Toledo,

Cleveland, Cedar Point [and] Lakeside via Put-in-Bay. [Detroit?, 1935]. 1 sheet folded to [12] p. Illus., map. MdBUS.

Ashley & Dustin Steamer Line, [the] Put-in-Bay route [operating] between Detroit, Sandusky, Toledo, Cleveland, Cedar Point [and] Lakeside via Put-in-Bay. [Detroit?, 1936]. 1 sheet folded to [12] p. Illus., map. MiD-D.

The Lake Erie Breeze. — Vol. 1, no. 1 (June 1936)-vol. 11, no. 1 (Summer 1946). — Detroit, 1936-1946. Illus., maps. Monthly during navigation season. CSFMM, CU-SB, MdBUS, MiD-D, OBgU, OV.

Ashley & Dustin Steamer Line, [the] Put-in-Bay route [operating] between Detroit, Sandusky, Toledo, Cleveland, Cedar Point [and] Lakeside via Put-in-Bay. [Detroit?, 1937]. 1 sheet folded to [12] p. Illus., map. OBgU.

Dear friend [promotional letter]. [Detroit?, 1937]. [4] p. Illus. MiD-B.

Ashley & Dustin Steamer Line, [the] Put-in-Bay route [operating] between Detroit, Sandusky, Toledo, Cleveland, Cedar Point [and] Lakeside via Put-in-Bay. [Detroit?, 1939]. 1 sheet folded to [12] p. Illus., map. MiD-D, WM.

Ashley & Dustin Steamer Line, [the] Put-in-Bay route [operating] between Detroit, Sandusky, Toledo, Cleveland, Cedar Point [and] Lakeside via Put-in-Bay. [Detroit?, 1940]. 1 sheet folded to [8] p. Map. WM, WMCHi.

Ashley & Dustin Steamer Line, [the] Put-in-Bay route [operating] between Detroit, Sandusky, Toledo, Cleveland, Cedar Point [and] Lakeside via Put-in-Bay. [Detroit?, 1941]. 1 sheet folded to [8] p. Map. MdBUS, MiD-D, WM.

Ashley & Dustin Steamer Line, [the] Put-in-Bay route [operating] between Detroit, Sandusky, Toledo, Cleveland, Cedar Point [and] Lakeside via Put-in-Bay. [Detroit?, 1942]. 1 sheet folded to [8] p. Illus., map. CU-SB, MiD-D, OFH, WM.

Ashley & Dustin Steamer Line, [the] Put-in-Bay route [operating] between Detroit, Sandusky, Toledo, Cleveland, Cedar Point [and] Lakeside via Put-in-Bay. [Detroit?, 1943]. 1 sheet folded to [8] p. Map. MiD-D, WM.

Ashley & Dustin Steamer Line, [the] Put-in-Bay route [operating] between Detroit, Sandusky, Toledo, Cleveland, Cedar Point [and] Lakeside via Put-in-Bay. [Detroit?, 1944]. 1 sheet folded to [8] p. Illus., map. CU-SB.

Ashley & Dustin Steamer Line, [the] Put-in-Bay route [operating] between Detroit, Sandusky, Toledo, Cleveland, Cedar Point [and] Lakeside via Put-in-Bay. [Detroit?, 1944]. 1 sheet folded to [8] p. Map. Second edition. CU-SB, MiD-D, WM.

Ashley & Dustin Steamer Line, [the] Put-in-Bay route [operating] between Detroit, Sandusky, Toledo, Cleveland, Cedar Point [and] Lakeside via Put-in-Bay. [Detroit?, 1945]. 1 sheet folded to [8] p. Illus., map. CU-SB, MiD-D, OBgU, OFH, WM.

Ashley & Dustin· Steamer Line, [the] Put-in-Bay route [operating] between Detroit, Sandusky, Toledo, Cleveland, Cedar Point [and] Lakeside via Put-in-Bay. [Detroit?, 1946]. 1 sheet folded to [8] p. Illus., map. CU-SB, MdBUS, MiD-D, OFH, WM.

Ashley & Dustin Steamer Line, [the] Put-in-Bay route [operating] between Detroit, Sandusky, Toledo, Cleveland, Cedar Point [and] Lakeside via Put-in-Bay. [Detroit?, 1947]. 1 sheet folded to [12] p. Illus., map. MiD-D.

S.S. Put-in-Bay lake cruises. [Detroit?, 1949]. 1 sheet folded to [12] p. Illus. CU-SB, MiD-D.

The big steamer Put-in-Bay, famous on the Great Lakes. [Detroit?, 1951?]. 1 sheet folded to [4] p. Illus. MdBUS, MiShM.

Moonlight cruise on Lake St. Clair. [Detroit?, 1952?]. 1 sheet folded to [6] p. Illus. MiD-D, MiShM, OFH.

New schedule and prices [for the] S.S. Put-in-Bay, the big excursion steamer. [Duluth?, 1953?]. 1 sheet folded to [4] p. Illus. MiD-D, MiShM.

ASHLEY & MITCHELL STEAMER LINE, DETROIT, MI

Founded around 1874 as successor to the Ashley, Lewis & Company. In 1887 the business name was changed to Ashley & Dustin Steamer Line.

Summer arrangement among the islands, Detroit, Put-in-Bay, Kelley's Island [and] Sandusky [on] the splendid, new "A-1" steamer Alaska. Detroit: Calvert Lith[ographing] Co., [1878?]. 1 sheet folded to [8] p. Illus., map. MiD-D.

AUTOMOBILE CLUB OF MICHIGAN, DETROIT, MI

Established 28 June 1916. Acquired the Bob-lo steamboats in March of 1983 and then sold them on 1 June 1988 to the International Broadcasting Corporation.

Cruise holidays [on the] Great Lakes, Georgian Bay, St. Lawrence and Saguenay rivers. [N.p., 1950]. 1 sheet folded to [6] p. Illus. MiD-D.

Boblo [sic] Island, take someone you love! [Detroit, 1983]. 1 sheet folded to [6] p. Illus., map. OBgU.

Boblo [sic] Island welcomes you. [N.p., 1985]. 1 sheet folded to [8] p. Map. MiD-D.

Boblo [sic] Island, come share the fun! [Detroit, 1987]. 1 sheet folded to [8] p. Illus., map. MiD-D.

BEAVER ISLAND BOAT COMPANY, CHARLEVOIX, MI

Incorporated on 13 February 1984. Still active as of 1990.

Cruise with us to beautiful...historic Beaver Island, America's Emerald Isle. [N.p., 1974]. 1 sheet folded to [4] p. Illus. OBgU.

People, pets, vehicles, [and] freight [served by this] 1990 ferry schedule. [Petoskey, MI: Little Traverse Printing, 1990]. 1 sheet folded to [4] p. Illus., map. MiD-D.

BENTON TRANSIT COMPANY, BENTON HARBOR, MI

Incorporated 30 September 1899. In 1927 it merged with the Chicago & South Haven Steamship Company to form the Chicago, Benton Harbor & South Haven Transit Company. Dissolved in 1931.

Compliments of [the] Benton Transit Co., operating the steamers "Frank Woods" and "Chas. McVea" on the Benton Harbor and Chicago route across Lake Michigan. Benton Harbor, MI: Ricaby & Smith, [1913]. [48] p. This volume consists of empty pages for taking notes. OBgU.

BOB-LO COMPANY, DETROIT, MI

Established on 10 May 1949 as successor to the Bob-lo Excursion Company to operate boats for the Island of Bob-lo Company. Ceased operations in 1983 when acquired by the Automobile Club of Michigan. Still a registered firm as of 1990.

Destination Bob-lo Island. [N.p., 1949?]. 1 sheet folded to [16] p. Illus., map. MdBUS, MiD-D, MiShM, OFH, ViNeM.

Come cruisin' down the river to magic [at] Bob-lo Island. [N.p., 1950]. 1 sheet folded to [16] p. Illus. MiD-D, OFH.

Come cruisin' down the river to magic Bob-lo Island. [N.p., 1951]. 1 sheet folded to [16] p. Illus. MdBUS, MiD-D, OFH, ViNeM.

Bob-lo 1952 sailing schedule. [N.p., 1952]. 1 sheet folded to [4] p. OBgU.

Bob-lo sailing schedule, 1953. [N.p., 1953]. 1 sheet folded to [4] p. Illus. MiD-D.

Bob-lo sailing schedule, 1954. [N.p., 1954]. 1 sheet folded to [4] p. Illus. MiD-D.

Bob-lo sailing schedule, season [1958]. [N.p., 1958]. 1 sheet folded to [4] p. MiD-D.

This is Bob-lo, the international playground. [N.p., 1958]. 1 sheet folded to [6] p. Illus. MiD-D.

For a quick sightseeing tour of Detroit go cruising on the Bob-lo steamers 3 hour ride on the Detroit River. [Detroit?, 1959?]. 1 sheet folded to [6] p. Illus., map. MiD-D, MiMtpC, OBgU.

For a quick sightseeing tour of Detroit go cruising on the Bob-lo steamers 3 hour ride on the Detroit River. [Detroit?, 1960?]. 1 sheet folded to [6] p. Illus., map. MiD-D, MiMtpC, MiShM, OBgU, ViNeM.

For a quick sightseeing tour of Detroit, go cruising on the Bob-lo steamers 3 hour ride on the Detroit River. [Detroit?, 1961?]. 1 sheet folded to [6] p. Illus. MiD-D, MiMtpC, MiShM, OBgU, ViNeM.

For a quick sightseeing tour of Detroit, go cruising on the Bob-lo steamers 3 hour ride on the Detroit River. [Detroit?, 1962?]. 1 sheet folded to [6] p. Illus. ViNeM.

In Detroit don't miss that Bob-lo cruise. [Detroit?, 1968?]. 1 sheet folded to [12] p. Illus., map. ViNeM.

In Detroit don't miss that Bob-lo cruise. [Detroit?, 1969?]. 1 sheet folded to [12] p. Illus., map. MiD-D.

In Detroit don't miss that Bob-lo cruise. [Detroit?, 1970?]. 1 sheet folded to [12] p. Illus., map. MiShM, OBgU.

Bob-lo, where fun begins. [N.p., 1973?]. 1 sheet folded to [8] p. Illus., map. MiD-D, MiMtpC, MiShM, OBgU, WManiM.

BOB-LO EXCURSION COMPANY, DETROIT, MI

Incorporated 13 December 1939 as successor to Bob-lo Steamers, Incorporated. Acquired in May of 1949 by Troy H. Browning (of Browning Steamship Company), who established the Bob-lo Company as a successor corporation. Dissolved on 11 January 1961.

Let's go to Bob-lo, the isle of rest and recreation. [N.p., 1940]. 1 sheet folded to [8] p. Illus., maps. CU-SB, MiD-D.

The story of Bob-lo Island by William A. Moffett. [N.p., 1940?]. 22, [2] p. Illus., map. MiD-D.

Let's go to Bob-lo. [N.p., 1941]. 1 sheet folded to [8] p. Illus., maps. MdBUS, MiD-D.

Let's go to Bob-lo, the isle of rest and recreation. [N.p., 1942]. 1 sheet folded to [8] p. Illus., maps. CU-SB, MiD-D, OFH.

Let's go to Bob-lo Island Park, "where the Detroit River enters Lake Erie". [N.p., 1942]. 1 sheet folded to [4] p. Illus., map. MiD-D, MiMtpC.

Let's go to Bob-lo, the isle of rest and recreation. [N.p., 1944]. 1 sheet folded to [8] p. Illus., map. CU-SB, MiD-D.

Let's go to Bob-lo, the isle of rest and recreation. [N.p., 1945]. 1 sheet folded to [8] p. Illus., maps. MiD-D.

Let's go to Bob-lo, the isle of rest and recreation. [N.p., 1946]. 1 sheet folded to [8] p. Illus., maps. MiD-D.

Let's go to Bob-lo, the isle of rest and recreation. [N.p., 1948]. 1 sheet folded to [8] p. Illus., maps. MiD-D.

Come to Bob-lo, the isle of rest and recreation. [N.p., 1949]. 1 sheet folded to [8] p. Illus., maps. MiD-D, OFH.

BOB-LO STEAMERS, INCORPORATED, DETROIT, MI

Formerly the Detroit & Windsor Ferry Company. Incorporated 20 September 1938. Dissolved 5 February 1940. Succeeded by the Bob lo Excursion Company.

Let's go to Bob-lo, the isle of rest and recreation. [N.p., 1939]. 1 sheet folded to [8] p. Illus., maps. MiD-D.

BRADLEY TRANSPORTATION COMPANY, ROGERS CITY, MI

Organized in 1923 as a West Virginia firm and successor to the Calcite Transportation Company. Became a part of the U.S. Steel Corporation in 1928. Dissolved as a company on 2 January 1952. Lost its identity on 1 July 1967 when it was made a part of U.S. Steel's Great Lakes Fleet.

St[eame]r John G[ephart] Munson christening ceremonies, Manitowoc, Wisconsin, November 28, 1951. [N.p., 1951]. 10, [2] p. Illus., map. MiD-D, WManiM.

Agreement between [the] Michigan Limestone Division [of the] United States Steel Corporation, Bradley Transportation Line, and District 50, United Mine Workers of America, and Local Union No. 14913, February 22, 1960. [N.p., 1960]. [2], 35, [3] p. OBgU.

Agreement between [the] Michigan Limestone Division [of the] United States Steel Corporation, Bradley Transportation Line, and District 50, United Mine Workers of America, and Local Union No. 14913, April 1, 1963, as amended September 20, 1963. [N.p., 1963]. [2], 59, [3] p. OBgU.

BROWN (WORTHY R.) & SON, INCORPORATED, LAKESIDE, OH

Established in 1910. Ceased operations in 1956.

Schedule of the motorship Lakeside III operating between Lakeside, Sandusky, [and] Put-in-Bay July 2 to Sept. 6, 1943. [N.p., 1943]. 1 sheet folded to [4] p. Illus. CU-SB.

Motorship Lakeside III, the sightseeing ship of the Lake Erie archipelago. [N.p., 1950]. 1 sheet folded to [8] p. Illus., map. MiD-D.

CANADA STEAMSHIP LINES, LIMITED, MONTREAL, QUE

Incorporated 17 June 1913 as Canada Transportation Lines, Limited. Acquired corporate name on 4 December 1913 by merger of the Northern Navigation Company, the Richelieu & Ontario Navigation Company, and others. Reorganized in 1937. Ceased Lake Ontario passenger service in 1952 and all passenger service on 10 November 1965. CSL sold the Hotel Tadoussac in 1966 and the Manoir Richelieu in 1968. In 1975 it became wholly owned by the Power Corporation of Canada, Limited. In January of 1980 it became a component of the CSL Group, Incorporated. Still active as of 1990. NOTE: materials from the Northern Navigation Division can be found under the heading of Northern Navigation Company.

Bay of Quinte, Thousand Islands, Montreal, [and] Quebec [via the Ontario, Bay of Quinte, and Quebec Division]. [Chicago: Poole Bros., 1914]. 1 sheet folded to [16] p. Illus., map. MSaP.

Canada Steamship Lines, Limited, Thousand Island Division local steamer service in effect June 28, 1914. [Montreal?, 1914]. 1 sheet folded to [6] p. CaOOA.

Niagara to the sea, official guide, 1914. Rochester, NY: John P. Smith Printing Co., [1914]. 144 p. Illus., folded map. CaOOA, CaOONL, CaOTU, MiD-D, KyLoU, MSaP, NBuHi.

Niagara to the sea [via] Thousand Islands, Rapids, Montreal, Quebec, [and] Saguenay River [with the] Richelieu & Ontario Division. Chicago: Poole Bros., [1914]. 38 [i.e. 20] p. Illus., maps. April issue. Folder A. MdBUS, MiD-D, ViNeM.

Niagara to the sea [via] Thousand Islands, Rapids, Montreal, Quebec, [and] Saguenay River [with the Richelieu & Ontario Division]. Chicago: Poole Bros., [1914]. 38 [i.e. 20] p. Illus., maps. July issue. Folder A. CaOOA, WM.

Addresses of James Carruthers, president, and J[oseph] W[illiam] Norcross, vice-president and managing director, at the annual meeting of shareholders held at Montreal March 25th, 1915. [Montreal?, 1915]. [4] p. NjP.

Lake Superior to the sea, by Garnault Agassiz. Chicago: Poole Bros., c1915. 96 p. Illus., folded map. Cover title: From the heart of the continent to the sea. DLC, MnHi.

The little red book, a guide and outline of the rapids and canals of the St. Lawrence River. Written for the Canada Steamship Lines, Ltd., by R.V. Fortune. [Montreal?, 1915?]. 16 p. CaOStCB, CaQQS, OBgU.

Niagara to the sea. [Montreal?], c1915. 104 p. Illus, map. CaOOA, CaOStCB.

Niagara to the sea, by Garnault Agassiz. Chicago: Poole Bros., c1915. 96 p. Illus., folded map. N, OO, ViNeM.

Niagara to the sea [via] Thousand Islands, Rapids, Montreal, Quebec, [and] Saguenay River [with the] Richelieu & Ontario Division. Chicago: Poole Bros., 1915. 38 [i.e. 20] p. Illus., maps. May issue. Folder A. MSaP, MdBUS, MiD-D, ViNeM.

Niagara to the sea [via] Thousand Islands, Rapids, Montreal, Quebec, [and] Saguenay River [with the Richelieu & Ontario Division]. Chicago: Poole Bros., [1915]. 38 [i.e. 20] p. Illus., map. July issue. Folder A. CaOStCB.

Report of the president and directors for the year ending December 31st, 1914, with which is incorporated the period December 15th to December 31st, 1913. [Montreal?, 1915]. [8] p. CtY, MH-BA, NjP.

Addresses of James Carruthers, president, and J[oseph] W[illiam] Norcross, vice-president and managing director, at the annual meeting of shareholders held at Montreal March 15th, 1916. [Montreal?, 1916]. [4] p. CtY, NjP.

Buffalo, Niagara Falls [and] Toronto [from] Hamilton [and] Grimsby. New York: M[artin] B. Brown Printing & Binding Co., [1916]. 1 sheet folded to 6, [2] p. Illus., map. ViNeM.

By-water Magazine. — Vol. 1, no. 1 (March 1916)-vol. 4, no. 9 (November 1919). — Montreal: Herald Press, 1916-1919. Illus., maps. Monthly. Continued by: Canadian Illustrated Monthly. CaOKQ, CaOONL, CaOStCB, CaOTAr, CaQMBN, CaQMMRB, CaQMU, CtY, MiD-B.

Niagara to the sea, by Garnault Agassiz. [Montreal?, 1916], c1915. 100 p. Illus., folded map. MiD-D, ViNeM.

Niagara to the sea, by Garnault Agassiz. [Montreal?, 1916], c1915. 132 p. Illus., folded map. CaOOA, CaOStCB, CaOLU, DLC, DPU, MSaP, WHi.

Niagara to the sea [via] Toronto, Thousand Islands, Rapids, Montreal, Quebec, [and] Saguenay River [with the] Richelieu & Ontario Division. Chicago: Poole Bros., [1916]. 38 [i.e. 20] p. Illus., maps. April issue. Folder A. CaOOA, MSaP, MdBUS, OBgU, ViNeM, WM.

Niagara to the sea [via] Toronto, Thousand Islands, Rapids, Montreal, Quebec, [and] Saguenay River [with the] Richelieu & Ontario Division. Chicago: Poole Bros., [1916]. 38 [i.e. 20] p. Illus., map. July issue. Folder A. CaOStCB, ViNeM.

Report of the president and directors for the year ending December 31st, 1915. [Montreal?, 1916]. [8] p. CtY, MH-BA, NjP.

The Thousand Islands of the St. Lawrence River, sight seeing trips among the islands by steamers of the Thousand Island Steamboat Company, Canada Steamship Lines (Limited). [Montreal?, 1916]. 1 sheet folded to [6] p. Illus. CaOOA.

Niagara to the sea [via] Toronto, Thousand Islands, Rapids, Montreal, Quebec, [and] Saguenay River. New York: M[artin] B. Brown Printing & Binding Co., [1917]. 38 [i.e. 20] p. Illus., maps. April issue? CaOOA, ViNeM.

Niagara to the sea [via] Toronto, Thousand Islands, Rapids, Montreal, Quebec, [and] Saguenay River. New York: M[artin] B. Brown Printing & Binding Co., [1917]. 38 [i.e. 20] p. Illus., maps. July issue. Folder A. CSmH, CaOStCB, MSaP.

Report of the president and directors for the year ending December 31st, 1916. [Montreal?, 1917]. [8] p. CtY, MH-BA, NjP.

American Express [promotes] three summer cruises [from] Niagara to the Saguenay without change of steamer. [New York?, 1918]. 1 sheet folded to [32] p. Illus., map. ViNeM.

Niagara to the sea [via] Toronto, Thousand Islands, Montreal, Quebec, [and] Saguenay River. Chicago: Poole Bros., [1918]. 38 [i.e. 20] p. Illus., map. May issue. Folder A. CaOKQ, CaOOA.

Niagara to the sea [via] Toronto, Thousand Islands, Montreal, Quebec, [and] Saguenay River. Chicago: Poole Bros., [1918]. 38 [i.e. 20] p. Illus., map. August issue. Folder A. CaOKQ, OClWHi.

Report of the president and directors for the year ending December 31st, 1917. [Montreal?, 1918]. [8] p. CtY, MH-BA, NjP.

Lake Superior to the sea, an inland water voyage on the Great Lakes and far-famed St. Lawrence and Saguenay Rivers, by Garnault Agassiz. [Montreal?, 1918?]. 96 p. Illus. CaOStCB, MiMtpC.

Niagara to the Saguenay, a summer cruise down the St. Lawrence [sponsored by the] American Express Travel Department. [New York?, 1918]. [16] p. Illus., map. ViNeM.

The Thousand Islands, sight seeing trips among the Thousand Islands by steamers of the Thousand Island Steamboat Co., Canada Steamship Lines (Limited). Rochester, NY: John P. Smith Printing Co., [1918?]. 1 sheet folded to [12] p. Illus., map. MdBUS

Canadian Illustrated Monthly. — Vol. 4 no. 10 (December 1919)-vol. 7, no. 3 (October 1922). — Montreal, 1919-1922. Illus. Monthly. Suspended publication from February-July, 1922. Continues: By-water Magazine. CaOONL, CaQMBN, CaQMMRB, CaQMU.

Niagara to the sea [via] Toronto, Thousand Islands, Montreal, Quebec, [and] Saguenay River, 1919. Chicago: Poole Bros., [1919]. 38 [i.e. 20] p. Illus., map. May issue. Folder A. CSmH, CaOOA, MSaP, MdBUS, MiD-D, OClWHi, ViNeM, WM.

Report of the president and directors for the year ending December 31st, 1918. [Montreal?, 1919]. [6] p. CtY, MH-BA, NjP.

Lake Superior to the sea, an inland water voyage on the Great Lakes and far-famed St. Lawrence and Saguenay rivers, by Garnault Agassiz. Montreal: Ronalds Press & Advertising Agency, [1920]. 96 p. Illus. MiD-D.

The little red book of the Thousand Islands, a guide and outline of the trip from Toronto and Prescott through the Thousand Islands, by R.V. Fortune. [Montreal?, 1920?]. 16 p. CaOONL.

Niagara to the sea [via] Toronto, Thousand Islands, Montreal, Quebec, [and] Saguenay River. Chicago: Poole Bros., [1920]. 46 [i.e. 24] p. Illus., maps. May issue. CaOOA, MiD-D, OBgU.

Niagara to the sea [via] Toronto, Thousand Islands, Montreal, Quebec, [and] Saguenay River. Chicago: Poole Bros., [1920]. 46 [i.e. 24] p. Illus., maps. July issue. CSmH, CaOStCB, MnDuC.

Proceedings of annual general meeting of shareholders, Montreal, March 2nd, 1920. [Montreal?, 1920]. [8] p. CtY.

Rapids of the St. Lawrence, Prescott to Montreal. [Montreal?, 1920?]. 20 p. Folded map. CaOKQ, MiD-D, OBgU.

Report of the president and directors for the year ending December 31st, 1919. [Montreal?, 1920]. [6] p. CtY, MH-BA, NjP.

Niagara to the sea, [offering] hundreds of miles of picturesque water trip from the thundering Niagara to the resounding Saguenay. [Montreal?, 1921?]. 1 sheet folded to [16] p. Illus., maps. MiD-D.

Niagara to the sea [via] Toronto, Thousand Islands, Montreal, Quebec, [and] Saguenay River. Montreal: T[homas] H. Best Printing Co., [1921]. 14 [i.e. 8] p. Illus., map. May issue. MiD-D.

Niagara to the sea [via] Toronto, Thousand Islands, Montreal, Quebec, [and] Saguenay River. [Chicago: Poole Bros., 1921]. 46 [i.e. 24] p. Illus., maps. May issue. CSmH, CaOOA, MiD-D, MiShM, ViNeM, WM.

Proceedings at annual general meeting of shareholders [in] Montreal, May 23rd, 1921, [being the annual report for 1920]. [Montreal?, 1921]. [6] p. CtY, NjP.

A modern voyage of discovery. [New York]: Smith, Sturgis & Moore, [1922?]. [16] p. Illus., map. MSaP, MdBUS, ViNeM.

Canada Steamship Lines, Limited, annual report [for] 1921. [Montreal?, 1922]. [4] p. CtY, MH-BA, NjP.

Niagara to the sea [via] Toronto, Thousand Islands, Montreal, Quebec, [and] Saguenay River. Chicago: Poole Bros., [1922]. 46 [i.e. 24] p. Illus., map. May issue. CaOOA, MiD-D, ViNeM, WM.

Two wonderful cruises, [from] Montreal to Quebec, Murray Bay, Tadousac [sic] [and] the Saguenay, [or] Montreal to [the] Gulf of St. Lawrence & Newfoundland. [Montreal?, 1922]. 1 sheet folded to [16] p. Illus., map. ViNeM.

Canada Steamship Lines, Limited, annual report [for] 1922. [Montreal?, 1923]. [4] p. CtY, CaOONL, MH-BA, NjP.

Niagara to the sea [via] Toronto, Thousand Islands, Montreal, Quebec, [and] Saguenay River. [Chicago: Poole Bros., 1923]. 46 [i.e. 24] p. Illus., maps. June edition. CSmH, CaOOA, CaOStCB, MSaP, MdBUS, MiD-D, ViNeM, WM.

The shrines of the St. Lawrence, [being] St. Joseph's Oratory, Cap-de-la-Madeleine, S[ain]te Anne-de-Beaupre, [and] Chapel of Perpetual Adoration. [Montreal?, 1923?]. 21, [1] p. Illus. CaOKQ, CaQMMRB, CaQQL.

Song book. [Montreal?]: Publication Distributors of Canada, [1923?]. 23, [1] p. Words only. MiD-D.

Canada Steamship Lines, Limited, annual report [for] 1923. [Montreal?, 1924]. [4] p. CtY, MH-BA, NjP.

Niagara to the sea [via] Toronto, Thousand Islands, Montreal, Quebec, [and] Saguenay River. [Chicago: Poole Bros., 1924]. 46 [i.e. 24] p. Illus., maps. March edition. CSmH, ViNeM, WM.

Niagara to the sea [via] Toronto, Thousand Islands, Montreal, Quebec [and] Saguenay River. Chicago: Poole Bros., [1924]. 46 [i.e. 24] p. Illus., map. June edition. CaOOA.

Canada Steamship Lines, Limited, annual report [for] 1924. [Montreal?, 1925]. [4] p. CtY, MH-BA, NjP.

Homespun, a tale of yesterday & today, by William Carless. [Montreal?, 1925?]. 16 p. Illus. CaOONL, CaQMM.

Niagara to the sea [via] Toronto, Thousand Islands, Montreal, Quebec, [and] Saguenay River. Chicago: Poole Bros., [1925]. 46 [i.e. 24]. Illus., maps. March edition. CSmH, CaOOA, MiD-D.

Special all-expense cruise [to the] St. Lawrence and Saguenay Rivers by chartered steamer "Cape Trinity" personally conducted [for Storey Tours]. [N.p., 1925]. 1 sheet folded to [4] p. Illus. MiD-D.

St. Lawrence and Saguenay Rivers [journey for] Storey Tours. [N.p., 1925]. 1 sheet folded to [8] p. Illus., map. MiD-D.

Canada Steamship Lines, Limited, annual report [for] 1925. [Montreal?, 1926]. [4] p. CtY, MH-BA, NjP.

Day line between Montreal, Three Rivers, [and] Quebec. [Montreal?], 1926. 1 sheet folded to [8] p. Illus., map. MdBUS.

Enjoy yourself, take a boat trip [on the] Buffalo-Niagara Falls-Toronto route [with the] Niagara Division. [Toronto?, 1926]. 1 sheet folded to [12] p. Illus., map. MdBUS, OBgU, ViNeM.

Niagara to the sea [via] Toronto, Thousand Islands, Montreal, Quebec, [and] Saguenay River. [Chicago: Poole Bros., 1926]. 46 [i.e. 24] p. Illus., maps. February edition. CSmH, CaOOA, CaOStCB, MdBUS, MiD-D, MiShM, WM.

S.S. "Cape Eternity" cruises, Montreal to Quebec, Murray Bay, Tadousac, [and] the Saguenay. [Montreal?, 1926]. 1 sheet folded to [8] p. Illus., map. MdBUS.

C.S.L. Chart. — Vol. 1, no. 1 (2 May 1927)-vol. 3, no. 12 (April/May 1930). Montreal, 1927-1930. Illus. Monthly (regularity varies). Note: Published in the interests of the company and its employees. CaOKMM, CaOTAr, CaOTHCA, MiD-B, OBgU.

Canada Steamship Lines, Limited, annual report [for] 1926. [Montreal?, 1927]. [8] p. CtY, MH-BA, NjP.

The little red book of Montreal, a few facts that are important and a few that are not about Montreal. Written for the Canada Steamship Lines, Ltd., by R.V. Fortune. [Montreal?, 1927?]. 15, [1] p. CaOTPB.

Niagara to the sea [via] Toronto, Thousand Islands, Montreal, Quebec, [and] Saguenay River. [Chicago: Poole Bros., 1927]. 46 [i.e. 24] p. Illus., map. March edition. CSmH, CaOOA, CaOONL, CaOStCB.

Through the land of the voyageurs, [being] descriptive notes & illustrations of Old World Canada [along] the route travelled by H[is] R[oyal] H[ighness] The Prince of Wales on the S.S. St. Lawrence of the Canada Steamship Lines, Limited. [Montreal?, 1927]. [48] p. Illus. Flyleaf title: Cruise of his royal highness The Prince of Wales on the S.S. St. Lawrence on the occasion of his visit to Canada, 1927. CaOKQ, CaOONL.

Canada Steamship Lines, Limited, annual report [for] 1927. [Montreal?, 1928]. [8] p. CtY, MH-BA, NjP.

Niagara to the sea [via] Toronto, Thousand Islands, Montreal, Quebec, [and] Saguenay River. [Chicago: Poole Bros., 1928]. 46 [i.e. 24] p. Illus., map. March edition. CaOOA, CaOStCB, MiD-D, OBgU, ViNeM.

Thousand Islands and St. Lawrence River, "the Venice of America." Watertown, NY: Santway Photo-craft Company, [1928?]. [32] p. Illus., map. CaOONL.

Canada Steamship Lines, Limited, annual report [for] 1928. [Montreal?, 1929]. [10] p. CtY, MH-BA, NjP.

Catalogue of marine museum collection of early and modern shipping and navigation aids on the Great Lakes, also plans, diagrams, maps, and sketches of naval dockyards, naval engagements, and fortifications. [Montreal?, 1929?]. 27, [1] p. Illus. MiD-B, NR, ViNeM.

The land of romance. Watertown, NY: Santway Photo-craft Company, [1929?]. [32] p. Illus., map. Cover title: Thousand Islands and the St. Lawrence River. CaOONL.

Niagara to the sea [via] Toronto, Thousand Islands, Montreal, Quebec, [and] Saguenay River. Chicago: Poole Bros., [1929]. 46 [i.e. 24] p. Illus., maps. CSmH, CaOOA, CaOStCB, CaQMMRB, MSaP, MdBUS, OFH, ViNeM, WM.

Personally conducted, all expense tours [from] Cleveland to the beautiful Saguenay [River]. [Montreal?, 1929]. 1 sheet folded to [8] p. Illus., map. OFH.

Song book. [Montreal, 1929]. 26, [2] p. Illus. Words only. CaOKMM, CaOTPB, CaQMBN, CaQMMRB, MiD-D, MiShM, OBgU.

All expense tours personally conducted [from] Toronto to the beautiful Saguenay and return. [Montreal?, 1930]. 1 sheet folded to [10] p. Illus. MiD-D.

Canada Steamship Lines, Limited, annual report [for] 1929. [Montreal?, 1930]. [10] p. CtY, MH-BA, NjP.

Catalogue of the Manoir Richelieu collection of Canadiana, compiled by Percy F[rancis] Godenrath, 1930. [Montreal, 1930]. [2], 73, [1] p. Cover title: The Manoir Richelieu collection of Canadiana. CaBVaU, CaMWU, CaNBFU, CaNBSM, CaNSHPL, CaOH, CaOHM, CaOKQ, CaOLU, CaOOA, CaOOCC, CaOOG, CaOOND, CaOONL, CaOORD, CaOOU, CaOTAG, CaOTY, CaOWA, CaQMBN, CaQMG, CaSRU, CaSSU, KyLoU, MH, NN, OClWHi, TxU.

The land of romance. Watertown, NY: Santway Photo-craft Co., [1930?]. [32] p. Illus., map. Cover title: Up the Saguenay, Canada's historic waterway. CaOKQ, CaOONL, MiD-D.

The Manoir Richelieu, Murray Bay, Province of Quebec, Canada, owned and operated by Canada Steamship Lines, Limited. [Montreal?, 1930?]. 16 p. Illus. Cover title: Winter sports at the Manoir Richelieu, Province of Quebec. CaQMBN.

Niagara to the sea [via] Toronto, Thousand Islands, Montreal, Quebec, [and] Saguenay River, season 1930. [Chicago: Poole Bros., 1930]. 46 [i.e. 24] p. Illus., maps. CaOOA, MiD-D, NBuHi, OBgU, WM.

Personally conducted, all expense tours [from] Cleveland to the beautiful Saguenay [River]. [Montreal?, 1930]. 1 sheet folded to [10] p. Illus., map. OFH.

Saguenay, "Saginawa," the river of deep waters, by Blodwen Davies, with illustrations by Paul Curon & G[eorge] A[drian] Cuthbertson. Toronto: McClelland & Stewart, c1930. 204 p. Illus., map. CaBVaU, CaBViP, CaOONL, DLC, ICU, KyLoU, NN, OCl, OLaK, TxU, WaSp.

All expense tours personally conducted [from] Toronto to the beautiful Saguenay and return, [offering] wonderful vacations mid scenic beauties unrivalled. [Montreal?, 1931]. 1 sheet folded to [10] p. Illus. ViNeM.

Canada Steamship Lines, Limited, annual report [for] 1930. [Montreal, 1931]. [8] p. CtY, MH-BA, NjP.

The land of romance. Watertown, NY: Santway Photocraft Co., [1931?]. [32] p. Illus., map. Cover title: Thousand Islands and St. Lawrence River. CaOKQ.

Niagara to the sea [via] Toronto, Thousand Islands, Montreal, Quebec, [and] Saguenay River, season 1931. [Chicago: Poole Bros., 1931]. 46 [i.e. 24] p. Illus., map. CaOOA, CaOONL, CaOStCB, MdBUS, MiD-D, N, ViNeM.

Personally escorted, deluxe all expense tours [of the] Saguenay River [and] eastern Canada [through] American Express travel service. Chicago: Poole Bros., [1931?]. 1 sheet folded to [12] p. Illus., map. ViNeM.

Supplementary catalogue of the Manoir Richelieu, Murray Bay, P[rovince] Q[uebec], historical collection of Canadiana, compiled by Percy F[rancis] Godenrath, 1931. [Montreal?, 1931]. 13, [1] p. CaBVaU, CaNBFU, CaNBSM, CaOH, CaOTAG.

Time tables [for] Niagara-Toronto, Toronto-Prescott-Montreal, Montreal-Quebec, Montreal-Saguenay divisions. [Montreal?, 1931]. 1 sheet folded to [6] p. March issue. CaOOA.

Toronto from Buffalo and Niagara Falls via Lewiston NY or Queenston Ont. [on the] Niagara River Line [of the] Niagara Division. [Toronto?], 1931. 1 sheet folded to [12] p. Illus., map. Issued April, 1931. ViNeM.

All expense tours personally conducted [from] Toronto to the beautiful Saguenay [River] and return. [Montreal?, 1932]. 1 sheet folded to [10] p. Illus. MdBUS, MiD-D.

Canada Steamship Lines, Limited, annual report [for] 1931. [Montreal?, 1932]. [8] p. CtY, MH-BA, NjP.

Catalogue of the Manoir Richelieu collection of North American Indians (1830-1840) compiled by Percy F[rancis] Godenrath. Montreal, 1932. [2], 30 p. Cover title: The Manoir Richelieu collection of North American Indians (1830-1840). CaNBSM, CaOH, CaOKQ, CaOLU, CaOOA, CaOONG, CaOONL, CaOTAG, CaOTY, CaQMBN, CaQMFA, DLC, NN, TxU.

Deluxe, all expense tours to the Saguenay River and eastern Canada from points in the New England states. Chicago: Poole Bros., [1932]. 1 sheet folded to [8] p. Illus., map. MdBUS.

Niagara to the sea [via] Toronto, Thousand Islands, Montreal, Quebec, [and] Saguenay River, season 1932. [Chicago: Poole Bros., 1932]. 38 [i.e. 20] p. Illus., map. CSFMM, CaOOA, MdBUS, MiD-D, OBgU, ViNeM, WM.

Personally escorted, deluxe all expense tours [to] Saguenay River [and] eastern Canada, season 1932. Chicago: Poole Bros., 1932. 1 sheet folded to [12] p. Illus., map. MiD-D.

Canada Steamship Lines, Limited, annual report [for] 1932. [Montreal?, 1933]. [8] p. CtY, MH-BA, NjP.

Deluxe, all expense tours to the Saguenay River and eastern Canada via Montreal, personally escorted from New York. Chicago: Poole Bros., [1933]. 1 sheet folded to [10] p. Illus., map. MdBUS.

Niagara to the sea [via] Toronto, Thousand Islands, Montreal, Quebec, [and] Saguenay River, season 1933. Chicago: Poole Bros., [1933]. 38 [i.e. 20] p. Illus., map. CU-SB, CaOOA, CaOStCB, MdBUS, OBgU, ViNeM, WM.

Niagara to the sea [via] Toronto, Thousand Islands, Montreal, Quebec, [and] Saguenay River, season 1933. Montreal: Ronalds Co., Limited, [1933]. 38 [i.e. 20] p. Illus., map. MiD-D.

All-expense tours through Canada's romantic inland waterway. New York: Wendell P. Colton Co., [1934?]. 1 sheet folded to [18] p. (6 panels are half-size). Illus., maps. ViNeM.

Canada Steamship Lines, Limited, annual report [for] 1933. [Montreal?, 1934]. [8] p. CaMWU, MH-BA, NjP.

Include a "cruise" through cool inland waters with your car or "garage" it near the pier. [Chicago?, 1934?]. 1 sheet folded to [16] p. Illus., map. ViNeM.

The Normandy of the New World, a description of an inland voyage through a northern land where yesterday lingers on the threshold of tomorrow. New York: Ronalds Re-sale Agency, c1934. 24 p. Illus., map. CU-SB, CaOKQ, CaOOA, CaQMMRB, MiD-D, OBgU, ViNeM.

Personally escorted, deluxe, all expense tours [to] Saguenay River [and] eastern Canada, season 1934. Chicago: Poole Bros., 1934. 1 sheet folded to [12] p. Illus., map. MdBUS.

Sailing schedule rates, information. Chicago: Poole Bros., [1934]. 1 sheet folded to [8] p. Illus., map. MdBUS, ViNeM.

The scenic water highway to Toronto from Buffalo and Niagara Falls [on the] (Niagara Division). Chicago: Poole Bros., [1934]. 1 sheet folded to [12] p. Illus., map. Issued April 1, 1934. MiD-D, ViNeM.

All-expense tours through Canada's romantic inland waterway, season 1935. New York: Wendell P. Colton Co., [1935]. 1 sheet folded to [18] p. (6 panels are half size). Illus., maps. [Folder C?]. ViNeM.

Canada Steamship Lines, Limited, annual report [for] 1934. [Montreal?, 1935]. [8] p. CaMWU, MH-BA, NjP.

Niagara to the sea, a scenic panorama of history, romance and charm. Chicago: Poole Bros., [1935]. 1 sheet folded to [16] p. Illus., map. March issue. Folder A. CU-SB, CaOOA, MdBUS, ViNeM.

Niagara to the sea, a scenic panorama of history, romance and charm. Montreal: Perrault Printing Company, [1935]. 1 sheet folded to [16] p. Illus., map. April issue. Folder A-1. MdBUS, ViNeM.

Personally escorted, deluxe, all expense tours [to] Saguenay River [and] eastern Canada, season 1935. Chicago: Poole Bros., 1935. 1 sheet folded to [12] p. Illus., map. Folder H. CaOOA, MdBUS.

Supplementary catalogue of the Manoir Richelieu collection of North American Indians (1830-1843) by Captain Percy F[rancis] Godenrath. [Montreal?, 1935]. [4] p. CaOKQ, CaOOA, CaOTAG.

All expense tours through Canada's romantic inland waterways. Chicago: Poole Bros., 1936. [12] p. Illus., maps. Form C. ViNeM.

Canada Steamship Lines, Limited, annual report [for] 1935. [Montreal?, 1936]. [4] p. CaMWU, CaOTP, MH-BA, NjP.

Canada Steamship Lines, Limited, general plan of reorganization dated April 18th, 1936. [Montreal?, 1936]. 11, [1] p. NNC.

Niagara to the sea, a scenic panorama of history, romance and charm. Chicago: Poole Bros., [1936]. [12] p. Illus., map. April issue. Folder A. CU-SB, MdBUS, MiD-D, OBgU, ViNeM.

Niagara to the sea, a scenic panorama of history, romance and charm. [Montreal?, 1936]. [12] p. Illus., map. Folder A-1. MiD-D, MiShM.

Personally escorted, all expense deluxe tours to the Saguenay River and eastern Canada, season 1936. Chicago: Poole Bros., 1936. 1 sheet folded to [12] p. Illus., map. Folder H. MdBUS, ViNeM.

Proposal of compromise or arrangement, including as part thereof the modified general plan of reorganization dated October 1st, 1936. [Montreal?, 1936]. 16 p. CaOKQAR, NNC.

The scenic water highway to Toronto from Buffalo and Niagara Falls [on the Niagara Division]. Chicago: Poole Bros., [1936]. 1 sheet folded to [12] p. Illus., map. Issued April 1, 1936. Folder R. MSaP, OBgU.

All expense tours personally escorted to the beautiful Saguenay River, wonderful vacations on the inland waterways of Canada, season 1937. [Montreal?, 1937]. 1 sheet folded to [10] p. Illus. Folder G. MiD-D.

All expense tours through Canada's romantic inland waterways, season 1937. Chicago: Poole Bros., [1937]. 16 [i.e. 12] p. Illus., maps. MdBUS.

Canada Steamship Lines annual report [for] 1936. [Montreal?, 1937]. [4] p. CaMWU, CaOTP, MH-BA, NjP.

The new Manoir Richelieu at Murray Bay, Province of Quebec, Canada, owned and operated by Canada Steamship Lines, Limited. Montreal: Ronalds Company, Limited, [1937?]. [16] p. Illus. MiD-D.

Niagara to the sea, a scenic panorama of history, romance and charm. Chicago: Poole Bros., 1937. [16] p. Illus., map. April issue. Folder A. CSFMM, CU-SB, MdBUS, MiD-D, OFH, ViNeM.

Niagara to the sea, a scenic panorama of history, romance and charm. [Montreal?, 1937]. [16] p. Illus., map. Folder A1. OBgU.

Personally escorted, all expense deluxe tours [to] Saguenay River and eastern Canada, season 1937. Chicago: Poole Bros., 1937. [8] p. Illus., map. Folder H. MiShM, OFH.

All expense tours personally escorted to the beautiful Saguenay River, season 1938. [Montreal?, 1938]. 1 sheet folded to [10] p. Illus. Folder G. MdBUS.

All expense tours through Canada's romantic inland waterways, season 1938. [Chicago?, 1938]. [12] p. Illus., maps. Form E-2. MiD-D, OBgU, ViNeM.

Canada Steamship Lines annual report [for] 1937. [Montreal, 1938]. [4] p. CaOTP, MH-BA, NjP.

Catalogue of the Walter H. Millen collection of Canadiana, comprising oil paintings, water colour drawings, prints, documents, and rare illustrated books in colour, compiled by Captain Percy F[rancis] Godenrath. [Toronto?, 1938]. 76 p. Illus. Cover title: Three centuries of Canadian history in picture and story, 1630-1930. CaNBSM, CaOTRM, CtY, NN.

Niagara to the sea, a scenic panorama of history, romance and charm. Montreal: Ronalds Company, [1938]. 1 sheet folded to [16] p. Illus., maps. CSmH.

Niagara to the sea, a scenic panorama of history, romance and charm. [Chicago?, 1938]. [16] p. Illus., map. Folder A. CSFMM, CU-SB, CaOOA, MdBUS, MiD-D, ViNeM, WM.

Personally escorted, all expense deluxe tours [to] Saguenay River and eastern Canada, season 1938. [Chicago?, 1938]. 1 sheet folded to [20] p. Illus., map. Folder H. MiD-D.

S.S. Richelieu cruises, shipboard vacations on the lower St. Lawrence and Saguenay Rivers, season 1938. [Chicago?, 1938]. [12] p. Illus., map. CU-SB, MSaP, MdBUS, MiD-D, OBgU.

The scenic water highway to Toronto from Buffalo and Niagara Falls [by the Niagara Division]. Chicago: Poole Bros., [1938]. 1 sheet folded to [12] p. Illus., map. Issued April 30, 1938. Folder R. MiD-D.

All-expense cruises on the Great Lakes, 7 days of pleasure on a deluxe cruise from Detroit, 1939. Chicago: Poole Bros., 1939. 1 sheet folded to [10] p. Illus., map. Folder J. CU-SB.

Canada Steamship Lines, Limited, annual report [for] 1938. [Montreal?, 1939]. [4] p. CaMWU, CaOTP, CtY, MH-BA, NjP.

Catalogue of the W[illiam] H[ugh] Coverdale historical collection of Canadiana and of North American Indians at the Manoir Richelieu, Murray Bay, P[rovince] Q[uebec], [for] 1930-1932-1935-1939, compiled by Captain Percy F[rancis] Godenrath, honorary curator. [Montreal?, 1939?]. 73, [1] p. Cover title: The Manoir Richelieu collection of Canadiana. CaOKQ.

Niagara to the sea, a scenic panorama of history, romance and charm, season 1939. [Chicago?, 1939]. [16] p. Illus., map. Folder A. CSmH, CU-SB, CaOOA, MdBUS, ViNeM.

Personally escorted, all expense deluxe tours [to] Saguenay River and eastern Canada, season 1939. [Chicago?, 1939]. 1 sheet folded to [20] p. Illus., map. Folder H. CSmH, CU-SB, MiD-D.

Richelieu cruises, shipboard vacations on the lower St. Lawrence and Saguenay Rivers, 1939. [Chicago?, 1939]. [12] p. Illus., map. Folder W. CU-SB, MdBUS, MiD-D, ViNeM.

Special 2 all expense cruise-tours through Canada's romantic inland waterways. [Chicago?, 1939]. 1 sheet folded to [12] p. Illus., map. Folder TT. CU-SB.

Supplementary catalogue and an abridged index of the Manoir Richelieu, Murray Bay, P[rovince] Q[uebec], historical collection of Canadiana, compiled by Captain Percy F[rancis] Godenrath, honorary curator, 1939. [Montreal, 1939]. 46 p. CaMWU, CaOH, CaOKQ, CaOLU, CaOOA, CaOTAG, CaQMBN, CaQMM, NN, OClWHi.

All-expense cruises on the Great Lakes, 7 days of pleasure on a deluxe cruise from Detroit, 1940. Chicago: Poole Bros., 1940. 1 sheet folded to [10] p. Illus., map. Folder J. CSmH, CU-SB.

All expense tours through Canada's romantic inland waterways, season 1940. [Chicago: Poole Bros.], 1940. 1 sheet folded to [24] p. Illus., maps. Edition of March 25, 1940. Form CDE. ViNeM.

By-laws of pension fund society of Canada Steamship Lines, Limited, incorporated 1940. [Montreal, 1940]. [2], 22 p. CaOKQAR, NNC.

Canada Steamship Lines, Limited, annual report [for] 1939. [Montreal, 1940]. [4] p. CaOTP, MH-BA, NjP.

Canada Steamship Lines raises the curtain for 1940 [with] schedules, escorted tours, [and] cruises. [Chicago: Poole Bros., 1940]. 1 sheet folded to [6] p. Illus. Two editions. MnDuLS, ViNeM.

Catalogue of a selection from the water-colour & sepia drawings (1760-1850) in the William H[ugh] Coverdale collection of historical Canadiana at the Manoir Richelieu, Murray Bay, P[rovince] Q[uebec], exhibited at the galleries of the Art Association of Montreal. [Montreal, 1940]. 11, [1] p. CaNBSM, CaOH, CaOOA, WHi.

Include a "cruise" through cool inland waters with your car or "garage" it near the pier. [N.p., 1940]. 1 sheet folded to [16] p. Illus., map. CU-SB, MiD-D.

The Manoir Richelieu at Murray Bay, Canada. [Montreal?, 1940?]. [20] p. Illus., map. CaOONL, CaQMBN, OBgU, OFH.

Niagara to the sea, a scenic panorama of history, romance and charm, season 1940. [Chicago?, 1940]. [16] p. Illus., map. Folder A. CSmH, CU-SB, CaOOA, MdBUS, MiD-D, OBgU.

Personally escorted, all expense deluxe tours [to] Saguenay River and eastern Canada, season 1940. [Chicago?, 1940]. 1 sheet folded to [20] p. Illus., map. Folder H. CSmH, CU-SB, MdBUS, MiD-D, MnDuLS, OFH.

Personally escorted, all expense tour through eastern Canada by rail and water. [Chicago?, 1940]. 1 sheet folded to [12] p. Illus., map. Folder T. CSmH, CU-SB, MiD-D, MnDuLS.

Richelieu cruises, America's most spectacular inland cruise, season 1940. [Chicago]: P[oole] B[ros.], [1940]. 1 sheet folded to [32] p. Illus., map. Folder W. CSmH, CU-SB, MdBUS, MiD-D, MiShM, ViNeM.

Romantic holidays. [Chicago?, 1940?]. 13, [3] p. Illus. CSmH, CU-SB, MiD-D.

All expense cruises, season 1941. [Montreal?, 1941]. 1 sheet folded to [6] p. Illus. Folder Z. MiD-D.

Canada Steamship Lines, Limited, annual report [for] 1940. [Montreal?, 1941]. [12] p. CaOTP, IEN-T, MH-BA, NjP.

Catalogue of a loan exhibition of water-colour drawings in the William H[ugh] Coverdale collection of historical Canadiana at the Manoir Richelieu, Murray Bay, P[rovince] Q[uebec], exhibited at the galleries of the Art Association of Montreal. [Montreal, 1941]. 11, [1] p. CaQMBN.

Cruise America's historic waterway to the sea through Canada. Chicago: P[oole] B[ros]., [1941]. [16] p. Illus., map. April issue. CU-SB, MSaP, MdBUS, MiD-D, ViNeM.

Cruise America's historic waterway to the sea through Canada. [Montreal?, 1941]. [16] p. Illus., map. May issue. Folder A-1. OFH, ViNeM.

Fascinating vacations on Canada's glorious inland waterways. [Chicago: Poole Bros., 1941]. 1 sheet folded to [16] p. Illus., maps. April issue. CU-SB.

Fascinating vacations on Canada's glorious inland waterways. [Chicago?, 1941]. [12] p. Illus., maps. CU-SB, MdBUS, MiD-D, OBgU, ViNeM.

Great Lakes cruises by steamer from Duluth, Minn., to Port Arthur, Sault S[ain]te Marie, Sarnia, Windsor, Detroit, and Buffalo. [Chicago?, 1941]. 1 sheet folded to [6] p. CU-SB.

Include a "cruise" through cool inland waters with your car or "garage" it near the pier. [Chicago?, 1941]. 1 sheet folded to [16] p. Illus., map. CU-SB.

S.S. Richelieu cruises. [Chicago?, 1941]. 1 sheet folded to [32] p. Illus., map. April issue. Folder W. CU-SB, ViNeM.

The Saguenay trip, by Damase Potvin with an appendix on the homespun industry by William Carless. Montreal: LaPatrie Printing, 1941. [2], 96, xii, [6] p. Illus., folded map. Eighth edition. CU-SB, CaQMBN, MiD-D.

Your fellow Americans will be off to Canada this summer, and we're ready! [Chicago?, 1941]. 1 sheet folded to [8] p. Illus., map. ViNeM.

Canada Steamship Lines, Limited, annual report [for] 1941. [Montreal?, 1942]. [12] p. CaOTP, IEN-T, MH-BA, NjP.

Catalogue of a loan exhibition of water-colour drawings in the William H[ugh] Coverdale collection of historical Canadiana at the Manoir Richelieu, Murray Bay, P[rovince] Q[uebec], 1942. [Montreal?, 1942]. 11, [1] p. CaOH, CaOOA.

Catalogue of a selection of water color drawings by G[eorge] A[drian] Cuthbertson of early and modern chipping, dockyards, naval engagements, and navigation aids of the Great Lakes from the Marine Collection, Canada Steamship Lines, Limited. [Montreal?, 1942]. 14, [2] p. Cover title: Catalogue of an exhibition from the Marine Collection, Canada Steamship Lines, held under the auspices of the Thunder Bay Historical Society, Fort William and Port Arthur, Ontario, 1942. CaNBSM, CaOKMM, MnDuU.

Catalogue of Canadiana, being a selection of prints, watercolour drawings, oil paintings and maps, drawn from the William H[ugh] Coverdale collection of historical Canadiana at the Manoir Richelieu, Murray Bay, P[rovince] Q[uebec], Canada, together with a group of oil paintings by contemporary Canadian artists, exhibited under the auspices of the Maple Leaf Fund, Inc., at the Grand Central Art Galleries, New York City, April 6th to 18th, 1942. New York: Grand Central Art Galleries, [1942]. 54 p. Cover title: Canadiana, an exhibition of historical prints, water-colour drawings, oil paintings, and maps. CaOHM, DLC, MB, MnHi, NN.

Cruise America's historic waterway through Canada, season 1942. [Chicago]: P[oole] B[ros.], [1942]. [16] p. Illus., map. May edition. Folder A. CSmH, CU-SB, MdBUS, OBgU, ViNeM.

Cruise America's historic waterway through Canada, season 1942. [Montreal?, 1942]. [16] p. Illus., map. May edition. Folder A-1. MiD-D.

Exhibition of Canadiana: a selection of prints, water-colour drawings, oil paintings, plans and maps of the city of Quebec and its environs, drawn from the William H[ugh] Coverdale collection of historical Canadiana at the Manoir Richelieu, Murray Bay, together with a group of early pieces of French-Canadian furniture from the Hotel Tadoussac, Tadoussac, [as] loaned by the Canada Steamship Lines, Limited, Montreal, P[rovince] Q[uebec], [and] exhibited at the Museum of the Province of Quebec, Quebec City, December 10, 1942 to January 31, 1943. [Montreal?, 1942]. 36 p. Cover title: Le vieux Quebec, Decembre 1942-Janvier 1943. CaNBSM, CaOH, CaOOA, CaOONG, DLC, MnHi, NN, OClWHi, WHi.

Exposition de gravures, aquarelles, peintures, plans et cartes de Quebec et de ses environs, tires de la collection William H[ugh] Coverdale deposee au Manoir-Richelieu, a la Malbaie, meubles anciens du Canada francais provenant de l'Hotel-Tadoussac pretes par les Canada Steamship Lines, Limited, de Montreal [et] tenue au Musee de la Province de Quebec du 10 Decembre 1942 au 31 Janvier 1943. [Montreal?, 1942]. 32 p. Cover title: Le vieux Quebec. CaNBSM, CaOOA, CaOONG, CaQMBN, DLC.

Fascinating all expense vacations on Canada's glorious inland waterways, season 1942. [Chicago: Poole Bros., 1942]. [8] p. Illus., map. Edition of May 10. CU-SB.

Fascinating all expense vacations on Canada's glorious inland waterways, season 1942. [Chicago]: P[oole] B[ros.], [1942]. [12] p. Illus., maps. Edition of May 12. CSmH.

Rapids of the St. Lawrence, Prescott to Montreal. Montreal: LaPatrie Printing, 1942. 20 p. Folded map. CSmH.

S.S. Richelieu cruises, one of America's unforgettable vacations. [Chicago?, 1942]. 1 sheet folded to [32] p. Illus., map. April issue. Folder W. CSmH, CU-SB, CaOKMM, MiD-D.

Canada Steamship Lines, Limited, annual report [for] 1942. [Montreal, 1943]. [12] p. Illus. CaMWU, CaOTP, IEN-T, MH-BA, NjP.

Catalogue of a selection of early views, maps, charts, and plans of the Great Lakes, the Far West, [and] the Arctic and Pacific Oceans, from the William H[ugh] Coverdale collection of historical Canadiana at the Manoir Richelieu, Murray Bay, P[rovince] Q[uebec], exhibited by the Thunder Bay Historical Society March 13th to April 30th, 1943. [Montreal?, 1943]. 22, [2] p. Illus., maps. Cover title: The Far West. CaNBSM, CaOH, CaOONG, DLC, MiD-B, MnHi, WHi.

Catalogue of a selection of paintings, drawings, prints, plans, etc. of early topographical views in Nova Scotia, New Brunswick, Quebec and Ontario from the conquest to confederation, embracing scenes of colonial settlements; building of roads, bridges and canals; shipping and the square-timber trade; naval and military events; sports and pastimes, etc., drawn from the William H[ugh] Coverdale collection of historical Canadiana at the Manoir Richelieu, Murray Bay, P[rovince] Q[uebec], [and] exhibited at the McIntosh Memorial Art Gallery, University of Western Ontario, London, Canada, November 1943 to January 1944. [Montreal?, 1943]. 50 p. Illus. Cover title: A century of pioneering. CaBViP, CaNBSM, CaOH, CaOKQ, CaOOA, DLC, MiU-C, NN, OClWHi, ViNeM.

Catalogue of a selection of water color drawings by G[eorge] A[drian] Cuthbertson and others and related items of early and modern shipping, dockyards, naval engagements, navigation aids, and maps, plans, ect. of the Great Lakes from the marine collection, Canada Steamship Lines, Limited, Montreal, Canada, and the Mariners' Museum, Newport News, Virginia, U.S.A. [Montreal?, 1943]. [4], 26, [10] p. Illus., maps. CSFMM, CaNBSM, CaOHM, CaOKQ, CaOOA, CaOONG, CaQMM, DLC, ICF, MHi, MSaP, MnHi, NBuHi, NN, OClWHi, ViN, ViNeM, WMCHi.

Catalogue of a selection of water color drawings by G[eorge] A[drian] Cuthbertson and others of early and modern shipping, dockyards, naval engagements, navigation aids, and maps, plans, etc. of the Great Lakes from the marine collection, Canada Steamship Lines, Limited. [Montreal?, 1943]. [6], 16, [6] p. Illus., maps. Cover title: The marine collection: an exhibition of historical water-colours and drawings, maps and plans relating to the Great Lakes. Note: supplied pagination may vary with edition. CaBViP, CaNBSM, CaOKQ, CaOOA, CaQMBN, MiU-C, WHi.

Cruise America's historic waterway through Canada, season 1943. [Chicago: Poole Bros., 1943]. [16] p. Illus., map. May issue. Folder A. CU-SB, MiD-D, ViNeM.

Fascinating all expense vacations on Canada's glorious inland waterways, season 1943. [Chicago: Poole Bros., 1943]. [16] p. Illus., maps. Edition of May 1. CU-SB, MiD-D, OBgU, ViNeM.

Rapids of the St. Lawrence, Prescott to Montreal. Montreal: LaPatrie Printing, 1943. 20 p. Illus., folded map. MiD-D.

S.S. Richelieu cruises, one of America's unforgettable vacations. [Chicago?, 1943]. 1 sheet folded to [32] p. Illus., map. April issue. Folder W. CSmH, CU-SB.

Ships of the Great Lakes, an exhibition of historical water colours and paintings, maps, plans, and prints from 1680 to 1942 on exhibit at the Mariners' Museum, Newport News, Virginia. [Montreal?, 1943]. 26, [10] p. Illus., maps. Title from cover. ICU, NN, OBgU.

Vacation cruises to suit wartime budgets and curtailed holidays. [Montreal?, 1943]. 1 sheet folded to [4] p. In French and English. ViNeM.

A selection of water color drawings by G[eorge] A[drian] Cuthbertson and others of early and modern shipping, dockyards, naval engagements, navigation aids, and maps, plans, etc. of the Great Lakes from the marine collection, Canada Steamship Lines, Limited. [Montreal?, 1944]. [6], 16, [6] p. Illus., maps. Cover title: The marine collection, an exhibition of historical water colours and drawings, maps and plans relating to the Great Lakes. Note: Supplied pagination may vary with edition. CaOKMM, CaQMBN, DLC, MiDA, MiD-B, MiD-D, MiU, MiU-H, MnHi, OClWHi, OFH.

The birds of America, by John James Audubon, exhibited at the Museum of the Province of Quebec, Quebec city, February 22nd to March 22, 1944, from the William H[ugh] Coverdale collection of historical Canadiana at the Manoir Richelieu, Murray Bay, P[rovince] Q[uebec]. [Montreal?, 1944]. 60 p. Illus. Cover title: Audubon. CaNBSM, CaOH, CaOHM, CaOOA, CaOONG, CaQMM, CtY, DLC, MnHi, NN, OClWHi, ViNeM.

Canada Steamship Lines, Limited, annual report [for] 1943. [Montreal?, 1944]. [12] p. Illus. CaMWU, CaOTP, IEN-T, MH-BA, NjP.

Canadiana, a selection of Quebec views drawn from the William H[ugh] Coverdale collection of historical Canadiana at the Manoir Richelieu, Murray Bay, P[rovince] Q[uebec], together with a group of French-Canadian furniture, handicrafts, and wood carvings from the Hotel Tadoussac, Tadoussac, P[rovince] Q[uebec], exhibited at the London Public Library and Art Museum November 10th to December 10th, 1944. [Montreal?, 1944]. 18, [2] p. Illus. CaBViP, CaNBSM, CaOH, DLC, MnHi, NN, OClWHi, ViNeM, WHi.

Catalogue of a selection of early views, maps, charts, and plans of the Great Lakes, the Far West, [and] the Arctic and Pacific Oceans from the William H[ugh] Coverdale collection of historical Canadiana at the Manoir Richelieu, Murray Bay, P[rovince] Q[uebec], exhibited by the Winnipeg Art Gallery Association in the art gallery, the Winnipeg auditorium, February 1st to February 29th, 1944. [Montreal?, 1944]. 22, [2] p. Illus., maps. Cover title: The last frontier. CaNBSM, CaOHM, CaOOA, CaOONG, CaQMBN, DLC, MnHi, NN, ViNeM, WHi.

Cruise America's historic waterway through Canada, season 1944. [Chicago: Poole Bros., 1944]. [16] p. Illus., map. April issue. Folder A. CU-SB, CaOONL, MdBUS, MiD-D, OFH, ViNeM.

Dear sir or madam [promotional piece]. [Chicago?], 1944. 1 sheet folded to [4] p. Illus., map. ViNeM.

Fascinating all expense vacations on Canada's glorious inland waterways, season 1944. [Chicago: Poole Bros., 1944]. [12] p. Illus., map. March 25 edition. Form CDE. CU-SB, MiD-D, OBgU, ViNeM.

Les oiseaux d'Amerique, par Jean Jacques Audubon, exposition au Musee de la Province de Quebec, Quebec, du 2 Mars au 2 Avril 1944, tiree de la collection de Canadiana William H[ugh] Coverdale, Manoir Richelieu, Murray Bay, P[rovince] Q[uebec]. [Montreal?, 1944]. 64 p. Illus. Cover title: Audubon. CaQMBN, DLC.

Rapids of the St. Lawrence, Prescott to Montreal. Montreal: LaPatrie Printing, 1944. 20 p. Folded map. OBgU.

S.S. Richelieu cruises, season 1944. [Chicago?], 1944. 1 sheet folded to [32] p. Illus., map. April issue. Folder W. CU-SB, MiD-D, OFH, ViNeM.

The Saguenay trip, by Damase Potvin, with an appendix on the homespun industry by William Carless. Montreal: LaPatrie Printing, 1944. [6], 96, xii, [4] p. Illus., folded map. [11th edition]. CaOONL, CaQMBN.

Time tables, 1944. [Montreal?, 1944]. 1 sheet folded to [6] p. Folder L. CU-SB.

World's largest inland water transportation company, Canada Steamship Lines, Limited, and its subsidiaries. Chicago: Poole Bros., [1944]. [2], 40, [2] p. Illus., map. CSmH, CU-SB, CaOKMM, CaOKQ, CaOKQAR, CaQMBN, MdBUS, MiD-D, OBgU, OClWHi, OV, ViNeM.

All-expense vacations on Canada's spectacular inland waterways, season 1945. [Chicago: Poole Bros., 1945]. 15, [1] p. Illus., maps. April issue. Folder CDEH. CU-SB, MdBUS, MiD-D, ViNeM.

Canada Steamship Lines, Limited, annual report [for] 1944. [Montreal?, 1945]. [12] p. Illus. CaMWU, CaOTP, IEN-T, MH-BA, NjP.

Cruise on Canada's scenic inland waterways, season 1945. [Chicago: Poole Bros., 1945]. 15, [1] p. Illus., maps. April issue. Folder A. CSmH, CU-SB, CaOPsM, MSaP, MdBUS, MiD-D, OBgU, ViNeM.

Rapids of the St. Lawrence. Montreal: LaPatrie Printing, 1945. [24] p. Illus., folded map. OFH.

Romantic Niagara. [Montreal?, 1945]. 20 p. Illus., folded map. CaOStCB.

S.S. Richelieu cruises, delightful all-expense ship and shore vacations on the St. Lawrence and Saguenay [Rivers] through lovely French Canada, season 1945. [Chicago?], 1945. 1 sheet folded to [32] p. Illus., map. April issue. Folder W. CU-SB, MdBUS, MiD-D, ViNeM.

The Saguenay trip, by Damase Potvin, with an appendix on the homespun industry by William Carless.

Montreal: LaPatrie Printing, [1945]. 98, xii p. Illus., folded map. [12th edition]. CaOKMM, CaQMBN, CaQMMRB.

A selection of water color drawings by G[eorge] A[drian] Cuthbertson and others of early and modern shipping, dockyards, naval engagements, navigation aids, and maps, plans, etc. of the Great Lakes from the marine collection [of the] Canada Steamship Lines, Limited, Montreal. [Montreal?, 1945]. [6], 16, [6] p. Illus., maps. Cover title: The marine collection, an exhibition of historical water-colors and drawings, maps and plans relating to the Great Lakes. CaOH, CaOKMM, MiD-B, OClWHi.

All-expense vacations on Canada's spectacular inland waterways, season 1946. [Chicago?, 1946]. 15, [1] p. Illus., maps. April issue. Folder CDEH. CU-SB, MdBUS, MiD-D, ViNeM.

Canada Steamship Lines, Limited, annual report [for] 1945. [Montreal?, 1946]. [12] p. Illus. CaMWU, CaOTP, IEN-T, MH-BA, NjP.

Cruise on Canada's scenic inland waterways, season 1946. [Chicago?, 1946]. 15, [1] p. Illus., map. May issue. Folder A. CSmH, CU-SB, CaOOA, MdBUS, MiD-D, OBgU, ViNeM.

Fascinating cruise vacations on Canada's scenic inland waterways. [Montreal?, 1946]. 1 sheet folded to [4] p. Illus., maps. Front blank except for letterhead. CU-SB.

Ideal summer scenic vacation cruise tours for 1946. [Chicago?, 1946]. 1 sheet folded to [4] p. Illus. MdBUS, ViNeM.

S.S. Richelieu cruises on the St. Lawrence and Saguenay [Rivers] through lovely French Canada, season 1946. [Chicago?, 1946]. 1 sheet folded to [32] p. Illus., map. April issue. Folder W. CSmH, CU-SB, MiD-D.

The Saguenay Cruise on Lake Ontario, the St. Lawrence, and the beautiful Saguenay River, it's a Berry Tour. [Chicago?, 1946]. 1 sheet folded to [8] p. Illus. CU-SB.

Saguenay River and eastern Canada visiting Toronto, Thousand Islands, Quebec, St. Anne de Beaupre, Montreal, Lake Ontario, St. Lawrence River, Detroit, Lake Erie, Niagara Falls [and] thrilling rapids. [Chicago, 1946]. 1 sheet folded to [8] p. Illus., map. Issued May 1 for Cartan Tours of Chicago. CU-SB.

Special S.S. Richelieu cruise on the St. Lawrence and Saguenay Rivers through picturesque French Canada. [Chicago?, 1946]. 1 sheet folded to [6] p. Illus. CU-SB, MiD-D.

All expense, personally escorted cruises, season 1947. [Chicago?, 1947]. [28] p. Illus., map. April edition. Folder C. Cover title: Set sail on your all-expense vacation cruise. MiD-D, ViNeM.

Canada Steamship Lines, Limited, annual report [for] 1946. [Montreal?, 1947]. [12] p. Illus. CaMWU, CaOTP, IEN-T, MH-BA, NjP.

Canada Steamship Lines presents the Inland Waterways Cruise, season 1947. [Chicago?, 1947]. [28] p. Illus., maps. Cover title: Up and down the river. April issue. Folder A. CSmH, MiD-D.

Cruise on Canada's scenic inland waterways, season 1947. [Montreal, 1947]. 11, [5] p. Illus., map. May edition. Folder A-1. MiD-D, OBgU, ViNeM.

S.S. Richelieu cruises on the St. Lawrence and Saguenay [rivers] through lovely French Canada, season 1947. [Chicago?, 1947]. 1 sheet folded to [32] p. Illus., map. April edition. Folder W. MiD-D, PPPMM.

The Saguenay trip, by Damase Potvin, with an appendix on the homespun industry by William Carless. Montreal: LaPatrie Printing, 1947. 118, xii p. Illus., map. [14th edition]. CaQMBN, OBgU.

Canada Steamship Lines, Limited, annual report [for] 1947. [Montreal?, 1948]. [12] p. Illus. CaMWU, CaOOT, CaOTP, IEN-T, MH-BA, NjP.

Canada Steamship Lines presents the Inland Waterways Cruise, season 1948. [Chicago?, 1948]. [28] p. Illus., maps. Cover title: Up and down the river. April issue. Folder A. CSmH.

Canada Steamship Lines time tables, 1948. [Chicago?, 1948]. 1 sheet folded to [6] p. Folder L. CSmH, MdBUS.

The Saguenay trip, by Damase Potvin, with an appendix on the homespun industry by William Carless. Montreal: LaPatrie Printing, 1948. 118, xii p. Illus., map. [15th edition]. MB, OBgU.

All expense, personally escorted cruises, season 1949. [Chicago?, 1949]. [26] p. (two folded). Illus., map. April edition. Folder C. Cover title: Set sail on your all-expense vacation cruise. MdBUS, MiD-D, ViNeM.

Canada Steamship Lines, Limited, annual report [for] 1948. [Montreal?, 1949]. [12] p. Illus. CaMWU, CaOOT, CaOTP, IEN-T, MH-BA, NjP.

Canada Steamship Lines presents the Inland Waterways Cruise, season 1949. [Chicago?, 1949]. [28] p. Illus., map. Cover title: Up and down the river. April issue. Folder A. MdBUS, MiD-D.

Canada Steamship Lines time tables, 1949. [Montreal?, 1949]. 1 sheet folded to [8] p. Map. April edition. Folder K. MiD-D.

Delightful all-expense ship and shore vacation [on a] S.S. Richelieu cruise through lovely French Canada, 1949. [Chicago?, 1949]. [16] p. Illus., map. March issue. MdBUS.

Canada Steamship Lines, Limited, annual report [for] 1949. [Montreal?, 1950]. [12] p. Illus. CaOOT, CaOTP, IEN-T, MH-BA, NjP.

Canada Steamship Lines presents the Inland Waterways Cruise, season 1950. [Chicago?, 1950]. [28] p. Illus., maps. Cover title: Up and down the river. ViNeM.

Canada Steamship Lines time tables, 1950. [Montreal?, 1950]. 1 sheet folded to [8] p. Map. March edition. Folder K. ViNeM.

The Saguenay trip, by Damase Potvin, with an appendix on the homespun industry by William Carless. Montreal: LaPatrie Printing, 1950. 120, xii p. Illus., folded map. [17th edition]. CaQMBN, CaQMMRB.

Canada Steamship Lines, Limited, annual report [for] 1950. [Montreal?, 1951]. [12] p. Illus. CaMWU, IEN-T, MH-BA, NjP.

Canada Steamship Lines presents the Inland Waterways Cruise, season 1951. [Chicago?, 1951]. [28] p. Illus., maps. Cover title: St. Lawrence/Saguenay River cruises. Folder A. CSmH, MiD-D, ViNeM.

Canada Steamship Lines time tables, 1951. [Chicago?, 1951]. 1 sheet folded to [4] p. CSmH.

Delightful, all-expense ship and shore vacation [on a] S.S. Richelieu cruise through lovely French Canada, 1951. [Chicago?, 1951]. [16] p. Illus., map. March issue. MdBUS.

S.S. Richelieu cruise through lovely French Canada, 1951. [Chicago?, 1951]. [16] p. Illus., map. March issue. Folder W. CSmH.

Time tables [for] Toronto, Niagara-on-the-Lake, [and] Queenston with connecting schedules to Niagara Falls and Buffalo, 1951. [Montreal?, 1951]. 1 sheet folded to [8] p. Map. February edition. Folder K. CU-SB, OFH.

Canada Steamship Lines, Limited, annual report [for] 1951. [Montreal?, 1952]. [12] p. Illus., map. CaOOT, CaOTP, IEN-T, MH-BA, NjP.

Canada Steamship Lines presents the Inland Waterways Cruise, season 1952. [Chicago?, 1952]. [28] p. Illus., map. Cover title: St. Lawrence/Saguenay River cruises. Folder A. CaOKMM, MdBUS, MiD-D.

Canada Steamship Lines time tables, 1952. [Montreal?, 1952]. 1 sheet folded to [8] p. Folder L. ViNeM.

Cook's escorted tours on board [the] S.S. Richelieu [visiting] Montreal, Quebec, S[ain]te Anne-de-Beaupre [and] Murray Bay, 1952. [Chicago?, 1952]. 1 sheet folded to [8] p. Illus., map. MiD-D.

The growth of a giant, a history of Canada Steamship Lines, Limited. [Montreal?, 1952?]. 22, [2] p. Illus. MSaP, OBgU, OV, ViNeM.

Vacation cruises, 1952. [Montreal?, 1952]. 1 sheet folded to [4] p. Illus. Text in French and English. ViNeM.

CSL News. — Vol. 1, no. 1 (1 April 1953?)-vol. ?, no. 368 (15 November 1968). — Montreal, 1953?-1968?. Illus. Semi-monthly. CaOKMM, OBgU.

Canada Steamship Lines, Limited, annual report [for] 1952. [Montreal?, 1953]. [12] p. Illus. CaOTP, IEN-T, MH-BA, NjP.

Consolidated by-laws of the company as at April 21, 1953. [Montreal?, 1953]. 43, [1] p. CaOKQAR, CaOKMM.

The Manoir. — Vol. 1, no. 1 (Spring 1953)-vol. 6, no. 1 (Summer 1957). — Montreal: Gazette Printing Company, 1953-1957. Illus. Annual. Continued by: Manoir and Colony Life Magazine. Note: Two editions were published in 1953. CaOONL, CaQMBN, OV.

The Saguenay trip, by Damase Potvin, with an appendix on the homespun industry by William Carless. Montreal: LaPatrie Printing, 1953. [4], 124, xii, [28] p. Illus., map in pocket. [20th edition]. CaOH, DLC, NN.

St. Lawrence-Saguenay River cruises, 1953. [Chicago?, 1953]. 27, [1] p. Illus. MdBUS.

Canada Steamship Lines, Limited, annual report [for] 1953. [Montreal?, 1954]. [16] p. Illus. IEN-T, MH-BA, NjP.

S.S. Richelieu cruises through lovely French Canada, 1954. [Montreal?, 1954]. [16] p. Illus., map. Folder W. CSmH.

St. Lawrence and Saguenay River cruises, 1954. [Chicago?, 1954]. 27, [1] p. Illus., map. Folder A. CSmH, MiD-D, MiShM, ViNeM.

St. Lawrence & Saguenay River cruises for an ideal vacation, season 1954. [Chicago?, 1954]. 1 sheet folded to [4] p. Illus. January edition. CSmH.

Canada Steamship Lines, Limited, annual report [for] 1954. [Montreal?, 1955]. [20] p. Illus. IEN-T, MH-BA, NjP.

Canada Steamship Lines time tables, 1955. [Montreal?, 1955]. 1 sheet folded to [8] p. Folder L. MiD-D, ViNeM.

Cook's escorted tours, cruise-tours to eastern Canada and Saguenay, including the famous S.S. "Richelieu" cruise-tour, 1955. [Chicago?], 1955. 11, [1] p. Illus., maps. MiD-D.

Cruises on the St. Lawrence and Saguenay rivers through French Canada, season 1955. [Chicago?, 1955]. 1 sheet folded to [4] p. Illus. February edition. MiD-D, MiShM.

Holiday cruises through French Canada [via the] St. Lawrence [and] Saguenay [rivers], 1955. [Montreal?], 1955. 1 sheet folded to [6] p. Illus. MiD-D.

S.S. Richelieu cruises through lovely French Canada, 1955. [Montreal?, 1955]. [2], 12, [2] p. Illus., map. Folder W. CSmH, MiD-D, MiShM, OBgU.

Vacation cruises [on the] St. Lawrence and Saguenay River [sic], 1955. [Chicago?, 1955]. 27, [1] p. Illus., map. Folder A. CSmH, MiD-D, MiShM, ViNeM.

Canada Steamship Lines, Limited, annual report [for] nineteen hundred fifty-five. [Montreal?, 1956]. [20] p. Illus. IEN-T, MH-BA, NjP.

Canada Steamship Lines time tables, 1956. [Montreal?, 1956]. 1 sheet folded to [8] p. Folder L. MiD-D, MiShM.

S.S. Richelieu cruises through lovely French Canada, 1956. [Montreal?, 1956]. [2], 12, [2] p. Illus., map. Folder W. CSmH.

Statement by T[homas] R[odgie] McLagan, Canada Steamship Lines, Ltd., before the Royal Commission of the Economic Prospects of Canada at the Montreal Hearings, January 18, 1956. [Montreal, 1956]. 7, [1] p. CaQMHE.

Vacation cruises [on the] St. Lawrence and Saguenay River [sic], 1956. [Chicago?, 1956]. 27, [1] p. Illus., map. Folder A. CSmH, MiD-D, ViNeM.

Canada Steamship Lines, Limited, annual report [for] 1956. [Montreal?, 1957]. [20] p. Illus. IEN-T, MH-BA, NjP.

French Canada cruises [along the] St. Lawrence and Saguenay rivers, season 1957. [Chicago?, 1957]. 1 sheet folded to [4] p. Illus. MdBUS, ViNeM.

S.S. Richelieu cruises through romantic French Canada, 1957. [Montreal?, 1957]. [2], 12, [2] p. Illus., map. Folder W. CaOKMM, MdBUS, MiD-D.

Vacation cruises on the majestic St. Lawrence and Saguenay River [sic], 1957. [Chicago?, 1957]. 27, [1] p. Illus. Folder A. MdBUS, MiD-D, ViNeM.

Canada Steamship Lines, Limited, annual report [for] 1957. [Montreal?, 1958]. [20] p. Illus. IEN-T, MH-BA, NjP, ViNeM.

Holiday cruises through French Canada [along the] St. Lawrence [and] Saguenay rivers, 1958. [Montreal?, 1958]. 1 sheet folded to [6] p. Illus. MdBUS.

Manoir and Colony Life Magazine. — Vol. 7, no. 1 (Summer 1958)-vol. 10, no. 1 (Summer 1961). — Montreal: Gazette Printing Company, 1958-1961. Illus. Annual. Continues: The Manoir. Continued by: Colony Life Magazine. CaOONL, CaQMBN.

1958 vacation cruises [to the] St. Lawrence & Saguenay rivers. [Montreal?, 1958]. 1 sheet folded to [4] p. Illus. Text in French and English. MiD-D.

S.S. Fort York [introduction sheet]. [Montreal?, 1958?]. 1 sheet folded to [4] p. Illus. MiD-D.

S.S. Richelieu cruises through romantic French Canada, 1958. [Montreal?, 1958]. [2], 12, [2] p. Illus., map. Folder W. CSmH, MiD-D, ViNeM.

Vacation cruises on the majestic St. Lawrence and Saguenay River [sic], 1958. [Chicago?, 1958]. 27, [1] p. Illus., map. Folder A. CSmH, MiD-D, ViNeM.

Canada Steamship Lines, Limited, 1958 annual report. [Montreal?, 1959]. [20] p. Illus. IEN-T, MH-BA, NjP, OV.

Canada Steamship Lines time tables, 1959. [Montreal?, 1959]. 1 sheet folded to [8] p. MdBUS.

Cook's escorted cruise-tours to eastern Canada, the St. Lawrence and the Saguenay, including cruise-tours aboard the famous S.S. "Richelieu," 1959. [New York?, 1959]. 22, [2] p. Illus., maps. ViNeM.

French Canada cruises [on the] St. Lawrence and Saguenay rivers, season 1959. [Chicago?, 1959]. 1 sheet folded to [4] p. Illus. MdBUS.

S.S. Richelieu cruises through romantic French Canada, 1959. [Montreal?, 1959]. [2], 12, [2] p. Illus., map. Folder W. CSmH, CaOKMM, MdBUS, MiD-D, ViNeM.

Vacation cruises on the majestic St. Lawrence and Saguenay rivers, 1959. [Montreal?, 1959]. 27, [1] p. Illus., map. Folder A. CSmH, MdBUS, ViNeM, WM.

Canada Steamship Lines, Limited, 1959 annual report. [Montreal?, 1960]. [20] p. Illus. IEN-T, MH-BA, NjP, OV.

French Canada cruises [on the] St. Lawrence and Saguenay rivers, season 1960. [Chicago?, 1960]. 1 sheet folded to [4] p. Illus. MiD-D.

Vacation cruises on the majestic St. Lawrence and Saguenay rivers, 1960. [Montreal?, 1960]. 27, [1] p. Illus., map. Folder A. MiD-D, ViNeM.

Canada Steamship Lines, Limited, annual report [for] 1960. [Montreal?, 1961]. [24] p. Illus., map. IEN-T, MH-BA, NN.

French Canada cruises [on the] St. Lawrence and Saguenay rivers, season 1961. [Chicago?, 1961]. 1 sheet folded to [4] p. Illus. MiD-D.

S.S. Richelieu cruises through historical French Canada, 1961. [Montreal]: Upton, [1961]. [2], 12, [2] p. Illus., map. Folder W. CSmH, ViNeM.

Vacation cruises on the majestic St. Lawrence and Saguenay rivers, 1961. [Montreal?, 1961]. 27, [1] p. Illus., map. Folder A. CSmH, MiD-D, ViNeM.

Canada Steamship Lines, Limited, annual report [for] 1961. [Montreal?, 1962]. [28] p. Illus., map. IEN-T, MH-BA, NN, NjP.

Colony Life Magazine. — Vol. 11, no. 1 (Summer 1962)-vol. 15, no. 1 (Summer 1966). — Montreal: Gazette Printing Company, 1962-1966. Illus. Annual. Continues: Manoir and Colony Life Magazine. CaOONL, CaQMBN.

French Canada and the Saguenay, soaring to new heights. [N.p., 1962]. 1 sheet folded to [4] p. Illus. No. 4. CSmH.

French Canada and the Saguenay, start sales soaring. [N.p., 1962]. 1 sheet folded to [4] p. Illus. No. 3. CSmH.

Hotel Tadoussac, Tadoussac P[rovince] Q[uebec]. [Montreal?, 1962]. 1 sheet folded to [12] p. Illus., map. MdBUS.

Manoir Richelieu, Murray Bay, Pointe-au-Pic, P[rovince] Q[uebec]. [Montreal?, 1962]. 1 sheet folded to [12] p. Illus., map. MdBUS.

Manoir Richelieu, Murray Bay, Pointe-au-Pic, P[rovince] Q[uebec]. [Montreal?, 1962]. 19, [1] p. Illus., maps. CaOKMM.

S.S. Richelieu cruises through romantic French Canada, 1962. [Montreal]: Upton, [1962]. [2], 12, [2] p. Illus., map. Folder W. CSmH, MiD-B.

Vacation cruises on the majestic St. Lawrence and Saguenay rivers, 1962. [Montreal?, 1962]. 27, [1] p. Illus., map. Folder A. MdBUS, MiD-B, MiD-D, ViNeM.

By-law "AA," by-law "BB," by-law "CC" of [the] Canada Steamship Lines, Limited. [Montreal?, 1963]. 30 p. Title from cover. CaOKMM, CaOKQAR.

Canada Steamship Lines, Limited, annual report [for] 1962. [Montreal?, 1963]. [22] p. Illus. IEN-T, MH-BA, NN, NjP.

French Canada cruises [on the] St. Lawrence and Saguenay rivers, season 1963. [Chicago?, 1963]. 1 sheet folded to [4] p. Illus. MdBUS, MiD-D.

The Paul Henry 36th Year Saguenay Cruise via the historic St. Lawrence, season 1963. [Detroit?, 1963]. 1 sheet folded to [8] p. Illus. MiD-D.

S.S. Richelieu cruises through romantic French Canada, 1963. [Montreal?, 1963]. 12, [2] p. Illus., map. Folder W. MdBUS, OBgU, ViNeM.

Saguenay and French Canada 9 & 15 day cruise tours [by] Cartan's, 1963. [Chicago?, 1963]. 1 sheet folded to [16] p. Illus., map. MiD-D.

Vacation cruises and tours on the majestic St. Lawrence and Saguenay rivers, 1963. [Montreal?, 1963]. 27, [1] p. Illus., map. Folder A. CSmH, MdBUS, ViNeM, WM.

Canada Steamship Lines, Limited, annual report [for] 1963. [Montreal?, 1964]. [26] p. Illus. IEN-T, MH-BA, NN, NjP.

French Canada cruises [to the] St. Lawrence and Saguenay rivers, season 1964. [Chicago?, 1964]. 1 sheet folded to [4] p. Illus. MiD-D.

Hotel Tadoussac, Tadoussac, P[rovince] Q[uebec]. [Montreal?, 1964]. 1 sheet folded to [12] p. Illus., map. Text in French and English. MiD-D.

Manoir Richelieu, Murray Bay, Pointe-au-Pic, P[rovince] Q[uebec]. [Montreal?, 1964]. 1 sheet folded to [12] p. Illus., map. Text in French and English. MiD-D.

S.S. Richelieu cruises, 1964. [Montreal]: Upton, 1964. 12, [4] p. Illus., map. Folder W. CSmH, MdBUS, MiD-D.

Vacation cruises and tours on the majestic St. Lawrence and Saguenay rivers, 1964. [Montreal?, 1964]. 27, [1] p. Illus., map. Folder A. CSmH, MdBUS, MiD-D.

Canada Steamship Lines, Limited, annual report [for] 1964. [Montreal?, 1965]. [28] p. Illus. IEN-T, MH-BA, NN, NjP.

Canada Steamship Lines time tables, 1965. [Montreal?, 1965]. 1 sheet folded to [8] p. Folder L. MiD-D.

French Canada cruises [to the] St. Lawrence and Saguenay rivers, season 1965. [Chicago?, 1965]. 1 sheet folded to [4] p. Illus. MiD-D.

S.S. Richelieu cruises, 1965. [Montreal]: Upton, 1965. 12, [4] p. Illus., map. Folder W. CSmH, CaOTPB.

St. Lawrence & Saguenay River [sic] cruises and tours, 1965. [Montreal?, 1965]. 27, [1] p. Illus. Folder A. CaOTPB, MdBUS, MiD-D.

Canada Steamship Lines, Limited, annual report [for] 1965. [Montreal?, 1966]. [26] p. Illus. IEN-T, MH-BA, NN, NjP.

Canada Steamship Lines, Limited, annual report [for] 1966. [Montreal?, 1967]. [28] p. Illus. IEN-T, MH-BA, NjP.

Interim report [to] June 30, 1967. [Montreal?, 1967]. 1 sheet folded to [8] p. OV.

Canada Steamship Lines, Limited, annual report [for] 1967. [Montreal?, 1968]. 28 p. Illus. IEN-T, MH-BA, NjP.

Manoir Richelieu, Murray Bay, Pointe-au-Pic, P[rovince] Q[uebec]., Canada. [N.p.]: Hotel Printing Co., [1968?]. 1 sheet folded to [24] p. Illus., map. CaOKMM.

Canada Steamship Lines, Limited, annual report [for] 1968. [Montreal?, 1969]. 22, [2] p. Illus. MH-BA, MnDuC.

Interim report [to] June 30, 1969. [Montreal?, 1969]. 1 sheet folded to [8] p. OV.

Canada Steamship Lines, Limited, annual report [for] 1969. [Montreal?, 1970]. 23, [1] p. Illus. IEN-T, MH-BA, MnDuC.

Interim report [to] June 30, 1970. [Montreal?, 1970]. 1 sheet folded to [8] p. OV.

Canada Steamship Lines, Limited, annual report [for] 1970. [Montreal?, 1971]. 19, [1] p. Illus. IEN-T, MH-BA, MnDuC, OV.

Interim report [to] June 30, 1971. [Montreal?, 1971]. 1 sheet folded to [8] p. OV.

Canada Steamship Lines, Limited, annual report [for] 1971. [Montreal?, 1972]. 24 p. Illus. CaOONL, IEN-T, MH-BA.

Canada Steamship Lines, Limited, annual report [for] 1972. [Montreal?, 1973]. 12 p. CaOONL, IEN-T, MH-BA.

The Scuttlebutt. — Vol. 1, no. 1 (August 1973)-vol. 14, no. ? (November 1977?). — Montreal, 1973-1977?. Illus. Irregular. OBgU.

Canada Steamship Lines, Limited, annual report [for] 1973. [Montreal?, 1974]. 12 p. CaOONL, IEN-T, MH-BA.

Canada Steamship Lines, Limited, notice of annual general meeting of shareholders. [Montreal?, 1974]. 4 p. IEN-T.

Rapport annuel, 1973. [Montreal?, 1974]. 12 p. Text in French. CaOONL.

A profile [of the firm's history, organization, and philosophy]. [Montreal?, 1975?]. [20] p. Text in French and English. CaOKMM, OBgU, OV.

Canada Steamship Lines, Limited, annual report [for] 1974. [Montreal?, 1975]. 12 p. CaOONL, IEN-T, MH-BA.

Notice of annual general meeting of shareholders. [Montreal?, 1975]. 4 p. IEN-T.

Rapport annuel, 1974. [Montreal?, 1975]. 12 p. Text in French. CaOColM, CaOONL.

The World. — Vol. 1, no. 1 (April 1975)-present. — Montreal, 1975-present. Illus. Monthly, then 8 times per year. In 1984 the frequency was reduced to bimonthly. Text in French and English. CaOONL, CaOPoCM, CaQMBN, OBgU.

M[otor] V[essel] "Atlantic Superior" [christening]. [Montreal?, 1982]. [8] p. Illus. Text in French and English. On cover: Canship. CaOKMM.

Etude du ballastage et des tuyauteries connexes dans les navires naviguant en eaux glacees: rapport sommaire prepare pour le Centre de Developpement des Transports, Transports Canada, par Societe Intercan avec Canada Steamship Lines, Inc., et Melville Shipping, Ltd. Montreal, 1983. vii, [1], 10 p. Text in French and English. CaQMBN.

Full speed ahead. [Montreal?, 1987?]. 1 sheet folded to [6] p. Illus. CaOColM, CaOKMM.

Self-unloading technology, [a] Canada Steamship Lines symposium, March, 1987. [Montreal?, 1987]. 13, [3] p. Illus. Text in English and Japanese. Cover title: Self-unloading technology by Canada Steamship Lines. CaOKMM.

Canada Steamship Lines, the fastest, most cost-effective distribution system in the world. [Montreal?, 1988?]. 11, [1] p. Illus. Includes some loose sheets in a back pocket. CaOKMM.

Commemorating the christening of the M[otor] S[hip] CSL Innovator, a self-unloading bulk carrier converted by Verolme Estaleiros for Canada Steamship Lines, April 19, 1988. [Montreal?, 1988]. [12] p. Illus. CaOKMM.

Passage to the sea: an exhibition commemorating the seventy-fifth anniversary of Canada Steamship Lines, 1913-1988. [Montreal?, 1988]. 1 sheet folded to [8] p. Illus., map. Also appears in French with title: Passage vers la Mer. CaOKMM, OV.

Canada Steamship Lines, "the self-unloader people." [Montreal?, 1989]. [12] p. Illus. Includes loose material in a back pocket. CaOKMM.

CANADIAN HOLIDAY COMPANY, INCORPORATED, ERIE, PA

Incorporated on 20 February 1963. Assets sold at U.S. Marshall's sale on 30 July 1964 to the Security-People's Trust Company. Still active as of 1990.

For floating fun, the S.S. North American offers you [a] floating hotel, supper club, dining & dancing, scheduled excursions, [and] charter cruises. [N.p., 1963]. 1 sheet folded to [4] p. Illus., map. MiD-D, OBgU.

A sparkling cruise-holiday [on] the S.S. North American. [N.p., 1964]. 1 sheet folded to [4] p. Illus. MiD-D, MiShM, OBgU, OFH.

CANADIAN NAVIGATION COMPANY, MONTREAL, QUE

Organized in 1857 as the successor to the Royal Mail Line. Merged early in 1875 with the Richelieu Company to form the Richelieu & Ontario Navigation Company.

Handbook of Canadian excursion tours via Grand Trunk Railway and Canadian Navigation Co., rates of fare for season of 1878. Boston: Rand, Avery & Co., [1878]. 17, [7] p. Illus., map. CaOKQ.

Handbook of Canadian excursion tours via Grand Trunk Railway and Canadian Navigation Co., rates of fare for season 1879. Boston: Rand, Avery & Co., [1879]. 17, [7] p. Illus., map. CaOKQ.

CANADIAN OIL COMPANIES, LIMITED, TORONTO, ONT

Incorporated on 4 December 1908. Became Canadian Oil Company, Limited, on 31 January 1963 then sold in the same year to Shell Canada, Limited.

M[otor] V[essel] W[illiam] Harold Rea, christened and commissioned August 25, 1962, by Mrs. W[illiam] Harold Rea at Collingwood, Ontario. [Toronto?, 1962]. [8] p. plus folded plan. Illus. MiD-D.

CANADIAN PACIFIC RAILWAY COMPANY, MONTREAL, QUE

Established a Great Lakes marine department in September of 1882. Began freight activities in 1883, and commenced passenger service on 11 May 1884. Discontinued passenger service on 28 November 1965. Ceased all shipping operations on 26 November 1967.

Upper lakes on the S.S. Alberta. [Chicago: Poole Bros., 1896]. 1 sheet folded to [20] p. Illus., map. MSaP.

Upper lake steamships Athabasca and Manitoba between Owen Sound, Sault S[ain]te Marie, Port Arthur, and Fort William in effect June 24th, 1897. [Chicago: Poole Bros., 1897]. 1 sheet folded to 12 [i.e. 16] p. Illus., map. OBgU.

Summer tours via [the] Canadian Pacific Railway to the upper lakes [from] Ottawa & Montreal, 1899. [Chicago?, 1899]. 40 p. Illus., maps (one folded). Volume 3. MiD-D.

Great Lakes steamship service. Chicago: Poole Bros., [1909]. [8] p. Illus., map. OBgU.

Great Lakes steamship service. [Chicago?, 1911]. 18 [i.e. 12] p. Illus., map. CaOOA.

Great Lakes steamship service, 1912. [Chicago?, 1912]. 22 [i.e. 12] p. Illus., map. ViNeM.

Great Lakes steamship service. [Montreal?, 1914]. 26 [i.e. 8] p. (each page covers 4 panels). Illus., map. ViNeM.

Great Lakes steamship service. [Montreal?, 1919]. 16 p. Illus., map. WManiM.

Great Lakes steamship service. [Montreal?, 1920]. 16 p. Illus., map. MiD-D.

Great Lakes steamship service. [Montreal?, 1922]. 16 p. Illus., map. CaOOA, MSaP.

Great Lakes steamship service. [Montreal?, 1923]. 16 p. Illus., map. CSmH, ViNeM.

Great Lakes steamship service. [Montreal?, 1924]. 16 p. Illus., map. CSmH.

Great Lakes steamship service. [Montreal?, 1925]. 16 p. Illus., map. CaQMCCA.

Great Lakes steamship service. [Montreal?], 1927. 16 p. Illus., map. CSmH, ViNeM.

Great Lakes steamship service, 1928. [Montreal?, 1928]. [8] p. Illus., map. April 20 edition. MiShM.

Great Lakes steamship service. [Montreal?], 1928. 16 p. Illus., maps. CaOOA, ViNeM, WM.

Great Lakes steamship service. [Montreal?], 1929. 16 p. Illus., maps. MSaP, ViNeM.

Leisurely days on Canada's inland seas twice weekly between Port McNicoll and Fort William. [Montreal?, 1930?]. 1 sheet folded to [12] p. Illus., map. OFH.

Canadian Pacific Great Lakes steamship service, summer 1936. [Montreal?], 1936. 4 p. Illus. ViNeM.

Cruise the Great Lakes. [Montreal?], 1936. [12] p. Illus., map. ViNeM.

Cruise the Great Lakes. [Montreal?, 1937]. [12] p. Illus., map. CSmH.

Cruise the Great Lakes. [Montreal?, 1938]. [12] p. Illus., maps. MdBUS, MiD-D.

Great Lakes steamship service, summer 1938. [Montreal?, 1938]. 4 p. Illus. MdBUS, MiD-D.

St. Lawrence Seaway 9-day cruises. [Montreal?, 1938]. 1 sheet folded to [12] p. Illus., map. CU-SB.

Cruise the Great Lakes. [Montreal?], 1939. [12] p. Illus., maps. ViNeM.

Great Lakes steamship service, summer 1939. [Montreal?, 1939]. 4 p. Illus. ViNeM.

Cruise the Great Lakes. [Montreal?], 1940. [12] p. Illus., map. MdBUS, ViNeM, WMCHi.

Great Lakes carefree cruises through inland seas. [Montreal?, 1940]. 1 sheet folded to [12] p. Illus., map. MdBUS.

Great Lakes steamship service, summer 1940. [Montreal?, 1940]. 4 p. Illus. MdBUS, ViNeM.

Cruise the Great Lakes. [Montreal?, 1941]. [12] p. Illus., map. CSFMM, CU-SB, ViNeM.

Great Lakes steamship service, summer 1941. [Montreal?, 1941]. 4 p. CSFMM, CU-SB, MiD-D.

Cruise the Great Lakes. [Montreal?, 1942]. [12] p. Illus., map. CSmH, CU-SB, MiD-D, OBgU, ViNeM.

Great Lakes Happy Holiday cruises through inland seas. [Montreal?], 1942. 1 sheet folded to [12] p. Illus., map. CU-SB, ViNeM.

Great Lakes steamship service, summer 1942. [Montreal?, 1942]. 4 p. CU-SB, ViNeM.

Cruise the Great Lakes. [Montreal?], 1943. [12] p. Illus., map. CU-SB, CaBVaMM, OFH, ViNeM.

Great Lakes steamship service, summer 1943. [Montreal?, 1943]. 4 p. CU-SB, ViNeM.

Great Lakes Happy Holiday cruises through inland seas. [Montreal?], 1944. 1 sheet folded to [12] p. Illus., map. CU-SB, MiD-D, OFH, ViNeM.

Great Lakes steamship service, summer 1944. [Montreal?], 1944. 4 p. May issue. ViNeM.

Go the Canadian Pacific Great Lakes way. [Montreal?, 1945]. 1 sheet folded to [6] p. Illus., map. MiD-D.

Great Lakes Happy Holiday cruises through inland seas. [Montreal?], 1945. 1 sheet folded to [12] p. Illus., map. MiD-D, OBgU.

Great Lakes steamship service, summer 1945. [Montreal?], 1945. 4 p. May issue. ViNeM.

Cruise the Great Lakes. [Montreal?], 1946. 1 sheet folded to [16] p. Illus., map. CU-SB, MiD-D, OBgU.

Cruise the Great Lakes. [Montreal?, 1947]. 1 sheet folded to [12] p. Illus., map. OBgU.

Great Lakes steamship service, summer 1947. [Montreal?], 1947. 4 p. Illus. OBgU.

Go the Canadian Pacific Great Lakes way. [Montreal?, 1948]. 1 sheet folded to [12] p. Illus., map. MiD-D.

Great Lakes steamship service, summer 1948. [Montreal?, 1948]. 4 p. Illus. MiD-D.

Go the Canadian Pacific Great Lakes way. [Montreal?, 1949]. 1 sheet folded to [12] p. Illus., map. OBgU.

Great Lakes steamship service, summer 1949. [Montreal?, 1949]. 4 p. Illus. OBgU.

Go the Canadian Pacific Great Lakes way. [Montreal?, 1950]. 1 sheet folded to [12] p. Illus., map. CSmH, OBgU.

Great Lakes steamship service, summer 1950. [Montreal?, 1950]. 4 p. Illus. CSmH, OBgU.

Go the Canadian Pacific Great Lakes way. [Montreal?, 1951]. 1 sheet folded to [12] p. Illus., map. MiD-D.

Great Lakes steamship service, summer 1951. [Montreal?, 1951]. 4 p. Illus. MiD-D, OBgU.

Go the Canadian Pacific Great Lakes way. [Montreal?, 1952]. 1 sheet folded to [12] p. Illus., map. OBgU.

Great Lakes steamship service, summer 1952. [Montreal?, 1952]. 4 p. Illus. OFH.

Great Lakes steamship service, summer holiday season 1953. [Montreal?, 1953]. 4 p. Illus. CSmH, OFH.

Go the Canadian Pacific Great Lakes way, leisurely days on Canada's inland seas twice weekly between Port McNicoll and Fort William. [Montreal?, 1953]. 1 sheet folded to [12] p. Illus., map. CSmH.

Go the Great Lakes way by Canadian Pacific. [Montreal?, 1954]. 1 sheet folded to [6] p. Illus., map. CaOTPB, OBgU.

Great Lakes steamship service, summer holiday season, 1954. [Montreal?, 1954]. 4 p. Illus. OBgU.

Go the Great Lakes way by Canadian Pacific. [Montreal?, 1955]. 1 sheet folded to [12] p. Illus., map. CSmH, MiD-D.

Great Lakes steamship service, summer holiday season 1955. [Montreal?, 1955]. 4 p. CSmH, MiD-D.

Go the Great Lakes way by Canadian Pacific. [Montreal?, 1956]. 1 sheet folded to [12] p. Illus., map. MiD-D, OBgU.

Great Lakes steamship service, summer holiday season 1956. [Montreal?, 1956]. 4 p. MiD-D.

Go the Great Lakes way by Canadian Pacific. [Montreal?, 1957]. 1 sheet folded to [12] p. Illus., map. MiD-D, OBgU.

Great Lakes steamship service, summer holiday season, 1957. [Montreal?, 1957]. 4 p. Illus. MiD-D, OBgU.

Go the Great Lakes way by Canadian Pacific. [Montreal?, 1958]. 1 sheet folded to [12] p. Illus., map. CSmH, MiD-D, MiShM.

Great Lakes steamship service, summer holiday season 1958. [Montreal?, 1958]. 4 p. CSmH, MiD-B, MiD-D, MiShM.

Your Great Lakes book mark, eastward edition. [Montreal?, 1958]. 1 sheet folded to [6] p. Maps. MiD-D.

Your Great Lakes book mark, westward edition. [Montreal?, 1958]. 1 sheet folded to [6] p. Maps. CSmH, MiD-D.

Great Lakes steamship service, summer holiday season 1959. [Montreal?, 1959]. 4 p. Illus. CaOKMM, MSaP, MiD-D.

Go the Great Lakes way by Canadian Pacific. [Montreal?, 1960]. 1 sheet folded to [12] p. Illus., map. MiD-D, OBgU.

Great Lakes steamship service, summer holiday season 1960. [Montreal?, 1960]. 4 p. Illus. MiD-D.

Go the Great Lakes way by Canadian Pacific. [Montreal?, 1961]. 1 sheet folded to [12] p. Illus., map. ViNeM.

Go the Great Lakes way by Canadian Pacific. [Montreal?, 1962]. 1 sheet folded to [12] p. Illus., map. CaOKMM, MiD-D, ViNeM.

Great Lakes steamship service, summer holiday season, 1962. [Montreal?, 1962]. 4 p. Illus. CaOKMM, MiD-D.

Go the Great Lakes way by Canadian Pacific. [Montreal?, 1963]. 1 sheet folded to [12] p. Illus., map. CSmH, MSaP, MdBUS, MiD-D.

Great Lakes steamship service, summer holiday season 1963. [Montreal?, 1963]. 4 p. Illus. MdBUS, MiD-D.

Go the Great Lakes way by Canadian Pacific. [Montreal?, 1964]. 1 sheet folded to [12] p. Illus., map. CaOKMM, MiD-D, MiShM.

Great Lakes steamship service, summer holiday season 1964. [Montreal?, 1964]. 4 p. Illus. CaOKMM, MiD-D, MiShM.

Go the Great Lakes way by Canadian Pacific. [Montreal?, 1965]. 1 sheet folded to [12] p. Illus., map. CaOKMM, MSaP, MdBUS, MiD-D, OFH, WManiM.

Great Lakes steamship service, summer holiday season 1965. [Montreal?, 1965]. 4 p. Illus. CaOKMM, MdBUS, MiD-D, MiShM, OFH.

Canadian Pacific afloat, 1883-1968, a short history and fleet list by George Musk. Warrington, England: Garside and Mackie, [1968]. vi, 106 p. Illus., maps. Revised edition. CaOKMM, NjP, OBgU, WHi.

CAYUGA STEAMSHIP COMPANY, LIMITED, TORONTO, ONT

Incorporated 26 March 1953 as a sort of successor to the Niagara Navigation Division of the Canada Steamship Lines. Commenced operations on 5 June 1954 and dissolved late in 1957.

Prospectus. [Toronto?, 1953]. [10] p. Illus. CaOPoCM, MiD-D.

Time table [for the] S.S. Cayuga, schedule of fares effective June 5th to September 12th, 1954. [Toronto?, 1954]. 1 sheet folded to [4] p. Illus., map. CaOTMMUC, MiD-D, OBgU.

Time table [for the] S.S. Cayuga, schedule of fares effective June 11th to September 5th, 1955. [Toronto?, 1955]. 1 sheet folded to [4] p. Illus., map. CaOTMMUC, MiD-D, MiShM, OBgU.

Sail across Lake Ontario on the S.S. Cayuga, save 85 miles of driving. [Toronto, 1956]. 1 sheet folded to [6] p. Illus. CaOTAr, CaOTMMUC, MiD-D, NBuHi.

Time table [for the] S.S. Cayuga, 1956. [Toronto, 1956]. 1 sheet folded to [4] p. Map. CaOTMMUC, MiD-D.

Time table [for the] S.S. Cayuga, effective June 19th to September 2nd, 1957. [Toronto?, 1957]. 1 sheet folded to [4] p. Map. CaOPoCM, CaOTMMUC, MiD-D.

CHARLEVOIX & BEAVER ISLAND TRANSIT COMPANY, CHARLEVOIX, MI

Established around 1945. Ceased to exist about 1952 and succeeded by the Beaver Island Transit Company.

Beaver Island-Charlevoix boat. [N.p., 1948]. 1 sheet folded to [4] p. Illus. MiD-D.

CHARLEVOIX-ST. JAMES TRANSIT COMPANY, CHARLEVOIX, MI

Incorporated 11 September 1923. Dissolved in 1935.

Beaver Island-Charlevoix boat schedule, effective from June 1 through Labor Day, 1938. Kalamazoo: Superior Printing Co., [1938]. [4] p. Illus. OFH.

CHESAPEAKE AND OHIO RAILWAY COMPANY, DETROIT, MI

Commenced ferry operations on 6 June 1947 when it took over the Pere Marquette Railway Company fleet. Acquired by the Chessie System on 15 June 1973.

Auto ferries, the short route in and out of Michigan and the Northwest. [Cleveland?, 1948]. 1 sheet folded to [6] p. Maps. Effective May 15, 1948. MiD-D, WManiM.

Auto ferries, the short route in and out of Michigan and the Northwest. [Cleveland?, 1949]. 1 sheet folded to [6] p. Maps. Effective April 20, 1949. MiD-D, MnDuC.

Auto ferries, the short route in and out of Michigan and the Northwest. [Cleveland?, 1949]. 1 sheet folded to [6] p. Illus., maps. Effective May 29, 1949. CU-SB, MSaP, OFH, WManiM.

Auto ferries, the short route in and out of Michigan and the Northwest. [Cleveland?, 1950]. 1 sheet folded to [6] p. Maps. Corrected to May 1, 1950. MiD-D.

Auto ferries, the short route in and out of Michigan and the Northwest. [Cleveland?, 1950]. 1 sheet folded to [6] p. Maps. Corrected to June 1, 1950. MiD-D, MiShM, MnDuC.

Auto ferries, the short route in and out of Michigan and the Northwest. [Cleveland?, 1951]. 1 sheet folded to [6] p. Maps. Corrected to March 1, 1951. MiD-D.

Auto ferries, the short route in and out of Michigan and the Northwest. [Cleveland?, 1951]. 1 sheet folded to [6] p. Maps. Corrected to June 1, 1951. MiD-D, ViCFC.

Auto ferries, the short route in and out of Michigan and the Northwest. [Cleveland?, 1951]. 1 sheet folded to [6] p. Maps. Corrected to September 30, 1951. MiD-D.

Auto ferries, the short route in and out of Michigan and the Northwest. [Cleveland?, 1952]. 1 sheet folded to [6] p. Maps. Corrected to May 1, 1952. WManiM.

[The Great Lakes railroad ferries]. [Cleveland, 1952]. 80 p. Illus., map. Special issue of *Tracks Magazine*, vol. 37, no. 10 (October, 1952). MiD-D, WManiM.

Auto ferries, the short route in and out of Michigan and the Northwest. [Cleveland?, 1953]. 1 sheet folded to [6] p. Maps. Effective February 1, 1953. MiD-D.

Auto ferries, the short route in and out of Michigan and the Northwest. [Cleveland?, 1953]. 1 sheet folded to [6] p. Maps. Effective May 1, 1953. MnDuC, ViCFC, WM.

Auto ferries, the short route in and out of Michigan and the Northwest. [Cleveland?, 1953]. 1 sheet folded to [6] p. Maps. Effective September 27, 1953. MiD-D.

Auto ferries, the short route in and out of Michigan and the Northwest. [Cleveland?, 1954]. 1 sheet folded to [6] p. Maps. Effective April 25, 1954. WM.

Auto ferries, the short route in and out of Michigan and the Northwest. [Cleveland?, 1954]. 1 sheet folded to [6] p. Maps. Effective September 26, 1954. ViNeM, WM.

Auto ferries, the short route in and out of Michigan and the Northwest. [Cleveland?, 1955]. 1 sheet folded to [8] p. Maps. Effective April 24, 1955. CSmH, MiD-D, ViNeM, WM.

Auto ferries, the short route in and out of Michigan and the Northwest. [Cleveland?, 1955]. 1 sheet folded to [8] p. Maps. Effective October 30, 1955. ViCFC.

Chesapeake and Ohio salutes Mason County. [Cleveland?, 1955]. 1 sheet folded to [4] p. Illus. MiLuRH.

Auto ferries, the short route in and out of Michigan and the Northwest. [Cleveland?, 1956]. 1 sheet folded to [8] p. Maps. Effective April 29, 1956. MiD-D, MiShM.

Auto ferries, the short route in and out of Michigan and the Northwest. [Cleveland?, 1956]. 1 sheet folded to [8] p. Maps. Effective October 28, 1956. WM, WMCHi.

Auto ferries, the short route in and out of Michigan and the Northwest. [Cleveland?, 1957]. 1 sheet folded to [8] p. Maps. Effective April 28, 1957. CSmH, OBgU, ViNeM, WM, WMCHi, WManiM.

Auto ferries, the short route in and out of Michigan and the Northwest. [Cleveland?, 1958]. 1 sheet folded to [8] p. Maps. Effective April 27, 1958. MiD-D, WM, WManiM.

Auto ferries, the short route in and out of Michigan and the Northwest. [Cleveland?, 1959]. 1 sheet folded to [8] p. Maps. Effective April 26, 1959. CSmH, ViCFC, WM, WManiM.

Auto ferries, the short route in and out of Michigan and the Northwest. [Cleveland?, 1960]. 1 sheet folded to [8] p. Maps. Effective April 24, 1960. MiD-D, ViCFC, WM.

C and O auto ferries, the short route in and out of Michigan and the Northwest. [Cleveland?, 1960]. 1 sheet folded to [8] p. Maps. Effective November, 1960. WM, WManiM.

Welcome aboard! Here is your personal facts folder [for the] Chesapeake and Ohio train and auto ferries [with] year-round service. [Cleveland?, 1960?]. 1 sheet folded to [4] p. Illus., map. Top edge scalloped. MiD-D, ViNeM.

C and O auto ferries, the short route in and out of Michigan and the Northwest. [Cleveland?, 1961]. 1 sheet folded to [8] p. Maps. Effective April, 1961. CSmH, MnDuC, ViCFC, ViNeM, WM, WManiM.

C and O auto ferries, the short route into and out of Michigan and the Northwest. [Cleveland?, 1961]. 1 sheet folded to [8] p. Maps. Winter schedule. OBgU.

C and O auto ferries, the short route into and out of Michigan and the Northwest. [Cleveland?, 1962]. 1 sheet folded to [8] p. Maps. Effective April, 1962. ViCFC, WManiM.

C and O auto ferries, the short route into and out of Michigan and the Northwest. [Cleveland?, 1962]. 1 sheet folded to [8] p. Maps. Effective November, 1962. WM, WManiM.

General operating and safety rules, Marine Department, Ludington and Port Huron, Michigan. [Cleveland?, 1962]. 12 p. WManiM.

C and O auto ferries, the short route into and out of Michigan and the Northwest. [Cleveland?, 1963]. 1 sheet folded to [8] p. Maps. Spring-summer schedule, April, 1963. CSmH, MiD-D, WM, WManiM.

C and O auto ferries, the short route into and out of Michigan and the Northwest. [Cleveland?, 1964]. 1 sheet folded to [8] p. Maps. Spring-summer schedule, April, 1964. CSmH, MiD-B, MiD-D, MiShM, MnDuC, OBgU, OFH, OV, ViNeM, WManiM.

C and O auto ferries, the short route into and out of Michigan and the Northwest. [Cleveland?, 1964]. 1 sheet folded to [8] p. Maps. Effective November, 1964. MiD-D, MiShM, WM, WManiM.

C and O auto ferries, the short route into and out of Michigan and the Northwest. [Cleveland?, 1965]. 1 sheet folded to [8] p. Maps. Spring-summer schedule, April, 1965. MiD-D, MiGr, MiLuRH, MiMtpC, MiShM, OBgU, OFH, ViCFC, ViNeM, WM, WManiM.

C and O auto ferries, the short route into and out of Michigan and the Northwest. [Cleveland?, 1965]. 1 sheet folded to [8] p. Maps. Winter-spring schedules, 1965-66. MiD-D, MiLuRH.

Presque Isle docks, Toledo, Ohio. [Cleveland?, 1965]. 1 sheet folded to [8] p. Illus., map. OBgU.

C and O cross Lake Michigan autoferry service, the short route between Michigan and the Northwest. [Cleveland?, 1966]. 1 sheet folded to [12] p. Illus., maps. Summer-fall schedules effective May 1, 1966. MiD-D, MiMtpC, MiShM, MnDuC, OBgU, ViCFC, ViNeM, WM, WManiM.

C & O cross Lake Michigan autoferry service, the short route between Michigan and the Northwest. [Cleveland?, 1966]. 1 sheet folded to [6] p. Maps. Winter-spring schedule, 1966-67. ViCFC, WManiM.

C & O cross Lake Michigan autoferry service, the short route between Michigan and the Northwest. [Cleveland?, 1967]. 1 sheet folded to [12] p. Illus., maps. Summer-fall schedules, 1967. MiD-D, ViCFC, ViNeM.

C & O cross Lake Michigan autoferry service, the short route between Michigan and the Northwest. [Cleveland?, 1967]. 1 sheet folded to [12] p. Illus., maps. Summer-fall schedules revised June 19, 1967. MiD-D, MiMtpC, MiShM, OBgU, ViCFC, WM, WMCHi, WManiM.

C & O cross Lake Michigan autoferry service, the short route between Michigan and the Northwest, 1968 schedules. [Cleveland?, 1968]. 1 sheet folded to [12] p. Illus., maps. Revised April 15, 1968. Effective May 24, 1968. CSmH, MiD-D, MiGr, MiMtpC, MiShM, OBgU, ViCFC, ViNeM, WM, WManiM.

C & O cross Lake Michigan autoferry service, 1969 schedules. [Cleveland?, 1969]. 1 sheet folded to [12] p. Illus., maps. Effective June 27, 1969. MiD-D, OBgU, OFH, ViNeM, WManiM.

C & O cross Lake Michigan autoferry service [connecting] Milwaukee, Manitowoc, Ludington, 1970 schedules. [Cleveland?, 1970]. 1 sheet folded to [12] p. Illus., maps. Effective May 29, 1970. CSmH, MiD-D, MiShM, OBgU, OFH, ViNeM, WM, WManiM.

C & O cross Lake Michigan autoferry service [to] Milwaukee-Manitowoc-Ludington, 1971. [Cleveland?, 1971]. 1 sheet folded to [12] p. Illus., maps. Effective May 28, 1971. MiD-D, MiMtpC, MiShM, MnDuC, OBgU, ViCFC, ViNeM, WManiM.

C & O cross Lake Michigan autoferry service [to] Milwaukee-Manitowoc-Ludington, 1972. [Cleveland?, 1972]. 1 sheet folded to [12] p. Illus., maps. Effective May 26, 1972. MiD-D, MnDuC, OBgU, ViCFC.

CHESSIE SYSTEM, INCORPORATED, BALTIMORE, MD

Incorporated 26 February 1973. Acquired the Chesapeake and Ohio Railway Company on 15 June 1973. Discontinued Ludington to Milwaukee service on 4 October 1980. Merged into CSX Corporation on 1 November 1980. Dropped Ludington to Manitowoc route in February of 1982. Ferry service acquired by the Michigan-Wisconsin Transportation Company on 1 July 1983.

Chessie System cross Lake Michigan autoferry service, May 25-Sept. 10, 1973. [Cleveland?, 1973]. 1 sheet folded to [6] p. Illus., maps. CSmH, MiD-D, MiMtpC, MiShM, OBgU, WM, WManiM.

Chessie System cross Lake Michigan autoferry service, May 24-Sept. 9, 1974. [Cleveland?, 1974]. 1 sheet folded to [6] p. Maps. MiD-D, MiShM, OBgU, OV, WM, WMCHi, WManiM.

Chessie System cross Lake Michigan autoferry service, May 23-Sept. 8, 1975. [Cleveland?, 1975]. 1 sheet folded to [6] p. Maps. MiD-D, OBgU, ViCFC, WM, WManiM.

Chessie System cross Lake Michigan autoferry service, June 11-Sept. 7, 1976. [Cleveland?, 1976]. 1 sheet folded to [6] p. Maps. MiD-D, MiLuRH, OBgU, WM, WManiM.

Chessie System cross Lake Michigan autoferry service, June 8-September 6, 1977. [Cleveland?, 1977]. 1 sheet folded to [6] p. Maps. Revised schedule June 2, 1977. MiD-D, MiShM, OBgU.

Chessie System cross Lake Michigan autoferry service, June 8-Sept. 6, 1977. [Cleveland?, 1977]. 1 sheet folded to [6] p. Maps. CaOKMM, MiD-D, MiLuRH, OBgU, ViCFC, WM, WManiM.

Chessie System Lake Michigan autoferry service, May 28-September 4, 1978. [Cleveland?, 1978]. 1 sheet folded to [4] p. Maps. MiD-D, MiLuRH, OBgU, ViCFC, WM, WManiM.

Chessie System Lake Michigan autoferry service, May 25-September 4, 1979. [Cleveland?, 1979]. 1 sheet folded to [4] p. Maps. MiLuRH, OBgU, WM, WManiM.

Chessie System Lake Michigan autoferry service, June 1-September 14, 1980. [Cleveland?, 1980]. 1 sheet folded to [4] p. Illus., maps. MiLuRH, MiMtpC, ViCFC, WM, WManiM.

Chessie System railroads Lake Michigan autoferry service, June 1-September 8, 1981. [Cleveland?, 1981]. 1 sheet folded to [4] p. Illus., maps. MiD-D, MiLuRH, MiMtpC, OBgU, ViCFC, WM, WManiM.

Chessie System railroads Lake Michigan autoferry service, May 28-September 7, 1982. [Cleveland?, 1982]. 1 sheet folded to [4] p. Illus., maps. CaOKMM, MiManiHi, MiMtpC, WM, WManiM.

Chessie System railroads Lake Michigan autoferry service, May 27-September 6, 1983. [Cleveland?, 1983]. 1 sheet folded to [4] p. Illus., maps. CSmH, MiD-D, MiMtpC, MiShM, OBgU, ViCFC, WM, WManiM.

CHICAGO AND DULUTH TRANSPORTATION COMPANY, CHICAGO, IL
Incorporated 1 March 1907. Dissolved 1 July 1920.

Lake Michigan and Lake Superior steamers. Chicago: Poole Bros., [1911]. 22 [i.e. 12] p. Illus., map. ViNeM, WM.

CHICAGO & MUSKEGON TRANSPORTATION COMPANY, CHICAGO, IL
Organized on 8 February 1900 as a division of the Barry Brothers Transportation Company. Assets sold at auction on 6 April 1905 and the firm dissolved on 21 September 1921. Succeeded in part by the Hackley Transportation Company.

Barry Muskegon line steamers between Chicago, Muskegon, Grand Haven, Grand Rapids, White Lake resorts, and all Michigan points. Grand Rapids: Dean-Hicks Printing Co., [1902]. 1 sheet folded to [16] p. Illus., maps. OBgU.

Coming and going through Michigan via Barry-Muskegon-Chicago steamers. [Grand Rapids, 1903?]. [40] p. Illus. Mi.

CHICAGO & SOUTH HAVEN STEAMSHIP COMPANY, CHICAGO, IL
Incorporated 3 May 1909 as a result of a merger of the Dunkley Williams Company and the Michigan Steamship Company. Ceased shipping operations in the fall of 1926. In 1927 it merged with the Benton Transit Company to form the Chicago, Benton Harbor & South Haven Transit Company. Dissolved in July, 1928.

South Haven and Michigan points, [the] shortest [and] most direct route from Chicago to Kalamazoo, Battle Creek, Jackson, Lake Cora, Paw Paw Lake & Lawton. Chicago: Faulkner-Ryan Co., [1909]. 15, [1] p. Illus. MSaP.

South Haven and Michigan points, [the] shortest [and] most direct route from Chicago to Kalamazoo, Battle Creek, Jackson, Lake Cora & Lawton. Chicago: Cahill-Igoe Co., [1914]. 19, [1] p. Illus., map. ViNeM.

South Haven and Michigan points, [the] shortest [and] most direct route from Chicago to Kalamazoo, Battle Creek, Jackson, Lake Cora & Lawton. [Chicago?, 1915]. 19, [1] p. Illus., map. WMCHi.

South Haven and Michigan points, [the] shortest [and] most direct route from Chicago to Kalamazoo, Battle Creek, Jackson, Lake Cora & Lawton, 1918. Chicago: Cahill-Igoe Co., [1918]. 7, [1] p. Illus., map. ViNeM.

South Haven and Michigan points, [the] shortest [and] most direct route from Chicago to Kalamazoo, Battle Creek, Jackson, Lake Cora & Lawton. Chicago: James T. Igoe Co., 1920. 11, [1] p. Illus., map. MiShM, WM.

South Haven and Michigan points, [the] shortest [and] most direct route from Chicago to Kalamazoo, Battle Creek, Jackson, Lake Cora & Lawton. Chicago: James T. Igoe Co., [1921]. 11, [1] p. Illus., map. MiD-D, MiShM, ViNeM.

South Haven and Michigan points, [the] shortest [and] most direct route from Chicago to Kalamazoo, Battle Creek, Jackson, Lake Cora & Lawton. Chicago: James T. Igoe Co., [1922]. 1 sheet folded to [4] p. Illus., map. ViNeM.

South Haven and Michigan points, [the] shortest [and] most direct route from Chicago to Kalamazoo, Battle Creek, Jackson, Lake Cora & Lawton. Chicago: James T. Igoe Co., [1923]. 1 sheet folded to [4] p. Illus., map. WM.

South Haven and Michigan points, [the] shortest [and] most direct route from Chicago to Kalamazoo, Battle Creek, Jackson, Lake Cora & Lawton. Chicago: James T. Igoe Co., [1924]. 1 sheet folded to [4] p. Illus., map. MiD-D, MiShM, OBgU, WM.

South Haven, the center of the play ground of a nation, 1926. [Chicago, 1926]. 1 sheet folded to [4] p. Illus. MiD-D.

CHICAGO, BENTON HARBOR & SOUTH HAVEN TRANSIT COMPANY, CHICAGO, IL

Established in the spring of 1927 by a merger of the Chicago & South Haven Steamship Company with the Benton Transit Company. Discontinued shipping operations on 6 June 1929.

South Haven and Michigan points, [the] shortest [and] most direct route from Chicago to Kalamazoo, Battle Creek, Jackson, Lake Cora & Lawton. Chicago: James T. Igoe Co., [1927]. 1 sheet folded to [4] p. Illus. MiD-D.

CHICAGO, DULUTH & GEORGIAN BAY TRANSIT COMPANY, CHICAGO, IL

Incorporated as an Indiana firm on 1 August 1912 and commenced operations on 20 June 1913. Adopted nickname of "Georgian Bay Line" in 1934. Moved head office to Detroit in 1935. Ceased operations on 23 October 1967 and dissolved on 7 March 1968.

Local passenger tariff. — No. 1 (January 20, 1913)-no. 794 (August 15, 1967) — Chicago?, 1913-1967. Irregular. ICC nos. 1-881. Map. MiD-B, MiD-D.

A week's cruise on four lakes, 2200 miles [on the] new steamship "North American." Detroit: Joseph Mack Printing House, [1914]. 11, [1] p. Illus. MiD-D, ViNeM.

A week's cruise. [Chicago?, 1915?]. 11, [1] p. Illus., folded map. MiU-H, ViNeM.

A week's cruise on four lakes, 2200 miles, season 1916. [Chicago?, 1916]. 11, [1] p. Illus., folded map. MiD-D, MSaP, ViNeM, WM, WMCHi.

A week's cruise on four lakes, 2200 miles, season 1917. [Chicago: Poole Bros., 1917]. 15, [1] p. Illus., map. MiD-D, ViNeM, WM, WMCHi.

A week's cruise on four lakes, 2200 miles, season 1918. Chicago: Wagner & Hanson Co., [1918]. 30 [i.e. 16] p. Illus., map. MiDbEI, ViNeM, WM.

Auditors' report and accounts [for] year ended December 31st, 1917. [Chicago?, 1918]. [4], 10, [5] leaves. Nearprint. MH-BA.

Auditors' report and accounts [for] year ended December 31st, 1918. [Chicago?, 1919]. [2], 5, [6] leaves. Nearprint. MH-BA.

Lake cruises, a week's cruise on four lakes, season 1919. Chicago: Wagner & Hanson Co., [1919]. [16] p. Illus., map. MSaP, MiD-D, MiGrM, WM.

Lake cruises, a week's cruise on four lakes, 2200 miles. [Chicago?, 1920]. 11, [1] p. Illus., map. OBgU.

Lake cruises, a week's cruise on four lakes, season 1920. Chicago: Wagner & Hanson Co., [1920]. [20] p. Illus., map. MiD-D, ViNeM.

Auditors' report and accounts [for period ending] December 31st, 1920. [Chicago?, 1921]. [1], 4, [5] leaves. MH-BA.

Lake cruises, a week's cruise on four lakes, season 1921. Chicago: Wagner & Hanson Co., [1921]. [20] p. Illus., map. MSaP, OBgU, ViNeM, WM.

Lake cruises, a week's cruise on four lakes, season 1922. Chicago: General Printing Co., [1922]. [20] p. Illus., map. WM.

Lake cruises, a week's cruise on four lakes, season 1923. Chicago: General Printing Co., [1923]. 19, [1] p. Illus., map. CSmH, MiD-B, ViNeM, WM.

How would you like to spend your vacation as these girls did? [Chicago?, 1924?]. 7, [1] p. MiD-D.

Lake cruises, a week's cruise on four lakes, season 1924. Chicago: Faulkner-Ryan Co., [1924]. 19, [1] p. Illus., map. CSmH, MiD-D, MiShM, NBuHi, WM.

Lake cruises, a week's cruise on four lakes, season 1925. Chicago: Chicago Rotoprint Co., [1925]. [20] p. Illus., map. MiD-D, OBgU, OFH, NBuHi, WM.

Lake cruises, a week's cruise on four lakes, season 1926. Chicago: Chicago Rotoprint Co., [1926]. [20] p. Illus., map. MiD-D, MiHolJA, NBuHi, ViNeM, WM.

Lake cruises, a week's cruise on 4 lakes, season 1927. Chicago: Walton & Spencer Co., 1927. 19, [1] p. Illus., map. CSmH, MiD-B, MiD-D, MiHolJA, NBuHi, WM.

Lake cruises, a week's cruise on 4 lakes, season 1928. Chicago: Walton & Spencer Co., 1928. 19, [1] p. Illus., map. MiD-D, WM.

A week on the Great Lakes with the Civic Council of Brooklyn fourth annual cruise. [Brooklyn?, 1929]. 11, [1] p. Illus., map. ViNeM.

Lake cruises, a week's cruise on 4 lakes, season 1929. Chicago: Walton & Spencer, 1929. 23, [1] p. Illus., map. MiD-B, MiD-D, ViNeM, WM.

Two perfect vacation weeks...one on S.S. Alabama...one at Rock Harbor Lodge on Isle Royale. [Chicago?, 1929?]. 1 sheet folded to [6] p. Illus., map. NBuHi.

Labor Day cruise thru the "Soo" locks, visiting White Fish Bay, Lake Superior [and] Mackinac Island [on the] S.S. South American. [Chicago?, 1930?]. 1 sheet folded to [4] p. Illus. MiShM.

Lake cruises, a week's cruise on 4 lakes, season 1930. Chicago: Walton & Spencer Co., 1930. 23, [1] p. Illus., map. MSaP, MiD-D, WM.

The Radio Press. — Vol. ?, no. 1 (1930?)- vol. ?, no. ? (1931?) — [Chicago, 1930-1931]? Daily during cruises. Published on board by the ship's wireless operators. Near-print. Continued by: The Wireless Press. MiD-D.

A week's cruise on the Great Lakes. Chicago: Poole Bros., [1931]. 23, [1] p. Illus., map. MiD-D.

Songs of the S.S. North American. [Chicago?, 1931?]. [16] p. Words only. MiD-D.

Songs of the S.S. South American. [Chicago?, 1931?]. [16] p. Words only. MiShM, OBgU.

A week's cruise on the Great Lakes. Chicago: Poole Bros., [1932]. 23, [1] p. Illus., map. CU-SB, MiD-D, MnDuC, NBuHi, OBgU, ViNeM, WM.

The Wireless Press. — Vol. ?, no. ? (1932?) — [Chicago, 1932]? Daily during cruises. Published on board by the ships' wireless operators. Near-print. Continues: The Radio Press. Continued by: The Daily Radio Press. MiD-D.

A week's cruise on the Great Lakes, 1933. Chicago: Poole Bros., [1933]. 23, [1] p. Illus., map. CU-SB, MiD-D, MiShM, ViNeM.

The Daily Radio Press. — Vol. ?, no. ? (1933)- vol. ?, no. ? (1938?) — [Chicago, 1933-1938]? Illus., maps. Daily during cruises. Published on board by the ships' wireless operators. Near-print. Continues: The Wireless Press. Continued by: Daily Radio News. MiD-D, MnDuU.

Day by day on the two Americans, 1933. Chicago: Hillison & Etten Co., [1933]. 1 sheet folded to [4] p. MiD-D

Eighth Annual Summer Cruise of the Civic Council of Brooklyn. [Brooklyn?, 1933]. 1 sheet folded to [10] p. Illus., map. ViNeM.

Summer vacation cruises. [Chicago?, 1933]. 1 sheet folded to [16] p. Illus. MiD-D, ViNeM.

World's Fair Championship Bridge Cruise, conducted by Edward C. Wolfe, America's foremost bridge lecturer. Chicago: Hillison & Etten Co., [1933]. 1 sheet folded to [12] p. Illus. WM.

All-expense Great Lakes cruises including World's Fair at Chicago. [Chicago?, 1934]. 23, [1] p. Illus., map. OBgU.

Lake cruises. [Chicago?, 1934]. 23, [1] p. Illus., map. CU-SB, MiD-D, MiGr, NBuHi, ViNeM, WM.

Rock Harbor Lodge on Isle Royale in Lake Superior via the S.S. Alabama. [Chicago?, 1934]. 1 sheet folded to [6] p. Illus., maps. MiShM.

All-expense vacation at the Muskoka Lakes via the Georgian Bay Line. [Detroit?], 1935. 1 sheet folded to [8] p. Illus., map. ViNeM.

Pleasure cruises for leisure days on the Great Lakes. [Chicago?, 1935]. 15, [1] p. Illus. CU-SB, MiD-D, NBuHi, ViNeM.

Annual Labor Day cruise to Mackinac Island, the "Soo," and return [for an] all-expense cruise [offering] glorious days [and] glamorous nights on the Georgian Bay Line. [Detroit?], 1936. 1 sheet folded to [4] p. Illus. MiD-D.

Pleasure cruises on the S.S. North American [and] S.S. South American. Detroit: C P[rinting] C[ompany], 1936. 19, [1] p. Illus., map. CSmH, MSaP, MiD-D, NBuHi, OBgU, ViNeM.

Pre-view of a perfect vacation on the Georgian Bay Line. [Detroit?], 1936. 1 sheet folded to [12] p. Illus., map. CU-SB, MiD-D, NBuHi, ViNeM.

Again we sail westward [with the] Erie Chamber of Commerce. [Erie?], 1937. 1 sheet folded to [6] p. Illus. MiD-B.

For a bang-up fourth [take an] all-expense 4th of July cruise to Charlevoix and Mackinac Island and return. [Detroit?, 1937]. 1 sheet folded to [4] p. Illus. MiD-D.

14-day, all-expense vacation, 7 days at the Muskoka Lakes [and] 7 days cruising on the Georgian Bay Line, season 1937. [Detroit?], 1937. 1 sheet folded to [8] p. Illus., map. MiD-D.

Great Lakes cruises [on the] S.S. North American [and the] S.S. South American, 1937. [Detroit?], 1937. 15, [1] p. Illus., map. CU-SB, MiD-D, NBuHi, OBgU, ViNeM.

Pleasure ahoy on the Great Lakes. [Detroit?], 1937. 1 sheet folded to [12] p. Illus., map. MiD-B, MiD-D, MiShM, OBgU, ViNeM.

Annual summer outing [by the] Electrical League of the Niagara Frontier. [Buffalo?, 1938]. 1 sheet folded to [4] p. Illus. Edges scalloped on three sides. MiD-B.

Archbishop McHale Council, Knights of Columbus, Annual Labor Day Cruise to the "Soo," Mackinac Island and return. [Detroit?, 1938?]. 1 sheet folded to [4] p. Illus. MiD-D.

14-day all-expense vacation, 7 days at the Muskoka Lakes [and] 7 days cruising on the Georgian Bay Line, season 1938. [Detroit?, 1938]. 1 sheet folded to [8] p. Illus., map. CSmH, MiD-D.

Georgian Bay Line-Mackinac Island all-expense vacations (season 1938) cruise to the Grand Hotel. [Detroit?, 1938]. 1 sheet folded to [6] p. Illus. CSmH, MiD-D.

Great Lakes cruises [on the] S.S. North American [and] S.S. South American, 1938. [Detroit?, 1938]. 19, [1] p. Illus., map. April edition. CSmH, CU-SB, MiD-D, NBuHi, OBgU, ViNeM.

Pleasure preview of a Great Lakes cruise. [Detroit?, 1938?]. 1 sheet folded to [8] p. Illus., map. MiD-D.

This summer cruise the Great Lakes. [Detroit?], 1938. 1 sheet folded to [12] p. Illus., map. MiD-B, MiD-D.

Ahoy, sailors! We're off [on the] 15th Annual Cruise [of the] Erie Chamber of Commerce, June 24-29, 1939. [Erie?, 1939]. 1 sheet folded to [4] p. Illus., map. MiD-B.

All-expense Labor Day cruises. [Detroit?, 1939?]. 1 sheet folded to [4] p. Illus. NBuHi.

All expense trip to Detroit - Greenfield Village and return. [Detroit?, 1939]. 1 sheet folded to [4] p. Illus. MiD-B.

Archbishop McHale Council, Knights of Columbus, Annual Labor Day All-Expense Cruise to Sault S[ain]te Marie, Mackinac Island and return. [Chicago?, 1939]. 1 sheet folded to [6] p. Illus. MiD-B.

Eleventh Good Fellowship Cruise [of the Harrisburg PA Chamber of Commerce]. [Harrisburg?, 1939]. 1 sheet folded to [6] p. Illus., map. MiD-B.

Georgian Bay Line-Mackinac Island all-expense vacations (season 1939) [with a] cruise to the Grand Hotel via the S.S. North American [and] S.S. South American. [Detroit?, 1939]. 1 sheet folded to [6] p. Illus. ViNeM.

Golden Horizon, by Rex [R.] Schwenneker. A brief history of the Great Lakes presented to you with the compliments of the Georgian Bay Line in memory of your cruise aboard the [firm's ship of your choice]. [Detroit?, 1939?]. [20] p. Illus. MiD-B.

Great Lakes cruises, Georgian Bay Line, season 1939. [Detroit?, 1939]. 23, [1] p. Illus., map. CSmH, CU-SB, Mi, MiD-B, MiD-D, MiMtpC, MiU-H, MnDuU, NBuHi, OBgU, ViNeM.

Guide to Chicago, Duluth & Georgian Bay Line 1939 sailings out of the Port of Detroit. [Detroit?, 1939]. 1 sheet folded to [4] p. MiD-D.

Here's your 14-day — all-expense royal Muskoka vacation... [including] 7 fun-filled days of Great Lakes cruising on the Georgian Bay Line's S.S. North American and S.S. South American. [Toronto?, 1939?]. 1 sheet folded to [12] p. Illus., map. MiD-D.

Holland [MI] men: here is your invitation to sail with us. [Chicago?, 1939]. 1 sheet folded to [4] p. Illus. MiD-B.

The pleasure way to the New York World's Fair! Rail and water circle cruise-tours. [Detroit?, 1939]. 1 sheet folded to [8] p. Illus., map. NBuHi.

6th Annual Cruise to Georgian Bay and Mackinac Island, Paul Henry Travel Service. [Detroit?, 1939]. 1 sheet folded to [4] p. Illus. MiD-D.

Third Order of St. Francis cruise to Jesuit Martyrs' Shrine at Midland, Ontario, and the beautiful Georgian Bay. [Detroit?, 1939?]. 1 sheet folded to [4] p. Illus. MiD-B.

Cruise the Great Lakes the American way with the Georgian Bay Line, season 1940. [Detroit?, 1940]. 15, [1] p. Illus., maps. CSmH, CU-SB, MSaP, MiD-B, MiD-D, MiHM, MiShM, MnDuLS, OBgU, ViNeM.

Cruise to the Grand Hotel via the S.S. North American [or] S.S. South American [and] enjoy several days at Mackinac Island. [Detroit?, 1940]. 1 sheet folded to [6] p. Illus. NBuHi.

Daily Radio News. — Vol. ?, no. ? (1940)-vol. ?, no. ? (1941?). — On board ship S.S. North American and S.S. South American. Daily during cruise season. Continues: The Daily Radio Press. Possibly continued by Cruise News. CSmH, MiD-B, MiD-D, PPPMM.

11-day super Great Lakes cruise tour to the New York World's Fair, July 14-24, 1940. [Detroit?, 1940]. 1 sheet folded to [8] p. Illus. CU-SB, MiD-D.

The log of the annual lake cruise, June 4th, 1940, [of] the Transportation Club of Buffalo. [Buffalo?, 1940]. [6] p. Illus. MiD-B.

Ship ahoy! A grand get-together [is the] Second Annual Cruise [of the] Sheboygan Association of Commerce, June 20-24, 1940. [Sheboygan?, 1940]. 1 sheet folded to [4] p. Illus. MiD-B, MiD-D.

Special 11 day cruise tour, July 20th to 31st - 1940, featuring 8 days on the Great Lakes. [Detroit?, 1940]. [12] p. Illus., map. NBuHi.

While summer lingers [take a] Labor Day cruise, [an] Indian summer cruise, including 1000 Islands, [or a] harvest time cruise. [Detroit?, 1940?]. 1 sheet folded to [12] p. Illus., maps. MiD-D.

All-America water-rail cruise of Great Lakes and Glacier National Park. [Detroit?, 1941]. 1 sheet folded to [8] p. Illus. NBuHi.

All-expense cruise to the Tulip-Time Festival, May 23-25, Georgian Bay Line. [Detroit?, 1941]. 1 sheet folded to [8] p. Illus. MiShM, WM.

"Early bird" cruises on Lake Michigan, 1941. [Detroit?, 1941]. 1 sheet folded to [4] p. Illus. CU-SB, MiD-D, MiShM.

8th Annual Special Cruise aboard the luxurious liner S.S. South American to Georgian Bay and Mackinac Island. [Detroit?, 1941]. 1 sheet folded to [4] p. Illus. MiD-D.

Enjoy a thrilling Georgian Bay Line Labor Day cruise in ocean liner luxury. [Detroit?, 1941?]. 1 sheet folded to [4] p. Illus., map. MiD-D.

Enjoy a thrilling Georgian Bay Line Labor Day cruise in ocean liner luxury. [Detroit?, 1941]. 1 sheet folded to [16] p. Illus. CU-SB, MiD-D, MiShM.

Flash: in 1941 for the first time you can take the new "adventure cruise" aboard the spotless, oil-fueled S.S. South American. [Detroit?, 1941]. 1 sheet folded to [4] p. Illus. MiD-D.

For a bang-up fourth [take an] all-expense 4th of July cruise, cruising Lake Erie [with] stops at Buffalo and Cleveland. [Detroit?, 1941]. 1 sheet folded to [4] p. Illus. MiD-D.

Great Lakes cruises [on the] S.S. North American, S.S. South American, [and] S.S. Alabama, season 1941. [Detroit?, 1941]. [12] p. Illus., maps. Pages are tri-folded. CSmH, CU-SB, MiD-D, MiHM, MiMtpC, MiShM, NBuHi, OBgU, OFH, PPPMM, ViNeM, WM.

On Wisconsin! All aboard for the time of your life on the gala Milwaukee Trade Tour and Good Will Cruise to Mackinac Island. [Milwaukee?, 1941]. 1 sheet folded to [4] p. Illus. MiD-B.

Sailors! We're off!...on the big 1941 summer cruise of the Illinois Dairy Products Association, June 27-28-29, aboard the S.S. Alabama. [Chicago?, 1941]. 1 sheet folded to [4] p. Illus., map. MiD-B.

17th Annual Erie Chamber of Commerce cruise, Erie, Pennsylvania, June 21-26, 1941, [with] three interesting ports to visit...and the time of your life aboard the S.S. South American. [Detroit?, 1941]. 1 sheet folded to [8] p. Illus., map. MiShM.

Shriners! and their ladies, all aboard for a grand vacation on the Gala Saladin Temple Cruise, June 29-July 3, 1941. [Detroit?, 1941]. 1 sheet folded to [4] p. Illus. MiD-B, MiHolJA.

Special bargain Indian summer cruise to Isle Royale [and] Mackinac Island, September 3-7, 1941. [Detroit?, 1941]. 1 sheet folded to [4] p. Illus., map. MiD-D, MiShM.

Special 11 day cruise tour featuring 8 days on the Great Lakes, 1941 season. [Detroit?, 1941]. 1 sheet folded to [12] p. Illus., map. MiD-D.

Week-end cruises to Mackinac Island and Sturgeon Bay. [Detroit?, 1941]. 1 sheet folded to [12] p. Illus., map. CU-SB, MiD-D, OFH, WM.

All-expense cruises to the Tulip-Time Festival, May 15-18-22 [on the] Georgian Bay Line. [Detroit?], 1942. 1 sheet folded to [8] p. Illus. CU-SB, MiD-D, MiShM.

Anchors aweigh! for the Second Annual Summer Cruise of the Illinois Dairy Products Association. [Chicago?, 1942]. 1 sheet folded to [4] p. Illus. Edges scalloped on three sides. MiD-B.

Announcing the senior cruises for 1942 [through] Youth Travel, Ann Arbor, Michigan. [Detroit?, 1942]. 1 sheet folded to [8] p. Illus. MiD-D.

Cruise from Chicago to the Rotary International Convention at Toronto aboard the S.S. Alabama, June 18-29, 1942. [Chicago?, 1942]. 1 sheet folded to [8] p. Illus., map. MiD-D.

"Early bird" cruises during the month of June from Cleveland and Detroit aboard the luxury liner S.S. South American, 1942. [Detroit?, 1942]. 1 sheet folded to [6] p. Illus., maps. MiD-D.

"Early bird" cruises on Lake Michigan from Chicago aboard the luxury liner S.S. North American, 1942.

[Chicago?, 1942]. 1 sheet folded to [6] p. Illus., maps. CU-SB, MiD-D, ViNeM.

Great Lakes cruises [on the] S.S. North American, S.S. South American, [and] S.S. Alabama. [Detroit?], 1942. [12] p. Illus., map. May edition. CSmH, CU-SB, MiD-D, MiShM, NBuHi, OBgU, OFH, ViNeM, WM.

Indian summer cruise through Michigan, Wisconsin and Canadian waters, September 8-13, 1942. [Detroit?], 1942. 1 sheet folded to [4] p. Illus., map. MiD-D.

Join the "gang" on our 2nd Annual Joliet Goodfellowship [sic] Cruise, Wednesday, June 10. [Joliet?, 1942]. 1 sheet folded to [4] p. Illus. MiD-B.

9th annual special cruise aboard the luxurious liner S.S. South American to Georgian Bay, Harbor Springs [and] Mackinac Island, sailing June 21, 1942. [Detroit?, 1942]. 1 sheet folded to [4] p. Illus. MiD-D.

Put your convention on the map with a Great Lakes convention cruise. [Detroit?, 1942]. 1 sheet folded to [4] p. Illus., map. Scalloped on 3 edges. MiD-D.

S.S. Alabama emergency stations and equipment book. [Detroit?, 1942?]. [12] p. Mi.

Saladin Great Lakes Cruise [on the] S.S. North America[n] June 18-22, 1942. [Grand Rapids?, 1942]. 1 sheet folded to [8] p. Illus. MiHolJA

Say good-bye to summer on a gala, all-expense Labor Day cruise to Harbor Springs and Mackinac Island aboard the spacious S.S. South American. [Detroit?, 1942?]. 1 sheet folded to [4] p. Illus., map. MiShM.

Vacation preview, "The Great Cruises of the Great Lakes." [Detroit?, 1942]. 1 sheet folded to [4] p. Illus., map. CU-SB, MiD-D.

Your choice of 2 thrilling all-expense Labor Day cruises from Chicago. [Chicago?, 1942]. 1 sheet folded to [4] p. Illus., maps. CU-SB, MiD-D.

Decoration Day cruise from Chicago aboard the luxury liner S.S. South American, 1943. [Chicago?, 1943]. 1 sheet folded to [4] p. Illus. CU-SB.

Georgian Bay Line Great Lakes cruises, season of 1943. [Detroit?, 1943]. 1 sheet folded to [20] p. Illus., maps. CU-SB, MiD-D, NBuHi, OBgU, OFH, ViNeM, WM.

1943 "early bird" cruise from Detroit aboard the luxury liner S.S. South American, June 11-14, 1943. [Detroit?, 1943]. 1 sheet folded to [4] p. Illus. MiD-D.

Preview of your 1943 V-cation [sic] on the Great Lakes aboard one of the cruise ships of the Georgian Bay Line. [Detroit?, 1943]. 1 sheet folded to [4] p. Illus., maps. MiD-D.

While summer lingers [take a] Labor Day cruise, Indian summer cruise, [or a] harvest time cruise on the luxury liner S.S. South American. [Chicago: Poole Bros.], 1943. 1 sheet folded to [8] p. Illus., maps. CU-SB, MiD-B, MiD-D.

While summer lingers [take a] Labor Day cruise, Indian summer cruise, [or a] harvest time cruise on the luxury liners S.S. North American [and] S.S. South American. [Chicago: Poole Bros., 1943]. 1 sheet folded to [8] p. Illus., maps. CU-SB, MiD-B, MiD-D.

Decoration Day cruise May 27th to 31st [on the] S.S. North American. [Detroit?, 1944]. 1 sheet folded to [4] p. Illus., map. MiD-D.

Great Lakes V-cation [sic] cruises, season 1944. [Detroit?], 1944. 1 sheet folded to [20] p. Illus., maps. CU-SB, MiD-B, MiD-D, NBuHi, ViNeM, WMCHi.

Week-end cruise aboard the luxury liner S.S. South American from Detroit and Cleveland to Port Colborne and return, May 27-29. [Detroit?], 1944. 1 sheet folded to [4] p. Illus. MiD-D.

While summer lingers [take a] Labor Day cruise, Indian summer cruise including 1,000 Islands, [or a] harvest time cruise on the luxury liners S.S. North American [and] S.S. South American. [Chicago: Poole Bros., 1944]. 1 sheet folded to [12] p. Illus., maps. CU-SB, MiD-B, MiD-D.

Great Lakes V-cation [sic] cruises [on the] S.S. North American [and] S.S. South American, season 1945. [Detroit?], 1945. 1 sheet folded to [20] p. Illus., maps. CSmH, CU-SB, MiD-B, MiD-D, MiHM, MiHolJA, MiMtpC, MiShM, NBuHi, OBgU, OFH, ViNeM.

7th Annual Graphic Arts Cruise to Georgian Bay. [Detroit?, 1945]. 1 sheet folded to [8] p. Illus. MiD-D.

2 delightful June cruises aboard the Georgian Bay Line's famous white luxury liner of the Great Lakes, S.S. North American. [Detroit?, 1945]. 2 p. Illus., map. MiD-D.

All-expense cruise to the Tulip-Time Festival. [Chicago?, 1946]. 1 sheet folded to [8] p. Illus. CU-SB, MiD-D.

8th Annual Graphic Arts Cruise to the Thousand Islands. [Detroit?, 1946]. 1 sheet folded to [8] p. Illus. MiD-D.

Gala Decoration Day cruise from Chicago on the luxury liner S.S. North American. [Detroit?], 1946. 1 sheet folded to [4] p. Illus., map. CU-SB, MiD-D.

Gala Decoration Day cruise to the Thousand Islands on the luxury liner S.S. South American. [Detroit?, 1946]. 1 sheet folded to [4] p. Illus., map. CU-SB.

Georgian Bay Line Indian summer (Thousand Islands) cruise. [Detroit?, 1946]. 1 sheet folded to [10] p. Illus., maps. CU-SB.

Georgian Bay Line special cruise to Tulip Land. [Chicago?, 1946]. 1 sheet folded to [8] p. Illus. CU-SB.

Golden horizon, by Rex [R.] Schwenneker. A brief history of the Great Lakes presented to you with compliments of the Georgian Bay Line. [Detroit?, 1946]. [20] p. Illus., map. NBuHi.

Great Lakes cruises [on the] Georgian Bay Line, 1946. [Detroit?], 1946. 1 sheet folded to [20] p. Illus., maps. CSmH, CU-SB, MiD-B, MiD-D, MiMtpC, MiShM, NBuHi, OBgU, OFH, ViNeM, WM.

"I AM" Ascended Master Youth Miracle Conclave aboard the S.S. North American, August 17 to August 31, 1946. [Chicago?, 1946]. 1 sheet folded to [8] p. Illus., map. MiD-D.

Looking ahead to your vacation on the Great Lakes. [Detroit?, 1946]. 1 sheet folded to [4] p. Illus., maps. MiD-D.

Reservation books open 1946 Georgian Bay Line pre-season, post-season, and regular summertime cruises. [Detroit?, 1946]. 1 sheet folded to [4] p. Illus. CU-SB, MiD-D.

Enjoy early September on the Great Lakes [with the] Georgian Bay Line. [Detroit?, 1947]. 1 sheet folded to [8] p. Illus. MiD-D.

Gala Decoration Day cruise to the Thousand Islands on the luxury liner S.S. South American, May 28-June 1, 1947. [Detroit?, 1947]. 1 sheet folded to [4] p. Illus., map. MiD-D, OBgU.

Great Lakes cruises, seven glorious days of sun, fun, rest. [Detroit?], 1947. 1 sheet folded to [20] p. Illus., maps. CU-SB, MiD-B, MiD-D, MiHM, NBuHi, OBgU, ViNeM, WM.

The Islington [resort] for "tops" in vacation pleasure via Georgian Bay Lines. [Detroit?, 1947]. 1 sheet folded to [4] p. Illus. MiD-D.

Looking ahead to your vacation on the Great Lakes. [Detroit?, 1947]. 1 sheet folded to [4] p. Illus., maps. CSmH, MiD-D, OBgU.

Tulip time in Holland, Michigan, May, 1947. [Chicago?, 1947]. 1 sheet folded to [12] p. Illus., map. CU-SB, MiD-D.

Enjoy early September on the Great Lakes Georgian Bay Line, special cruises capture the thrills of the inland seas at their best! [Detroit?], 1948. 1 sheet folded to [8] p. Illus. CSmH, MiD-D, OBgU.

Great Lakes cruises on the sister queens of the Great Lakes, 1948. [Detroit?, 1948]. 7, [1] p. Illus., maps. Pages vary in size. CSmH, CU-SB, MiD-B, MiD-D, MiShM, NBuHi, OBgU, PPPMM, ViNeM, WM.

Plan now...a carefree vacation on the Great Lakes in 1948. [Detroit?, 1948]. 1 sheet folded to [6] p. Illus., maps. CSmH, MiD-D, OBgU.

Sail away over Decoration Day on a Georgian Bay Line gala cruise to Mackinac Island, sailing on May 28, 1948. [Detroit?, 1948]. 1 sheet folded to [4] p. Illus. CSmH, CU-SB, MiD-D, WManiM.

Burlington [Railroad] Great Lakes cruise, weekly [during] season 1949. [Chicago?, 1949]. 1 sheet folded to [10] p. Illus., map. MiD-B, MiD-D.

Georgian Bay Line Mackinac Island all-expense vacations, 1949. [Detroit?, 1949]. 1 sheet folded to [8] p. Illus. CSmH, CU-SB, MiD-B, MiD-D, MnDuC, NBuHi, OBgU.

The Georgian Bay Line 1949 Great Lakes cruises. [Detroit?, 1949]. 7, [1] p. Illus., maps. CSmH, CU-SB, CaOOA, MSaP, MiD-D, MiShM, NBuHi, OBgU.

Join the fun on this special week-end cruise aboard the S.S. North American from Chicago to Soo Locks and return, June 17 to 20, 1949. [Chicago?, 1949]. 1 sheet folded to [8] p. Illus. MiShM.

Labor Day and Indian summer Great Lakes cruises, 1949. [Detroit?, 1949]. 1 sheet folded to [8] p. Illus. CU-SB, MiD-B, MiD-D, MnDuC, NBuHi.

Sail away over Decoration Day on a Georgian Bay Line gala cruise to Mackinac Island. [Detroit?, 1949]. 1 sheet folded to [4] p. Illus. MiD-B.

Special pilgrimage cruise to historic Fort S[ain]te Marie, 1649-1949, the Third Centenary of the Jesuit Martyrs of North America. [Detroit?, 1949]. 1 sheet folded to [4] p. Illus. CU-SB.

All-expense vacations [on the] Georgian Bay Line [to] Mackinac Island, 1950. [Detroit?, 1950]. 1 sheet folded to [8] p. Illus. MiD-B, MiD-D, MiShM.

4 glorious days of fun afloat! aboard the S.S. South American for the Ohio State Automobile Association's 1950 Convention Cruise. [Detroit?, 1950]. 1 sheet folded to [6] p. Illus. OBgU.

The Georgian Bay Line Great Lakes cruises, 1950. [Detroit?, 1950]. 7, [1] p. Illus., maps. Pages vary in size. CSmH, CaOOA, MiD-B, MiD-D, MiHM, OBgU, WM.

Great Lakes cruises [on the] S.S. North American, S.S. South American, [and] S.S. Alabama. [Detroit?, 1950]. [12] p. Illus., maps. OBgU.

Great Lakes vacation via United Air Lines and Georgian Bay Line, combine the convenience of flying with the pleasure of cruising. [Detroit?, 1950]. 1 sheet folded to [4] p. Illus. MiD-D.

17th Annual Friendship Cruise aboard the luxurious liner S.S. South American to Harbor Springs, Mackinac Island, Georgian Bay [and the] Jesuit Martyrs' Shrine. [Detroit?, 1950]. 1 sheet folded to [4] p. Illus. MiD-B, MiD-D.

Top fun on the Great Lakes [with] special Labor Day week-end cruises to Mackinac Island and other points of interest. [Detroit?, 1950]. 1 sheet folded to [4] p. Illus. MiD-D, OBgU.

A chamber of commerce good-fellowship cruise. [Detroit?, 1951?]. 1 sheet folded to [4] p. Illus. ViNeM.

All-expense vacations [on the] Georgian Bay Line [to] Mackinac Island, 1951. [Detroit?, 1951]. 1 sheet folded to [8] p. Illus. MiD-D.

Georgian Bay Line Great Lakes cruises, have fun [and] relax, 1951. [Detroit?, 1951]. 1 sheet folded to [16] p. Illus., map. CSmH, MiD-B, MiD-D, MiShM, OBgU, ViNeM, WM.

Georgian Bay Line Mackinac Island all-expense vacations, 1951. [Detroit?, 1951]. 1 sheet folded to [8] p. Illus. MiD-D, ViNeM.

Great Lakes Labor Day cruise [on the] S.S. North American [from] Chicago to Charlevoix, Mackinac Island, Escanaba and return. [Chicago?, 1951]. 1 sheet folded to [4] p. Illus. MiD-D, MiHoljA.

Lackawanna Great Lakes cruises. [N.p., 1951]. 1 sheet folded to [12] p. Illus., map. MiD-D.

Medinah's star-studded pleasure cruise for other nobles and their families. [Chicago?, 1951]. 1 sheet folded to [8] p. Illus. MiD-D.

Attention Rotarians, come aboard for the 6th Annual Rotary Great Lakes Cruise [on the] S.S. North American. [Michigan City?, 1952]. 1 sheet folded to [4] p. Illus., map. MiD-B.

Breezy Point Lodge-Georgian Bay Line combination Great Lakes cruise. [Chicago?, 1952]. 1 sheet folded to [12] p. Illus., map. MiD-D.

Come aboard for a grand Great Lakes cruise [on the] S.S. North American. [Chicago?, 1952]. 1 sheet folded to [4] p. Illus., map. MiD-B.

Cruise News. — Vol. 1, no. 1 (1952?)-vol. ?, no. ? (1967). — [Detroit?, 1952?-1967]. Irregular. Mainly boiler plate issued with each cruise. Near-print. Possible successor to the Daily Radio News. MiD-B, MiD-D, OBgU.

Cruise with the stars from WLS to Mackinac - Sault Ste. Marie [and] Midland, June 6-11, 1952. [Chicago?, 1952]. 1 sheet folded to [8] p. Illus., map. MiD-B.

Georgian Bay Line-Mackinac Island all-expense vacations. [Detroit?, 1952]. 1 sheet folded to [8] p. Illus. MiD-B, MiD-D.

Great Lakes cruises, top measure in cruise pleasure on the inland seas, 1952. [Detroit?, 1952]. 1 sheet folded to [16] p. Illus., map. CSmH, MiD-B, MiD-D, MiMtpC, MiShM, MiU-H, OBgU, ViNeM.

Labor Day and Indian summer Great Lakes cruises, 1952. [Detroit?, 1952]. 1 sheet folded to [16] p. Illus., map. MiD-B, MiD-D, MiShM, WM.

Special Georgian Bay week-end June cruise. [Detroit?, 1952?]. 1 sheet folded to [4] p. Illus. MiD-B.

Tip for a trip, a cruise for you in '52 on the Great Lakes, "America's great inland seas." [Detroit?, 1952]. 1 sheet folded to [4] p. Illus., map. CSmH, MiD-B, MiD-D, MiShM, OBgU.

The twentieth is tops! Embark on the 1952 Good Fellowship Cruise [of the] Harrisburg Chamber of Commerce. [Detroit?, 1952]. 1 sheet folded to [8] p. Illus., map. MiD-D.

All-expense vacations [on the] Georgian Bay Line [to] Mackinac Island, 1953. [Detroit?, 1953]. 1 sheet folded to [8] p. Illus. MiD-D.

Fortieth Anniversary Cruise September 8-11, 1953, [and] passenger list aboard the S.S. South American. [Detroit?, 1953]. [2], 8 leaves. Near-print. MiD-B, MiD-D.

Georgian Bay Line Mackinac Island all-expense vacations, 1953. [Detroit?, 1953]. 1 sheet folded to [8] p. Illus. CSmH, MiD-D.

Give your next convention, sales meeting, district meeting [or] group get-togethers new appeal [and] charter your own Great Lakes cruise on the Georgian Bay Line. [Detroit?, 1953?]. 1 sheet folded to [6] p. Illus., map. ViNeM.

Great Lakes cruises, top measure in cruise pleasure on the inland seas, 1953. [Detroit?, 1953]. 1 sheet folded to [16] p. Illus., map. CSmH, MiD-B, MiD-D, MiMtpC, MiShM, NBuHi, OBgU, ViNeM.

Special Great Lakes Labor Day weekend cruises to famous Mackinac Island. [Detroit?, 1953]. 1 sheet folded to [4] p. Illus. MiD-B, OBgU.

Cruising the Great Lakes, 1954. [Detroit?, 1954]. [8] p. Illus., map. Pages differ in size. CSmH, Mi, MiD-B, MiD-D, MiHM, MiHolJA, MiShM, MnDuC, NBuHi, OBgU, ViNeM.

Georgian Bay Line Mackinac Island all-expense vacations, 1954. [Detroit?, 1954]. 1 sheet folded to [8] p. Illus. MiD-B, ViNeM.

Join this gay tulip-time — cherryland weekend cruise [to] Holland, Michigan [and] Sturgeon Bay, Wisconsin, May 14-17, 1954, from Chicago. [Chicago?, 1954]. 1 sheet folded to [4] p. Illus. CSmH, MiD-D.

Special Great Lakes Labor Day week-end cruises to famous Mackinac Island, 1954. [Detroit?, 1954]. 1 sheet folded to [4] p. Illus. MiD-D.

Special June Great Lakes cruise [to the] Jesuit Martyrs' Shrine, Midland, Ont., Canada [plus] Georgian Bay [and] Mackinac Island. [Detroit?, 1954]. 1 sheet folded to [4] p. Illus. MiD-D, ViNeM.

Special Rotary International Golden Anniversary convention cruises [in 1955]. [Chicago?], 1954. 1 sheet folded to [8] p. Illus., map. CSmH, MiD-D, MiShM.

Tip for a trip, cruise the Great Lakes [and see] America's water wonderland [where you can] relax [and] have fun, 1954. [Detroit?, 1954]. 1 sheet folded to [4] p. Illus., map. MiD-B.

Great Lakes cruise ship S.S. South American, queen of the Great Lakes. [Detroit?, 1955]. 1 sheet folded to [4] p. Illus. MiD-D.

Great Lakes cruises, 1955. [Detroit?, 1955]. [8] p. Illus., map. Pages differ in size. CSmH, MiD-B, MiD-D, MiMtpC, MiShM, MnDuC, NBuHi, OBgU, ViNeM.

Join this gay tulip-time — cherryland week-end cruise [to] Holland, Michigan [and] Sturgeon Bay, Wisconsin, May 14-16, 1955, from Chicago. [Chicago?, 1955]. 1 sheet folded to [4] p. Illus. MiD-B, MiD-D.

Special early September Great Lakes cruises at extra special low rates to famous Mackinac Island. [Detroit?, 1955]. 1 sheet folded to [4] p. Illus. MiD-B, MiD-D, OBgU.

Special Great Lakes Labor Day week-end cruises to famous Mackinac Island, 1955. [Detroit?, 1955]. 1 sheet folded to [4] p. Illus. MiD-B, MiD-D.

Your job with the Georgian Bay Line. [N.p., 1955?]. 17, [1] p. Illus. MiHolJA.

Join this gay tulip-time — cherryland week-end cruise to Holland, Michigan [and] Sturgeon Bay, Wisconsin, May 18-21, 1956. [Chicago?, 1956]. 1 sheet folded to [4] p. Illus. MiD-B, MiD-D.

Passenger list [of] the Georgian Bay Line St. Lawrence Seaway — Pan-American Games Conference Cruise aboard the S.S. South American, September 7-10, 1956. [Detroit?, 1956]. 7 leaves. MiD-B.

Special Great Lakes Labor Day week-end cruises to famous Mackinac Island, 1956. [Detroit?, 1956]. 1 sheet folded to [4] p. Illus. MiD-D.

Tip for a trip, you owe it to yourself to cruise the Great Lakes (America's great inland seas) in 1956. [Detroit?, 1956]. 1 sheet folded to [4] p. Illus. MiD-B, MiD-D.

Vacation cruises on the Great Lakes, 1956. [Detroit?, 1956]. 1 sheet folded to [24] p. Illus., map. CSmH, MSaP, MiD-B, MiD-D, MiShM, MnDuC, NBuHi, OBgU, OV, ViNeM.

All-expense cruise to the Tulip-Time Festival. [Chicago?, 1957?]. 1 sheet folded to [8] p. Illus. OFH.

The Chicago Association of Commerce & Industry sponsors a preview luxury cruise of the St. Lawrence Seaway. [Chicago?, 1957]. 1 sheet folded to [10] p. Illus., map. MiD-B, MiD-D.

Emergency stations and equipment book [for the] S.S. North American, 1957. [Detroit?, 1957]. [12] p. MiD-B, MiHoIJA.

Emergency stations and equipment book [for the] S.S. South American, 1957. [Detroit?, 1957]. [12] p. MiD-B.

Join this gay tulip-time — cherryland week-end cruise May 17-20, 1957, from Chicago. [Chicago?, 1957]. 1 sheet folded to [4] p. Illus. CSmH, MiD-B.

Pontiac Area Chamber of Commerce 1st Annual Cruise June 7-10, 1957. [Pontiac?, 1957]. 1 sheet folded to [4] p. Illus., map. ViNeM.

Special Great Lakes Labor Day week-end cruises to famous Mackinac Island, 1957. [Detroit?, 1957]. 1 sheet folded to [4] p. Illus. MiD-D, MnDuC, OBgU.

Tip for a trip: cruise the Great Lakes (America's great inland seas) in 1957. [Detroit?, 1957]. 1 sheet folded to [4] p. Illus. CSmH, MiD-B, MiD-D.

Vacation cruises on the Great Lakes, 1957. [Detroit?, 1957]. 1 sheet folded to [24] p. Illus., maps. CSmH, MiD-B, MiD-D, MiShM, OBgU, OV, ViNeM, WM.

Passenger list [and] room directory [for the] Second Pontiac Area Chamber of Commerce Cruise of the Great Lakes, June 5-8, 1958. [Pontiac]: Gen[eral] Ptg. Co., [1958]. 15, [1] p. Illus. ViNeM.

Pontiac Area Chamber of Commerce 2nd Annual Cruise, June 5-8, 1958. [Pontiac?, 1958]. 1 sheet folded to [4] p. Illus. ViNeM.

Special June Great Lakes cruise [to the] Jesuit Martyrs' Shrine [at] Midland, Ont., Canada [plus] Georgian Bay [and] Mackinac Island. [Detroit?, 1958]. 1 sheet folded to [4] p. Illus. MiD-B, MiD-D, OBgU.

Special Labor Day week-end and St. Lawrence Seaway Great Lakes cruises on the S.S. North American [and] S.S. South American, 1958. [Detroit?, 1958]. 1 sheet folded to [16] p. Illus., map. MiD-D, MiShM, OBgU.

3 special week-end Great Lakes cruises at bargain rates! [Detroit?, 1958]. 1 sheet folded to [6] p. Illus. CSmH, MiD-D, MnDuC.

Tip for a trip, cruise the Great Lakes (America's great inland seas) in 1958. [Detroit?, 1958]. 1 sheet folded to [4] p. Illus., map. MiD-B, MiD-D.

Vacation cruises on the Great Lakes, 1958. [Detroit?, 1958]. 1 sheet folded to [24] p. Illus., maps. CSmH, MiD-B, MiD-D, MiHoIJA, MiMtpC, MiShM, MiU-H, OBgU, ViNeM, WM.

Announcing Greater Lansing's First Annual Fellowship Cruise, 1959, [by the] Chamber of Commerce of Greater Lansing. [Lansing?, 1959]. 1 sheet folded to [4] p. Illus. ViNeM.

The Detroit Free Press Great Lakes-St. Lawrence Seaway cruise [during] May 31-June 7 [on the] S.S. South American. [Detroit, 1959]. 1 sheet folded to [4 whole and 4 half] p. Illus., map. MiD-B, MiD-D.

Inaugural cruise on the St. Lawrence Seaway for Hoosiers from Lake Michigan to Montreal, Canada, May 31 to June 14. [Gary IN?, 1959]. 1 sheet folded to [6] p. Illus., map. MiD-B.

Join this gay tulip-time — cherryland week-end cruise [to] Holland, Michigan [and] Sturgeon Bay, Wisconsin, May 15-18, 1959, from Chicago. [Chicago?, 1959]. 1 sheet folded to [4] p. Illus. MiD-D.

The Seaway Press, the newspaper that serves its readers on the Seaway holiday cruise. — Vol. 1, no. 1 (1959)- vol. ?, no. ? (1965?). — [Detroit, 1959-1965]? Illus., maps. Daily during cruises. Printed on board by the wireless operators. Near-print. MiD-D.

Special Great Lakes-St. Lawrence Seaway cruises, be aboard! on the first trip of a passenger cruise ship to sail from Great Lakes ports to Montreal and return. [Detroit?, 1959]. 1 sheet folded to [8] p. Illus., map. CSmH, MiD-B, MiD-D, OBgU, ViNeM.

Special Great Lakes-St. Lawrence Seaway September color cruise. [Detroit?, 1959]. 1 sheet folded to [8] p. Illus., map. CSmH, MiD-D, MnDuC, OBgU.

Special June Great Lakes cruise [to the] Jesuit Martyrs' Shrine [at] Midland, Ont., Canada [plus] Georgian Bay [and] Mackinac Island. [Detroit?, 1959]. 1 sheet folded to [4] p. Illus. MiD-D.

Special Labor Day week-end Great Lakes cruises to famous Mackinac Island and other scenic points of interest, 1959. [Detroit?, 1959]. 1 sheet folded to [4] p. Illus. MiD-B, MiD-D, MnDuC, OBgU.

Tip for a trip, cruise the Great Lakes (America's great inland seas) in 1959. [Detroit?, 1959]. 1 sheet folded to [4] p. Illus., map. MiD-D.

Vacation cruises on the Great Lakes, 1959. [Detroit?, 1959]. 1 sheet folded to [24] p. Illus., maps. CSmH, MiD-B, MiD-D, MiShM, OBgU, OV, ViNeM, WM.

You are invited to be aboard the S.S. North American for the new St. Lawrence Seaway dedication cruise June 20-July 2 and attend the international Seaway dedication ceremonies [with] President Eisenhower and Queen Elizabeth [at the] St. Lambert Lock, Montreal, Quebec, June 26, [sponsored by the] Chicago Association of Commerce and Industry. [Chicago?, 1959]. 1 sheet folded to [6] p. Maps. MiHoIJA.

Great Lakes vacation cruises, 1960. [Detroit?, 1960]. 1 sheet folded to [24] p. Illus., maps. CSmH, MiD-B, MiD-D, MiHoIJA, MiMtpC, MiShM, MnDuC, OBgU, ViNeM, WM.

Log of my Great Lakes cruise [on the] S.S. South American. West Nyack NY: Dexter Press, [1960?]. [38] p. spiral bound. Illus., maps. MiD-B.

Special, First Great Lakes-St. Lawrence Seaway September Color Cruise to Quebec city via Toronto and Montreal, 1960. [Detroit?, 1960]. 1 sheet folded to [16] p. Illus., map. MiD-B, MiD-D, WManiM.

Special June, 1960, Great Lakes-St. Lawrence Seaway cruises. [Detroit?, 1960]. 1 sheet folded to [8] p. Illus., map. MiD-B, MiD-D, MiShM.

Special Labor Day week-end Great Lakes cruises to famous Mackinac Island and other scenic points of interest, 1960. [Detroit?, 1960]. 1 sheet folded to [4] p. Illus. MiD-B, MiD-D, OBgU.

3 special week-end Great Lakes cruises at bargain rates!. [Detroit?, 1960]. 1 sheet folded to [6] p. Illus. MiD-B, MiD-D, MnDuC, OBgU.

2 special 3-day Great Lakes cruises [on the] S.S. South American, 1960. [Detroit?, 1960]. 1 sheet folded to [4] p. Illus. MiD-B, MiD-D, MnDuC.

Great Lakes all-expense vacation cruises, 1961. [Detroit?, 1961]. 1 sheet folded to [24] p. Illus., maps. CSmH, MiD-B, MiD-D, MnDuC, OBgU, ViNeM, WM, WManiM.

Great Lakes cruises, 1961. [Detroit?, 1961]. 1 sheet folded to [24] p. Illus., maps. OBgU.

Great Lakes vacation cruises, 1961. [Detroit?, 1961]. 1 sheet folded to [6] p. Illus., map. CSmH, MdBUS, MiD-D, MiMtpC, MnDuC, OBgU, OFH, ViNeM, WM.

Martin-Empire independent cruise-tours, including a one week Great Lakes cruise combined with a choice of a week's tour of scenic national park areas, 1961. [New York?, 1961]. 1 sheet folded to [10] p. Illus., map. MiD-D.

Rent a ship [to] hold your big meetings, sales conventions, [and] company get-togethers on the Great Lakes. Consult Executive Travel. [Detroit?, 1961?]. 1 sheet folded to [6] p. Illus. MiD-D.

Special Great Lakes-St. Lawrence Seaway cruises [from] Chicago, Detroit, Cleveland [and] Buffalo to Toronto, Montreal, Quebec City, and return, 1961. [Detroit?, 1961]. 1 sheet folded to [16] p. Illus., map. CSmH, MiD-B, MiD-D, MiShM, OBgU, ViNeM.

Special June Great Lakes cruise [to the] Jesuit Martyrs' Shrine, Midland, Ont., Canada, and Georgian Bay [from] June 12 thru 14, 1961. [Detroit?, 1961]. 1 sheet folded to [4] p. Illus. MiD-D, OBgU.

Special Labor Day week-end Great Lakes cruises, 1961, to famous Mackinac Island. [Detroit?, 1961]. 1 sheet folded to [4] p. Illus. MiD-B, MiD-D, MiShM, WM.

All-expense Great Lakes vacation cruises, 1962. [Detroit?, 1962]. 1 sheet folded to [12] p. Illus., map. CSmH, CaOOA, MiD-B, MiD-D, MiMtpC, MiShM, MnDuC, OBgU, OFH, OV, ViNeM, WM.

Bruce-Terminix 35th Anniversary Convention Cruise, September 13-17, 1962. [Memphis TN?, 1962]. 1 sheet folded to [6] p. Illus. MiD-B.

Magnificent Great Lakes all-expense cruises, 1962. [Detroit?, 1962]. 1 sheet folded to [36] p. Illus., map. CSmH, MiD-B, MiD-D, MiMtpC, MiShM, MnDuC, OBgU, ViNeM.

Marian pilgrimage cruise via Georgian Bay Lines, 1962. [Detroit?, 1962]. 1 sheet folded to [16] p. Illus., map. Panels vary in size. MiD-B.

Passenger agreement between [the] Seafarers International Union, Great Lakes District, A[merican] F[ederation] [of] L[abor]–C[ongress] [of] I[ndustrial] O[rganizations], and [the] Great Lakes Association of Marine Operators representing [the] Chicago, Duluth & Georgian Bay Company. Detroit, [1962]. 21, [1] p. MiD-B.

Senior Cruise No. 2 [by Youth Travel]. [Ann Arbor?, 1962]. 1 sheet folded to [4] p. Illus. MiD-B.

Senior Cruise No. 5 [by Youth Travel]. [Ann Arbor?, 1962]. 1 sheet folded to [4] p. Illus. MiD-B.

Sing a song as you sail along on the Eleventh Annual [Cleveland] Chamber of Commerce Cruise June 11-15, 1962. [Cleveland: Pickands Mather & Co., 1962]. [2], 16, [2] p. Words only. MiHo]JA.

Special Great Lakes cruise August 26, 1962, from Cleveland. [Cleveland?, 1962]. 1 sheet folded to [4] p. Illus. MiD-D.

Special Great Lakes-Seaway cruise to Quebec City. [Detroit?, 1962]. 1 sheet folded to [4] p. Illus. MiD-B, MiD-D.

Special Great Lakes-St. Lawrence Seaway cruises [from] Chicago, Detroit, Cleveland, [and] Buffalo to Toronto, Montreal, and return, 1962. [Detroit?, 1962]. 1 sheet folded to [16] p. Illus., map. MiD-B, MiD-D, MiMtpC, OBgU, ViNeM, WM.

Special Labor Day week-end cruise-tour to Toronto, Ont., Canada, 1962. [Detroit?, 1962]. 1 sheet folded to [4] p. Illus. MiD-B, MiD-D, OBgU.

Special new Georgian Bay Line Great Lakes cruise, explore America's great inland seas. [Buffalo?, 1962]. 1 sheet folded to [4] p. Illus., map. MiD-B.

Teen-Tour Cruise, [an] all-expense cruise of the magnificent Great Lakes from Sault S[ain]te Marie, Mich., June 22, 1962. Sault S[ain]te Marie: Sault News, [1962]. 1 sheet folded to [6] p. Illus. MiD-B.

Youth Travel Senior Skip Day Cruise No. 4. [Ann Arbor?, 1962]. 1 sheet folded to [4] p. Illus. MiD-B.

Cook's escorted cruise-tours of the Great Lakes, 1963. [Chicago?], 1963. 1 sheet folded to [10] p. Illus., map. MiD-D.

For adventure...pleasure...relaxation...cruise the Great Lakes with a Roamer Tour party on the S.S. South American. [Reading PA?], 1963. 1 sheet folded to [4] p. Illus. MiD-B.

Great Lakes all-expense cruises, 1963. [Detroit?, 1963]. 1 sheet folded to [16] p. Illus., map. CSmH, MSaP, MiD-B, MiD-D, MiMtpC, MiShM, MnDuC, OBgU, ViNeM, WM.

Join this gay tulip-time — cherryland week-end Great Lakes cruise [to] Holland, Michigan - Sturgeon Bay, Wisconsin, May 17-20, 1963, from Chicago. [Chicago?, 1963]. 1 sheet folded to [4] p. Illus. MiD-B, MiD-D, MiShM, WM.

Land and sea tours [via the] New York Central [Railroad and the] Georgian Bay Line, 1963. [N.p., 1963]. 1 sheet folded to [6] p. Illus., map. MiD-D.

Passenger agreement between Seafarers International Union, Great Lakes District, A[merican] F[ederation] [of] L[abor]-C[ongress] [of] I[ndustrial] O[rganizations], and Great Lakes Association of Marine Operators representing [the] Chicago, Duluth & Georgian Bay Company, 1963-1965. [Detroit, 1963]. 14, [2] p. MiD-B, MiHoJA.

Sing a song as you sail along on the Twelfth Annual [Cleveland] Chamber of Commerce Cruise, June 17-21, 1963. [Cleveland?, 1963]. [2], 16, [2] p. Words only. MiHoJA

16th [annual] Great Lakes Cruise [by the] Greater Bay City Chamber of Commerce [to] Milwaukee [and] Charlevoix [during] June 6-9, 1963, [on the] S.S. South American. [Bay City: Ambrose J. Maxwell, 1963]. 28 p. Illus. MiD-B, MiHoJA.

Special Great Lakes - St. Lawrence Seaway cruises [from] Detroit, Cleveland [and] Buffalo to Toronto, Montreal and return, 1963. [Detroit?, 1963]. 1 sheet folded to [16] p. Illus., map. CSmH, MSaP, MiD-B, MiD-D, MiHoJA, MiShM, MnDuC, OBgU, ViNeM, WM.

Special Labor Day week-end Great Lakes cruise to famous Mackinac Island and beautiful Harbor Springs, Michigan, 1963. [Chicago?, 1963]. 1 sheet folded to [4] p. Illus. MiD-B, MiD-D, OBgU.

Special 6-day Great Lakes cruise-tour, 1963. [Buffalo, 1963]. 1 sheet folded to [4] p. Illus. MiD-B.

Vacation tip, cruise the Great Lakes [on the] queen of the Great Lakes, S.S. South American, 1963. [Detroit?, 1963]. 1 sheet folded to [4] p. Illus. MiD-B, MiD-D, ViNeM.

Cook's cruise tours of the Great Lakes and a visit to the New York World's Fair, every Sunday - 15 days, June 21 through August 23 from Detroit, 1964 LF series. [Detroit?, 1964]. 1 sheet folded to [6] p. Illus. MiD-D.

Cruise directory [for the] 13th Annual "Cruise With a Purpose" [by the] Cleveland Chamber of Commerce, June 15-19, 1964. [Cleveland?, 1964]. 24 p. Illus. MiD-D, MiHoJA.

Great Lakes cruises, 2200 miles of vacation fun, 1964. [Detroit?, 1964]. 1 sheet folded to [16] p. Illus., map. CSmH, MSaP, MdBUS, Mi, MiD-B, MiD-D, MiHoJA, MiMtpC, MiShM, MnDuC, OBgU, OFH, OV, ViNeM, WM.

Join this gay tulip-time — cherryland week-end Great Lakes cruise [to] Holland, Michigan, Sturgeon Bay [and] Green Bay, May 15-18, 1964, from Chicago. [Chicago?, 1964]. 1 sheet folded to [4] p. Illus., map. MiD-B, MiD-D.

Land and sea tours [via the] New York Central [Railroad and the] Georgian Bay Line, 1964. [N.p., 1964]. 1 sheet folded to [6] p. Illus., map. MiD-D.

17th Great Lakes Cruise [by the] Greater Bay City Chamber of Commerce [to] Erie PA, Lorain, O[hio] [and] Detroit, June 4-7, 1964. [Detroit?, 1964]. 24 p. Illus. MiD-D.

Special Great Lakes-St. Lawrence Seaway cruise [from] Detroit, Cleveland [and] Buffalo to Toronto, Montreal and return, 1964. [Detroit?, 1964]. 1 sheet folded to [16] p. Illus., map. CSmH, MSaP, MiD-B, MiD-D, OFH, ViNeM.

Special June Great Lakes cruise [to] Jesuit Martyrs' Shrine, Midland, Ont., Canada, Georgian Bay, June 8 thru 10, 1964. [Detroit?, 1964]. 1 sheet folded to [4] p. Illus. MiD-B, MiD-D, MnDuC, OBgU.

Special Labor Day week-end Great Lakes cruise to famous Mackinac Island, 1964. [Detroit?, 1964]. 1 sheet folded to [4] p. Illus. MiD-B, MiD-D, OBgU.

Special 6-day Great Lakes cruise, 1964. [Buffalo: Anderson & Wahl, 1964]. 1 sheet folded to [4] p. Illus. MiD-B.

Vacation tip, cruise the Great Lakes [on the] S.S. South American, 1964. [Detroit?, 1964]. 1 sheet folded to [4] p. Illus. MiD-B, MiD-D, OBgU, ViNeM.

Come along on a 1965 Great Lakes cruise. [Detroit?, 1965]. 1 sheet folded to [16] p. Illus., map. CSmH, MiD-B, MiD-D, MiHoJA, MnDuC, OBgU, OFH, ViNeM, WM.

Cruise Conference, District 633, May 14, 15, 16, 1965. [Detroit?, 1965]. [16] p. Cover title: District 633, Rotary International, cruise conference [from] Marine City, Michigan. MiD-B, MiD-D.

Exercise a tonsil [singing] with Cleveland's City Council as you sail to Port Arthur and return on the Fourteenth Annual Cleveland Chamber of Commerce Cruise, June 21-25, 1965. [Cleveland?, 1965]. [2], 15, [3] p. Words only. MiHoJA.

For an extra special 1965 vacation, cruise the Great Lakes..., America's Mediterranean Sea, aboard the S.S. South American. [Detroit?, 1965]. 1 sheet folded to [4] p. Illus. MiD-B, ViNeM.

Great Lakes 7 or 9-day ship 'n shore cruise [with Berry World Travel, Inc.], 1965. [N.p., 1965]. 1 sheet folded to [12] p. Illus., map. MiD-B, MiD-D.

Special Great Lakes-St. Lawrence Seaway cruise [from] Detroit, Cleveland [and] Buffalo to Toronto, Montreal and return, 1965. [Detroit?, 1965]. 1 sheet folded to [16] p. Illus., map. CSmH, MiD-B, MiD-D, MiShM, MnDuC, OBgU, WM.

Special June Great Lakes cruise [to] Jesuit Martyrs' Shrine, Midland, Ont., Canada, [and] Georgian Bay. [Detroit?, 1965]. 1 sheet folded to [4] p. Illus. MiD-B, MiD-D, MiShM, OBgU, OFH.

Special Labor Day week-end Great Lakes cruise to famous Mackinac Island, 1965. [Detroit?, 1965]. 1 sheet folded to [4] p. Illus. MiD-B, MiD-D, OBgU.

Special 6-day Great Lakes cruise, 1965. [Detroit?, 1965]. 1 sheet folded to [4] p. Illus. MiD-D, OBgU.

The 25th Silver Anniversary Business Development Cruise [on] June 3, 4 & 5, 1965, sponsored by the Greater Grand Rapids Chamber of Commerce. [Grand Rapids?, 1965]. 1 sheet folded to [4] p. Illus., map. MiD-B, MiD-D.

Youth Travel senior cruises. [Ann Arbor?, 1965]. 1 sheet folded to [6] p. Illus. MiD-B.

Autumn color cruise tour, 1966. [Detroit?, 1966]. 1 sheet folded to 9, [1] p. Illus., map. Issued for Finlay Fun-Time Tours. CSmH.

Cruise directory [for the] 15th Annual "Cruise with a Purpose" [by the] Cleveland Chamber of Commerce, June 13-17, 1966. [Cleveland?, 1966]. 24 p. Illus. MiD-B, MiD-D.

Cruise the Great Lakes in '66. [Detroit?, 1966]. 1 sheet folded to [16] p. Illus., map. CSmH, MiD-B, MiD-D, MiHolJA, MiMtpC, MiShM, MnDuC, OBgU, ViNeM.

8th Annual Business Development Cruise sponsored by [the] Chamber of Commerce of Greater Lansing. [Detroit?, 1966]. 14 p. Illus., map. MiD-D.

"Georgie" welcomes you aboard a sister queen of the Great Lakes, S.S. South American. [Detroit?, 1966?]. 1 sheet folded to [4] p. MiD-B.

Hit high C's [with this song book] as you sail the inland seas on the Fifteenth Annual Cleveland Chamber of Commerce Cruise June 13-17, 1966. [Cleveland?, 1966]. [2], 15, [3] p. Words only. MiD-D.

Join one of these gay tulip-time — cherryland Great Lakes cruises to Holland, Michigan. [Chicago?], 1966. 1 sheet folded to [4] p. Illus., map. MiD-B, MiD-D, MiHolJA, MiShM, OBgU, WM, WManiM.

Passenger list-room directory [for the] 19th Greater Bay City Chamber of Commerce Cruise of the Great Lakes, June 9-12, 1966. [Detroit?, 1966]. 24 p. Illus. MiD-D.

Preview of '66 Great Lakes cruises. [Detroit?, 1966]. 1 sheet folded to [4] p. Illus. MiD-D, OBgU, ViNeM.

Special Great Lakes-St. Lawrence Seaway cruises [from] Detroit, Cleveland [and] Buffalo to Toronto, Montreal and return, 1966. [Detroit?], 1966. 1 sheet folded to [16] p. Illus., map. CSmH, MiD-B, MiD-D, MiHolJA, MiShM, MnDuC, OBgU, ViNeM.

Special June Great Lakes cruise [to the] Jesuit Martyrs' Shrine [at] Midland, Ont., Canada [plus] Georgian Bay. [Detroit?], 1966. 1 sheet folded to [4] p. Illus. MiD-B, MiD-D, MiShM, OBgU.

Special Labor Day week-end Great Lakes cruise to famous Mackinac Island, 1966. [Detroit?], 1966. 1 sheet folded to [4] p. Illus. MiD-B, MiD-D, MiHolJA, MiShM, MnDuC, OBgU, ViNeM, WM.

Special Labor Day week-end Great Lakes cruise to famous Mackinac Island, 1967. [Detroit?], 1966. 1 sheet folded to [4] p. Illus. MiD-B, MiD-D, MiHolJA, ViNeM.

1967 Great Lakes cruises and special St. Lawrence Seaway cruises to Montreal & Expo 67. [Detroit: Vanderkloot Press, 1966]. 1 sheet folded to [24] p. Illus., map. CSmH, MiD-B, MiD-D, MiHM, MiHolJA, MnDuC, OBgU, OFH, ViNeM, WM.

Cook's escorted 9-day cruises to Montreal and Expo 67 by way of the Great Lakes and the St. Lawrence Seaway, 1967. [N.p., 1967]. 1 sheet folded to [10] p. Illus., map. MiD-D.

Especially arranged!! Buffalo Evening News Great Lakes-St. Lawrence Seaway cruise to Expo 67 in Montreal May 29 - June 4, 1967. [Buffalo, 1967]. 1 sheet folded to [8] p. Illus. MiD-D.

Extra Expo 67 cruise. [Detroit?, 1967]. 1 sheet folded to [6] p. Illus. MiD-B, MiD-D.

"Georgie" welcomes you aboard the queen of the Great Lakes, S.S. South American. [Detroit?, 1967]. [16] p. Illus. MiD-D, MiHolJA, MnDuC, OV.

Great Lakes or the St. Lawrence Seaway, including Montreal's Expo 67. [Detroit?, 1967]. 1 sheet folded to [12] p. Illus., map. Issued for Berry World Travel, Inc. WManiM.

9th Annual Business Development Cruise sponsored by [the] Chamber of Commerce of Greater Lansing. [Lansing?, 1967]. 1 sheet folded to [4] p. Illus. MiD-D.

Now 14 big Great Lakes-St. Lawrence Seaway cruises to Expo 67. [Detroit?, 1967]. 1 sheet folded to [8] p. Illus. MiD-B, MiD-D, OBgU, OFH, WM.

Passenger list-room directory [on the] S.S. South American [for the] 20th Greater Bay City Chamber of Commerce Cruise of the Great Lakes, May 11-14, 1967. [Detroit?, 1967]. 24 p. Illus. MiHolJA.

CHICAGO-MILWAUKEE STEAMSHIP LINE, CHICAGO, IL

Commenced business around 1933 upon the demise of the Goodrich Transit Company, operating one of the defunct firm's ships and a segment of its system of routes. Apparently controlled from 1933 to 1936 by the Michigan Trust Company and from 1936 to 1942 by Edward E. Taylor, of Duluth.

Chicago-Milwaukee lake excursions. [Chicago?, 1934]. 1 sheet folded to [4] p. Illus. WM.

Chicago-Milwaukee Steamship Line, in sight of land all the way [with] daily lake excursions [and] moonlight cruises. [Chicago?, 1937]. 1 sheet folded to [6] p. Illus. OBgU.

Chicago-Milwaukee Steamship Line, in sight of land all the way [with] daily lake excursions [and] moonlight cruises, season 1938. [Chicago?, 1938]. 1 sheet folded to [6] p. Illus. CU-SB.

Chicago-Milwaukee Steamship Line [with] daily lake excursions [and] moonlight cruises. [Chicago?, 1939]. 1 sheet folded to [6] p. Illus. OFH, WM.

Milwaukee-Chicago all-expense cruise [for] vacationists! [Chicago?, 1939?]. 1 sheet folded to [4] p. Illus. MiD-D.

Chicago-Milwaukee Steamship Line, in sight of land all the way [with] daily lake excursions [and] moonlight cruises, season 1940. [Chicago?, 1940]. 1 sheet folded to [6] p. Illus. CU-SB, MiD-D, OFH, WMCHi.

Chicago-Milwaukee Steamship Line, in sight of land all the way [with] daily lake excursions [and] moonlight cruises, season 1941. [Chicago: Poole Bros., 1941]. 1 sheet folded to [6] p. Illus. CU-SB, MiD-D, OBgU, WM, WManiM.

CHICAGO ROOSEVELT STEAMSHIP COMPANY, MANITOWOC, WI

Created on 1 June 1927 as a Delaware corporation and initially operated by the Goodrich Transit Company. Dissolved on 27 May 1949.

Delightful short lake outings [and] every day cross lake cruises, June, 1933. [Chicago?, 1933]. 1 sheet folded to 11, [1] p. Illus. MiD-D, OFH.

Delightful short lake outings [and] every day cross lake cruises, July, 1933. [Chicago?, 1933]. 1 sheet folded to 11, [1] p. Illus. MiD-D.

Delightful short lake outings [and] every day cross lake cruises, August, 1933. [Chicago?, 1933]. 1 sheet folded to 11 [1] p. Illus. MdBUS, WM.

The most entrancing views of the Century of Progress Exposition and the skyline of metropolitan Chicago. [Chicago?, 1933?]. 1 sheet folded to [4] p. Illus. ViNeM.

Feast your eyes, rest your feet. [Chicago?, 1934]. 1 sheet folded to [6] p. Illus. MSaP, MdBUS.

A word or two about the steamship Roosevelt. [Chicago?, 1935?]. 1 sheet folded to [6] p. ViNeM.

Lake cruises via the spacious S.S. Theodore Roosevelt. [Chicago?, 1936]. 1 sheet folded to [8] whole and [8] half p. Illus., map. MdBUS, MiD-D, ViNeM.

Delightful lake cruises [on the] S.S. Theodore Roosevelt. [Chicago?, 1937]. 1 sheet folded to [16] p. Illus., map. Edition of June 15, 1937. CU-SB, OBgU.

Daily lake cruises [on the] S.S. Theodore Roosevelt. [Chicago?, 1938]. 1 sheet folded to 8 p. Illus., maps. MiShM.

Daily lake cruises [and] nightly dance cruises [on the] S.S. Theodore Roosevelt. [Chicago?, 1939]. 1 sheet folded to [16] p. Illus., maps. Edition of June 1, 1939. CU-SB.

Daily lake cruises [and] nightly dance cruises [on the] S.S. Theodore Roosevelt. [Chicago?, 1940]. 1 sheet folded to [16] p. Illus., maps. Edition of June 1, 1940. CU-SB, MiD-D.

CHICAGO STEAMSHIP LINES, INCORPORATED, CHICAGO, IL

Apparently created in 1922. Ceased to exist about 1927.

Chicago Steamship Lines, Inc., and Northern Trust Company, appellants, vs. United States Lloyds, Inc., et al., appellees in the United States Circuit Court of Appeals for the Seventh Circuit, October term, A.D. 1924, no. 3630. Chicago: Gunthorp-Warren Printing Company, [1924]. [2], 82 p. OBgU.

CLEVELAND & BUFFALO TRANSIT COMPANY, CLEVELAND, OH

Incorporated 13 September 1892 as an Ohio business and began service in 1893. Reorganized as a Delaware enterprise on 17 November 1927. Went bankrupt on 29 April 1937 and reorganized on 10 August 1938. Ceased operations at the end of the 1938 season, and cruises conducted thereafter by the Cleveland and Buffalo Transit Company of Illinois. Liquidated in May of 1945.

Summer tours [on the] daily line between Cleveland and Buffalo. Cleveland: Clark-Britton Printing Co., c1893. 60 p. Illus. CtY, OBgU.

C & B Line summer tours, 1895. [Cleveland?, 1895]. 90 p. Illus., map. OHi.

C & B Line connecting Buffalo, Cleveland, and Toledo while you sleep, season 1896. [Cleveland?, 1896]. 1 sheet folded to [4] p. Illus. NBuHi.

C & B Line summer tours, 1896. Chicago: Poole Bros., c1896. 115, [1] p. Illus., maps. OBgU.

An ideal journey. New York: Frank Presbrey, [1897]. 29, [3] p. Illus. NBuHi.

C & B Line summer tours, 1897. Cleveland: J.S. Savage Print, c1897. 110 p. Illus., map. CaOStCB.

C & B Line summer tours, 1898. Chicago: Poole Bros., c1898. 119, [1] p. Illus., map. OClWHi.

C & B Line summer tours, 1899. [Cleveland?], c1899. 84, xxxvi p. Illus., maps. OClWHi.

Summer tours for 1900. [Cleveland?, 1900]. 112 p. Illus., maps. DLC, MiD-D.

C & B Line connecting Buffalo, Cleveland and Toledo while you sleep, season 1901. Chicago: Poole Bros., [1901]. 1 sheet folded to [6] p. Illus. OBgU.

Summer tours for 1901 to the Pan-American Exposition, Buffalo. [Cleveland?], c1901. 112 p. Illus., maps. MSaP, MiD-B, MiD-D.

C & B Line connecting Buffalo, Cleveland and Toledo while you sleep, season 1902. Chicago: Poole Bros., [1902]. 1 sheet folded to [6] p. Illus. MdBUS.

Summer tours, 1902. [Cleveland?], c1902. 112 p. Illus., maps. DLC, MiD-B, NN, OClWHi.

Summer tours for 1903. Detroit: John Bornman & Son, [1903]. 112 p. Illus., maps. OBgU.

Summer tours, MCMIV [1904]. Buffalo: Matthews-Northrup Works, c1904. 112 p. Illus. OClWHi.

The Cleveland & Buffalo Transit Company. Buffalo: Matthews-Northrup Works, [1905]. 24 p. Illus., maps. OBgU.

Summer tours, 1905. Chicago: Poole Bros., c1905. 111, [1] p. Illus. NBuHi, OBgU.

C [&] B Line, season 1906, connecting while you sleep [with] Buffalo, Cleveland and Toledo. Chicago: Poole Bros., [1906]. 14 [i.e. 8] p. Illus., map. MdBUS, MiD-B.

Summer tours, 1906. Chicago: Poole Bros., c1906. 110, [2] p. Illus., map. MiD-B, MiD-D, OBgU, WM.

Vacation cruises via the C & B Line, 1906. Chicago: Poole Bros., [1906]. [28] p. Illus. MiD-D.

Summer tours, 1907. Chicago: Poole Bros., c1907. 112 p. Illus. DLC, OBgU.

C & B Line connecting while you sleep [with] Buffalo, Cleveland and Toledo, season 1908. Chicago: Poole Bros., [1908]. 22 [i.e. 12] p. Illus., map. OClWHi, ViNeM.

Summer tours, 1908. [Chicago?], c1908. 112 p. Illus. MiMtpC, ViNeM.

C & B Line, season 1910, between Buffalo, Erie, Cleveland, and Toledo. Chicago: Poole Bros., 1910. 22 [i.e. 12] p. Illus., map. MdBUS, MiD-D.

Summer tours, 1910. [Buffalo: Matthews-Northrup Works, 1910]. 138 p. Illus., map. DLC, OBgU.

C & B Line between Buffalo, Erie, Cleveland, and Toledo, season 1912. Chicago: Poole Bros., [1912]. 22 [i.e. 12] p. Illus., map. MSaP, MiD-D.

Summer tours, 1912. Chicago: Poole Bros., c1912. 136 p. Illus., maps. WM.

C & B Line between Buffalo, Erie, Cleveland, Port Stanley, and Put-in-Bay, season 1913. Chicago: Poole Bros., [1913]. 30 [i.e. 16] p. Illus., map. OHi.

The building of the great ship "Seeandbee" — the largest and most costly passenger steamer on inland waters of the world, for daily service [between] Cleveland and Buffalo, 1913. [Cleveland?, 1913]. [16] p. Illus. MSaP, OClWHi.

The great ship Seeandbee, daily service [between] Cleveland & Buffalo. Cleveland: Gardner Printing Co., [1913?]. 26, [2] p. Illus. CSFMM, MdBUS, MiD-D, MiShM.

Summer tours, 1913. [Chicago?], c1913. 164 p. Illus., maps. OBgU (in the catalog but not found).

C & B Line between Buffalo, Cleveland, Port Stanley and Put-in-Bay, season 1914. Chicago: Poole Bros., [1914]. 30 [i.e. 16] p. Illus., map. MiD-D, OClWHi.

Summer tours, 1914. [Buffalo: Matthews-Northrup Works, 1914]. 142 p. Illus., maps. DLC.

C & B Line between Buffalo, Cleveland, Cedar Point, Put-in-Bay and Port Stanley, season 1915. Chicago: Poole Bros., [1915]. 30 [i.e. 16] p. Illus., map. ViNeM.

The Cleveland & Buffalo Transit Co. [Buffalo?, 1915?]. 24 p. Illus., maps. OFH.

The Cleveland & Buffalo Transit Co. [Buffalo: Matthews-Northrup Works, 1915]. 168 p. Illus., folded map. Cover title: Summer tours, 1915. NBuHi.

The Cleveland & Buffalo Transit Co. [Buffalo: Matthews-Northrup Works, 1916]. 139, [1] p. Illus., maps. Cover title: Summer tours, 1916. MiD-D.

A vacation trip to Niagara Falls on the great ship "Seeandbee" [during the 1918 season]. [Buffalo]: Gies & Co., c1917. 1 sheet folded to [8] p. Illus., maps. ViNeM.

C & B Line between Buffalo, Cleveland, Cedar Point, Put-in-Bay and Port Stanley, season 1917. Chicago: Poole Bros., [1917]. 14 [i.e. 8] p. Illus., map. ViNeM.

Cleveland to Buffalo or Niagara Falls and return on the great ship "Seeandbee." [Cleveland?, 1917]. [8] p. Illus., map. OClWHi.

The Cleveland & Buffalo Transit Co., season 1917. [Buffalo: Matthews-Northrup Works, 1917]. 128 p. Illus., maps. Cover title: Summer tours, 1917. MiD-D.

Niagara Falls excursions, including a lake trip on the great ship "Seeandbee." [Buffalo]: Gies & Co., c1917. 1 sheet folded to [16] p. Illus., maps. Optional title: Excursions to Niagara Falls on the great ship "Seeandbee." MiD-D.

C & B Line [to] Buffalo, Cleveland, Cedar Point [and] Put-in-Bay. Buffalo: Matthews-Northrup Works, [1918]. 14 [i.e. 8] p. Illus., map. MSaP.

The great ship "Seeandbee" and sister-ships "City of Buffalo," "City of Erie," [and] "State of Ohio," season 1918. Buffalo: Matthews-Northrup Works, [1918]. 31, [1] p. Illus., maps. ViNeM.

C & B Line [to] Buffalo, Cleveland, Cedar Point [and] Put-in-Bay. Buffalo: Matthews-Northrup Works, [1919]. 14 [i.e. 8] p. Illus., map. CtY, MSaP, MiD-D.

The great ship "Seeandbee" and sister-ships "City of Buffalo," "City of Erie," [and] "State of Ohio," season 1919. Buffalo: Matthews-Northrup Works, [1919]. 31, [1] p. Illus., maps. OHi, ViNeM.

C & B Line [to] Buffalo, Cleveland, Cedar Point [and] Put-in-Bay. [Buffalo?, 1920]. 14 [i.e. 8] p. Illus., map. CSmH.

The great ship "Seeandbee" and sister-ships "City of Buffalo," "City of Erie," [and] "State of Ohio," season 1920. Buffalo: Matthews-Northrup Works, [1920]. 31, [1] p. Illus., maps. OBgU, OHi.

C & B Line [to] Buffalo, Cleveland, Cedar Point [and] Put-in-Bay. [Buffalo: Matthews-Northrup Works, 1921]. 14 [i.e. 8] p. Illus., map. CSmH, OBgU.

A vacation trip to Niagara Falls on the great ship "Seeandbee." [Buffalo]: American Lithographing Co., c1923. 1 sheet folded to [8] p. Illus., maps. ViNeM.

C & B Line daily steamers [to] Buffalo, Cleveland, Cedar Point, Put-in-Bay [and] Toledo. [Buffalo?, 1923]. 14 [i.e. 8] p. Illus., map. ViNeM.

C & B Line route maps of auto tours East or West, take your car by steamer [and pay] low rates for tourist automobiles. Buffalo: Matthews-Northrup Works, [1923]. 1 sheet folded to [16] p. Illus., maps. CtY, MiD-D.

The great ship "Seeandbee" and sister ships "City of Buffalo," "City of Erie," [and] "State of Ohio," season 1923. Buffalo: Matthews-Northrup Works, [1923]. 32 p. Illus., map. ViNeM.

C & B Line daily steamers [to] Buffalo, Cleveland, Cedar Point, Put-in-Bay [and] Toledo. [Buffalo?, 1924]. 14 [i.e. 8] p. Illus., map. CSmH.

Cedar Point and Put-in-Bay lake resorts. [Buffalo?, 1924]. 1 sheet folded to [12] p. Illus., map. MiD-D, OClWHi.

C & B Line [to] Buffalo, Cleveland, Cedar Point [and] Put-in-Bay. [Buffalo?, 1925]. 14 [i.e. 8] p. Illus., map. CSmH, MiD-D, OLimaACH, ViNeM.

Lake cruise deluxe on the great ship "Seeandbee," Chicago and return with short stops at Cleveland, Sault Ste. Marie, and Mackinac Island, September 8-15, 1925. Buffalo: Matthews-Northrup Works, [1925]. [12] p. Illus., map. WManiM.

The great ship "Seeandbee" and sister ships "City of Buffalo" [and] "City of Erie," a new day-excursion steamer, the finest on the Great Lakes, in service June 14th, season 1926. Cleveland: Britton-Gardner Printing Co., [1926]. 32 p. Illus., map. OSandF.

New $5.00 auto rate, take your car by steamer to Buffalo and back for two days motor tour. [Buffalo?, 1926?]. 1 sheet folded to [6] p. Illus., maps. MiD-D.

Announcing the 1927 lake cruise deluxe on the great ship "Seeandbee," Buffalo and Cleveland to Chicago and return, September 6th to 13th. [Buffalo?, 1927]. 1 sheet folded to [6] p. Illus., map. MiD-D.

Auto rates $5.00 and up. [Buffalo?, 1927]. 1 sheet folded to [4] p. Illus., map. CSmH.

C & B Line [to] Buffalo, Cleveland, Cedar Point [and] Put-in-Bay. Buffalo: J[ames] W. Clement Co., [1927]. 30 [i.e. 8] p. Illus., maps. CSmH, MiD-D.

The Cleveland and Buffalo Transit Co., season 1927. [Buffalo?, 1927]. 32 p. Illus., map. OHi.

C & B Line [to] Buffalo, Cleveland, Cedar Point [and] Put-in-Bay. [Buffalo?, 1928]. 30 [i.e. 16] p. Illus., maps. OHi.

C & B Line [to] Cleveland, Buffalo, Port Stanley, Cedar Point [and] Put-in-Bay. [Buffalo?, 1929]. 1 sheet folded to 39 [i.e. 24] p. Illus., map. CU-SB, ViNeM.

For your vacation, a Great Lakes cruise on the S.S. Seeandbee, the world's greatest "showboat." Cleveland: Hubbell Advertising Agency, [1929?]. 1 sheet folded to [16] p. Illus., map. MiU-H, WM.

C & B Line lake cruise deluxe on the great ship "Seeandbee," September 7th to 14th, 1930. [Buffalo?, 1930]. 1 sheet folded to [4] p. Illus., map. MiD-D.

C & B Line special tours [to] Cedar Point, Put-in-Bay and Port Stanley, Canada. [Buffalo?, 1930]. 24 p. Illus., maps. MSaP.

C & B Line special tours [to] Cleveland, Buffalo [and] Port Stanley, Canada. [Buffalo?, 1930]. 24 p. Illus., maps. MiD-D, OClWHi, OFH, ViNeM.

Daily express service [and] lowest freight rates, mark and ship your freight via the Cleveland & Buffalo Transit Co. [Buffalo?, 1930]. 1 sheet folded to 8 p. ViNeM.

Cleveland - Buffalo - Port Stanley, Canada, circle tours. [Buffalo, 1931]. 11, [1] p. Illus., map. MiD-D, ViNeM.

Lake cruises [on] the great S.S. Seeandbee. Cleveland: Hubbell Advertising Agency, [1931?]. 1 sheet folded to [16] p. Illus., map. MiD-D.

Travel on Lake Erie via the C & B Line to or from Cleveland, Buffalo, Niagara Falls, Port Stanley, Canada, Cedar Point [and] Put-in-Bay. [Cleveland?, 1932]. [12] p. Illus., maps. MdBUS, MiD-D, NBuHi, OBgU, OClWHi, ViNeM.

Tour by lake, save a day. [Cleveland?, 1933]. 1 sheet folded to [12] p. Illus., map. CU-SB, MiD-B, ViNeM.

Your 1933 convention. [Cleveland?, 1933]. 1 sheet folded to [8] p. Illus. OClWHi.

DeLuxe [sic] lake cruises [offering] rest, romance, and high adventure. [Cleveland?, 1934]. 1 sheet folded to [12] p. Illus., map. MiD-D.

Joyous, carefree adventure, Great Lakes cruises on the S.S. Seeandbee, the world's greatest "showboat." [Cleveland?, 1934]. 1 sheet folded to [16] p. Illus., map. OV, ViNeM.

Travel by steamer for vacation or business, take your car [and] save a day! [Cleveland?, 1934]. 1 sheet folded to [12] p. Illus., map. CU-SB, MiD-D, ViNeM.

For your vacation, a Great Lakes cruise on the S.S. Seeandbee. Cleveland: Hubbell Advertising Agency, [1935?]. 1 sheet folded to [16] p. Illus., map. CSmH, ViNeM.

Here's your deck plan of the S.S. Seeandbee, the world's largest cruising liner. [Cleveland?, 1935?]. 1 sheet folded to [16] p. Illus., map. MiShM, ViNeM.

Travel by steamer for vacation or business, take your car [and] save a day! [Cleveland?, 1935]. 1 sheet folded to [12] p. Illus., map. CSmH, CU-SB, MiD-D, ViNeM.

Enjoy 7 glorious days on the Great Lakes absolutely free as the guest of your General Electric vacuum cleaner distributor. [Chicago?, 1936?]. 1 sheet folded to [4] p. Illus., map. Title on verso: The S.S. Seeandbee pictorial ship news. MiD-D.

Greater success for your conventions and sales promotions with chartered Great Lakes cruises on the S.S. Seeandbee. [Cleveland?, 1936?]. [8] p. Illus., map. OV.

Lake cruises [on] the great S.S. Seeandbee. Cleveland: Hubbell Advertising Agency, [1936]. 1 sheet folded to [16] p. Illus., map. CU-SB, MiD-D.

Lake steamers for vacations, pleasure tours, [and] business trips. [Cleveland?, 1936]. 1 sheet folded to [12] p. Illus. MiD-D, OBgU, ViNeM.

For your convention or sales promotion, a chartered cruise on the S.S. Seeandbee, the largest passenger

steamship on the Great Lakes exclusively in cruise service. [Cleveland?, 1937?]. [8] p. Illus., map. OV.

Lake cruises. [Cleveland, 1937]. 1 sheet folded to [16] p. Illus., map. MSaP, ViNeM.

Lake steamers, the way to go. Take your car [to] Cleveland, Buffalo, Port Stanley, Cedar Point [and] Put-in-Bay. [New York, 1937]. 1 sheet folded to [12] p. Illus., map. OBgU, ViNeM.

Your dream come true, 7 great days on the largest lake cruise ship S.S. Seeandbee. Cleveland: Hubbell Advertising Agency, [1937?]. [8] p. Illus., map. MiU-H.

Choose your lake cruise. [Cleveland?, 1938?]. 1 sheet folded to [4] p. Illus. WManiM.

Lake cruises. [Cleveland, 1938]. 1 sheet folded to [12] p. Illus., map. CU-SB, MiU-H, ViNeM.

Swell news about a good time over July 4th. [Cleveland?, 1938]. 1 sheet folded to [12] p. Illus. OBgU.

Travel by steamer for business or vacation tours, use the liners of the Lakes [to] Cleveland, Buffalo, Port Stanley, Canada [and] Niagara Falls. [Cleveland?, 1938]. 1 sheet folded to [8] p. Illus., map. MSaP, MiD-D, MiU-H, OBgU, ViNeM.

Your dream come true, 7 great days on the largest lake cruise ship, S.S. Seeandbee. Cleveland: Printed by Bassett Co. for the Hubbell Advertising Agency, [1938]. [8] p. Illus., map. MiD-D, MiU-H.

Announcing the 1939 cruise service [for] the S.S. Seeandbee. [Cleveland?, 1939]. 1 sheet unfolded. Illus., map. OBgU.

For your vacation, 7 happy days on the S.S. Seeandbee. Cleveland: Great Lakes Litho Co., [1939]. [8] p. Illus., map. CU-SB, MiD-D.

The S.S. Seeandbee, the largest lake cruise ship, a luxury cruise on a luxury liner at an amazingly low cost. Cleveland: Great Lakes Litho Co., [1939?]. [8] p. Illus., map. MiD-D, OV.

Swell news about a good time over Labor Day. [Chicago?, 1939]. 1 sheet folded to [12] p. Illus. CSmH.

Here's your deck plan of the S.S. Seeandbee, the world's largest cruising liner. [Chicago?, 1940]. 1 sheet folded to [16] p. Illus., map. CU-SB, MiD-D.

7 day vacation cruises on the Great Lakes [by] S.S. Seeandbee. [Chicago?, 1940]. 1 sheet folded to [24] p. Illus., map. CSmH, CU-SB, MiD-D, OFH, ViNeM.

7 day Great Lakes vacation cruises [on the] luxury liner "Seeandbee." [Chicago?, 1940]. 1 sheet folded to [24] p. Illus., map. CU-SB, MiD-D.

Swell news about your summer vacation. [Chicago?, 1940?]. 1 sheet folded to [6] p. Illus., map. MiD-D.

Special cruises for shopping news readers. Mackinac Island - Soo on the S.S. Seeandbee June 15-20. [Chicago?, 1941?]. 1 sheet folded to [12] p. Illus. MiShM.

CLEVELAND & BUFFALO STEAMSHIP COMPANY, CHICAGO, IL

Commenced operations around 1942 as a sort of successor to the Cleveland & Buffalo Transit Company, but did not incorporate until 15 January 1943. Went into voluntary bankruptcy in 1951 and the firm's charter revoked on 11 November 1951.

Afternoon lake cruises [on the] S.S. City of Grand Rapids. [Chicago]: Carl Gorr Printing Co., [1942]. 1 sheet folded to [8] p. Illus. CSmH.

One day lake cruises [from] Chicago to Benton Harbor - St. Joe. [Chicago]: Carl Gorr Printing Co., 1942. 1 sheet folded to [8] p. Illus. CU-SB, OFH.

One day lake cruises [from] Chicago to Benton Harbor - St. Joe and return. [Chicago?, 1943]. 1 sheet folded to [8] p. Illus. MiD-D.

One day lake cruises [on the] S.S. City of Grand Rapids [from] Benton Harbor - St. Joe to Chicago and return. [Chicago?, 1944]. 1 sheet folded to [4] p. Illus. MiD-D, OBgU, OFH.

Take a victory cruise for your summer vacation. [Chicago?, 1944?]. 1 sheet folded to [6] p. Illus. ViNeM.

Lake cruises [to] Benton Harbor every day, moonlight cruises every night. [Chicago?, 1945]. 1 sheet folded to 12 p. Illus. MiD-D, OFH.

Picnic lake cruises for your organization or club [on the] S.S. City of Grand Rapids. [Chicago?, 1945]. 1 sheet folded to [12] p. Illus. ViNeM.

Choose your lake cruise [on the] S.S. Theodore Roosevelt. [Chicago?, 1946]. 1 sheet folded to [4] p. MiD-D, CU-SB.

3 great vacation cruises on 2 big lake liners. [Chicago?, 1946]. 1 sheet folded to [16] p. Illus. CU-SB, MiD-D, OBgU, OFH, WManiM.

Choose your lake cruise [on the] S.S. City of Grand Rapids. [Chicago?, 1947]. 1 sheet folded to [4] p. Illus. CU-SB, OBgU.

Lake cruises every day [and] every night [on the] S.S. City of Grand Rapids. [Chicago?, 1947]. 1 sheet folded to 12 p. Illus. CU-SB, MiD-D, ViNeM.

3 day Chicago all expense vacation. [Chicago?, 1947?]. 1 sheet folded to [12] p. Illus. ViNeM.

Choose your cruise [on the] S.S. City of Grand Rapids. [Chicago?, 1948]. 1 sheet folded to [4] p. Illus. CU-SB.

Lake cruises every day [and] every night [on the] S.S. City of Grand Rapids. [Chicago?, 1948]. 1 sheet folded to 12 p. Illus. CU-SB, MdBUS, MiD-D, OFH, ViNeM.

Sail on a full day lake cruise. [Chicago?, 1950]. 1 sheet folded to 6 p. Illus. MdBUS, MiD-D.

CLEVELAND & CANADA NAVIGATION COMPANY, CLEVELAND, OH

Incorporated on 29 March 1927 as successor to the Western Reserve Navigation Company. Ceased to exist on 15 November 1929.

"The short route to Canada" between Cleveland and Port Stanley. Cleveland: J[ohn] B. Savage Co., 1928. 14 [i.e. 8] p. Illus., map. Time table no. 2. MiD-D.

CLEVELAND-CANADA STEAMSHIP COMPANY, CLEVELAND, OH

Incorporated 29 June 1946. Commenced service in 1947. Went bankrupt in 1949 and dissolved on 16 October 1950.

2 new all steel ships, 3 services. [Cleveland]: Vernels Service, [1947]. 1 sheet folded to [4] p. Illus., map. CSmH, MiD-D, OFH.

S.S. Cadillac [is an] all-steel ship — completely fireproof [and offering the] shortest route to Canada [by connecting] Cleveland, Ohio to Erieau, Ont. [Cleveland?, 1948]. 1 sheet folded to [4] p. Illus., map. MiD-D.

CLEVELAND-CEDAR POINT STEAMSHIP COMPANY, CLEVELAND, OH

Established on 1 May 1944 and apparently never incorporated. Ceased operations in 1945.

Good news! about your get-together picnic. [Cleveland?, 1944]. 1 sheet folded to [6] p. Illus. MiD-D, OFH, WM.

Lake cruises [to] Cedar Point every day, moonlight cruises every night. [Cleveland?, 1945]. 1 sheet folded to [12] p. Illus. MiD-D, OFH.

CLEVELAND-CLIFFS IRON COMPANY, MARINE DEPARTMENT, CLEVELAND, OH

Though it chartered ships as early as 1855, it did not acquire its first vessel until 1867 when it was the Cleveland Iron Mining Company. In 1891 Cleveland Iron merged with the Iron Cliffs Company to form the Cleveland-Cliffs Iron Company. In November of 1984 the fleet was discontinued and the remaining vessels sold to the Interlake Steamship Company.

Welcome aboard [the] S.S. Edward B[elden] Greene. [Cleveland?, 1952?]. [16] p. MnDuC.

Group life insurance, sickness and accident insurance, and hospitalization insurance plan for licensed officers and stewards of the Cleveland-Cliffs Iron Company, Marine Department, as amended, effective November 1, 1957. [Cleveland?, 1958]. 21, [3] p. OBgU.

Contract between the Cleveland-Cliffs Iron Company and the Lake Sailors Union, Independent, July 1, 1959, amended May 6, 1960, ratified May 27, 1960. [Cleveland, 1960]. 39, [1] p. OBgU.

Labor contract between the Cleveland-Cliffs Iron Company and [the] United Steelworkers of America, A[merican] F[ederation] [of] L[abor]-C[ongress] [of] I[ndustrial] O[rganizations], and its Local 5000, September 1, 1965. [Cleveland?, 1965]. 75, [1] p. OBgU.

Labor contract between the Cleveland-Cliffs Iron Company and [the] United Steelworkers of America, A[merican] F[ederation] [of] L[abor]-C[ongress] [of] I[ndustrial] O[rganizations], and its Local 5000, August 1, 1971. [Cleveland?, 1971]. [2], 101, [1] p. OBgU.

Marine safety booklet, 1972. [Cleveland?, 1972]. 26 p. OBgU.

Cliffs News Letter (marine edition). — Vol. 1, no. 1 (April 1973)-vol. 7, no 3 (September 1979)? — Cleveland, 1973-1979. Bimonthly. Illus. Continued by: Cliffs Clipper. MnDuC, OBgU.

S.S. Walter A[dam] Sterling [commissioning]. [N.p., 1978]. 1 sheet folded to [4] p. Illus. MiD-D.

Cliffs Clipper. — Vol. 7, no. 4 (October 1979)?-vol. 10, no. 1 (Spring 1982)? — Cleveland, 1979-1982. Irregular. Illus. Continues: Cliffs News Letter (marine edition). OBgU.

On deck. [Cleveland?, 1979?]. [8] p. Illus., map. OBgU.

75th [celebration], the anniversary banquet for Cleveland-Cliffs' masters and chief engineers, past and present, [at] Quail Hollow, March 26, 1980. [Cleveland, 1980]. [8] p. Illus. MnDuC, OBgU.

Vessel procedures. [Cleveland, 1980]. 168 leaves. Illus., map. Title from cover. Contained in a 3-ring notebook, pagination may vary. MiD-D.

Vessel safety procedures. [Cleveland, 1980]. 128 leaves. Illus., map. Title from cover. Contained in a 3-ring notebook, pagination may vary. MiD-D.

CLEVELAND ERIEAU STEAMSHIP COMPANY, CLEVELAND, OH

Incorporated on 2 December 1919. Ceased to exist about 1926.

Time tables and general information. Cleveland: Roger Williams Press, [1920?]. 1 sheet folded to [8] p. Illus. OBgU.

CLEVELAND STEAMSHIP COMPANY, CLEVELAND, OH

Incorporated on 3 November 1898. Its fleet was sold to the Interlake Steamship Company on 30 December 1915, and the firm dissolved on 10 August 1922.

First Annual Meeting of the Engineers, First Annual Joint Meeting of the Captains and Engineers, and Third Annual Meeting of the Masters of the Cleveland Steamship Company and the Buffalo Steamship Company. Cleveland: Mediator Printery, 1912. 149, [1] p. Cover title: Third Annual Meeting of the Masters and First Annual Meeting of the Engineers of the Cleveland Steamship Co. and the Buffalo Steamship Co. OCl.

CLEVELAND TANKERS, INCORPORATED, MARINE DEPARTMENT, CLEVELAND, OH

Incorporated in March of 1933. Still active in 1990.

Marine safety booklet. [Cleveland?, 1974?]. 29 [i.e. 40] p. Illus. OBgU.

COLLINGWOOD STEAMSHIP COMPANY, LIMITED, COLLINGWOOD, ONT

Incorporated on 13 August 1917. Dissolved 31 December 1962.

Summer steamer schedule, 1918. [N.p., 1918]. 1 sheet folded to [4] p. Illus. CaOOA.

COLONIAL STEAMSHIPS, LIMITED, PORT COLBORNE, ONT

Incorporated on 5 December 1933. Commenced operations in 1934. On 31 December 1958, it changed its name to Scott Misener Steamships, Limited.

A souvenir of the formal christening and commissioning of the S.S. Scott Misener, June, 1951. St. Catharines: St. Catharines Standard, [1951]. 20 p. Illus. MiD-D, MnDuC, OBgU.

COLUMBIA TRANSPORTATION COMPANY, CLEVELAND, OH

Formerly the Columbia Steamship Company, its name was changed in 1931. Acquired the fleet of the Valley Camp Steamship Company in 1935. It merged with the Oglebay Norton Company on 31 October 1957, and was operated as a division of that firm.

The Columbia Shipmate. — Vol. 1, no. 1 (May 1941)-vol. 17, no. ? (November-December 1957). — Cleveland, 1941-1957. Illus. Monthly during the navigation season. Continued by: Fore 'n' Aft. MiD-D, OBgU, OV.

Great Lakes cruise. [Cleveland?, 1954?]. 9 [i.e. 20] leaves. MnDuC, MnDuU.

Fore 'n' Aft. — Vol. 1, no. 1 (August 1959)-vol. 4, no. ? (June 1963). — Cleveland, 1959-1963. Illus. Quarterly. Continues: Columbia Shipmate. MnDuC, OBgU, OV.

CROSBY TRANSPORTATION COMPANY, MILWAUKEE, WI

Incorporated on 30 March 1903. Succeeded by the Wisconsin & Michigan Transportation Company in March of 1925 and ceased to exist as of 1 January 1926.

Grand Trunk Railway system, the shortest route between Milwaukee and all Michigan, Canadian and eastern points, season 1911. Chicago: Poole Bros., [1911]. 12 [i.e. 8] p. Illus., map. MSaP.

Summer tours [for] 1911, a book illustrating and describing our unique and pleasant vacation tours. Milwaukee: Cramer-Krasselt Co., c1911. 96 p. Illus. WM.

Crosby Transportation Co. [and] Grand Trunk Railway system Grand Haven route, the shortest route between Milwaukee and all Michigan, Canadian and eastern points, season 1912. Chicago: Poole Bros., [1912]. 12 [i.e. 8] p. Illus., map. WM.

A week's lake trip [for] $40.00, including transportation, meals, and berth. Milwaukee: Braband-Voss Co., [1913]. [8] p. Illus., maps. MiD-D, WMCHi.

Summer tours, a book illustrating and describing our unique and pleasant vacation tours. Milwaukee: Wright & Joys Co., [1913]. 96 p. Illus. ViNeM, WM.

A week's lake trip including transportation, meals, and berth [covering] 2,000 miles of blue sky and water. Milwaukee: Wright & Joys Co., [1914]. [8] p. Illus., map. OBgU, ViNeM.

Crosby Line steamers, the Grand Haven route, the shortest route between Milwaukee and all Michigan, Canadian, and eastern points, season 1914. Milwaukee: Wright & Joys Co., [1914]. 1 sheet folded to 4 [i.e. 8] p. Map. WMCHi.

Crosby Transportation Company, "the Grand Haven route" to Spring Lake. [Milwaukee, 1920]? 1 sheet folded to [4] p. Illus., map. MiGrH.

Crosby Line steamers, the popular short line across Lake Michigan between Milwaukee, Wis., and Muskegon, Mich., season 1922. [Milwaukee?, 1922]. [4] p. MSaP.

The Crosby Line, the Milwaukee-Muskegon route. Chicago: Poole Bros., [1923]. 1 sheet folded to [8] p. Illus. WM.

The Crosby Line, the Milwaukee-Muskegon route. Chicago: Poole Bros., [1924]. 1 sheet folded to [4] p. WM.

DETROIT & BUFFALO STEAMBOAT COMPANY, DETROIT, MI

Incorporated 13 February 1901. Acquired by the Detroit & Cleveland Navigation Company on 2 February 1909. Dissolved 26 February 1910.

The lake route to the Niagara frontier connecting the East and the West via Detroit and Buffalo. Chicago: Poole Bros., [1902?]. 1 sheet folded to 16 [i.e. 32] p. Illus., map. CaOOA, MSaP, MiD-D.

$3.00 saved to all points East and West via the D & B Line, "just two boats" between Detroit and Buffalo. Detroit: John Bornman & Son, [1903?]. 1 sheet folded to [4] p. Illus., map. Mi.

Lake and rail route to the World's Fair, St. Louis, 1904. Chicago: Poole Bros., [1904]. 14, [2] p. Illus., map. WManiM.

The lake route to the Niagara frontier connecting the East and the West via Detroit and Buffalo. Chicago: Poole Bros., [1905]. 1 sheet folded to 16 [i.e. 32] p. Illus., map. MSaP, MdBUS.

DETROIT & CLEVELAND NAVIGATION COMPANY, DETROIT, MI

Incorporated 8 December 1897 as successor to the Detroit & Cleveland Steam Navigation Company. Vessel operations were officially suspended on 9 May 1951, though no ships operated after the 1950 season. Dissolved 5 October 1960, and merged with the Denver-Chicago Trucking Company. Name changed to DC International, Incorporated, on 25 February 1966.

Col[onel] Clayton's lake tour, a summer trip via [the] Detroit & Cleveland Navigation Co., the coast line to Mackinac (a novel). Detroit: John Bornman & Son, c1898. 67, [149] p. Illus., maps. MiD-D, OBgU, WM.

Lake tours via the D & C, the coast line to Mackinac. Detroit: John Bornman & Son, [1898]. [24] p. Illus., maps. Mi.

A hero of Manila, a summer trip via [the] Detroit & Cleveland Navigation Company. Detroit: John Bornman & Son, 1899. 76, [158] p. Illus., maps. Has scalloped edges on 3 sides. Mi, MiD-B, MiMtpC, NN, OBgU, OFH.

Lake tours via the D & C daily between Detroit & Cleveland. Detroit: John Bornman & Son, [1899]. 48 p. Illus., maps. Mi, MiMtpC.

A hero of Manila, a summer trip via [the] Detroit & Cleveland Navigation Company. Detroit: John Bornman & Son, c1899, [1900]. 76, [158] p. Illus., maps. OBgU.

Lake tours via the D & C, [offering] day and night trips between Detroit & Cleveland, the coast line to Mackinac, daily between Cleveland, Put-in-Bay and

Toledo [plus] four trips per week between Toledo, Detroit, and Mackinac. Detroit: John Bornman & Son, [1900]. 48 p. Illus., maps. MiU-H.

Tours on the D & C [with] day and night trips between Detroit & Cleveland, the coast line to Mackinac, daily between Cleveland, Put-in-Bay and Toledo [plus] four trips per week between Toledo, Detroit, and Mackinac. Detroit: John Bornman & Son, [1900]. 48 p. Illus., maps. MiD-B.

Day and night trips [on the] Detroit and Cleveland [route], the coast line to Mackinac. Detroit: John Bornman & Son, [1901]. 64 p. Illus., maps. MiD-D.

The spirit of the inland seas: a story of a summer tour on the Great Lakes. Detroit: John Bornman & Son, c1901. 79, [189] p. Illus., maps. MSaP, MiD-B, OO.

Day & night trips [on the] Detroit & Cleveland [route], the coast line to Mackinac. Detroit: John Bornman & Son, [1902]. 64 p. Illus., maps. OBgU.

Passenger tariff from Cleveland, Toledo, [and] Detroit to points in Michigan, Ontario, Quebec, Wisconsin, Minnesota, Ohio, Pennsylvania, and New York via lake or rail. Detroit: John Bornman & Son, [1902]. 26 p. Illus. In effect April 28th. OBgU.

The spirit of the inland seas: [the] story of a summer tour on the Great Lakes via the Detroit & Cleveland Navigation Co. Detroit: John Bornman & Son, 1902. 77, [1], cxii, [4] p. Illus., maps. MiD-D, NBu.

Day & night trips [on the] Detroit & Cleveland [route], the coast line to Mackinac. Detroit: John Bornman & Son, [1903]. 64 p. Illus., maps. MSaP, MiD-D, NN, OBgU.

The mystery of the monogram, [the] story of a summer tour on the Great Lakes. Detroit: John Bornman & Son, c1904. 78, [90], cxxx p. Illus., maps. MiD-D, MiU-H.

Day and night trips [to] Detroit and Cleveland [on the] queen of [the] lake routes. Detroit: John Bornman & Son, [1905]. 64 p. Illus. Mi.

Time table between Detroit and Cleveland, the coast line to Mackinac, Toledo, Detroit and St. Ignace. Detroit: John Bornman & Son, [1905]. 1 sheet folded to [4] p. Illus., map. OBgU.

After many years, [the] story of a tour on the Great Lakes via the Detroit & Cleveland Navigation Company, "the coast line to Mackinac." Detroit: John Bornman & Son, 1906. 176, 108, [4] p. Illus., maps. Cover title: Water way tales. DLC, MiD-D, OO.

Specifications for the building of a side paddle wheel steel steamboat for the Detroit & Cleveland Navigation Company, Frank E[ugene] Kirby, naval architect, April, 1906. [Detroit?, 1906]. viii, 70 leaves. MiD-D.

After many years, [the] story of a tour on the Great Lakes. Detroit: John Bornman & Son, c1907. 248, [4] p. Illus.,

maps. Cover title: Water way tales. MiD-D, MiU-H, OBgU, OHi.

Day and night trips [between] Detroit and Cleveland [plus] daily service to Mackinac via the coast line. Detroit: John Bornman & Son, [1907]. 68 [i.e. 36] p. Illus., maps. MiD-D, ViNeM.

The waterway between Detroit and Buffalo connecting East and West via the Niagara frontier [with] daily service. Chicago: Poole Bros., [1907?]. 1 sheet folded to 16 [i.e. 32] p. Illus., map. MSaP.

Day and night trips [between] Detroit and Cleveland [plus] daily service to Mackinac via the coast line. Detroit: John Bornman & Son, [1908]. 68 [i.e. 36] p. Illus., maps. MiManiHi.

Mackinac Island, Detroit, Cleveland, Buffalo & Niagara Falls [plus] Toledo, Alpena, Saginaw, Bay City, St. Clair, Port Huron, Harbor Beach, Oscoda, Cheboygan [and] St. Ignace. Detroit: John Bornman & Son, [1909]. 76 [i.e. 40] p. Illus., map. MiU-H.

Water-way tales, the magazine of the Great Lakes. Detroit: John Bornman & Son, c1909. 100, [6], 152 p. Illus., maps. DLC.

Steamer schedules, 1910. Detroit: John Bornman & Son, [1910]. 76 [i.e. 40] p. Illus., map. Cover title: Mackinac Island, Detroit, Cleveland, Buffalo and Niagara Falls. Mi, MiU-H, WM.

Waterway tales, the magazine of the Great Lakes. [Detroit: John Bornman & Son], c1910. 155, [3], 116 p. Illus., maps. DLC, WHi, WMCHi.

Detroit & Cleveland Navigation Company rules and regulations. Detroit: Frank H. West, 1911. 92 p. CaOKMM, MiD-D.

Steamer schedules, 1911. Detroit: John Bornman & Son, [1911]. 76 [i.e. 40] p. Illus., map. Cover title: Mackinac Island, Detroit, Cleveland, Buffalo and Niagara Falls. Mi, MiD-D, MiU-H, ViNeM.

Water way tales, the magazine of the Great Lakes. Detroit: John Bornman & Son, 1911. 168, [76] p. Illus., maps. OClWHi.

Steamer schedules, 1912. Detroit: John Bornman & Son, [1912]. 76 [i.e. 40] p. Illus., folding map. Cover title: D & C lake lines [to] Mackinac Island, Detroit, Cleveland, Buffalo, Niagara Falls, & way ports. MSaP, ViNeM.

Water way tales, the magazine of the Great Lakes. Detroit: John Bornman & Son, [1912]. 160, 101, [1] p. Illus., maps. MiD-D, OO.

Steamer schedules, 1913. Detroit: John Bornman & Son, [1913]. 76 [i.e. 40] p. Illus., folding map. Cover title: D & C lake lines [to] Detroit, Cleveland, Buffalo, Niagara Falls, Mackinac Island and way ports. MSaP, MiD-D, MiShM, OBgU, WM.

Water way tales, the magazine of the Great Lakes. Detroit: John Bornman & Son, c1913. 162, [6], 100 p. Illus., maps. OBgU, OHi.

Steamer schedules, 1914. Detroit: John Bornman & Son, [1914]. 76 [i.e. 40] p. Illus., folding map. Cover title: D & C lake lines [to] Detroit, Cleveland, Buffalo, Niagara Falls, Toledo, Mackinac Island, and way ports. ViNeM.

Water way tales, the magazine of the Great Lakes. Detroit: John Bornman & Son, 1914. 151, 104, [7] p. Illus., maps. MiD-D, OO, ViNeM.

New steamer City of Detroit III costing $1,500,000, the largest and finest sidewheel steamer in the world operating between Detroit and Buffalo. Detroit: John Bornman & Son, [1915?]. [16] p. Illus. MiD-D, MiMtpC.

Steamer schedules, 1915. Detroit: John Bornman & Son, [1915]. 76 [i.e. 40] p. Illus., map. Cover title: D & C lake lines, two giants of the Great Lakes, steamer City of Detroit III [and] steamer City of Cleveland III [serving] Detroit, Cleveland, Buffalo, Niagara Falls, Toledo, Mackinac Island, and way ports. WM.

Two giants of the Great Lakes, steamer City of Detroit III [and] steamer City of Cleveland III. Detroit: John Bornman & Son, [1915]. 1 sheet folded to [8] p. Illus., map. MSaP, ViNeM.

Vacation days on the Great Lakes, Niagara Falls, Mackinac Island [and] St. Ignace. Detroit: John Bornman & Son, [1915?]. 23, [1] p. Illus., map. MiD-B.

Water way tales, the magazine of the Great Lakes. Detroit: John Bornman & Son, c1915. 153, 104, [5] p. Illus., maps. MiD-D, OBgU.

D & C lake lines, two giants of the Great Lakes, steamer City of Detroit III [and] steamer City of Cleveland III [serving] Detroit, Cleveland, Buffalo, Niagara Falls, Toledo, Mackinac Island and way ports. Detroit: John Bornman & Son, [1916]. 1 sheet folded to [4] p. Illus., map. MiMtpC.

Steamer schedules, 1916. [Detroit, 1916]. 76 [i.e. 40] p. Illus., map. Cover title: D & C lake lines, two giants of the Great Lakes, steamer City of Detroit III [and] steamer City of Cleveland III [serving] Detroit, Cleveland, Buffalo, Niagara Falls, Toledo, Mackinac Island, and way ports. MiD-D, ViNeM.

Steamer schedules, 1917. [Detroit, 1917]. 68 [i.e. 36] p. Illus., map. Cover title: D & C lake lines [serving] Detroit, Cleveland, Buffalo, Niagara Falls, Toledo, Mackinac Island, and way ports. MiD-D.

Two giants of the Great Lakes, steamer City of Detroit III [and] steamer City of Cleveland III [serving] Detroit, Cleveland, Buffalo, Niagara Falls, Toledo, Mackinac Island, and way ports. [Detroit, 1917]. 1 sheet folded to [8] p. Illus., map. MdBUS, MiD-D.

Water way tales, the magazine of the Great Lakes. Detroit: John Bornman & Son, c1917. 94, [2], 160 p. Illus. MnHi.

Steamer schedules, 1918. [Detroit, 1918]. 62 [i.e. 32] p. Illus., map. Cover title: D & C lake lines [serving] Detroit, Cleveland, Buffalo, Niagara Falls, Mackinac Island, and way ports. MiD-D, MiDbEI, OBgU.

Vacation days on the Great Lakes. Detroit: John Bornman & Son, [1918?]. 23, [1] p. Illus., map. ViNeM.

Water way tales, the magazine of the Great Lakes. [Detroit: John Bornman & Son, 1918]. 32, 118, [36] p. Illus., map. OBgU.

D & C lake lines [serving] Detroit, Cleveland, Buffalo, Niagara Falls, Toledo, Mackinac Island, and way ports. Detroit: John Bornman & Son, [1919]. 1 sheet folded to [4] p. Illus., map. MiD-D.

Steamer schedules, 1919. Detroit: John Bornman & Son, [1919]. 68 [i.e. 36] p. Illus., map. Cover title: D & C lake lines [serving] Detroit, Cleveland, Buffalo, Niagara Falls, Mackinac Island, and way ports. MiD-D, ViNeM, WM.

Steamer schedules, 1920. Detroit: John Bornman & Son, [1920]. 68 [i.e. 36] p. Illus., map. Cover title: D & C lake lines [serving] Detroit, Cleveland, Buffalo, Niagara Falls, Mackinac Island and way ports. MiD-D, OBgU.

Water way tales, the magazine of the Great Lakes. [Detroit, 1920]. 34, 122, [22] p. Illus., map. MiD-B.

D & C Lake Lines [serving] Detroit, Cleveland, Buffalo, [and] Niagara Falls. [Detroit, 1921]. 1 sheet folded to [4] p. Illus. OBgU.

Steamer schedules, 1921. [Detroit, 1921]. 52 [i.e. 28] p. Illus., map. Cover title: D & C lake lines [to] Detroit, Cleveland, Buffalo [and] Niagara Falls. Mi, MiD-D, MiShM, OBgU.

Water way tales, the magazine of the Great Lakes. Detroit: John Bornman & Son, c1921. 102, 58 p. Illus., map. MiD-D, OBgU.

Steamer schedules, 1922. [Detroit, 1922]. 52 [i.e. 28] p. Illus., map. Cover title: D & C lake lines [serving] Detroit, Cleveland, Buffalo [and] Niagara Falls. MdBUS, MiD-D, ViNeM.

The water way, a tale of three cities, the magazine of the Great Lakes, 1922. Detroit: John Bornman & Son, c1922. 32, 108, [36] p. Illus., maps. MiD-D, OBgU.

D & C Lines [serving] Detroit, Cleveland, Buffalo [and] Niagara Falls. [Detroit?, 1923?]. 27, [1] p. Illus., map. ViNeM.

Souvenir of steamer Greater Detroit. [Detroit]: National Railway News Co., [1923?]. [32] p. Illus. ViNeM, WManiM.

Travel the D & C water-way this year. [Detroit, 1923]. 27, [1] p. Illus., map. Cover title: D & C lake lines [to] Detroit, Cleveland, Buffalo [and] Niagara Falls. MiD-D, MiShM.

The water way, a tale of three cities, the magazine of the Great Lakes. Detroit: John Bornman & Son, [1923]. 32, 112, [36] p. Illus., maps. MiD-B, MiD-D.

The D & C waterway is the better way on the Great Lakes of America. [Detroit, 1924]. 116 [i.e. 60] p. Illus., map. Cover title: D & C lake lines [serving] Detroit, Cleveland, Buffalo [and] Niagara Falls. MSaP, MdBUS, Mi, MiD-D, OBgU.

D & C lake lines [serving] Detroit, Cleveland, Buffalo [and] Niagara Falls. [Detroit?, 1925?]. 1 sheet folded to [8] p. Illus., map. WM.

The D & C lake lines waterway is the better way on the Great Lakes of America [to see] Mackinac Island, the summer wonderland, [plus] Niagara Falls, Buffalo, Cleveland, Detroit, St. Ignace [and] Chicago. [Detroit, 1925]. 134 [i.e. 68] p. Illus., maps. Optional cover title: D & C lake lines [to] Detroit, Cleveland, Buffalo, Niagara Falls, Mackinac Isl[and] [and] Chicago. CSmH, MSaP, Mi, MiD-B, MiD-D, MiShM, OBgU, ViNeM, WM.

Greater Detroit [and] Greater Buffalo, the two largest steamers of their type in the world. [Detroit]: J[ohn] B[ornman] & S[on, 1925?]. 1 sheet folded to [12] p. Illus., map. MiD-D.

The D & C lake lines is the popular way on the inland seas of America. [Detroit, 1926]. 134 [i.e. 68] p. Illus., maps. Cover title: D & C lake lines [to] Detroit, Cleveland, Buffalo, Niagara Falls [and] Chicago. MiD-D.

Vacation days on the Great Lakes [to] Niagara Falls, Mackinac Island [and] St. Ignace. Detroit: John Bornman & Son, [1926]. 22 p. Illus., map. MiD-D.

Vacation days on the Great Lakes [to] Niagara Falls, Mackinac Island [and] St. Ignace. [Detroit, 1926]. 134 [i.e. 68] p. Illus., maps. CSmH, WManiM.

A vacation extraordinary aboard these new steamers. Detroit: Bornman Offset, [1927]. 132 [i.e. 66] p. Illus., maps. CSmH, MiD-B, MiD-D, WM.

D & C lake lines [to] Mackinac Island, St. Ignace, Chicago, Detroit, Cleveland, Buffalo, [and] Niagara Falls. Detroit: John Bornman & Son, [1927?]. [4] p. Illus. MiD-D.

D & C lake lines [to] Mackinac Island, St. Ignace, Chicago, Detroit, Cleveland, Buffalo [and] Niagara Falls. Detroit: John Bornman & Son, [1927]. 1 sheet folded to [8] p. Illus., map. MiD-D.

Vacation days on the Great Lakes [to] Niagara Falls, Mackinac Island [and] St. Ignace. Detroit: John Bornman & Son, [1927]. 23, [1] p. Illus., map. CSmH, MiD-D.

D & C lake lines [serving] Mackinac Island, St. Ignace, Chicago, Detroit, Cleveland, Buffalo [and] Niagara Falls. Detroit: John Bornman & Son, [1928]. 1 sheet folded to [8] p. Illus., map. CSmH, WM.

D & C lake lines [serving] Detroit, Cleveland, Buffalo, Niagara Falls, Mackinac Island, St. Ignace [and] Chicago. Detroit: Bornman, [1928]. 132 [i.e. 68] p. Illus., maps. Mi, MiD-D, OBgU.

Souvenir of [the] steamer Greater Detroit. [Detroit]: National Railway News Co., [1928]. [32] p. Illus. MiD-D.

Vacation days on the Great Lakes. Detroit: John Bornman & Son, [1928]. 23, [1] p. Illus., map. MiD-D.

Attractive new low fare, all expense D & C cruises between Detroit and Mackinac Island and St. Ignace. [Detroit?, 1929?]. 1 sheet folded to [4] p. MiD-D.

Comfort in travel, new daylight service between Detroit and Cleveland. Detroit: Bornman, [1929]. 132 [i.e. 68] p. Illus., maps. Cover title: D & C lake lines [serving] Mackinac Island, St. Ignace, Chicago, Detroit, Cleveland, Buffalo [and] Niagara Falls. DSI, MSaP, MiD-D, ViNeM, WM.

D & C lake lines [serving] Detroit, Cleveland, Buffalo, Niagara Falls, Mackinac Island, St. Ignace [and] Chicago. Detroit: John Bornman & Son, [1929]. 1 sheet folded to [8] p. Illus., map. MiD-D, ViNeM.

Detroit and Cleveland Navigation Company annual statement [for the years] 1928-1927. [Detroit, 1929]. [4] p. CtY.

Vacation days on the Great Lakes. [Detroit, 1929]. 23, [1] p. Illus., map. MSaP, MiD-D.

D & C lake lines [to] Detroit, Cleveland, Buffalo, Niagara Falls, Mackinac Island, St. Ignace [and] Chicago. Detroit: John Bornman & Son, [1930]. 1 sheet folded to [8] p. Map. MiD-D, ViNeM, WM.

D & C lake lines [to] Detroit, Cleveland, Buffalo, Niagara Falls, Mackinac Island, St. Ignace [and] Chicago. Detroit: John Bornman & Son, [1930]. 68 [i.e. 32] p. Illus., map. MiD-D, ViNeM.

Detroit and Cleveland Navigation Company annual statement [for the years] 1929-1928. [Detroit, 1930]. [4] p. CtY, MH-BA.

Detroit and Cleveland Navigation Company annual statement [for the years] 1930-1929. [Detroit, 1931]. [4] p. MH-BA.

Pleasure days on the blue Great Lakes, 1931. Detroit: John Bornman & Son, [1931]. 36 [i.e. 20] p. Illus. MiD-D, MiPhM, MiShM, ViNeM.

Lake tours, vacation days [and] business trips, 1932. Detroit: John Bornman & Son, c1932. 19, [1] p. Illus., map. MiD-D, MiMtpC, MiShM, OBgU, ViNeM, WM.

All-expense tours [from] Detroit-Cleveland-Buffalo to Mackinac Island or Chicago, Chicago to Mackinac Island, or Niagara Falls Ont. via Mackinac Island, Detroit [and] Buffalo. [Detroit?, 1933?]. 1 sheet folded to 9, [1] p. Illus. ViNeM.

Lake tours, vacation days [and] business trips, 1933. Detroit: John Bornman & Son, c1933. 19, [1] p. Illus., map. MiD-B, MiD-D, MiMtpC, MiShM, OBgU, ViNeM, WM, WManiM.

Chicago Exposition, a new six-day Great Lakes cruise, 1934. [Detroit, 1934]. 39, [1] p. Illus., maps. MiD-B, MiD-D, MiShM, MiU-H, OBgU, ViNeM, WM.

D & C Lake Lines [to] Detroit, Cleveland, Buffalo, Niagara Falls, Mackinac Island, [and] Chicago. [Detroit]: J[ohn] B[ornman] & S[on], [1934?]. 1 sheet folded to [12] p. Illus., map. OBgU.

Detroit and Cleveland Navigation Company annual statement [for the years] 1933-1932. [Detroit, 1934]. [4] p. MH-BA.

Annual report [of the] Detroit and Cleveland Navigation Company [for year ending] December 31, 1934. [Detroit, 1935]. [8] p. CtY, MH-BA.

Summer tours, season 1935. [Detroit, 1935]. 1 sheet folded to [16] p. Illus., map. CSmH, ViNeM.

Summer tours [to] Detroit, Cleveland, Buffalo, Niagara Falls, Mackinac Island, St. Ignace [and] Chicago, season 1935. Detroit: Howe Printing Co., [1935]. 38 [i.e. 40] p. Illus., map. MSaP, MdBUS, Mi, MiD-D, ViNeM.

D & C lake lines, the grand fleet of the Great Lakes, 1936. [Detroit, 1936]. 15, [1] p. Illus., map. MiD-D, MiShM, OBgU, ViNeM, WManiM.

Detroit and Cleveland Navigation Company (a Michigan corporation), and subsidiary company Detroit and Cleveland Steamship Company, consolidated financial statements [for the year ending] December-31, 1935. [Detroit, 1936]. [8] p. MH-BA.

Travel in comfort via the water way, condensed schedules and rates of the D & C lake lines. [Detroit?, 1936?]. 1 sheet folded to [4] p. MiD-D, OBgU.

Vacation cruises on the Great Lakes. [Detroit]: Howe Printing Co., [1936?]. 1 sheet folded to [16] p. enveloping an 8 p. booklet. Illus., map. Included folded deck plans. OBgU.

Detroit and Cleveland Navigation Company (a Michigan Corporation), and subsidiary company Detroit and Cleveland Steamship Company, consolidated financial statements [for the year ending] December 31, 1936. [Detroit, 1937]. [8] p. MH-BA.

The grand fleet of the Great Lakes [serving] Detroit, Cleveland, Buffalo, Niagara Falls, Mackinac Island, St.

Ignace [and] Chicago, 1937. [Detroit, 1937]. 15, [1] p. Illus., map. CSmH, CU-SB, MdBUS, MiD-D, OBgU, ViNeM.

Great Lakes cruises [can] be carefree, go D & C, America's greatest vacation values! [Detroit?, 1937?]. 1 sheet folded to [24] p. Illus., map. MiD-D.

Travel in comfort via the D & C lake lines, condensed schedules and fares, 1937. [Detroit, 1937]. 1 sheet folded to [4] p. MiD-D, OBgU.

All expense trip to Niagara Falls and return. [Detroit?, 1938]. 1 sheet folded to [4] p. Illus., map. Optional title: The bargain cruise of the year! MiD-D.

Detroit and Cleveland Navigation Company (a Michigan corporation), and subsidiary company Detroit and Cleveland Steamship Company, consolidated financial statements [for the year ending] December 31, 1937. [Detroit, 1938]. [8] p. MH-BA.

The grand fleet on the Great Lakes [offering] new low-cost all-expense cruises, low week-end round-trip rates, special holiday cruises, low party rates, [and] charter cruises throughout [the] season, 1938. [Detroit, 1938]. 11, [1] p. Illus., map. CSmH, MiD-B, MiShM, MiU-H, OBgU, ViNeM, WM.

Life can be fun, a short history of 80 years of D & C pleasure giving. By George W[ashington] Stark, Detroit's official historian. [Detroit, 1938]. 1 sheet folded to [6] p. Illus., map. OBgU.

New low-cost, all-expense cruises, low week-end round-trip rates, special holiday cruises, low party rates, [and] charter cruises throughout [the] season. [Detroit, 1938]. 11, [1] p. Illus., map. CU-SB.

Travel in comfort via the D & C lake lines, the finest ships on the Great Lakes, 1938 schedules and fares. [Detroit, 1938]. 1 sheet folded to [6] p. Illus. CSmH, MiD-D, MiU-H, ViNeM.

All expense trip to Niagara Falls and return. [Detroit, 1939]. 1 sheet folded to [4] p. Illus., map. CSmH.

Cruise to Georgian Bay, Manitoulin Island, Parry Sound & Killarney [on] all-expense cruises from Buffalo. [Detroit, 1939]. 1 sheet folded to [8] p. Illus., map. MiManHi.

D & C lake lines, the Great Lakes route to the world's fairs. [Detroit, 1939]. 1 sheet folded to [6] p. Illus. CSmH, CU-SB, MdBUS, OBgU, OLimaACH, ViNeM.

D & C lake lines, the Great Lakes route to the world's fairs. [Detroit, 1939]. 1 sheet folded to [16] p. Illus., map. CU-SB, MSaP, MdBUS, MiD-D, MiShM, MiU-H, ViNeM, WM.

D & C lake lines boat and railroad to New York World's Fair. [Detroit, 1939]. 1 sheet folded to [24] p. Illus., maps. CSmH, MdBUS, MiD-D, MiMtpC, MiShM, OBgU.

Detroit and Cleveland Navigation Company and Detroit and Cleveland Steamship Company consolidated financial statements [for the year ending] December 31, 1938. [Detroit, 1939]. [8] p. Folded map. CtY, MH-BA.

Eleventh Good Fellowship Cruise [of the Harrisburg, PA Chamber of Commerce]. [Harrisburg?, 1939]. 1 sheet folded to [6] p. Illus., map. MiD-D.

Sail away to Put-in-Bay, round trip excursions from Detroit to Put-in-Bay on Lake Erie. [Detroit?, 1939?]. 1 sheet folded to [4] p. Illus. MiShM, OBgU, WM.

The season's smartest week-end cruise to Mackinac Island and return via D & C. [Detroit, 1939]. 1 sheet folded to [4] p. Illus. CSmH.

Boat and railroad to New York World's Fair. [Detroit, 1940]. 1 sheet folded to [8] p. Illus., map. WM.

Boat and railroad to New York World's Fair. [Detroit, 1940]. 1 sheet folded to [16] p. Illus., maps. CU-SB, OBgU, ViNeM.

D & C all-expense trip to Niagara Falls and return. [Detroit?, 1940?]. 1 sheet folded to [4] p. Illus., map. MiD-D, OBgU.

D & C lake lines big Labor Day week-end cruise. [Detroit?, 1940]. 1 sheet folded to [4] p. Illus. MiD-D.

D & C lake lines [to] Detroit, Cleveland, Buffalo, Niagara Falls, Mackinac Island [and] Georgian Bay by boat and railroad to New York World's Fair, 1940. [Detroit, 1940]. 1 sheet folded to [8] p. Illus., map. CSmH, MiD-D.

Detroit and Cleveland Navigation Company and Detroit and Cleveland Steamship Company consolidated financial statements [for the year ending] December 31, 1939. [Detroit, 1940]. [8] p. MH-BA.

For your vacation, 2 gloriously gay D & C cruises. [Detroit, 1940]. 1 sheet folded to [4] p. Illus. CU-SB, MiD-D, OBgU.

Visit beautiful Grand Hotel, Mackinac Island, Michigan, on a cruise. [Detroit?, 1940?]. 1 sheet folded to [4] p. Illus. MiD-D, OBgU.

When you make your vacation plans for next summer, include these 2 gay D & C cruises. [Detroit?, 1940?]. 1 sheet folded to [4] p. Illus. MiD-D, OBgU.

Detroit and Cleveland Navigation Company annual report for year ended December 31, 1940. [Detroit, 1941]. [8] p. CtY, MH-BA.

Fun afloat on this big D & C 4th of July cruise. [Detroit?, 1941]. 1 sheet folded to [4] p. Illus., map. MiD-D.

Go by boat, it's fun afloat! from Detroit overnight every night to Cleveland and Buffalo [including] low-cost, all-expense Great Lakes cruises [from] Detroit to Niagara Falls, Mackinac Island, Harbor Springs [and] Georgian Bay. [Detroit, 1941]. 7, [1] p. Illus. CSmH, MiD-D, OBgU, WM.

Go by boat...it's fun afloat! [with] low-cost, all-expense Great Lakes cruises [from] Buffalo to Mackinac Island, Harbor Springs, Georgian Bay, Detroit and Greenfield Village, 1941. [Detroit, 1941]. 7, [1] p. Illus. Blue folder. MdBUS, MiD-D, OBgU, ViNeM.

Go by boat...it's fun afloat! [with] low-cost, all-expense Great Lakes cruises [from] Cleveland to Mackinac Island, Harbor Springs, Georgian Bay, Detroit and Greenfield Village, 1941. [Detroit, 1941]. 7, [1] p. Illus. OBgU.

Go by boat, it's fun afloat! [sailing] overnight every night between Buffalo and Detroit [or] Cleveland and Detroit [or on] low cost, all-expense Great Lakes cruises to Niagara Falls, Mackinac Island, Georgian Bay [and] Greenfield Village. [Detroit, 1941]. 19, [1] p. Illus., map. Yellow folder. CSmH, MdBUS, MiD-D, MiShM, MnDuLS, OBgU, ViNeM, WM.

An invitation to fun! [in] 1942. [Detroit?, 1942]. 1 sheet folded to [4] p. Illus. MiD-D.

D & C big 4th of July cruise, 1942. [Detroit?, 1942]. 1 sheet folded to [4] p. Illus. MiD-D.

D & C lake lines low cost, all-expense romance cruises to Mackinac Island, Harbor Springs [and] Georgian Bay, 1942. [Detroit, 1942]. 8 p. Illus., map. Two editions: one yellow and one green. MdBUS, MiD-D, MiShM, MiU-H, OBgU, ViNeM, WM, WMCHi.

Detroit and Cleveland Navigation Company annual report for year ended December 31, 1941. [Detroit, 1942]. [8] p. CtY, MiD-D.

Go by boat, it's fun afloat, 1942. [Detroit, 1942]. 1 sheet folded to [8] p. Illus., map. Back title: Overnight every night between Buffalo and Detroit. CtY, MiD-D, WManiM.

Go by boat, it's fun afloat, 1942. [Detroit, 1942]. 1 sheet folded to [8] p. Illus., map. Back page: Ride and rest, East or West. MiD-D, OBgU.

Low cost, all-expense romance cruises to Mackinac Island, Harbor Springs [and] Georgian Bay. [Detroit, 1942]. 8 p. Illus., map. CSmH, MSaP, MiD-D.

Low cost, all-expense romance cruises to Mackinac Island, Harbor Springs [and] Georgian Bay [plus] visit Buffalo and Niagara Falls. [Detroit, 1942]. 8 p. Illus., map. April edition. CSmH, MiD-D, MiShM, OBgU.

Announcing D & C lake lines waterways vacations for war workers, 1943. [Detroit?, 1943]. 1 sheet folded to [4] p. Illus. Note: Red brochure. MiD-D.

Announcing daily D & C lake lines waterways vacations for war workers between Buffalo and Detroit, 1943. [Detroit?, 1943]. 1 sheet folded to [4] p. Illus. Note: Green brochure. MiD-D.

Economical passenger and freight transportation, 1943. [Detroit, 1943]. 1 sheet folded to [8] p. Illus., map. CSmH, MiD-D, MiMtpC, MiShM, NBuHi, OBgU, ViNeM, WM, WMCHi.

September cruises to Mackinac Island, Georgian Bay, Harbor Springs [and] Midland, Ont., on the big cruise steamer Western States. [Detroit, 1943]. 2 p. Illus. MiD-D.

Cruises on the famous cruise ship "Western States" to Mackinac Island, Harbor Springs, Georgian Bay [and] Midland, Ont., 1944. [Detroit, 1944]. 1 sheet folded to [6] p. Illus. MiD-D, ViNeM.

D & C lake lines [are active during] good months to travel by boat, 1944. [Detroit?, 1944]. 1 sheet folded to [4] p. Illus. MiD-D.

The grand fleet of the Great Lakes, overnight service between Detroit and Cleveland and between Detroit and Buffalo, 1944. [Detroit, 1944]. 1 sheet folded to [8] p. Illus., map. CtY, MiD-D, MiMtpC, MiShM, OBgU, ViNeM, WM.

1944 mid-week cruise on the famous cruise steamer "Western States." [Detroit, 1944]. 1 sheet folded to [4] p. Illus. MiD-D.

Overnight every night between Detroit and Cleveland, overnight every night between Detroit and Buffalo, [plus] mid-week and week-end cruises, lake rides, charters, [and] express freight. [Detroit, 1944]. 1 sheet folded to [4] p. Illus. MiD-D.

Buffalo and Niagara Falls, leave every Monday...starting June 4 - last date September 3, 1945 [by Fords Travel Service]. [Chicago?, 1945]. 1 sheet folded to [4] p. Illus. MiD-B.

D & C lake lines presents roaming around America by the old AAA traveler [Jim Welsh]. [Detroit], c1945. 48 p. Illus. First edition, June 1945. Cover title: Roaming around America by the old traveler. CSmH, MiD-B, OClWHi.

Detroit & Cleveland Navigation Company annual report for the year ended December 31, 1944. [Detroit, 1945]. [8] p. Map. MiD-D.

The grand fleet of the Great Lakes, overnight service between Detroit and Cleveland and between Cleveland and Buffalo, 1945. [Detroit, 1945]. 1 sheet folded to [8] p. Illus., map. CSmH, MiD-D, MiShM, OBgU, OFH, ViNeM.

September-October-November between Detroit and Cleveland, September-October between Detroit and Buffalo. [Detroit, 1945]. 1 sheet folded to [8] p. Illus., map. CSmH, WM, WManiM.

Water-way Tales. — Vol. 1, no. 1 (September 1945)-vol. 6, no. ? (1950?). — Detroit, 1945-1950? Illus. Monthly?

Cataloging based on September, 1945 issue. CSmH, MiD-D.

Attractive new low fare all expense D & C cruises. [Detroit?, 1946?]. 1 sheet folded to [4] p. MiD-D.

D & C 1946 mid-week cruise on the famous cruise steamer "Western States." [Detroit?, 1946]. 1 sheet folded to [4] p. Illus. MiD-D.

Sail the inland seas with D & C, overnight and daylight trips [plus] northern cruises, 1946. [Detroit, 1946]. 1 sheet folded to [8] p. Illus., map. Issued March, 1946. CSmH, CaOOA, CtY, MiD-D, MiMtpC, MiShM, OBgU, OFH, ViNeM, WM.

D & C cruises, 1 Labor Day week end cruise [to] Sault S[ain]te Marie, Georgian Bay [and] Mackinac Island, [plus] 2 post-season cruises to Goderich, Ontario. [Detroit, 1947]. 1 sheet folded to [6] p. Illus. MiD-D, OBgU.

D & C lake lines all-expense cruise to Detroit-Greenfield Village and return, 1947. [Detroit?, 1947]. 1 sheet folded to [4] p. Illus. MiD-D, OBgU.

Delightful cruises on the Great Lakes, 1947. [Detroit, 1947]. 1 sheet folded to [12] p. Illus., map. MdBUS, MiD-D, OBgU, OFH, ViNeM, WM.

Detroit & Cleveland Navigation Company annual report for the year ended December 31, 1946. [Detroit, 1947]. 9, [1] p. Map. MiD-D, OFH.

Detroit & Cleveland Navigation Company annual report for the eleven months ended November 30, 1947. [Detroit, 1947?]. [8] p. Map. Mi, MiD-D.

New 7-day cruise [plus] midweek and weekend cruises on the grand fleet of the Great Lakes, 1947. [Detroit, 1947]. 1 sheet folded to [4] p. Illus., map. May edition. MdBUS, MiD-D, MiMtpC, OBgU, ViNeM, WM.

Great Lakes cruises, 1948. [Detroit, 1948]. 1 sheet folded to [4] p. Illus., map. CSmH, MiD-D, OBgU.

Great Lakes cruises: be carefree, go D & C. [Detroit, 1948]. 1 sheet folded to [24] p. Illus., map. MiD-D, NBuHi, OBgU, WM.

Life can be fun, a short short [sic] story of 80 years of D & C pleasure giving, by George W[ashington] Stark. [Detroit, 1948]. 1 sheet folded to [6] p. Illus., map. MiD-D.

Your carefree dining hour [offering] delicious cuisine, you're carefree when you go D & C. [Detroit?, 1948?]. 1 sheet folded to [4] p. Illus., map. Includes tour advertisements on verso and Great Lakes statistics on page [2]. MiD-D, OBgU.

D & C graduation cruises, class of '49. [Detroit, 1949]. 1 sheet folded to [6] p. MiD-D.

D & C Great Lakes cruises for a carefree 1949 vacation. [Detroit, 1949]. [16] p. Illus., map. CSmH, MSaP, MiD-D, MiMtpC, MiShM, OBgU, OV, ViNeM.

Detroit and Cleveland Navigation Company annual report for the fiscal year ended November 30, 1949. [Detroit?, 1949?]. 1 sheet folded to [6] p. MiD-D.

Adventure ahoy! The biggest and best graduation class cruises on the Great Lakes exclusively for graduates, class of 1950. [Detroit, 1950]. 1 sheet folded to [24] p. Illus., map. MiD-D.

America's greatest vacation values, D & C 7-day Great Lakes cruise to Mackinac Island, the Soo Locks, Detroit, Buffalo (Niagara Falls), [and] Harbor Springs. [Detroit?, 1950?]. 1 sheet folded to [4] p. Illus., maps. CSmH, MiD-D, MiShM, OBgU, OFH, ViNeM.

D & C 5-star Great Lakes cruises, America's greatest vacation values for 1950. [Detroit, 1950]. 1 sheet folded to [24] p. Illus., map. Appears in three editions colored green, yellow, and red. CSmH, MdBUS, MiD-D, MiShM, OBgU, ViNeM.

Round trip excursions [from] Detroit to Put-in-Bay. [Detroit?, 1950?]. 1 sheet folded to [4] p. Illus. MiD-D, OBgU, OFH, ViNeM.

Your D & C 5-star Great Lakes cruise travel-log. [Detroit, 1950]. 1 sheet folded to [16] p. Illus., map. MiD-D, ViNeM.

Annual report for the fiscal year ended November 30, 1950. [Detroit?, 1951?]. 1 sheet folded to [6] p. MH-BA.

DETROIT & CLEVELAND STEAM NAVIGA-TION COMPANY, DETROIT, MI

Incorporated 27 April 1868. Acquired by the Detroit & Cleveland Navigation Company on 5 January 1898.

Michigan Railroad Guide. — Vol. 1, no. 1 (August 1877)-vol. 5, no. 53 (December 1881)? — Detroit, 1877-1881? Monthly. Maps. MiD-D.

The Detroit and Cleveland Steam Navigation Co.'s daily line [of] elegant sidewheel passenger steamers. Detroit: Calvert Lith[ographing] Co., [1881]. 1 sheet folded to [10] p. Illus., map. MiD-D.

Daily line palace steamers. Detroit: Calvert Lith[ographing] Co., [1882], c1881. 1 sheet folded to [20] p. Illus., maps. MiMtpC.

Steamers City of Mackinac and City of Cleveland for Mackinac. Detroit: Calvert Lith[ographing] Co., [1883], c1881. 1 sheet folded to [20] p. Illus., maps. MiMtpC.

A lake tour to picturesque Mackinac, historical and descriptive, by C[ummings] D[avis] Whitcomb. Detroit: O[rin] S. Gulley, Bornman & Co., c1884. [2], 111, [1] p. Illus., folding maps. CaOOONL, CtY, DLC, MSaP, MiD-B,

MiD-D, MiMarqHi, MiMtpC, MiU, MiU-T, MnHi, NN, OBgU, OClWHi.

A lake tour to picturesque Mackinac, historical and descriptive, by C[ummings] D[avis] Whitcomb. — Revised edition. — Detroit: O[rin] S. Gulley, Bornman & Co., 1884. [116] p. Illus., maps. Cover title: Lake tours via picturesque Mackinac. MiD-B, MiMtpC, MiU-H.

Steamers City of Mackinac and City of Cleveland for Mackinac [with the] Lake Huron Division. Detroit: Gulley Printing House, [1884]. 1 sheet folded to [20] p. Illus., maps. Second cover title: Palace steamers [of the] Lake Erie Division. OBgU.

Detroit and Cleveland Steam Navigation Co. [on] Lake Erie [and] Lake Huron. Detroit: O[rin] S. Gulley, Bornman & Co., [1885]. [24] p. Illus., maps. CtY, DSI, MSaP, OBgU, OClWHi, ViNeM.

Detroit and Cleveland Steam Navigation Co. [on] Lake Erie [and] Lake Huron. Detroit: O[rin] S. Gulley, Bornman & Co., [1886]. [16] p. Illus., maps. MSaP, Mi, MiD-B, MiU-H.

Detroit and Cleveland Steam Navigation Co. [on] Lake Erie [and] Lake Huron. Detroit: O[rin] S. Gulley, Bornman & Co., [1886]. [24] p. Illus., maps. CaOOA, CaQQS, OBgU.

A lake tour to picturesque Mackinac, historical and descriptive, by C[ummings] D[avis] Whitcomb. Detroit: O[rin] S. Gulley, Bornman & Co., 1887. [74] p. Illus., maps. Cover title: Lake tours via picturesque Mackinac. OClWHi.

A lake tour to picturesque Mackinac, historical and descriptive, by C[ummings] D[avis] Whitcomb. Detroit: O[rin] S. Gulley, Bornman & Co., 1888. [150] p. Illus., maps. Cover title: Lake tours via picturesque Mackinac. MiD-B, MiMtpC.

Midsummer voyages on northern seas. Detroit: O[rin] S. Gulley, Bornman & Co., [1888]. [24] p. Illus., maps. MiD-B, MiU-T, OClWHi.

A lake tour to picturesque Mackinac via the D & C, written by Frank H[amilton] Taylor. New York: Giles Litho[graphy] & Liberty Printing Co., c1889. [156] p. Illus., maps. DLC, MiU-T, OBgU.

Fares from Detroit, March 15th, 1889. Detroit: O[rin] S. Gulley, Bornman & Co., [1889]. [4] p. MiD-D.

Midsummer voyages on northern seas. Detroit: Van Leyen & Co., [1889?]. [24] p. Illus., maps. MiU-H, OClWHi, OO.

A lake tour to picturesque Mackinac via the D & C, written by Frank H[amilton] Taylor. Detroit: O[rin] S. Gulley, Bornman & Co., c1890. [122] p. Illus., maps. DLC, MiGr, OO.

Midsummer voyages on the D & C. Detroit: O[rin] S. Gulley, Bornman & Co., [1890?]. [24] p. Illus., maps. MiD-D, MiU-T, OFH, OLimaACH.

To the members of the National Educational [sic] Association and teachers generally. [Detroit, 1890]. 1 sheet folded to [4] p. Illus. MiD-D.

A lake tour to picturesque Mackinac via the D & C. Detroit: O[rin] S. Gulley, Bornman & Co., c1891. [160] p. Illus., maps. Cover title: Picturesque Mackinac via the D & C. DLC, MiD-B, MiU-H, MnHi, OBgU, OClWHi, OO.

Midsummer voyages on the D & C. Detroit: O[rin] S. Gulley, Bornman & Co., [1891]. [24] p. Illus., maps. Mi.

A lake tour to picturesque Mackinac via the D & C. Detroit: O[rin] S. Gulley, Bornman & Co., 1892. [128] p. Illus., maps. Cover title: Picturesque Mackinac via the D & C. MiD-B, MiMarqHi.

Midsummer voyages on the D & C. Detroit: O[rin] S. Gulley, Bornman & Co., [1892?]. Illus., maps. MiD-D.

Midsummer D & C voyages. Detroit: John Bornman & Son, [1893]. [28] p. Illus., maps. MiD-B, MiD-D, ViNeM.

A lake tour to picturesque Mackinac via the D & C. Detroit: John Bornman & Son, 1894. [166] p. Illus., maps. Cover title: Lake tours via the D & C. MiD-B.

Midsummer D & C voyages. Detroit: John Bornman & Son, [1894]. [28] p. Illus., map. MiMtpC, OO.

Midsummer D & C voyages. Detroit: John Bornman & Son, [1895]. [28] p. Illus., maps. MiD-D.

Search light effect as the D & C sister ships pass on Lake Huron. Spend your vacation on the D & C Line. Detroit: John Bornman & Son, [1895?]. 23, [1] p. Illus., map. MSaP.

Three on a tour. Detroit: John Bornman & Son, c1895. 120, [34] p. Illus., maps. DLC, MiD-D, Mi-MISPC, OBgU.

Three on a tour, by Helen K. Ingram. Detroit: John Bornman & Son, 1895. 120, [34] p. Illus., maps. MiD-D.

Lake tours via the D & C, the coast line to Mackinac. Detroit: John Bornman & Son, [1896]. [24] p. Illus., maps. MiD-D.

Three on a tour. Detroit: John Bornman & Son, [1896], c1895. 120, [74] p. Illus., maps. MiD-D, OBgU.

Col[onel] Clayton's lake tour. Detroit: John Bornman & Son, 1897. 123, [79] p. Illus., maps. DLC, MiD-D, MiGr.

DETROIT AND GEORGIAN BAY NAVIGATION COMPANY, LIMITED, DETROIT, MI
Incorporated on 3 December 1937. Dissolved on 25 October 1951. Associated with the Seaway Lines, Limited.

Fiords of the inland seas and Georgian Bay on the Seaway Lines. [Detroit?, 1938]. 1 sheet folded to [8] p. Illus., map. CSmH, MiD-D.

Cruise to Georgian Bay, Manitoulin Island, Parry Sound & Killarney, all-expense cruises from Detroit. [Detroit?, 1939]. 1 sheet folded to [8] p. Illus., map. MdBUS, MiD-D, OFH.

Georgian Bay, North Channel, Manitoulin Isl[and] [and] Parry Sound. [Detroit?, 1939]. 1 sheet folded to [8] p. Illus., map. CSmH.

Complete circle cruise of Georgian Bay [through] Paul Henry Travel Service. [Detroit?, 1940?]. 1 sheet folded to [6] p. Illus., map. MiD-D.

Complete circle cruise of Georgian Bay [through] Paul Henry Travel Service. [Detroit?, 1941?]. 1 sheet folded to [8] p. Illus., map. MiD-D.

DETROIT AND MILWAUKEE RAILWAY AND STEAMSHIP COMPANY, DETROIT, MI
Organized on 21 April 1855 by confederation of the Detroit & Pontiac Railroad Company and the Oakland & Ottawa Railroad Company. Commenced shipping operations in 1858 by chartering two steamers from the Lake Michigan Transit Company. The Company began operating its own boats late in 1859. Went into receivership on 10 April 1860, and was sold to the Detroit & Milwaukee Railroad Company on 4 October 1860.

Pocket guide for passengers by the Detroit and Milwaukee Railway & Steamship Line, the great northwestern U.S. mail route [offering] express, package, and freight line in connection with the Great Western, Grand Trunk, Buffalo & Lake Huron, and other connecting railroads & steamboats East, 1860. Buffalo: Clapp, Matthews & Co.'s Steam Printing House, [1860]. 11, [1] p. Folding map with text. CaOOA.

DETROIT AND ST. CLAIR RIVER TOWING ASSOCIATION, DETROIT, MI
Apparently an informal name given to a group of individuals and firms who banded together to establish more uniform towing fees for vessels being towed between Lakes Erie and Huron.

[List of ships, along with their tonnage, owners, and port of hail]. [N.p., 1867]. 48 p. MnDuC.

[Roster of ships, owners, ports, and charges], 1882. Detroit: Thorndike Nourse, [1882]. 57, [1] p. MiPh

DETROIT & WINDSOR FERRY COMPANY, DETROIT, MI
Formerly the Detroit, Belle Isle & Windsor Ferry Company. Incorporated 13 December 1910. Dissolved

20 September 1938, because of competition from the Detroit-Windsor tunnel and the Ambassador Bridge. Succeeded by Bob-lo Steamers, Incorporated.

Bob-lo Island, where fun begins. [Detroit?, 1925?]. 1 sheet folded to [8] p. Illus. MiD-D.

Bob-lo Island, where fun begins. [Detroit, 1926]. 1 sheet folded to [8] p. Illus. MiD-D.

Bob-lo Island, where fun begins. [Detroit, 1927]. [8] p. Illus., maps. MiD-D.

Bob-lo Island, where fun begins. [Detroit?, 1928?]. [8] p. Illus., maps. MiD-D.

Bob-lo Island park. [Detroit], c1929. 24 p. Illus., map. Cover title: The greatest spot on earth. MiD-D.

In all the world no day like this, the river ride to Bob-lo. [Detroit?, 1930?]. [12] p. Illus., map. MiD-D.

Come with us to Bob-lo (date goes here) and you'll have a wonderful time! (name of your church, organization or society goes here). [Detroit, 1931]. [16] p. Illus. MiD-D.

Rest while you ride [on the] ferry service between Detroit and Windsor for automobile and driver. [Detroit?, 1932?]. [8] p. Illus., map. MiD-D.

Come with us to Bob-lo and you'll have a wonderful time! [Detroit, 1935]. [16] p. Illus., map. MiD-D.

Bob-lo Island, the river ride to Bob-lo. [Detroit, 1936]. 1 sheet folded to [8] p. Illus., map. MiD-D

Bob-lo Island, the river ride to Bob-lo. [Detroit, 1937]. 1 sheet folded to [8] p. Illus., map. MiD-D.

DETROIT, BELLE ISLE & WINDSOR FERRY COMPANY, DETROIT, MI
Incorporated 12 May 1881. Opened Bois Blanc Island Amusement Park on 18 June 1898. Reorganized as the Detroit & Windsor Ferry Company. Dissolved 6 May 1911.

Bois Blanc Park, situated at the mouth of the Detroit River with Lake Erie lying in full view. Detroit: Winn & Hammond, [1898]. [16] p. Illus., map. MiD-D.

River rides out of Detroit [to] Bois Blanc Park [and] Belle Isle Park, Amherstburg and Windsor, Ont. [Detroit?, 1901]. [12] p. Illus., map. MiD-D.

River rides out of Detroit [to] Bois Blanc and Belle Isle Parks, Amherstburg, Windsor, Ont. [Detroit?, 1904?]. [16] p. Illus., map. OBgU.

DETROIT-ST. CLAIR NAVIGATION COMPANY, DETROIT, MI
Incorporated 18 June 1937. Dissolved in 1947.

Modern steel steamer City of Hancock summer schedule. [Detroit?, 1939?]. 1 sheet folded to [4] p. Illus. MiD-D.

DETROIT-WALLACEBURG STEAMSHIP LINE, DETROIT, MI
Established around 1916 and apparently operated only during that year.

Detroit, Walpole Island [and] Wallaceburg route. [Detroit?, 1916?]. 1 sheet folded to [12] p. Illus., map. MiD-B, MiDbEI.

DOMINION TRANSPORTATION COMPANY, LIMITED, OWEN SOUND, ONT
Incorporated 26 October 1909, as successor to the Dominion Fish Company fleet. Joined with the Owen Sound Transportation Company in 1936. Purchased by the Detroit & Cleveland Navigation Company in 1955. Dissolved on 26 January 1981.

Spring-summer steamer schedules, 1920. Owen Sound: R[ichardson], B[ond] & W[right], Limited, [1920]. 1 sheet folded to [4] p. Illus. MiD-D.

Spring-summer steamer schedules, 1925. [N.p., 1925]. 1 sheet folded to [6] p. Illus., map. OBgU.

Local passenger tariff no. J1[-J13]? between Owen Sound and Sault S[ain]te Marie and intermediate ports, and between Owen Sound and Providence Bay and intermediate ports, and between Owen Sound and Meaford and Collingwood. [N.p., 1936-1948?]. 1 sheet folded to [4] p. Annual release. MiD-D.

Sailing schedule, 1936 season. [N.p., 1936]. 1 sheet folded to [8] p. Illus. Published jointly with the Owen Sound Transportation Company. MiD-D.

Sailing schedule, 1937 season. [N.p., 1937]. 1 sheet folded to [8] p. Illus. Published jointly with the Owen Sound Transportation Company. MiD-D.

1000 mile Great Lakes cruise, summer 1939. [N.p., 1939]. 1 sheet folded to [12] p. Illus., map. Published jointly with the Owen Sound Transportation Company. OBgU.

Great Lakes cruise 1000 miles, 5 or 6 days, summer 1940. [N.p., 1940]. 1 sheet folded to [12] p. Illus., map. Published jointly with the Owen Sound Transportation Company. CaOONL, MiD-D.

The national emergency demands you "keep fit" [with a] 5 day, 1000 mile cruise on Georgian Bay, St. Mary's River [and] Whitefish Bay. [N.p., 1941]. 1 sheet folded to [12] p. Illus., map. Published jointly with the Owen Sound Transportatiion Company. MiD-D.

Cruise 1000 miles on Georgian Bay, St. Mary's River [and] Whitefish Bay. [Toronto?, 1943]. 1 sheet folded to [12] p. Illus., map. Published jointly with the Owen Sound Transportation Company. MiD-D, OBgU, OFH.

Summary of sailings, 1943. [N.p., 1943]. [2] p. Published jointly with the Owen Sound Transportation Company. MiD-D.

Cruise 1000 miles on Georgian Bay, St. Mary's River [and] Whitefish Bay. [Toronto?, 1944]. 1 sheet folded to [12] p. Illus., map. Published jointly with the Owen Sound Transportation Company. MiD-D, OFH.

Cruise 1000 miles on Georgian Bay, St. Mary's River [and] Whitefish Bay. [Toronto?, 1945]. 1 sheet folded to [12] p. Illus., map. Published jointly with the Owen Sound Transportation Company. MiD-D, OFH.

Cruise 1000 miles on Georgian Bay, St. Mary's River [and] Whitefish Bay. [Toronto?, 1946]. 1 sheet folded to [12] p. Illus., map. Published jointly with the Owen Sound Transportation Company. MiD-D, OFH.

Cruise 1000 miles on Georgian Bay, St. Mary's River [and] Whitefish Bay. [Toronto?, 1947]. 1 sheet folded to [12] p. Illus., map. Published jointly with the Owen Sound Transportation Company. MiD-D, MiShM, OBgU.

Summary of sailings, 1947. [N.p., 1947]. [2] p. Published jointly with the Owen Sound Transportation Company. MiD-D.

Cruise 1000 miles on Georgian Bay, St. Mary's River [and] Whitefish Bay. [Toronto?, 1948]. 1 sheet folded to [12] p. Illus., map. Published jointly with the Owen Sound Transportation Company. MiD-D, OBgU.

Summary of sailings, 1948. [N.p., 1948]. [2] p. Published jointly with the Owen Sound Transportatiion Company. MiD-D.

DULUTH LAKE TRANSPORTATION COMPANY, DULUTH, MN

Organized in March of 1874. Ceased to exist in April of 1876.

Lake Superior south shore line, [with] the splendid passenger steamers Manistee and Metropolis, will form a semi-weekly line between Duluth, Bayfield, Ashland, Ontonagon, Isle Royale, Eagle Harbor, Houghton, Hancock, L'Anse and Marquette. Duluth: Daily Herald Stop-cylinder Steam Press, [1874]. 1 sheet folded to [6] p. ViNeM.

DUNKLEY-WILLIAMS COMPANY, CHICAGO, IL

Incorporated 29 April 1902, as successor to the Henry W. Williams Transportation Company. Became the Chicago & South Haven Steamship Company on 3 May 1909, when it merged with the Michigan Steamship Company.

South Haven and Michigan points, [the] shortest, most direct route from Chicago to Kalamazoo, Battle Creek,

Jackson, Lake Cora, Paw Paw Lake & Lawton. Chicago: Faulkner-Ryan Co., [1908]. 15, [1] p. Illus. MiD-D.

ERIE & WESTERN TRANSPORTATION COMPANY, BUFFALO, NY

Incorporated as a Pennsylvania firm on 21 June 1865. Called the Anchor Line, it was a subsidiary of the Pennsylvania Railroad Company. Taken over by the Great Lakes Transit Corporation on 1 April 1916.

Anchor Line [serving] Buffalo, Mackinac Island, Duluth, and intermediate ports [on] the Great Lakes route, 1895. Buffalo: Matthews-Northrup Co., [1895]. 1 sheet folded to [32] p. Illus., map. MSaP.

Anchor Line [serving] Buffalo, Mackinac Island, Duluth, and intermediate points [on] the Great Lake route, 1896. Buffalo: Matthews-Northrup Co., [1896]. 1 sheet folded to [32] p. Illus., map. MSaP.

Anchor Line [serving] Buffalo, Mackinac Island, Duluth, and intermediate ports [on] the Great Lake route, 1897. Buffalo: Matthews-Northrup Co., [1897]. 1 sheet folded to [32] p. Illus., map. MSaP.

Anchor Line [serving] Buffalo, Mackinac Island, Duluth, and intermediate ports [on] the Great Lake route, 1898. Buffalo: Matthews-Northrup Co., [1898]. 1 sheet folded to [24] p. Map. MiD-B.

Anchor Line [serving] Buffalo, Mackinac Island, Duluth, and intermediate ports [on] the Great Lake route, 1899. Buffalo: Matthews-Northrup Co., [1899]. [24] p. Illus., map. MSaP.

Anchor Line [serving] Buffalo, Mackinac Island, Duluth, and intermediate ports [on] the Great Lake route, 1900. Chicago: Poole Bros., [1900]. 1 sheet folded to 23, [1] p. Illus., map. MSaP, NBuHi.

Anchor Line [serving] Buffalo, Mackinac Island, Duluth, and intermediate ports [on] the Great Lake route, 1901. Chicago: Poole Bros., [1901]. 1 sheet folded to 23, [1] p. Illus., map. MiD-D, ViNeM.

Anchor Line [serving] Buffalo, Mackinac Island, Duluth, and intermediate ports [on] the Great Lake route, 1902. Buffalo: Matthews-Northrup Works, [1902]. 1 sheet folded to 24 p. Map. MiD-D.

Anchor Line [serving] Buffalo, Mackinac Island, Duluth, and intermediate ports [on] the Great Lake route, 1903]. Chicago: Poole Bros., [1903]. 32 [i.e. 16] p. Illus., maps. NBuHi.

Anchor Line [serving] Buffalo, Mackinac Island, Duluth, and intermediate points [on] the Great Lake route, 1904. Buffalo: A[lbert] T. Brown Press, [1904]. 32 [i.e. 16] p. Illus., maps. MSaP, MiD-D.

Some items of information regarding the Anchor Line ports of call, with a few points of interest at each port that may be visited en route. [Buffalo?, 1904?]. 1 sheet folded to [10] p. ViNeM.

Anchor Line [serving] Buffalo, Mackinac Island, Duluth, and intermediate points [on] the Great Lakes route, 1905. Buffalo: Matthews-Northrup Works, [1905]. 40 [i.e. 20] p. Illus., maps. ViNeM.

Four per cent. [sic], twenty-year guaranteed gold loan of $1,500,000 of January 1st, 1905, [being a] deed of trust of the Erie and Western Transportation Company, [a] traffic and guaranty agreement, [and] deed of trust of Western Warehousing Company, Girard Trust Company, trustee. [Buffalo?, 1905]. [4], 47, [1] p. NNC.

Some items of information regarding the Anchor Line ports of call, with a few points of interest at each port that may be visited en route. [Buffalo?, 1905?]. 1 sheet folded to [6] p. MiD-D.

Anchor Line [serving] Buffalo, Mackinac Island, Duluth, and intermediate points [on] the Great Lakes route, 1906. Chicago: Poole Bros., [1906]. 40 [i.e. 20] p. Illus., maps. ViNeM, WM

Anchor Line [serving] Buffalo, Mackinac Island, Duluth and intermediate points [on] the Great Lakes route, 1907. Chicago: Poole Bros., [1907]. 40 [i.e.20] p. Illus., maps. ViNeM.

The Anchor Line intended sailings of passenger steamers, season of 1907. [Buffalo?, 1907]. 27, [1] p. Illus. Cover title: Summer schedule, 1907. ViNeM.

Pennsylvania Railroad through the Great Lakes and back via [the] Anchor Line. Philadelphia: Allen, Lane & Scott, [1907]. 1 sheet folded to 19, [3] p. Illus., map. ViNeM.

Anchor Line (Pennsylvania Railroad steamers) [serving] Buffalo, Mackinac Island, Duluth, and intermediate points [on] the Great Lakes route, 1909. Chicago: Poole Bros., [1909]. 40 [i.e. 20] p. Illus., maps. MiD-D, MiU-H.

Anchor Line, "the Great Lakes route," [intended sailings]. Chicago: Poole Bros., [1910]. 19, [1] p. Illus., maps. MSaP, Mi, MiU-H.

Anchor Line, "the Great Lakes route," season 1912. Chicago: Poole Bros., [1912]. 19, [1] p. Illus., maps. ViNeM, WM.

Anchor Line, "the Great Lakes route," 1913. Chicago: Poole Bros., [1913]. 19, [1] p. Illus., maps. MnHi, NBuHi.

Anchor Line, "the Great Lakes route," 1914. Chicago: Poole Bros., [1914]. 19, [1] p. Illus., maps. ViNeM.

Ports of call, with a few points of interest at each port that may be visited en route. Buffalo: Kenworthy Printing Co., [1914?]. 1 sheet folded to [14] p. MiD-D, NBuHi.

Anchor Line, "the Great Lakes route," 1915. Chicago: Poole Bros., [1915]. 19, [1] p. Illus., map. MSaP, MiD-D, OBgU, ViNeM.

ERIE ISLE FERRY COMPANY, PUT-IN-BAY, OH

Incorporated on 28 May 1930. Went into receivership on 7 February 1961.

Auto and passenger ferry, St[eame]r Erie Isle, [to] Put-in-Bay and Middle Bass. [N.p., 1937]. 1 sheet folded to [12] p. Illus., map. WM.

Season's schedule (eastern standard time) automobile and passenger ferry to Put-in-Bay and Middle Bass. [N.p., 1939]. 1 sheet folded to [12] p. Illus., map. MiD-D, OSandF.

Progressive changes in island transportation. [N.p., 1940?]. 1 sheet folded to [4] p. Illus., map. OFH.

Auto and passenger ferry to Put-in-Bay from Catawba Point. [N.p., 1942?]. 1 sheet folded to [6] p. Illus., map. OBgU.

Mystic Isle, [the] new auto and passenger ferry to Put-in-Bay from Catawba Point, Ohio. [N.p., 1943?]. 1 sheet folded to [6] p. Illus., map. MiD-D.

Mystic Isle, [the] new auto and passenger ferry to Put-in-Bay from Catawba Point, Ohio, 1944 summer schedule. [N.p., 1944]. 1 sheet folded to [8] p. Illus., map. MiD-D, OBgU, OFH, WM.

Mystic Isle, [the] new auto and passenger ferry to Put-in-Bay from Catawba Point, Ohio, 1945 summer schedule. [N.p., 1945]. 1 sheet folded to [8] p. Illus., map. MiD-D, OFH.

Mystic Isle, [the] largest auto and passenger ferry to Put-in-Bay from Catawba Point, Ohio, 1946 summer schedule. [N.p., 1946]. 1 sheet folded to [6] p. Illus., map. MiD-D, OFH, WM.

Mystic Isle, [the] largest [and] fastest auto and passenger ferry [from] Port Clinton, Ohio, to Put-in-Bay, 1947 schedule. [N.p., 1947]. 1 sheet folded to [6] p. Illus., map. MiD-D, OBgU, OFH.

Ferry Mystic Isle from Port Clinton to Put-in-Bay, Ohio, 1949 schedule. [N.p., 1949]. 1 sheet folded to [4] p. Illus., map. OBgU.

Fast ferry Mystic Isle from Port Clinton to Put-in-Bay, Ohio, 1950 schedule. [N.p., 1950]. 1 sheet folded to [4] p. Illus., map. MiD-D, OFH.

Auto and passenger ferry to Put-in-Bay from Catawba Point. [N.p., 1951]. 1 sheet folded to [6] p. Illus., map. MiD-D.

ERIE RAILROAD COMPANY, NEW YORK, NY

Incorporated 14 November 1895. Acquired the Union Steamboat Company on 30 June 1896. The lake line was made part of the Great Lakes Transit Corporation on 22 March 1916.

Erie Railroad lake line rules for masters and engineers effective July 1, 1913. [N.p., 1913]. [2], 12 p. N.

FJELL-ORANJE LINES, ROTTERDAM, HOL

Created in April of 1956 by a partial merger of the Norwegian Fjell Line and the Dutch Oranje Line. Represented in the United States by Great Lakes Overseas, Incorporated, of Chicago. In May of 1959, its Princess Irene was the first foreign vessel to offer regular passenger service on the Great Lakes. Became part of the Trans-Atlantic Lakes Line in January of 1968. Dissolved on 31 December 1970.

Great Lakes-St. Lawrence Seaway cruises aboard ocean-going passenger cargo ships of the Fjell-Oranje Lines. [Detroit?, 1959?]. 1 sheet folded to [12] p. Illus., map. MiD-B.

Great Lakes-St. Lawrence Seaway cruises aboard ocean-going passenger cargo ships of the Fjell-Oranje Lines, 1960. [Detroit?, 1960]. 1 sheet folded to [12] p. Illus., map. CSmH, MiD-B, MiD-D, OBgU, WManiM.

Fjell-Oranje Lines [Great Lakes service]. [Amsterdam?, 1961?]. 1 sheet folded to [24] p. Illus. MiD-D.

Great Lakes-St. Lawrence Seaway cruises aboard ocean-going passenger cargo ships of the Fjell-Oranje Lines. [N.p., 1963?]. 1 sheet folded to [12] p. Illus., map. MiShM, ViNeM.

Great Lakes-St. Lawrence Seaway cruises aboard ocean-going passenger cargo ships of the Fjell-Oranje Lines. [N.p., 1964]. 1 sheet folded to [12] p. Illus., map. ViNeM.

FORD MOTOR COMPANY, MARINE DIVISION, DEARBORN, MI

Established in 1924 when improvements to the River Rouge allowed Great Lakes ships access to the Dearborn plant. In the spring of 1982 the fleet was transferred to a Ford subsidiary, the Rouge Steel Company. Ceased operations in 1989 when the fleet was sold to Lakes Shipping, Incorporated, a subsidiary of the Interlake Steamship Company.

Welcome aboard [ships of the fleet]. [N.p., 1958?]. [12] p. Illus., map. MiD-D.

Naming ceremonies [for the] S.S. Ernest R[obert] Breech, Detroit, Michigan, April 11, 1962. [N.p., 1962]. [12] p. Illus., map. MiD-B, MiD-D.

Steel Division [of the] Ford Motor Company, in connection with Michigan Week May 19-25, 1963, welcomes you aboard the S.S. William Clay Ford Saturday, May 25, 1963. [N.p., 1963]. 1 sheet folded to [4] p. Illus., map. MiD-D.

Naming ceremonies [for the] S.S. John Dykstra, Dearborn, Michigan, May 11, 1966. [N.p., 1966]. [12] p. Illus., map. MiD-D.

New employe [sic] orientation booklet [for] marine operations, Ford Steel Division. [N.p., 1970?]. [12] p. Illus. Title from back cover. MiD-D.

GARTLAND STEAMSHIP COMPANY, CHICAGO, IL

Incorporated on 8 November 1929. Generally a freight-carrying firm, it operated a passenger vessel during the Chicago World's Fair. Acquired by the American Steamship Company on 28 July 1986.

Gartland Steamship Company [sailings between] Chicago-Muskegon. [Chicago: Poole Bros., 1933]. 1 sheet folded to [6] p. Illus., map. OBgU, ViNeM, WM.

GEORGIAN BAY NAVIGATION COMPANY, LIMITED, DETROIT, MI

Established about 1897. Known as the Windsor, Detroit & Soo Line. Ceased operations around 1904.

Georgian Bay route [from] Cleveland to the Soo and return. [Detroit?, 1898]. [12] p. Illus. CaOOA.

Georgian Bay route, Detroit to the Soo. [Detroit?, 1899?]. [12] p. Illus., map. MiD-B.

Summer on the Georgian Bay and the 30,000 islands, America's greatest scenic route. [Detroit?, 1899]. [16] p. Illus., map. MSaP, MiD-D.

Georgian Bay route on the Windsor, Detroit and Soo Line, sailing weekly between Lake Erie ports and the Soo via the 30,000 islands of Georgian Bay. [Detroit?, 1901]. [12] p. Illus., map. MiD-D, OBgU.

Lake tours of the Georgian Bay Navigation Co., Limited, sailing tri-weekly between Lake Erie ports and the Soo via the 30,000 islands of Georgian Bay. [Detroit?, 1902]. [16] p. Illus., map. MSaP, ViNeM.

Lake tours of the Cleveland and Georgian Bay Line, sailing between Lake Erie ports and the Soo via the 30,000 islands of Georgian Bay. Detroit: Calvert Lith[ographing Company], [1903?]. [16] p. Illus., map. MiD-D.

GEORGIAN BAY TOURIST & STEAMSHIPS, LIMITED, PENETANG, ONT

Incorporated 27 April 1949, as apparent successor to the Georgian Bay Tourist Company of Midland. May have filed for bankruptcy in 1954. Dissolved on 4 January 1960.

30,000 Islands cruises from Penetang, Ontario. [Midland, ONT, 1949]. 1 sheet folded to [6] p. Illus., maps. CaOPsM.

30,000 Island cruises from the heart of historic Huronia through the winding channels of Georgian Bay's famous inside passage. [Midland, ONT]: Midland Press, [1949?]. 1 sheet folded to [6] p. Illus., map. OBgU.

30,000 Island cruises from Penetang, Midland and Parry Sound through the protected channels of Georgian Bay's historic inside passage. Midland, ONT: Midland Press, [1950?]. 1 sheet folded to [6] p. Illus., map. OFH.

30,000 Island cruises. Midland, ONT: Midland Press, [1950?]. 1 sheet folded to [4] p. Illus., map. OFH.

30,000 Island cruises. Midland, ONT: Midland Press, [1952]. 1 sheet folded to [6] p. Illus., map. MiD-D.

30,000 Island cruises. Midland, ONT: Midland Press, [1953]. 1 sheet folded to [4] p. Illus., map. CSmH, MiD-D.

GEORGIAN BAY TOURIST COMPANY OF MIDLAND, LIMITED, MIDLAND, ONT

Incorporated 6 May 1921, as successor to the Northern Navigation Company's 30,000 Island route. In 1949 it began operating under the name of Georgian Bay Tourist & Steamships, Limited? Dissolved on 5 January 1953.

30,000 Island route 1923 time table of steamers operated by the Georgian Bay Tourist Co. of Midland, Limited, Ontario, and Honey Harbour Navigation Company, Limited. [Midland, ONT?, 1923]. [20] p. Illus. CaOOA.

The 30,000 Islands [of] Georgian Bay, Canada's summer playground [serviced by] boat trips between Midland and Parry Sound. [Midland, ONT?, 1927]. 1 sheet folded to [16] p. Illus., map. OBgU.

The 30,000 Islands [of] Georgian Bay, Canada's summer playground [served by] boat trips between Midland, Parry Sound, and Point-au-Baril. Midland, ONT: Midland Free Press, [1929]. 1 sheet folded to [16] p. (8 are half panels). Illus., map. CaOOA.

The 30,000 Islands [of] Georgian Bay, "Canada's summer playground." Midland, ONT: Free Press, [1931]. 1 sheet folded to [6] p. Illus. MiD-D.

Take a boat trip through the beautiful 30,000 Islands [in] Georgian Bay from Midland and Parry Sound. [Midland, ONT?, 1933]. 1 sheet folded to [8] p. Illus. MiD-D.

Take a boat trip through the beautiful 30,000 Islands [in] Georgian Bay from Midland and Parry Sound. [Midland, ONT?, 1934]. 1 sheet folded to [8] p. Illus. MiD-D, WM.

Travel by boat [to] 30,000 Islands [in] Geogian Bay, 1935 time table. [Midland, ONT?, 1935]. 1 sheet folded to [4] p. Illus. MiD-D.

Travel by boat [to] 30,000 Islands [in] Georgian Bay, 1936 time table. [Midland, ONT?, 1936]. 1 sheet folded to [4] p. Illus. MiD-D.

Travel by boat [to] 30,000 Islands [in] Georgian Bay, 1937 time table. [Midland, ONT?, 1937]. 1 sheet folded to [6] p. Illus. MiD-D.

30,000 islands all-expense cruises from Midland. [Midland, ONT?, 1938?]. 1 sheet folded to 8 p. Illus., map. OBgU.

Time table [to] 30,000 Islands [in] Georgian Bay, season of 1940. [Midland, ONT?, 1940]. 1 sheet folded to [6] p. Illus. MiD-D.

30,000 Islands, all-expense cruises from Midland. [Midland, ONT?, 1940]. 1 sheet folded to [8] p. Illus., maps. MiD-D.

30,000 Islands, all-expense cruises from Midland. [Midland, ONT?, 1941]. 1 sheet folded to [6] p. Illus., maps. MiD-D.

30,000 Islands, all-expense cruises from Midland. [Midland, ONT?, 1942]. 1 sheet folded to [6] p. Illus., maps. MiD-D.

This is your vacation time table, 1942 cruises [to] 30,000 Islands of the Georgian Bay. [Midland, ONT, 1942]. 1 sheet folded to [6] p. Illus. MiD-D.

30,000 Islands, all-expense cruises from Midland. [Midland, ONT?, 1943]. 1 sheet folded to [6] p. Illus., maps. MiD-D, OBgU.

This is your vacation time table, 1943 cruises [to] 30,000 Islands of the Georgian Bay. [Midland, ONT?, 1943]. 1 sheet folded to [6] p. Illus. MiD-D.

30,000 Islands, cruises from Midland. [Midland, ONT?, 1944]. 1 sheet folded to [6] p. Illus., maps. MiD-D, OFH.

30,000 Islands, cruises from Midland. [Midland, ONT?, 1945]. 1 sheet folded to [6] p. Illus., maps. MiD-D, OFH.

30,000 Islands, cruises from Midland. [Midland, ONT?, 1947]. 1 sheet folded to [6] p. Illus., maps. MiD-D.

30,000 Islands, cruises from Midland. [Midland, ONT?, 1948]. 1 sheet folded to [6] p. Illus., maps. MiD-D.

GOODRICH TRANSIT COMPANY, CHICAGO, IL

Incorporated 25 May 1906, in Maine. Reincorporated under the same name 1 February 1921, as a Delaware corporation. Acquired the Graham & Morton Line in October of 1924. Bought the Chicago, Racine & Milwaukee Line in 1926. Merged with the West Ports Steamship Company on 1 January 1930. Filed bankruptcy on 20 December 1932, and dissolved on 10 May 1933, when its assets were sold at auction.

Goodrich boats on Lake Michigan & Green Bay, from Chicago to Milwaukee, Grand Haven, Muskegon, White Lake, and Michigan and Wisconsin summer resorts, summer 1907. Milwaukee: Evening Wisconsin Co., [1907]. 30 [i.e. 16] p. Illus., maps. MiManiHi.

Goodrich boats on Lake Michigan & Green Bay, from Chicago to Milwaukee, Grand Haven, Muskegon, White Lake, Mackinac Island, [plus] Michigan and Wisconsin summer resorts, summer 1908. Milwuakee: Evening Wisconsin Printing Co., [1908]. 30, [i.e. 16] p. Illus., maps. WM.

Goodrich boats on Lake Michigan & Green Bay, from Chicago to Milwaukee, Grand Haven, Muskegon, White Lake, Mackinac Island, [plus] Michigan and Wisconsin summer resorts, summer 1909. Milwaukee: Evening Wisconsin Co., [1909]. 30 [i.e. 16] p. Illus., map. MiD-D.

Goodrich boats on Lake Michigan and beautiful Green Bay. Chicago: Poole Bros., [1910]. 30 [i.e. 16] p. Illus., map. MiU-H.

Goodrich boats on Lake Michigan and beautiful Green Bay, 1912. Chicago: Poole Bros., [1912]. 30 [i.e. 16] p. Illus., map. WM.

A week's cruise from Milwaukee to Put-in-Bay, Lake Erie, and return for the centennial celebration of Perry's victory on Lake Erie, September 10, 1913, on the steamer Alabama of the Goodrich Steamship Lines. [Chicago: Poole Bros., 1913]. 12 p. Illus., map. WHi, WM.

A week's cruise from Chicago through beautiful Green Bay to Mackinac Island, the Soo, North Channel, [the] thirty thousand islands of Georgian Bay, and return on the steamship Arizona of the Goodrich Steamship Lines. Chicago: Poole Bros., [1914]. 15, [1] p. Illus., map. Cover title: A week's cruise. ViNeM, WM.

Goodrich Steamship Lines on Lake Michigan and Green Bay, 1914. Milwaukee: Wright & Joys Co., [1914]. 1 sheet folded to [4] p. Illus., map. MiD-B.

Goodrich Steamship Lines on Lake Michigan and picturesque Georgian Bay, 1914. Chicago: Poole Bros., [1914]. 38 [i.e. 20] p. Illus., map. WMCHi.

Goodrich Steamship Lines on Lake Michigan and picturesque Georgian Bay, 1915. Chicago: Poole Bros., [1915]. 38 [i.e. 20] p. Illus., maps. ViNeM, WMCHi.

Goodrich Steamship Lines on Lake Michigan and Green Bay, 1916. Milwaukee: Evening Wisconsin Co., [1916]. 1 sheet folded to [8] p. Illus., map. ViNeM.

Goodrich Steamship Lines on Lake Michigan and picturesque Georgian Bay. Chicago: Poole Bros., [1916]. 30, [i.e. 16] p. Illus., map. OBgU.

The Goodrich way from Chicago to Spring Lake resorts via Grand Haven. [Chicago?, 1917?]. 1 sheet folded to [4] p. Illus., map. MiGrH.

Goodrich Steamship Lines on Lake Michigan and Green Bay, 1917. Milwaukee: Evening Wisconsin Co., [1917]. 1 sheet folded to [8] p. Illus., map. ViNeM.

Goodrich Steamship Lines on Lake Michigan and picturesque Mackinac, 1917. Chicago: Poole Bros., [1917]. 30 [i.e. 16] p. Illus., map. ViNeM.

Goodrich Steamship Lines on Lake Michigan and picturesque Mackinac, 1918. Chicago: Poole Bros., [1918]. 14 [i.e. 8] p. Illus., map. MiDbEI, ViNeM.

The beauty spots of two states invite you to rest and recuperate. Chicago: Poole Bros., [1918]. 23, [1] p. Illus., maps. Cover title: What about your vacation? Michigan & Wisconsin ideal resorts. WM.

Goodrich Steamship Lines on Lake Michigan and picturesque Mackinac, 1919. Chicago: Poole Bros., [1919]. 14 [i.e. 8] p. Illus., map. ViNeM, WM.

A day on the Christopher Columbus, Chicago - Milwaukee, a day's outing in sight of land all the way. [N.p., 1920?]. 1 sheet folded to [6] p. Illus. ViNeM, WM.

Goodrich Steamship Lines on Lake Michigan and picturesque Mackinac, 1920. Chicago: Poole Bros., [1920]. 14 [i.e. 8] p. Illus., map. ViNeM.

The beauty spots of two states invite you to rest and recuperate. Chicago: Poole Bros., [1921]. 22 p. Illus., maps. Cover title: What about your vacation? Michigan & Wisconsin ideal resorts. Mi.

Goodrich Steamship Lines on Lake Michigan and picturesque Mackinac, 1921. [Chicago, 1921]. 14 [i.e. 8] p. Illus., map. ViNeM, WM.

The beauty spots of two states invite you to rest and recuperate. Chicago: Poole Bros., [1922]. 23, [1] p. Illus., maps. Cover title: What about your vacation? Michigan & Wisconsin ideal resorts. WM.

Goodrich Steamship Lines on Lake Michigan and picturesque Mackinac, 1922. [Chicago, 1922]. 14 [i.e. 8] p. Illus., map. Mi-MISPC, MiD-D, ViNeM, WM.

The beauty spots of two states invite you to rest and recuperate. Chicago: Poole Bros., 1923. 23, [1] p. Illus., maps. Cover title: What about your vacation? Michigan & Wisconsin ideal resorts. MSaP, MiShM, WM.

Goodrich Steamship Lines on Lake Michigan and picturesque Mackinac, 1923. [Chicago, 1923]. 14 [i.e. 8] p. Illus., map. ViNeM, WM.

The beauty spots of two states invite you to rest and recuperate. Chicago: Poole Bros., [1924]. 23, [1] p. Illus., maps. Cover title: What about your vacation? Michigan & Wisconsin ideal resorts. ViNeM.

Goodrich Steamship Lines on Lake Michigan and picturesque Mackinac, 1924. Chicago: Poole Bros., [1924]. 14 [i.e. 8] p. Illus., map. ViNeM, WM.

Beauty spots of Michigan and Wisconsin, Goodrich vacation suggestions. Chicago: Poole Bros., [1925]. 26, [2] p. Illus., maps. WM.

Goodrich [plus] Graham and Morton Steamship Lines, 1925. Chicago: Pryor Press, [1925]. 20 [i.e. 12] p. Illus., map. CSmH, OBgU, WM, WManiM.

Goodrich [plus] Graham and Morton Steamship Lines, 1926. Chicago: Pryor Press, [1926]. 22 [i.e. 12] p. Illus., map. WM.

Mackinac Island cruises through beautiful Green Bay, delightful 3 1/2 day shore trips. Chicago: Pryor Press, [1926]. 1 sheet folded to [8] p. Illus., map. WM.

Beauty spots of western Michigan. Chicago: Poole Bros., [1927]. 27, [1] p. Illus., maps. MiD-B.

The Goodrich Anchor. — Vol. 1, no.1 (December 1927?)- vol. 6?, no. ? (1932?). — Chicago, 1927-1932? Monthly. Cataloging based on edition for October, 1928. WManiM.

Goodrich [plus] Graham and Morton Steamship Lines, 1927. Chicago: Pryor Press, [1927]. 22 [i.e. 12] p. Illus., map. CSmH, ViNeM, WM.

Goodrich Steamship Lines, 1928. Chicago: Pryor Press, [1928]. 20 [i.e. 12] p. Illus., map. MSaP, WM.

Goodrich vacation suggestions: beauty spots of western Michigan. Chicago: Poole Bros., [1928]. 27, [1] p. Illus., maps. Mi.

Shoreline cruises [to] 'Mackinac' — "Snow" Islands [and] Green Bay, 1928. [Chicago, 1928]. 1 sheet folded to [4] p. Illus., map. ViNeM.

Shore line cruises [to] 'Mackinac' [the] "Snow" Islands [and] Green Bay, 1928. Chicago: Poole Bros., [1928]. 1 sheet folded to [8] p. Illus., map. MiD-D.

Goodrich Steamship Lines, 1929. Chicago: Pryor Press, [1929]. 28 [i.e. 20] p. Illus., map. ViNeM, WM.

Go the Goodrich way [with] S.S. Theodore Roosevelt daylight excursions, perfect service between Milwaukee and Chicago. [Chicago?, 1930]. 1 sheet folded to [4] p. Illus. WM.

Goodrich Steamship Lines. [Chicago?, 1930]. 15, [1] p. Illus., maps. ViNeM, WM.

Goodrich Steamship Lines. [Chicago: Poole Bros., 1931]. 1 sheet folded to [8] p. Illus., map. MiD-D, MiShM, ViNeM.

Goodrich Steamship Lines. Chicago: Poole Bros., [1932]. 1 sheet folded to [8] p. Map. MiD-B, MiD-D, OFH, ViNeM, WM.

GOODRICH TRANSPORTATION COMPANY, CHICAGO, IL

Established on 18 April 1868, as a Wisconsin firm. Reincorporated as a Maine business on 7 April 1906, and name changed to Goodrich Transit Company.

The finest and only lines of side-wheel passenger steamers on the upper lakes are those of the "Goodrich Transportation Co.," 1880. Chicago: J[udson] M.W. Jones Stationery and Printing Co., [1880]. 1 sheet folded to [16] p. Illus., map. WMCHi.

The Goodrich Line to all the principal ports and summer resorts of Lake Michigan, season of 1884. Chicago: J[udson] M.W. Jones Stationery and Printing Co., [1884]. 1 sheet folded to [16] p. Illus., map. OBgU.

The steamship "Virginia." [Chicago?, 1891?]. [16] p. Illus. WManiM.

The summer time table of the Goodrich Line to the principal ports on Lake Michigan, season of 1893. Chicago: Stromberg, Allen & Co., [1893]. 1 sheet folded to [24] p. Illus., map. Mi.

The Goodrich Line to all the principal ports and summer resorts on Lake Michigan, season 1897. Chicago: Stromberg, Allen & Co., [1897]. 1 sheet folded to [20] p. Illus., map. WMCHi.

Log book recording the adventures of the up-to-date argonautic Chicago veteran pill-rollers [being the Chicago Veteran Druggists' Association]. Chicago: W[illshire] G. Russell & Co., [1899]. 11, [1] p. ViNeM.

GRAHAM & MORTON TRANSPORTATION COMPANY, BENTON HARBOR, MI

Established in 1875. Incorporated 17 February 1903. Merged with the Goodrich Transit Company in October of 1924 and then dissolved on 25 November 1925.

"The Favorite." Chicago: Corbitt-Skidmore Company, [1899?]. 1 sheet folded to [4] p. MiShM.

Something about the Graham and Morton Line, and some pictures of river and lake around St. Joseph and Benton Harbor, Michigan. St. Joseph, MI: A[rthur] B. Morse Company, [1900?]. [32] p. Illus. Cover title: Graham & Morton Line [to] Chicago, St. Joseph, and Benton Harbor. MiD-D.

The Graham & Morton Line to all Michigan. St. Joseph, MI: A[rthur] B. Morse Company, [1901]. 48 p. Illus. MiStj.

The Graham and Morton Line to all Michigan. St. Joseph, MI: A[rthur] B. Morse Company, c1902. 67, [1] p. Illus., map. MiD-D, MiMtpC, MiShM, MiU-T.

Some pictures of the beautiful summering places reached by the Graham & Morton Line. Chicago: Illinois Engraving Co., [1902?]. [56] p. Illus., map. Cover title: When the boat comes in. MiMtpC.

Lake and rail, [the] Grand Rapids Short Line, 2 trips daily connecting with the Pere Marquette Railway for all northern and eastern Michigan resorts, 3 round trips daily [to] St. Joseph & Benton Harbor, [the] line to all Michigan and Indiana points, 1904. [St. Joseph, MI?, 1904]. 1 sheet folded to [4] p. Illus., map. WManiM.

Lake and rail, [the] Grand Rapids Short Line, 2 trips daily connecting with the Pere Marquette Railway for all northern and eastern Michigan resorts, 3 round trips daily [to] St. Joseph & Benton Harbor, [the] line to all Michigan & Indiana points, 1906. [St. Joseph, MI?, 1906]. 1 sheet folded to [4] p. Illus., map. WManiM.

Graham & Morton Line to all Michigan. [St. Joseph, MI?, 1907]. [20] p. Illus., map. WM.

G[raham] & M[orton] T[ransportation] Co. rules governing employees. [St. Joseph, MI?, 1907]. 44 p. MiKW.

G[raham] & M[orton] Line 1909 time table. Chicago: Regensteiner Colortype Co., [1909]. 1 sheet folded to [4] p. Illus. Effective June 21, 1909. ViNeM.

Graham & Morton Line to all Michigan. St. Joseph, MI: A[rthur] B. Morse Co., [1910]. [24] p. Illus., map. MiU-H.

Graham & Morton Line to all Michigan. St. Joseph, MI: [Arthur B.] Morse Company, [1911]. [28] p. Illus., maps. MSaP, OBgU.

Graham & Morton Line to all Michigan. St. Joseph, MI: A[rthur] B. Morse Co., [1912]. [28] p. Illus., map. MSaP, MiD-D, WM.

Graham & Morton Line to all Michigan. St. Joseph, MI: A[rthur] B. Morse Co., [1913]. [28] p. Illus., map. WM.

Graham and Morton Line. St. Joseph, MI: A[rthur] B. Morse Co., [1914]. [28] p. Illus., map. MiGrM, ViNeM, WM, WMCHi.

Graham and Morton Line. St. Joseph, MI: A[rthur] B. Morse Company, [1915]. [24] p. Illus., map. DLC, ViNeM.

The dustless way to happy land. St. Joseph, MI: A[rthur] B. Morse Co., [1917]. [16] p. Illus., map. MiD-D, ViNeM.

Graham and Morton Line. St. Joseph, MI: A[rthur] B. Morse Co., [1918]. [16] p. Illus., map. WM.

Graham and Morton Line, the steel fleet of white flyers, season 1922. St. Joseph, MI: A[rthur] B. Morse Company, [1922]. 22 p. Illus., map. MiD-D.

The Graham & Morton Transportation Co. $750,000 first mortgage 6% gold bonds. [St. Joseph, MI?, 1923]. [4] p. Illus., map. NNC.

Graham and Morton Line, the steel fleet of white flyers, 1874-1924 golden anniversary. St. Joseph, MI: Power Farming Press, [1924]. [22] p. Illus., map. MiD-D.

Goodrich [plus] Graham and Morton steamship lines, 1925. Chicago: Pryor Press, [1925]. 20 [i.e. 12] p. Illus., map. CSmH, WM, WManiM.

Goodrich [plus] Graham and Morton steamship lines, 1926. Chicago: Pryor Press, [1926]. 22 [i.e. 12] p. Illus., map. WM.

Beauty spots of western Michigan. Chicago: Poole Bros., [1927]. 27, [1] p. Illus., maps. MiD-B.

Goodrich [plus] Graham and Morton steamship lines, 1927. Chicago: Pryor Press, [1927]. 22 [i.e. 12] p. Illus., map. CSmH, ViNeM, WM.

GRAND PORTAGE-ISLE ROYALE TRANSPORTATION LINE, INCORPORATED, DULUTH, MN
Incorporated on 27 April 1967. Still active as of 1990.

Cruise to beautiful Isle Royale National Park aboard the motor vessel Voyageur II or Wenonah, 1986. [Duluth: Pro-print, 1986]. 1 sheet folded to [8] p. Illus., maps. MiD-D.

Cruise to beautiful Isle Royale National Park aboard the motor vessel Wenonah or cruise around Isle Royale aboard the Voyageur II. [Virginia, MN: W[illiam] A. Fisher Co., 1988]. 1 sheet folded to [6] p. Illus., maps. MiD-D.

Cruise to beautiful Isle Royale National Park aboard the motor vessel Wenonah or cruise around Isle Royale aboard the Voyageur II. [Virginia, MN: W[illiam] A. Fisher Co., 1989]. 1 sheet folded to [6] p. Illus., maps. MiD-D.

GRAND TRUNK MILWAUKEE CAR FERRY COMPANY, MILWAUKEE, WI
Organized 10 November 1905, as a Wisconsin firm under the control of the Detroit, Grand Haven & Milwaukee Railway. On 1 January 1929, it was acquired by the newly formed Grand Trunk Western Railroad Company. All passenger service was terminated in 1971, and the fleet ceased operations on 1 November 1978.

Grand Trunk Railway system, the shortest route between Milwaukee and all Michigan, Canadian and eastern points, season 1911. Chicago: Poole Bros., [1911]. 12 [i.e. 8] p. Illus., map. MSaP.

GRAND TRUNK WESTERN RAILROAD COMPANY, DETROIT, MI
Incorporated on 1 November 1928, as a Canadian-owned business. Created the Grand Trunk-Pennsylvania Transportation Company as a Wisconsin firm on 12 December 1931. On 17 July 1933, its Michigan port was changed from Grand Haven to Muskegon. The Pennsylvania Railroad Company withdrew from this arrangement at the end of the 1953 season.

Agreement between the Grand Trunk Western Railroad Company and the Pennsylvania Railroad Company, October 28, 1931, granting Pennsylvania R.R. Co. use of car ferry terminal facilities at Milwuakee, Wisconsin. Philadelphia: Allen, Lane & Scott, [1931]. 11, [1] p. MiU-H.

Agreement between [the] Grand Trunk Western Railroad Company and the Pennsylvania Railroad Company, October 28, 1931, providing for the incorporation of [the] "Grand Trunk-Pennsylvania Transportation Company." Philadelphia: Allen, Lane & Scott, [1931]. 20 p. MiU-H.

Applicant's return to questionnaire no. 1 before the Interstate Commerce Commission in the matter of the application of [the] Grand Trunk Western Railroad Company...[for] the extension of the line of railroad operated by it (1) by car ferry between Muskegon, Michigan, and Manitowoc, Wisconsin.... Detroit: Detroit Free Press, 1932. 32 p. MiU-H.

Application before the Interstate Commerce Commission...of Grand Trunk Western Railroad Company for authority...to control Grand Trunk Milwaukee Car Ferry Company through stock ownership. [Detroit?, 1935]. 13, [1] p. MiU-H.

GREAT LAKES CRUISE BUREAU, CHICAGO, IL

Associated with the B.J. Kennedy Travel Service, an agent for various cruise lines. This was not a shipping firm, per se, but it did produce promotional literature for various navigation companies.

Suggestions for your 1943 summer vacation. [Chicago?, 1943]. 1 sheet folded to [4] p. Illus. MiD-D.

Take a lake trip for your 1944 summer vacation. [Chicago?, 1944]. 1 sheet folded to [6] p. Illus. MiD-D.

Kennedy's [Travel Service] suggestions for your 1945 summer vacation trip. [Chicago?, 1945]. 1 sheet folded to [4] p. Illus. MiD-D.

Vacation travel suggestions for 1946. [Chicago?, 1946]. 1 sheet folded to [6] p. Illus. MiD-D.

GREAT LAKES STEAMSHIP COMPANY, INCORPORATED, CLEVELAND, OH

Incorporated 19 May 1911, as a Maine corporation and successor to the United States Transportation Company through a merger of the Brown fleet, L.C. Smith Transit, American Transit Company, Cowle Transit Company, and the Wilkinson Transportation Company. Reincorporated under the same name as a Delaware Corporation on 26 February 1924. Its fleet was acquired by the Wilson Marine Transit Company on 8 April 1957, and the firm liquidated on 3 February 1958.

Great Lakes Steamship Company fourth annual report [for year ending] December 31, 1914. [Cleveland?, 1915]. [8] p. MH-BA.

Great Lakes Steamship Company fifth annual report [for year ending] December 31, 1915. [Cleveland?, 1916]. [8] p. MH-BA.

Great Lakes Steamship Company sixth annual report [for year ending] December 31, 1916. [Cleveland?, 1917]. [8] p. MH-BA, NNC.

Great Lakes Steamship Company seventh annual report [for year ending] December 31, 1917. [Cleveland?, 1918]. [8] p. MH-BA.

Great Lakes Steamship Company eighth annual report [for year ending] December 31, 1918. [Cleveland?, 1919]. [8] p. MH-BA.

Great Lakes Steamship Company ninth annual report [for year ending] December 31, 1919. [Cleveland?, 1920]. [8] p. MH-BA.

Tenth annual report of the Great Lakes Steamship Company [for year ended] December 31, 1920. [Cleveland?, 1921]. [8] p. MH-BA.

Eleventh annual report of the Great Lakes Steamship Company [for year ended] December 31, 1921. [Cleveland?, 1922]. [8] p. CtY, MH-BA.

Twelfth annual report of the Great Lakes Steamship Company [for year ended] December 31, 1922. [Cleveland?, 1923]. [8] p. MH-BA.

Annual report of the Great Lakes Steamship Company, Inc., [for year ended] December 31, 1925. [Cleveland?, 1926]. [8] p. NNC.

Annual report of the Great Lakes Steamship Company, Inc., [for year ended] December 31, 1926. [Cleveland?, 1927]. [8] p. MH-BA, NNC.

Annual report of the Great Lakes Steamship Company, Inc., [for year ended] December 31, 1926. [Cleveland?, 1928]. [8] p. MH-BA, NNC.

Annual report of the Great Lakes Steamship Company, Inc., [for year ended] December 31, 1928. [Cleveland?, 1929]. [8] p. MH-BA.

Annual report of the Great Lakes Steamship Company, Inc., for the fiscal year ending December 31, 1929. [Cleveland?, 1930]. [12] p. MH-BA.

Annual report of the Great Lakes Steamship Company, Inc., for the fiscal year ending December 31, 1930. [Cleveland?, 1931]. [12] p. MH-BA.

Annual report of the Great Lakes Steamship Company, Inc., for the fiscal year ending December 31, 1931. [Cleveland?, 1932]. [12] p. MH-BA.

Annual report of the Great Lakes Steamship Company, Inc., for the fiscal year ending December 31, 1932. [Cleveland?, 1933]. [12] p. MH-BA.

Annual report of the Great Lakes Steamship Company, Inc., for the fiscal year ending December 31, 1933. [Cleveland?, 1934]. [12] p. MH-BA.

Annual report of the Great Lakes Steamship Company, Inc., for the fiscal year ending December 31, 1934. [Cleveland?, 1935]. [12] p. MH-BA.

Annual report of the Great Lakes Steamship Company, Inc., for the fiscal year ending December 31, 1935. [Cleveland?, 1936]. [12] p. MH-BA.

Annual report of the Great Lakes Steamship Company, Inc., for the fiscal year ending December 31, 1936. [Cleveland?, 1937]. [12] p. MH-BA, NNC.

Annual report of the Great Lakes Steamship Company, Inc., for the fiscal year ending December 31, 1937. [Cleveland?, 1938]. [12] p. MH-BA, NNC.

Annual report of the Great Lakes Steamship Company, Inc., for the fiscal year ended December 31, 1938. [Cleveland?, 1939]. [12] p. MH-BA.

Annual report of the Great Lakes Steamship Company, Inc., for the fiscal year ended December 31, 1939. [Cleveland?, 1940]. [12] p. MH-BA.

Annual report of the Great Lakes Steamship Company, Inc., for the fiscal year ended December 31, 1940. [Cleveland?, 1941]. [12] p. CtY, MH-BA.

Annual report of the Great Lakes Steamship Company, Inc., for the fiscal year ended December 31, 1941. [Cleveland?, 1942]. [12] p. MH-BA.

The Richard M[ather] Marshall. [Cleveland?, 1953?]. [8] p. Illus., map. MnDuC.

Annual report of the Great Lakes Steamship Company, Inc., for the fiscal year ended December 31, 1954. [Cleveland?, 1955]. [12] p. OBgU.

GREAT LAKES TOWING COMPANY, CLEVELAND, OH

Incorporated as a New Jersey firm on 6 July 1899. Acquired by the American Ship Building Company on 20 June 1972.

Tariff of the Great Lakes Towing Company, effective October 5, 1950. [Cleveland?, 1950]. 14 leaves. OBgU.

Tug service on the Great Lakes. [Cleveland?, 1956?]. 12 p. Illus. MnDuC.

The Great Lakes Towing Company annual report, 1956. [Cleveland?, 1957]. [8] p. IEN-T.

General tariff of the Great Lakes Towing Company, effective May 12, 1960. [Cleveland?, 1960]. 15, [1] p. OBgU.

The Great Lakes Towing Company annual report, 1960. [Cleveland?, 1961]. [8] p. IEN-T.

General tariff of the Great Lakes Towing Company, effective May 1, 1969. [Cleveland?, 1969]. 15, [1] p. OBgU.

General tariff of the Great Lakes Towing Company, effective April 18, 1975. [Cleveland?, 1975]. 15, [1] p. OBgU.

General tariff of the Great Lakes Towing Company, effective April 1, 1976. [Cleveland?, 1976]. 15, [1] p. OBgU.

General tariff of the Great Lakes Towing Company, effective April 1, 1977. [Cleveland?, 1977]. 15, [1] p. OBgU.

General tariff of the Great Lakes Towing Company, effective May 1, 1978. [Cleveland?, 1978]. 15, [1] p. OBgU.

The Great Lakes Towing Company means towing on the Great Lakes...anywhere. [Cleveland?, 1980?]. 1 sheet folded to [6] p. Illus., map. OBgU.

GREAT LAKES TRANSIT COMPANY, CHICAGO, IL

Incorporated on 3 February 1971. Dissolved on 9 April 1987.

Lake Michigan cruise, stay on Mackinac Island. [Chicago?, 1971?]. 1 sheet folded to [6] p. Illus., map. MdBUS, MiD-D, WManiM.

New! Lake Michigan cruise. [Chicago?, 1973?]. 1 sheet folded to [6] p. Illus., map. WManiM.

Excursion cruises on Lake Michigan, the Clipper Line. [N.p., 1977]. 1 sheet folded to [4] p. Illus. MiShM, WM.

GREAT LAKES TRANSIT CORPORATION, BUFFALO, NY

Records show a Great Lakes Transit Company being established on 23 February 1916. The Great Lakes Transit Corporation was incorporated 22 March 1916, in response to the Panama Canal Act of 24 August 1912, and the subsequent ICC ruling in May of 1915 that prohibited railroads from operating fleets. Acquired by purchase the vessels of the Western Transit Company, Erie & Western Transportation Company, Mutual Transit Company, and the Erie Railroad Lake Line. Commenced operations on 1 April 1916. Ceased passenger service at the end of the 1936 season. Absorbed the Minnesota-Atlantic Transit Company in 1941. Ceased operating ships in 1945. Dissolved on 22 November 1950.

Great Lakes Radio News. — Vol 1, no. 1 (1916?)-vol. ?, no. ? (1936?) — Published on board ship, 1916?-1936? Illus. Daily during cruise season. Alternate title: Radio News Bulletin. Cataloging based on 1928 edition. MiD-D.

G[reat] L[akes] T[ransit] C[orporation], [season] 1916. Chicago: Poole Bros., [1916]. 19, [1] p. Illus., maps. MiD-B, ViNeM, WManiM.

Great Lakes cruise, the finest in the world, [season 1917]. New York: Rand, McNally & Co., [1917]. 30 [i.e. 16] p. Illus., map. MiShM, OBgU, ViNeM.

Great Lakes cruise, finest in the world, season 1918. Chicago: Poole Bros., [1918]. 30 [i.e. 16] p. Illus., map. OBgU.

Great Lakes cruise, finest in the world, season 1919. Chicago: Poole Bros., [1919]. 30 [i.e. 16] p. Illus., map. MSaP, MiD-D, MnHi, WHi.

Great Lakes cruise, finest in the world, season 1920. Chicago: Poole Bros., [1920]. 30 [i.e. 16] p. Illus., map. OBgU, ViNeM.

Great Lakes cruise, finest in the world, season 1921. Chicago: Poole Bros., [1921]. 30 [i.e. 16] p. Illus., map. MSaP, MiD-D.

Great Lakes Transit Corporation, season 1921. [N.p., 1921]. 1 sheet folded to [4] p. Maps. CSmH.

Great Lakes cruise, finest in the world, season 1922. Chicago: Poole Bros., [1922]. 30 [i.e. 16] p. Illus., map. CSmH, MiD-D, MnHi, NBuHi, ViNeM.

The "ship's log," [a souvenir magazine]. [N.p.]: William J. Dalton, c1922. 68 p. Illus., map. OBgU.

Great Lakes cruise, finest in the world, season 1923. New York: Rand, McNally & Co., [1923]. 30 [i.e. 16] p. Illus., map. MiD-B, ViNeM.

Great Lakes cruise, finest in the world, season 1924. New York: Rand, McNally & Co., [1924]. 30 [i.e. 16] p. Illus., map. CSmH, MiD-D, ViNeM, WM.

Great Lakes cruise, finest in the world, season 1925. New York: Andrew H. Kellogg Co., [1925]. 38 [i.e. 20] p. Illus., map. CSmH, MiD-D, MiPhM, NNC, OBgU, ViNeM, WM, WManiM.

Great Lakes cruise, finest in the world, season 1926. New York: Andrew H. Kellogg Co., [1926]. 38 [i.e. 20] p. Illus., map. CSmH, MSaP, MiD-B, ViNeM, WM.

Great Lakes cruise, finest in the world, season 1927. New York: Charles Francis Press, [1927]. 23, [1] p. Illus., map. CSmH, MiD-B, PPPMM, ViNeM, WM.

Great Lakes cruise, finest in the world, season 1928. New York: Charles Francis Press, [1928]. 23, [1] p. Illus., map. MiD-D, MiShM, MnDuC, OBgU, ViNeM, WM.

Guide book [of] what you will see as the guest of the Great Lakes Transit Corporation. New York: Charles Francis Press, [1928?]. 14, [2] p. Illus., maps. MiD-B, MnDuC, OBgU.

Great Lakes cruise, what you will see as the guest of the Great Lakes Transit Corporation. [Buffalo?, 1929?] 14, [2] p. Maps. CtMyMHi, MiU-H, ViNeM.

Great Lakes cruise, finest in the world, season 1929. New York: Charles Francis Press, [1929]. 23, [1] p. Illus., map. MSaP, MiD-B, MiD-D, MnDuU, PPPMM, ViNeM, WMCHi.

Great Lakes cruise, finest in the world, season 1930. [N.p., 1930]. 23, [1] p. Illus., map. MiD-B, MiD-D, MnHi, ViNeM, WM.

Great Lakes cruise, finest in the world, season 1931. Lockport, NY: Corson Co., [1931]. 31, [1] p. Illus., map. MiD-D, MiMtpC, MiShM, OBgU, ViNeM.

Great Lakes cruise, finest in the world, season 1932. [N.p., 1932]. 1 sheet folded to [8] p. Illus. NBuHi.

Great Lakes cruise, finest in the world, season 1932. Lockport, NY: Corson Co., [1932]. 23, [1] p. Illus., map. MiD-D, OBgU, ViNeM, WM.

Great Lakes cruise, season 1933. [N.p., 1933]. 1 sheet folded to [16] p. Illus., map. MSaP, MdBUS, MiD-D, ViNeM, WM.

Great Lakes cruise, season 1933. Lockport, NY: Corson Mfg. Co., [1933]. 23, [1] p. Illus., map. MiD-B, MiD-D, MiShM, NBuHi, OBgU, ViNeM, WM, WManiM.

The log of the steamships Tionesta, Juniata [and] Octorara. [N.p., 1933?]. 1 sheet folded to [4] p. Illus., maps. MiD-D.

All-expense Great Lakes cruises, including World's Fair at Chicago. [N.p., 1934]. 23, [1] p. Illus., map. OBgU.

Great Lakes cruise, season 1934. Lockport, NY: Corson Mfg. Co., [1934]. 24 p. Illus., map. CaOOA, MiD-D, MiMtpC, MiShM, MiU-H, MnDuC, NBuHi, OBgU, ViNeM, WManiM.

Great Lakes cruise, season 1934, the finest cruise to or from [the] World's Fair [in] Chicago. [N.p., 1934]. 1 sheet folded to [16] p. (4 panels are diagonally trimmed). Illus. MdBUS, ViNeM, WM.

Great Lakes cruise, season 1935. Lockport, NY: Corson Mfg. Co., [1935]. 24 p. Illus., map. MSaP, MiD-D, ViNeM, WM.

Great Lakes Transit Corporation cruise, season 1936. Buffalo: J[ames] W. Clement Co., 1936. 23, [1] p. Illus., map. MSaP, MiD-D, MiShM, OBgU, OFH, ViNeM.

GREAT NORTHERN TRANSIT COMPANY, LIMITED, COLLINGWOOD, ONT

Established in 1881 as successor to the Georgian Bay Transit Company. Merged in 1899 with the North Shore Navigation Company to form the Northern Navigation Company of Ontario, Limited. Popularly known as the White Line.

Great Northern Transit Co.'s steamboat line running in close connection with the G[rand] T[runk] R[ailroad] and C[anadian] P[acific] R[ailroad] companies. Toronto: Mail

Job Print, [1891]. 1 sheet folded to [20] p. Illus., map. CaOOA.

Great Northern Transit Co.'s steamboat line running in close connection with the G[rand] T[runk] R[ailroad] and C[anadian] P[acific] R[ailroad] companies. Toronto: Mail Job Print, [1892]. 1 sheet folded to [20] p. Illus., map. CaOONL.

Great Northern (White Line) Transit Co., Limited, season 1898. Toronto: Murray Printing Co., [1898]. 1 sheet folded to [16] p. Illus., map. MiD-B.

GREEN BAY TRANSPORTATION COMPANY, GREEN BAY, WI

Incorporated on 26 April 1905, as successor to the Hart Steamboat Line. Dissolved on 10 January 1912.

The land locked route to Mackinac Island, Petoskey & Soo. [N.p., 1909]. 23 [i.e. 12] p. Illus., map. MiD-D.

GRUMMOND'S MACKINAC LINE, DETROIT, MI

The firm was founded about 1867. The Mackinac Line was created around 1881. Became a part of the White Star Line in 1896.

The popular route to Mackinac Island, St. Ignace Cheboygan, Alpena, Oscoda, and other Lake Huron west shore ports from P[or]t Huron, St. Clair River landings, Detroit, Cleveland, and Toledo is via Grummond's Mackinac Line steamers Flora and Atlantic. Detroit: Raynor & Taylor, [1890?]. 1 sheet folded to [12] p. Illus. MiD-D, OBgU.

The popular route to Mackinac via Grummond's Mackinac Line from Cleveland, Toledo, Detroit, and Port Huron. [N.p., 1891?]. [8] p. Folded map. MiD-D.

HALL CORPORATION SHIPPING, LIMITED, MONTREAL, QUE

Originally the George Hall Coal Company of Canada, Limited, in April of 1927 it became known as Hall Corporation of Canada, Limited. Acquired name shown above in 1973. Became Halco, Incorporated, around 1980, and its fleet sold to Enerchem in 1987.

The story of Hall Corporation of Canada, Limited, and Hall Corporation Shipping, Limited. [Montreal?, 1977]. 15, [1] p. Illus., map. Cover title: Hall Corporation Shipping, Limited, 1927-1977. CaOKMM, MdBUS, MiD-D, MnDuC, OBgU.

The Post Cliffe. — Vol. 1, no. 1 (October 1979)-vol. 7, no. 2 (August 1986). — Westmont QUE, 1979-1986. Illus. Quarterly. Text in French and English. MiD-D, MnDuC, OBgU.

HAMILTON HARBOUR COMMISSIONERS, HAMILTON, ONT

Established on 1 April 1912. Still active in 1990.

Heat bothering you? Cool, pleasant cruises on S.S. Lady Hamilton or the S.S. Macassa. [Hamilton?, 1955]. 1 sheet folded to [6] p. Illus. CaOOA.

HANNA COMPANY (M.A.), CLEVELAND, OH

Incorporated in Ohio on 9 December 1922. In October of 1961 it was acquired by the Hanna Mining Company.

Agreement between the M[arcus] A[lonzo] Hanna Co., agent, and the Lake Sailors Union, February 28, 1955. [Cleveland, 1955]. 30 p. OBgU.

Agreement between the M[arcus] A[lonzo] Hanna Co., agent, and the Lake Sailors Union, July 1, 1957. [Cleveland, 1957]. 39, [1] p. OBgU.

Group insurance benefits plan for licensed officers and stewards, effective April 1, 1960. [Cleveland?, 1960]. 28 p. OBgU.

Picture story of the S.S. Paul H[arvey] Carnahan. [Cleveland?, 1961?]. 1 sheet folded to [8] p. Illus. MiD-D.

HANNA MINING COMPANY, CLEVELAND, OH

Incorporated in Delaware on 27 March 1927, as the Franklin Steamship Corporation. Acquired the name of Hanna Mining Company in 1958. Name changed to Hanna (M.A.) Company on 3 May 1985.

Labor contract between the Hanna Mining Company and United Steelworkers of America, A[merican] F[ederation] [of] L[abor]-C[ongress] [of] I[ndustrial] O[rganizations] and its Local 5000, [for the Hansand Steamship Corporation effective] September 1, 1965. [N.p., 1965]. 74 p. OBgU.

Labor contract between the Hanna Mining Company and United Steelworkers of America, A[merican] F[ederation] L[abor]-C[ongress] [of] I[ndustrial] O[rganizations] and its Local 5000, [for the Hansand Steamship Corporation effective] August 1, 1968. [N.p., 1968]. 84 p. WManiM.

Marine safety booklet, 1972. [Cleveland?, 1972]. 26 p. Illus. OBgU.

Labor contract between the Hanna Mining Company and United Steelworkers of America, A[merican] F[ederation] [of] L[abor]-C[ongress] [of] I[ndustrial] O[rganizations] and its Local 5000, [for the Hansand Steamship Corporation in] 1980. [Cleveland, 1980]. 128 p. OBgU.

HANNAH MARINE CORPORATION, BURR RIDGE, IL

Formerly the Hannah Inland Waterways Corporation, it became the Hannah Marine Corporation on 10 September 1979. Still active as of 1990.

The Hannah Line. — Volume 1, number 1 (December 1980)- volume 3, number 2 (August 1982)? — N.p., 1980-1982? Illus. Semi-annual. OBgU.

HANSAND STEAMSHIP CORPORATION, CLEVELAND, OH

Incorporated as a Delaware firm on 21 June 1951. Operated as an affiliate of the Hanna Company, the Hanna Mining Company, and the M.A. Hanna Company in joint ownership with the Sand Products Corporation. Though inactive in 1990, the enterprise had not been dissolved.

From salt water to freshwater [a history of the Joseph Hamilton Thompson]. [N.p., 1950]. [20] p. Illus. CSFMM, MnDuC, OBgU.

HART STEAMBOAT LINE, GREEN BAY, WI

Incorporated on 23 June 1896. Name changed to Green Bay Transportation Company on 26 April 1905.

Hart's Steamboat Line time table, season 1898. Green Bay: Gazette Print, [1898]. 1 sheet folded to [16] p. Illus., map. WGrM.

Hart's Steamboat Line time table, season 1899. Green Bay: Gazette Publishing Co., [1899]. 1 sheet folded to [8] p. Illus., map. MSaP.

You could easily go fourteen on this hand of "harts," but you would be fourteen times better satisfied if you would go one trip on Hart's Steamboat Line. Green Bay: Gazette Pub[lishing] Co., [1900]. 1 sheet folded to [16] p. Illus., map. MiD-D.

HART TRANSPORTATION COMPANY, STURGEON BAY, WI

Incorporated on 21 October 1905. Dissolved on 17 March 1919.

1909 time card of the Hart Transp[ortation] Co. [N.p., 1909]. 1 sheet folded to [4] p. Illus. WM

Schedule of the Hart Transportation Co. on the waters of Green Bay, summer 1914. [N.p., 1914]. 1 sheet folded to [4] p. Illus. MiD-B.

HOLLAND & CHICAGO TRANSPORTATION COMPANY, HOLLAND, MI

Incorporated 1 December 1892. Purchased by the Graham & Morton Steamship Company in 1901 and ceased business on 26 February 1902.

Holland and Chicago Line operating the well-known and popular steamers "Soo City" and "City of Holland." Chicago: Poole Bros., [1898]. 1 sheet folded to [6] p. Illus. MiU-H.

HOOPER MOTORSHIPS, LIMITED, SCUDDER, ONT

Incorporated on 14 July 1959. Commenced operations in 1960. Ceased activities in 1976. Dissolved on 14 September 1987.

M[otor] S[hip] Leamington schedule [connecting] Pelee Island and Leamington, Ontario. [N.p., 1967?]. 1 sheet folded to [8] p. Illus., map. OBgU, OFH.

INDIANA TRANSPORTATION COMPANY, CHICAGO, IL

Created around 1900 and known as the Michigan City-Chicago Line. Ceased to exist about 1916 as a result of the death of the firm's founder on 1 March 1914, and the Eastland disaster on 24 July 1915.

Pleasant trips via Chicago's newest and greatest ships [offering] short enjoyable excursions between Chicago & Michigan City, 1912. [Chicago?, 1912]. 1 sheet folded to [12] p. Illus. June edition. MiD-D.

Pleasant trips [on the] Theodore Roosevelt, Chicago's best and most popular ship. Chicago: Wallace Press, [1914]. 1 sheet folded to [12] p. Illus. ViNeM.

Saugatuck and Douglas, Michigan's delightful summer resorts reached direct via [the] steamship "United States." Chicago: Wallace Press, [1914]. 15, [1] p. Illus., maps. ViNeM.

INLAND STEEL COMPANY, CHICAGO, IL

Incorporated as a Delaware firm on 6 February 1917. Shipping activities began around 1924 with the creation of the Inland Steamship Company. Still active as of 1990.

Welcome aboard the S.S. Wilfred Sykes, flagship of the Inland Steel fleet. [N.p., 1949]. [12] p. Illus., map. MiD-B, MiD-D, MnDuC.

S.S. Edward L[arned] Ryerson, new flagship of the Inland Steel fleet. [Chicago, 1960]. [16] p. Illus., map. ICHi, MiD-D, WManiM.

The Ship's Log. — Vol. 1, no. 1 (September 1977)-vol.9, no.2 (Summer 1986). — Chicago, 1977-1986. Illus. Monthly. OBgU.

The Inland fleet. [Chicago?, 1978?]. [12] p. Illus., map. MiD-D, MnDuC.

Welcome aboard. [Chicago?, 1981?]. [12] p. Illus., maps. MiD-D, OBgU.

INTERLAKE STEAMSHIP COMPANY, CLEVELAND, OH

Incorporated in Ohio on 1 April 1913, as successor to the Lackawanna Steamship Company. Purchased the Cleveland Steamship Company fleet in 1916 and the Youngstown Steamship Company in 1929. Reincorporated with the same name as a Delaware firm on 28 October 1931. Merged with Pickands Mather Company on 31 August 1966, though it had long been associated with the firm. Acquired the Ford Motor Company fleet in 1989. Still active in 1990.

First mortgage or deed of trust dated May 1, 1913, the Interlake Steamship Company to the Guardian Savings and Trust Company, trustee, securing $3,000,000 first mortgage, $1,000 six per cent coupon gold bonds, maturing $250,000 on November 1 each year 1914 to 1925, inclusive. [Cleveland?, 1913]. 107, [1] p. NNC.

First Annual Meeting of the Interlake Steamship Co.'s Masters, Engineers, and Officers held at [the Hollenden Hotel in] Cleveland, Ohio, March 30-31, 1914. [Cleveland, 1914]. 50 p. MiU-H.

[Rule book for ships and officers]. Cleveland: Marine Review Print, 1916. 36 p. MiD-D.

Balance sheet and profit and loss account [for year ending] December 31, 1927. [Cleveland?, 1928]. [4] p. CtY, MH-BA.

Balance sheet and profit and loss account [for year ending] December 31, 1928. [Cleveland?, 1929]. [4] p. CtY, MH-BA.

Balance sheet and profit and loss account [for year ending] December 31, 1930. [Cleveland?, 1931]. [4] p. CtY, MH-BA.

Balance sheet and profit and loss account [for year ending] December 31, 1931. [Cleveland?, 1932]. [4] p. CtY, IEN-T, IU, MH-BA.

Balance sheet and profit and loss account [for year ending] December 31, 1932. [Cleveland?, 1933]. [4] p. IEN-T, IU, MH-BA.

Balance sheet and profit and loss account [for year ending] December 31, 1933. [Cleveland?, 1934]. [4] p. IEN-T, IU, MH-BA.

Balance sheet and profit and loss account [for year ending] December 31, 1934. [Cleveland?, 1935]. [8] p. IEN-T, IU, MH-BA, OClWHi.

Balance sheet and profit and loss account [for year ending] December 31, 1935. [Cleveland?, 1936]. [8] p. IEN-T, IU, MH-BA, OBgU.

Balance sheet and profit and loss account [for year ending] December 31, 1936. [Cleveland?, 1937]. [8] p. IEN-T, IU, MH-BA, OBgU.

Balance sheet and profit and loss account [for year ending] December 31, 1937. [Cleveland?, 1938]. [8] p. IEN-T, IU, MH-BA, OBgU.

Balance sheet and profit and loss account [for year ending] December 31, 1938. [Cleveland?, 1939]. [8] p. IEN-T, IU, MH-BA, OBgU.

Interlake Steamship Log. — Vol. 1, no. 1 (November 1938)-vol. 18, no. 1 (November 1955). — Cleveland, 1938-1955. Illus. Monthly. Continued by: Interlake Log. MiD-D, OBgU, OV.

Balance sheet and profit and loss account [for year ending] December 31, 1939. [Cleveland?, 1940]. [6] p. IEN-T, IU, MH-BA, OBgU.

Balance sheet and profit and loss account [for year ending] December 31, 1940. [Cleveland?, 1941]. [8] p. CtY, IEN-T, IU, MH-BA, OBgU.

Balance sheet and profit and loss account [for year ending] December 31, 1941. [Cleveland?, 1942]. [8] p. IEN-T, MnDuC.

Annual report for the year ended December 31, 1942. [Cleveland?, 1943]. [10] p. IEN-T, IU.

Annual report for the year ended December 31, 1943. [Cleveland?, 1944]. [10] p. IEN-T, IU.

Annual report for the year ended December 31, 1944. [Cleveland?, 1945]. [10] p. IEN-T, IU.

Annual report for the year ended December 31, 1945. [Cleveland?, 1946]. [12] p. IEN-T, IU, MH-BA, OBgU.

Annual report for the year ended December 31, 1946. [Cleveland?, 1947]. [12] p. IEN-T, IU, MH-BA, OBgU.

Annual report for the year ended December 31, 1947. [Cleveland?, 1948]. [10] p. IEN-T, IU, OBgU.

Annual report for the year ended December 31, 1948. [Cleveland?, 1949]. [10] p. IEN-T, IU, OBgU.

Annual report for the year ended December 31, 1949. [Cleveland?, 1950]. [10] p. IEN-T, IU, OBgU.

Employees pension plan effective January 1, 1951, the Interlake Steamship Company. [Cleveland, 1950]. 15, [1] p. OBgU.

Annual report for the year ended December 31, 1950. [Cleveland?, 1951]. [10] p. IEN-T, IU, OBgU.

Notice of annual meeting of stockholders, May 1, 1951. [Cleveland?, 1951]. 8 p. OBgU.

Annual report for the year ended December 31, 1951. [Cleveland?, 1952]. [10] p. IEN-T, IU, OBgU.

Notice of annual meeting of stockholders, May 1, 1952. [Cleveland?, 1952]. 4 p. OBgU.

Annual report for the year ended December 31, 1952. [Cleveland?, 1953]. [10] p. IEN-T, IU, OBgU.

Annual report for the year ended December 31, 1953. [Cleveland?, 1954]. [10] p. IEN-T, IU, OBgU.

Annual report for the year ended December 31, 1954. [Cleveland?, 1955]. [10] p. IEN-T, IU.

Annual report for the year ended December 31, 1955. [Cleveland?, 1956]. [10] p. IEN-T, IU, OBgU.

Group insurance program for hourly paid employees, the Interlake Steamship Company, Cleveland, Ohio, as amended, effective December 1, 1956. [Cleveland, 1956]. 28 p. OBgU.

Group insurance program for salaried paid licensed officers and stewards, the Interlake Steamship Company, Cleveland, Ohio, as amended, effective December 1, 1956. [Cleveland, 1956]. 28 p. OBgU.

The Interlake Log. — Vol. 1, no. 1 (May 1956)-vol. 24, no. 4 (Winter 1979). — Cleveland: Pickands Mather & Co., 1956-1979. Illus. Monthly thru 1956, then quarterly. Continues: Interlake Steamship Log. Continued by: The Log. CaOKMM, MnDuC, OBgU, OV.

Sailing with Interlake: a handbook for Interlake sailors. [Cleveland?, 1956?]. 22, [2] p. OBgU, OV.

The Interlake Steamship Company annual report [for the year] 1956. [Cleveland?, 1957]. [12] p. Illus. IEN-T, IU, MnDuC, OV.

Mid-year report for the six months ended June 30, 1957. [Cleveland?, 1957]. 1 sheet folded to [4] p. OBgU.

The Interlake Steamship Company annual report [for the year] 1957. [Cleveland?, 1958]. [12] p. Illus. IEN-T, IU, OV.

The Interlake Steamship Company annual report [for the year] 1958. [Cleveland?, 1959]. [12] p. Illus. IEN-T, IU, OV.

The Interlake Steamship Company annual report [for the year] 1959. [Cleveland?, 1960]. [12] p. Illus. IEN-T, IU, MiD-D.

Mid-year report for the six months ended June 30, 1960. [Cleveland?, 1960]. 1 sheet folded to [6] p. OBgU.

The Interlake Steamship Company annual report [for the year] 1960. [Cleveland?, 1961]. [12] p. Illus. IEN-T, IU, MnDuC.

Mid-year report for the six months ended June 30, 1961. [Cleveland?, 1961]. 1 sheet folded to [6] p. OBgU.

The Interlake Steamship Company annual report [for the year] 1961. [Cleveland?, 1962]. [12] p. Illus. IEN-T, IU.

Mid-year report for the six months ended June 30, 1962. [Cleveland?, 1962]. 1 sheet folded to [6] p. OBgU.

Notice of annual meeting of stockholders, March 23, 1962. [Cleveland?, 1962]. [6] p. OBgU.

The Interlake Steamship Company annual report [for the year] 1962. [Cleveland?, 1963]. [12] p. Illus. IEN-T, IU.

Mid-year report to [the] stockholders, 1963. [Cleveland?, 1963]. 1 sheet folded to [6] p. MnDuC.

Notice of annual meeting of [the] stockholders, March 22, 1963. [Cleveland?, 1963]. [6] p. OBgU.

The Interlake Steamship Company annual report [for the year] 1963. [Cleveland?, 1964]. [12] p. Illus. IEN-T, IU, OV.

Notice of annual meeting of [the] stockholders, March 20, 1964. [Cleveland?, 1964]. [8] p. OBgU.

The Interlake Steamship Company annual report [for the year] 1964. [Cleveland?, 1965]. 11, [1] p. Illus. IEN-T, IU, MnDuC, OV.

Mid-year report to [the] stockholders, 1965. [Cleveland?, 1965]. 1 sheet folded to [6] p. MnDuC

The Interlake Steamship Co. annual report [for the year] 1965. [Cleveland?, 1966]. [16] p. Illus. IEN-T, IU, OV.

The Interlake Steamship Company proxy statement [relating to the merger of the company with Pickands Mather]. [Cleveland?, 1966]. [92] p. MnDuC.

Mid-year report to [the] stockholders, 1966. [Cleveland?, 1966]. 1 sheet folded to [6] p. MnDuC, OV.

Directory of Interlake Steamship pensioners, November, 1972. [Cleveland?, 1972]. [4] p. OBgU.

Safety news. [Cleveland?, 1973]. 13 leaves. Illus. OBgU.

Log Line. — Vol. 1, no. 1 (April 1974)-vol. 5, no. 8 (December 1978). — Cleveland, 1974-1978. Monthly. Continued by: The Log. OBgU.

The Interlake Steamship Company. [Cleveland?, 1980?]. 1 sheet folded to [8] p. Illus., map. WManiM.

The Log. — Vol. 1, no. 1 (Spring 1980)-vol. 7, no. 3 (Fall 1986). — Cleveland: Pickands Mather & Co., 1980-1986. Illus. Quarterly. Continues: The Interlake Log. CaOKMM, OBgU, OV, WM.

Directory of Interlake pensioners, Fall, 1981. [Cleveland?, 1981]. [4] p. OBgU.

Welcome aboard the M[otor] V[essel] William J[ohn] DeLancey, April 1, 1981. [Cleveland?, 1981]. 1 sheet folded to [4] p. Illus. MiD-D, OBgU.

The Interlake Steamship Company, operated by Pickands Mather & Co. [Cleveland?, 1982?]. [12] p. Illus., map. MnDuC, OV, WManiM.

ISLAND TRANSPORTATION COMPANY, ST. IGNACE, MI

Commenced business around 1899. Merged with the Arnold Transit Company in May of 1946.

Schedule of St[eame]r Algomah between Mackinaw City and Mackinac Island. [N.p., 1932]. 1 sheet folded to [4] p. Illus. MiD-D.

Mackinac Island ferry service from Mackinaw City via St[eame]r Algomah, effective June 1st, 1933. [N.p., 1933]. 1 sheet folded to [4] p. Illus. MiD-D, Mi-MISPC.

ISLANDS-BAY STEAMSHIP COMPANY, CLEVELAND, OH

Operated only during the year 1945.

One day luxury cruises [on the] S.S. Alabama to Put-in-Bay and Canada. [Cleveland?, 1945]. 1 sheet folded to [8] p. Illus. CU-SB, MiD-D, OBgU, OFH.

ISLE ROYALE TRANSPORTATION COMPANY, CHICAGO, IL

A subsidiary of the Duke Transportation Company of New Orleans, it apparently operated only in 1933.

Wonder cruises to a magic isle. [Chicago]: Wilson-Hall Co., 1933. 1 sheet folded to [8] p. Illus. MiD-D.

Wonder cruises to a magic isle. [Chicago]: Wilson-Hall Co., 1933. 1 sheet folded to [16] p. Illus., map. MiD-D, MiHM.

JOURNEYS, INCORPORATED, CHICAGO, IL

Incorporated on 10 January 1933. Involuntarily dissolved on 11 June 1936.

Plan of [the] S.S. Isle Royale. [N.p., 1933]. 1 sheet folded to [6] p. Illus. ViNeM.

Plan of [the] S.S. Alabama. [N.p., 1934?]. 1 sheet folded to [6] p. Illus. MiD-D.

Wonder cruises to a magic isle, [the] S.S. Alabama chartered to Journeys, Inc. Rockford, IL: Wilson-Hall Co., [1934]. 1 sheet folded to [32] p. Illus., map. CU-SB, MdBUS, MiHM, MiShM, ViNeM, WManiM.

KIRBY LINE, INCORPORATED, DETROIT, MI

Incorporated 2 April 1937, as successor to Kirby's Travel Bureau, Incorporated. Dissolved on 27 December 1939.

Announcing the wonder cruise of the S.S. Alabama to Isle Royale, Fort William, Georgian Bay, 30,000 Islands, Mackinac, [and] Saulte [sic] S[ain]te Marie from Cleveland and Detroit. [Detroit?, 1936?]. 1 sheet folded to [8] p. Illus., map. CU-SB, MiD-D, OBgU.

The "early bird" cruise of the S.S. Alabama to Isle Royale, Sault S[ain]te Marie, [and] Mackinac Island June 29 to July 4, 1937. [Detroit?, 1937]. 1 sheet folded to [4] p. Illus. MiD-D, OBgU.

Wonder cruise to Isle Royale, Georgian Bay, Fort William, North Channel, Mackinac, [and] Sault S[ain]te Marie on the S.S. Alabama. [N.p., 1937]. 1 sheet folded to [16] p. Illus., map. MiD-D, OBgU, WM.

The "early bird" cruise of the S.S. Alabama to Isle Royale, Sault S[ain]te Marie, [and] Mackinac Island June 28 to July 3, 1938. [N.p., 1938]. 1 sheet folded to [4] p. Illus. MiHM.

Wonder cruise to Isle Royale. [N.p., 1938]. [12] p. Illus., map. CU-SB, MiD-D, MiHM, MiShM, MiU-H, MnDuC.

LACKAWANNA RAILROAD COMPANY, NEW YORK, NY

Incorporated as the Delaware, Lackawanna & Western Railroad on 30 April 1853. Acquired the Lackawanna Railroad Company on 24 December 1911. Merged with the Erie Railroad Company on 17 October 1960, to form the Erie-Lackawanna Railroad Company.

Lackawanna wanderlust cruises on the Great Lakes and St. Lawrence River. [N.p., 1939]. 1 sheet folded to [24] p. Illus., map. NBuHi.

Lackawanna wanderlust cruises on the Great Lakes and St. Lawrence River. [N.p., 1941]. 1 sheet folded to [24] p. Illus., map. ViNeM.

LACKAWANNA TRANSPORTATION COMPANY, BUFFALO, NY

Incorporated on 1 September 1887. Ceased operations on 1 September 1907.

Steamer "Saginaw Valley" general average statement [regarding] disaster [of] Oct[ober] 28, 1893, westbound. [Buffalo, 1894]. 70, [2] p. N.

LAKE ERIE NAVIGATION COMPANY, LIMITED, WALKERVILLE, ONT

Chartered in 1898 as a subsidiary of the Lake Erie & Detroit River Railway. Incorporated on 5 July 1899, and ceased operations around 1908. Reactivated in 1927 by the Pere Marquette Railway Company, then dissolved on 2 January 1970.

Official time tables in effect June 17th, season 1899, [for the] Port Stanley, Rond Eau [sic], Cleveland route. [N.p., 1899]. 1 sheet folded to [8] p. Maps. CaOOA.

LAKE ERIE TRANSPORTATION COMPANY, TOLEDO, OH

Incorporated 12 November 1889. Owned and operated by the Wabash Railroad Company. Ceased operations in 1911.

Steamer S[heldon] C[lark] Reynolds, west bound, cargo on fire and was stranded [on] November 23, 1890. [Buffalo, 1891]. 20 p. N.

Steamer "J[ohn] C. Gault" general average [for] westbound [incident when her] cargo [was] discovered on fire November 25, 1891. [N.p., 1892]. 16 p. N.

Steamer "S[heldon] C[lark] Reynolds" and cargo, general average statement [of] east-bound [trip when she] stranded May 2d, 1893. Buffalo: Hartman & DeCoursey, [1893]. 9, [1] p. N.

LAKE MICHIGAN & LAKE SUPERIOR TRANSPORTATION COMPANY, CHICAGO, IL

Established in 1879 through a merger of Leopold & Austrian's Lake Superior Line with the Spencer Line. Ceased to exist about 1905.

Lake Superior tourist's guide, 1883. Chicago: Jones Litho. Co., [1883]. 19, [1] p. Illus., map. MiU-H.

A guide to the health, pleasure, game, and fishing resorts on the northern lakes reached by the steamers of the Lake Michigan and Lake Superior Transportation Co. and connections, with map, routes, rates, time cards, and general information. Chicago: J[udson] M.W. Jones Stationery and Printing Co., 1884. 33, [7] p. Illus., maps. Cover title: Lake Superior tours, presented by the Lake Michigan & Lake Superior Transportation Co., Chicago. Mi.

Tourists [sic] guide to the summer resorts of Lake Superior, 1885. Chicago: J[udson] M.W. Jones Sta[tionery] & Ptg. Co., [1885]. 39, [1] p. Illus., maps. IHi.

The new steel steamship Manitou. Chicago: J[oseph] C. Winship & Co., [1893?]. [16] p. Illus. ViNeM.

Souvenir of the World's Columbian Exposition, Chicago, with street guide, compliments of the Passenger Department. Chicago: Vandercook Engraving and Pub[lishing] Co., [1893]. 1 sheet folded to [24] p. in covers. Illus., map. ViNeM.

Summer tours on the great inland lakes, season 1893. Chicago: J[oseph] C. Winship & Co., [1893]. 53 [i.e. 52] p. Illus., folded map. OBgU.

The Lake Superior Line via the Great Lakes, 1896. Chicago: Stromberg, Allen & Co., [1896]. 31 [i.e. 16] p. Illus., map. MiD-D.

Lake tours [on] the Lake Superior Line, northern summer resorts. Chicago: Stromberg, Allen & Co., [1900]. 26 p. Illus., folded map. MiD-D.

Travel the pioneer way to the great Lake Superior country for comfort, recreation and health. Chicago: Stromberg, Allen & Co., [1903]. 31 [i.e. 16] p. Illus., maps. MiD-D.

LAKE MICHIGAN TRANSIT COMPANY, MILWAUKEE, WI

Established on 15 May 1858, as a Wisconsin firm to carry freight and passengers across Lake Michigan for the Detroit & Milwaukee Railway Company. Appears to have discontinued business in 1869.

Charter and by-laws of the Lake Michigan Transit Company, August, 1859. Milwaukee: Jermain & Brightman, 1859. 10 p. MWA, MiD-B.

LAKE NAVIGATION COMPANY, BUFFALO, NY

Incorporated on 25 February 1856. Ceased operations on 25 February 1858.

Catalogue of the valuable property belonging to the Lake Navigation Co. to be sold at auction by order of the receivers on Tuesday, April 13th, at 11 o'clock A.M. in the rotunda of the Merchants Exchange, Buffalo. Buffalo: Commercial Advertiser Steam Press, 1858. 16 p. NBuHi.

LAKE ONTARIO & BAY OF QUINTE STEAMBOAT COMPANY, LIMITED, KINGSTON, ONT

Incorporated in 1893. Known as the Bay of Quinte Line. Merged on 4 December 1913, with the Canada Steamship Lines.

The Bay of Quinte route to the Thousand Islands. Kingston: Jackson Press, [1890?]. 1 sheet folded to [18] p. Illus., map. CaOOA.

The Bay of Quinte route to the Thousand Islands. [Rochester?, 1893?]. 1 sheet folded to [18] p. Illus., map. CaOOA.

The Bay of Quinte route to the Thousand Islands. [Rochester?, 1894?]. 1 sheet folded to [18] p. Illus., map. CaOKQ, CaOOA, MSaP.

The Bay of Quinte route to the Thousand Islands. [Rochester?, 1895?]. 1 sheet folded to [18] p. Illus., map. CaOOA, MSaP.

The Bay of Quinte route to the Thousand Islands. Rochester: Vredenburg & Co., [1896?]. 1 sheet folded to [18] p. Illus., map. CaOOA.

The Bay of Quinte route to the Thousand Islands. [Rochester?, 1898?]. 1 sheet folded to [18] p. Illus., map. CaOOA, NR.

Steamer North King daily between Port Hope, Cobourg, Ont., and Rochester, N.Y., connecting Grand Trunk and N[ew] Y[ork] C[entral] railways, etc., July 1899. [Rochester?, 1899]. 1 sheet folded to [6] p. Illus., map. CaOOA, NR.

Scenic and...sporting tours descriptive of the Bay of Quinte, the Kawartha Lakes region, and the hunting and fishing grounds on the shores of Lake Ontario and the Bay of Quinte, Central Canada. Rochester, NY: Union and Advertiser Press, [1900]. 83, [5] p. Illus., map. CaOKQ, CaOTAr.

The Bay of Quinte route to the Thousand Islands. Rochester, NY: Union & Adv[ertising] Press, [1901?]. 1 sheet folded to [18] p. Illus., map. MSaP, ViNeM.

Scenic and...sporting tours descriptive of the Bay of Quinte, the Kawartha Lakes region, and the hunting and fishing grounds on the shores of Lake Ontario and the Bay of Quinte, Central Canada, season 1901. Rochester, NY: Union & Advertising Press, [1901]. [2], 75, [5] p. Illus., folding maps. MSaP.

Kawartha Lakes, Bay of Quinte, [and] 1000 Islands. Toronto: W[esley] S[andfield] Johnston & Co., [1907]. 32 p. Illus., folded map. CaOOA.

Kawartha Lakes, Bay of Quinte, [and] 1000 Islands [where] summer and fishing resorts [are] reached by the Lake Ontario & Bay of Quinte Steamboat Co., Limited. Toronto: W[esley] S[anfield] Johnston & Co., [1911?]. 32 p. Illus., folded map. CaOOA.

LAKE ONTARIO NAVIGATION COMPANY, LIMITED, TORONTO, ONT
Incorporated on 23 April 1892. Apparently went out of existence around 1920.

Niagara Falls Line steamer Empress and Grand Trunk Railway System for Toronto, the Muskoka District, Kingston, Thousand Islands, Montreal, Quebec, and all points in Ontario and Quebec. [N.p., 1898]. 1 sheet folded to [4] p. Map. CaOOA.

St[eame]r Argyle sailing tri-weekly between the 1000 Islands of the St. Lawrence River and Alexandria Bay, Rockport, Ont., Gananoque, Kingston, Oswego, Sodus Point, Charlotte, [and] Toronto. [N.p., 1899]. 1 sheet folded to [6] p. Illus. Effective June 24. CaOOA.

Steamer Argyle sailing tri-weekly between Toronto, Charlotte, Sodus Point, Oswego, Kingston, Rockport, Ont., Alexandria Bay and the 1000 Islands of the St. Lawrence River. [N.p., 1899]. 1 sheet folded to [6] p. Illus. Effective June 24. CaOOA.

St[eame]r Argyle [sailing schedule]. [N.p., 1900]. 1 sheet folded to [6] p. Illus. CaOOA.

LAKE SUPERIOR LINE, CITY UNKNOWN
Appears to be issued by the Pioneer Lake Superior Line.

Lake Superior Line, 1865. [Cleveland?, 1865]. 1 sheet folded to [8] p. Illus., map. CaOOA.

Lake Superior Line, 1866. Cleveland: Fairbanks, Benedict & Co., [1866]. 1 sheet folded to [8] p. Illus., map. CaOOA.

LAKE SUPERIOR TRANSIT COMPANY, BUFFALO, NY
Incorporated on 11 February 1878, as a pool fleet of the Union, Western, and Anchor steamboat lines. Dissolved in the fall of 1892.

Attractions of an excursion upon the Great Lakes, presented by the Lake Superior Transit Co., 1878. Buffalo: Clay & Company, [1878]. 30, [12] p. Illus. MiD-B, Mi-MISPC, OBgU.

Time table of the Lake Superior Transit Company line of steamers, 1878. [Buffalo, 1878]. 1 sheet folded to [12] p. MiU-H.

Attractions of an excursion upon the Great Lakes, routes & rates for summer tours, 1880. Buffalo: Clay & Richmond, [1880]. 64 p. Illus., map. DLC, Mi, MnDuU, WManiM.

Lake Superior Transit Company time tables, 1880. Buffalo: The Courier Company, [1880]. [24] p. MiD-D.

Points of interest on the route of the Lake Superior Transit Company's steamers. Buffalo: The Courier Company, [1881]. 66 p. Illus., folded map. Cover title: Presented by Lake Superior Transit Company. MSaP, MiMtpC, MiU-H, MiU-T, MnDuU, ViNeM.

Lake Superior Transit Co. [excursions]. Buffalo: The Courier Company, [1882]. 80 p. Illus., folded map. CaOONL, WM.

Lake Superior Transit Company intended sailings. Buffalo: The Courier Company, [1882]. [28] p. MiD-D.

Summer tours via the Great Lakes. [Buffalo: Matthews, Northrup & Co., 1883]. 95, [1] p. Illus., folded map. CaOONL, DLC, ICHi, Mi-MISPC, OO.

Intended sailings, 1884. Buffalo: Courier Company, [1884]. [28] p. Illus. OBgU.

Lake Superior Transit Company intended sailings, 1884. Buffalo: The Courier Company, [1884]. [30] p. Illus. OBgU.

Summer tours via the Great Lakes. [Buffalo: Matthews-Northrup Co., 1884]. 95, [1] p. Illus., folded map. MSaP, MiGr, MiMtpC, MnHi, NN, OBgU.

"Excursion" routes and rates from Buffalo, Erie, Cleveland, Detroit, Port Huron, Marquette, Portage and Duluth. Buffalo: The Courier Company, [1885?]. 31, [1] p. MnHi, OBgU.

A summer sail on the great inland seas. [Buffalo?, 1886?]. 30, [2] p. Illus., maps. MSaP.

Lake Superior Transit Co., the Great Lake route between Buffalo, Duluth, and intermediate points. Buffalo: Matthews, Northrup & Co., [1887]. 1 sheet folded to [24] p. Illus., map. MnHi.

Summer tours via the Great Lakes, 1887. Buffalo: Matthews, Northrup & Co., [1887]. 23, [1] p. Illus. MiD-D, MnHi.

Lake Superior Transit Co., the Great Lake route between Buffalo, Duluth, and intermediate ports, 1889. Buffalo: Matthews, Northrup & Co., [1889]. 1 sheet folded to [32] p. Illus., map. MSaP, MnHi, ViNeM.

Summer tours via the Great Lakes [with] routes and rates, 1889. Buffalo: Matthews, Northrup & Co., [1889]. 23, [1] p. Illus. ViNeM.

Lake Superior Transit Co. between Buffalo, Duluth, and intermediate ports, 1890. Buffalo: Matthews-Northrup & Co., [1890]. 1 sheet folded to [32] p. Map. OBgU, ViNeM.

Summer tours via the Great Lakes [with] routes and rates, 1890. Buffalo: Matthews, Northrup & Co., [1890]. 23, [1] p. Illus. ViNeM.

Lake Superior Transit Co., the Great Lake route between Buffalo, Duluth, and intermediate ports, 1891. Buffalo: Matthews-Northrup Co., [1891]. 1 sheet folded to [32] p. Map. MnHi.

Buffalo, Duluth, and intermediate ports, 1892. Buffalo: Matthews-Northrup Co., [1892]. 1 sheet folded to [32] p. Illus., map. MSaP, MiU-H.

LEHIGH VALLEY RAILROAD COMPANY, BETHLEHEM, PA
Organized on 7 January 1853. The Lehigh Valley Transit Company fleet was established in 1881. Ceased to exist in 1920 when it merged with the Great Lakes Transit Corporation.

Lehigh tour [to] 1000 Islands [and] Saguenay River, Canada. [N.p., 1932]. 1 sheet folded to [12] p. Illus., map. CaOOA.

MCQUEEN MARINE, LIMITED, AMHERSTBURG, ONT
Incorporated on 15 June 1945. On 31 December 1979, it became part of the Malden Development Corporation, Limited.

Marine contractors [offering] towing dredging, salvaging, lightering, diving, surveying, [and] dock builders. [N.p., 1968?]. [12] p. Illus., maps. MiD-D, OBgU.

MACKINAC ISLAND FERRY COMPANY, MACKINAW CITY, MI
Incorporated on 25 June 1954. Acquired by Straits Transit, Incorporated, in 1959.

The Welch ferry line, Mackinaw City, Michigan. [N.p., 1957?]. 1 sheet folded to [4] p. Illus., map. MiD-D.

MACKINAC TRANSPORTATION COMPANY, ST. IGNACE, MI
Established on 10 October 1881. Operated the first railroad car ferry on the Great Lakes. Reorganized 10 October 1911. Discontinued operations in 1976, when its route was taken over by the Straits Car Ferry Service. Dissolved on 29 January 1980.

Brief of the Mackinac Transportation Company and interveners before the Interstate Commerce Commission [regarding] Mackinac Transportation Company abandonment of entire line (finance docket no. 22917). Chicago: Scheffer Press, [1965]. ii, 62 p. MiU-H.

Joint exceptions of the Mackinac Transportation Company, Soo Line Railroad Company, Michigan Central Railroad Company, the New York Central Railroad Company, Penndel Company, and the Pennsylvania Railroad Company to the examiner's report and recommended order before the Interstate Commerce Commission [regarding] Mackinac Transportation Co. abandonment of entire line (finance docket no. 22917). [Chicago]: Scheffer Press, [1965]. iii, [1], 42 p. MiU-H.

MANITOU ISLAND TRANSIT, LELAND, MI
Formerly Manitou Mail Service, it acquired this name around 1980 according to the owner. Still active in 1990.

Take a boat cruise to the Manitou Islands on the "Manitou Isle," Leland, Michigan. [N.p., 1967?]. 1 sheet folded to [6] p. Illus., map. CSmH.

Take a boat cruise to the Manitou Islands on the Manitou Isle or Island Clipper, Leland, Michigan. [N.p., 1970]. 1 sheet folded to [6] p. Illus., map. CSmH.

Take a boat cruise to Manitou Islands in beautiful Lake Michigan. [N.p., 1981]. 1 sheet folded to [4] p. Illus. CSmH.

Cruise to the Manitou Islands. [N.p., 1982]. 1 sheet folded to [4] p. Illus. CSmH.

Cruise to South Manitou Island. [N.p., 1988?]. 1 sheet folded to [12] p. Illus., map. MiD-D.

Cruise to South Manitou Island. [N.p., 1990]. 1 sheet folded to [12] p. Illus., map. MiD-D, MiMtpC, MiShM.

MANITOU STEAMSHIP COMPANY, CHICAGO, IL
Established about 1900. Ceased to exist around 1908.

The Great Lakes route to northern summer resorts, 1900. Chicago: Poole Bros., [1900]. 24 [i.e. 12] p. Illus., map. MiD-D

The Great Lakes route to northern summer resorts, season 1901. Chicago: Poole Bros., [1901]. 24 [i.e. 12] p. Illus., map. MSaP, MiD-D.

Routes and rates for summer tours, season 1902. Chicago: Stromberg, Allen & Co., [1902]. 24 p. Map. MiD-D.

The Mackinac Line to all northern summer resorts, season 1903. Chicago: Poole Bros., [1903]. 24 [i.e. 12] p. Illus., map. MSaP.

MEDUSA PORTLAND CEMENT COMPANY, CEMENT TRANSIT DIVISION, CLEVELAND, OH
Established on 2 April 1929, with the Cement Transit Company as a subsidiary. Became the Medusa Corporation on 31 March 1972. Still active in 1990.

Welcome aboard the S.S. Medusa Challenger. [N.p., 1967?]. [8] p. Illus., map. WManiM.

MICHIGAN. DEPARTMENT OF ADMINISTRATION. LANSING, MI
Created on 24 May 1948. Became the Department of Management and Budget on 23 May 1973.

State of Michigan, Department of Administration, Purchasing Division, Lansing, Michigan, offering for sale 5 ferry boats. [Lansing?, 1958?]. [10] p. Illus. MiLuRH.

MICHIGAN. STATE HIGHWAY DEPARTMENT. LANSING, MI
Authorized by Public Act 106 of 1923, ferry service was commenced on 31 July of that year. Commonly known as the White Fleet. Ferry operations ceased on 1 November 1957, with the opening of the Mackinac Bridge.

Michigan state ferry service schedule between Mackinaw City and Sainte Ignace, effective April 10th, 1932. [Lansing?, 1932]. 1 sheet folded to [4] p. Illus. Mi.

Michigan state ferry service schedule between Mackinaw City and Sainte Ignace, effective April 10th, 1933. [Lansing?, 1933]. 1 sheet folded to [4] p. Illus. WM.

Michigan state ferry service schedule between Mackinaw City and Sainte Ignace, effective April 16th, 1934. [Lansing?, 1934]. 1 sheet folded to [4] p. Mi, MiD-D, MiU-H, WM.

Michigan state ferry service schedule between Mackinaw City and Sainte Ignace, effective April 16th, 1936. [Lansing?, 1936]. 1 sheet folded to [4] p. Illus. WM.

Michigan State Highway Department announces the inauguration of a special state ferry service between Mackinaw City and St. Ignace for truckers, effective July 1st to September 9th, inc. [Lansing?, 1937]. 1 leaf. WM.

Michigan state ferries service schedule, effective April 16th, 1938. Lansing, [1938]. 1 sheet folded to [8] p. Map. Mi.

Michigan state ferries year 'round service schedule, effective April 15, 1939. Lansing, [1939]. [8] p. Illus., map. CSmH, CU-SB, MSaP, Mi, WM.

Michigan state ferries year 'round service schedule, effective April 15, 1940. Lansing, [1940]. 1 sheet folded to [16] p. Map. Mi.

Michigan state ferries service schedule, effective April 15, 1941. Lansing, [1941]. 1 sheet folded to [8] p. Mi.

Michigan state ferry service schedule, effective April 15, 1942. [Lansing, 1942]. 1 sheet folded to [4] p. CU-SB.

Michigan state ferry schedule. [Lansing, 1945]. 1 sheet folded to [6] p. Illus., map. CU-SB, MiD-D.

Michigan state ferry schedule, summer 1946. [Lansing, 1946]. 1 sheet folded to [4] p. Illus., map. CSmH, CU-SB, MiD-D.

Michigan state ferry schedule through April 30, 1948. [Lansing, 1947]. 1 sheet folded to [6] p. Illus., map. CU-SB, MiU-H.

Michigan state ferry schedule through April 15, 1949. [Lansing, 1948]. 1 sheet folded to [6] p. Illus., map. CU-SB, Mi, MiD-D, MiMtpC, OBgU.

Michigan state ferry schedule through April 15, 1950. [Lansing, 1949]. 1 sheet folded to [6] p. Illus., map. CSmH, CU-SB, MiD-D, OFH.

Michigan state ferry schedule through April 15, 1951. [Lansing, 1950]. 1 sheet folded to [6] p. Illus., map. Mi, MiD-D, MiMtpC, OBgU.

Vacationland trial run, December 8, 1951. [Lansing?, 1951]. [4] p. Illus. MiD-D.

Michigan state ferry schedule through April 15, 1952. [Lansing, 1951]. 1 sheet folded to [6] p. Illus., map. MiD-D.

Michigan state ferry schedules, 1953. [Lansing, 1953]. 1 sheet folded to [4] p. Illus., map. Mi, MiD-D.

Michigan state ferry schedules, 1955. [Lansing, 1954]. 1 sheet folded to [6] p. Illus., map. Mi, MiD-D.

Michigan state ferry schedules, 1955-1956. [Lansing, 1955]. 1 sheet folded to [6] p. Illus., map. Mi, MiD-D.

Michigan state ferry schedules, 1956-1957. [Lansing, 1956]. 1 sheet folded to [6] p. Illus., map. CSmH, Mi, MiD-D, MiShM, MiU-H, OBgU.

History of the Michigan state ferries. [Lansing, 1971?]. 4 p. (verso of all pages is blank). Illus. Mi, OBgU.

MICHIGAN INTERSTATE RAILWAY COMPANY, OWOSSO, MI

Established on 2 September 1977. On 1 October 1977, it took over operation of the Ann Arbor car ferries under state subsidy. Ceased operating the ferries on 26 April 1982. Filed bankruptcy in 1983 and taken over by the Ann Arbor Railroad on 7 October 1988.

The Lake Michigan short cut, Ann Arbor car ferry 1977 summer schedule, effective June 7 through September 18. [Lansing, 1977]. 1 sheet folded to [6] p. Maps. MiD-D, MiShM, OBgU, WM.

Your Lake Michigan short cut between Michigan and Wisconsin, now at reduced fares, 1978 summer schedule effective May 30-Sept. 16. [Lansing, 1978]. 1 sheet folded to [8] p. Illus., maps. MiD-D, MiMtpC, MiShM.

Your Lake Michigan short cut between Michigan and Wisconsin, Ann Arbor car ferry 1979 summer car ferry schedule effective May 30-Sept. 16. [Lansing, 1979]. 1 sheet folded to [8] p. Maps. Mi, MiD-D, MiShM, WM.

Your Lake Michigan short cut between Michigan and Wisconsin, Ann Arbor car ferry 1980 summer car ferry schedule effective May 23-Sept. 1. [Lansing, 1980]. 1 sheet folded to [8] p. Maps. CSmH, MiShM, WM.

Your short cut to lower operating costs. Save energy, money and time [if you] truck on the Ann Arbor car ferry. Lansing, 1980. 1 sheet folded to [6] p. Maps. MiMtpC.

Your Lake Michigan short cut between Michigan and Wisconsin, Ann Arbor car ferry 1981 summer car ferry schedule, Memorial Day thru Labor Day. [Lansing, 1981]. 1 sheet folded to [8] p. Illus., maps. CSmH, MdBUS, MiD-D, MiShM, OBgU, WM.

MICHIGAN-OHIO NAVIGATION COMPANY, DETROIT, MI

First created in 1954 as Waterways, Incorporated. Established on 6 July 1955 and owned by the Sand Products Corporation. Its ship did not sail in 1955. Ceased operations at the end of the 1962 season. Dissolved in 1964.

Inaugural cruise souvenir program [of the] S.S. Aquarama. [Detroit?, 1955?]. [16] p. Illus. Mi, MiD-D, NBuHi, OBgU, OClWHi, WmaniM.

Welcome aboard the spectacular Aquarama. [Detroit?, 1955?]. 1 sheet folded to [6] p. Illus., map. MiShM.

Welcome aboard! [the] S.S. Aquarama, your guide to fun and entertainment aboard ship. [Detroit?, 1956?]. 1 sheet folded to [4] p. Illus. MiShM, OFH.

Welcome aboard the fabulous, new, eight million dollar passenger ship S.S. Aquarama. [Detroit?, 1956]. 1 sheet folded to [6] p. Illus. MiD-D, NBuHi, WManiM.

Detroit, Michigan, to Cleveland, Ohio, daily summer service, 1957. [Detroit?, 1957]. 1 sheet folded to [4] p. Illus. MdBUS, MiD-D, MiShM, ViNeM.

Detroit to Cleveland [and] Cleveland to Detroit, [the] new auto short-cut across Lake Erie saves 180 driving miles. [Detroit?, 1957]. 1 sheet folded to [16] p. Illus., maps. MiD-D, MiMtpC, MiShM, MiU-H, ViNeM.

A guide to a new era in summer pleasure, we'll meet aboard the S.S. Aquarama. [Detroit?, 1958]. 1 sheet folded to [6] p. Illus. MiD-D.

Detroit to Cleveland [and] Cleveland to Detroit, [the] new auto short-cut across Lake Erie saves 180 driving miles. [Detroit?, 1958]. 1 sheet folded to [16] p. Illus., maps. CSmH, MiD-D, MiShM, OBgU.

Welcome aboard the fabulous S.S. Aquarama [offering] fast, fascinating travel continuous 1-day cruising [between] Detroit [and] Cleveland. [Detroit?, 1958]. 1 sheet folded to [6] p. Illus. MiD-D, MiMtpC, MiShM, OBgU.

Detroit to Cleveland [and] Cleveland to Detroit, [the] new auto short-cut across Lake Erie saves 180 driving miles. [Detroit?, 1959]. 1 sheet folded to [16] p. Illus., map. MiD-D, MiShM, OBgU.

Welcome aboard, the spectacular Aquarama is yours to enjoy. [Detroit?, 1959?]. 1 sheet folded to [6] p. Illus., map. MiD-D, MiShM, ViNeM.

Detroit to Cleveland [and] Cleveland to Detroit, [a] new auto short-cut across Lake Erie saves 180 driving miles. [Detroit?, 1960]. 1 sheet folded to [8] p. Illus. MiD-B, MiD-D, MiMtpC, MiShM, OBgU, OFH, WM, WManiM.

Detroit to Cleveland [and] Cleveland to Detroit, [a] new auto short-cut across Lake Erie saves 180 driving miles.

[Detroit?, 1961]. 1 sheet folded to [8] p. Illus. MiD-D, ViNeM, WM, WManiM.

Detroit to Cleveland [and] Cleveland to Detroit [on the] S.S. Aquarama, [this] auto short cut across Lake Erie saves 180 driving miles. [Detroit?, 1962]. 1 sheet folded to [4] p. Illus., maps. CSmH, MiD-D, OFH, WM.

MICHIGAN STEAMSHIP COMPANY, SOUTH HAVEN, MI

Organized in January of 1903. Established a working relationship with the Dunkley-Williams Company in March of 1906. Merged with the Dunkley-Williams Company on 3 May 1909, to form the Chicago & South Haven Steamship Company.

Michigan Steamship Co. schedule, season of 1903. Chicago: Marsh & Grant, [1903]. [40] p. Illus., map. ICHi.

MICHIGAN TRANSIT COMPANY, CHICAGO, IL

Originally the Merchants Transit Company, it acquired this name on 2 May 1918, when it merged with the Northern Michigan Transportation Company. Reorganized on 16 January 1928, as the Michigan Transit Corporation.

East shore resorts [along] Lake Michigan, 1919. [Chicago: Poole Bros., 1919]. 30 [i.e. 16] p. Illus., map. MiD-D, ViNeM, WM.

Summer sailings to [20 ports, the] popular line to Mackinac Island. [Chicago?, 1919]. 1 sheet folded to [6] p. Illus., map. ViNeM.

Michigan Transit Co., the direct line between Chicago and all northern Michigan summer resorts. [Chicago: Poole Bros., 1920]. 30 [i.e. 16] p. Illus., map. MiD-D, MiShM, ViNeM.

Michigan Transit Co., the direct line between Chicago and all northern Michigan summer resorts, 1921. [Chicago: Poole Bros., 1921]. 30 [i.e. 16] p. Illus., map. MSaP, MiD-D, ViNeM, WM.

Michigan Transit Co., [the] direct steamship service between Chicago and all northern Michigan summer resorts, 1922. [Chicago: Poole Bros., 1922]. 30 [i.e. 16] p. Illus., map. ICHi, MSaP, ViNeM, WM.

Michigan Transit Co., [the] direct steamship service between Chicago and all northern Michigan summer resorts, 1923. Chicago: Poole Bros., [1923]. 22 [i.e. 12] p. Illus., map. WM.

Trips just long enough, 1924. Chicago: Poole Bros., [1924]. 22 [i.e. 12] p. Illus., map. MSaP, MiD-D, ViNeM, WM.

Trips just long enough, 1925. Chicago: Poole Bros., [1925]. 22 [i.e. 12] p. Illus., map. ViNeM, WM, WManiM.

Travel via the direct lake route between Chicago and all northern Michigan summer resorts [on] large modern steel steamships, 1926. Chicago: Poole Bros., [1926]. 1 sheet folded to [4] p. WM.

Trips just long enough, 1926. Chicago: Poole Bros., [1926]. 22 [i.e. 12] p. Illus., map. MiD-B, ViNeM, WM.

Lake cruises aboard the Manitou, "just long enough," [on a] Sault Ste. Marie cruise, 1927. Chicago: Poole Bros., [1927]. 1 sheet folded to [8] p. Illus. WM.

Vacation lake trips "just long enough." Chicago: Poole Bros., [1927]. 22 [i.e. 12] p. Illus., map. MiD-D, ViNeM.

MICHIGAN TRANSIT CORPORATION, CHICAGO, IL

Formerly the Michigan Transit Company, it incorporated on 16 January 1928. Ceased to exist on 17 January 1933.

Spring schedule, advance announcement summer schedule [of the] Michigan Transit Corporation, [the] Chicago-northern west Michigan direct lake route, 1928 season. [Chicago?, 1928]. 1 sheet folded to [4] p. MiD-D.

Vacation lake trips "just long enough" [on the] Chicago-northern Michigan lake route, 1928. [Chicago: Poole Bros.], 1928. 30 [i.e. 16] p. Illus., map. April 20 edition. MiD-B, MiD-D, ViNeM, WM.

Chicago-northern Michigan lake route, vacation lake trips just long enough, 1929. [Chicago: Poole Bros.], 1929. 30 [i.e. 16] p. Illus., map. Mi, ViNeM.

Chicago-northern west Michigan direct lake route. Chicago: Poole Bros., [1929]. 1 sheet folded to 6 p. Illus. MiD-D.

Chicago-northern Michigan lake route, vacation lake trips just long enough, 1930. [Chicago: Poole Bros.], 1930. 30 [i.e. 16] p. Illus., map. MSaP, Mi, ViNeM, WM, WManiM.

Chicago-Muskegon and northern Michigan summer resorts, 7 sailings every week, 1931. Chicago: Poole Bros., [1931]. 12 [i.e. 8] p. Illus., map. MiD-D, ViNeM, WM.

Chicago-Muskegon and northern Michigan summer resorts, 6 sailings every week. Chicago: Poole Bros., [1931]. 1 sheet folded to 6 [i.e. 8] p. Revised summer schedule effective July 24, 1931. OBgU, ViNeM.

MICHIGAN TRUST COMPANY, GRAND RAPIDS, MI

Incorporated on 2 July 1889. Acquired most of the Goodrich fleet at auction on 10 May 1933, and may have subsequently formed the Chicago-Milwaukee Steamship Line. Consolidated with Old Kent Bank on 31 December 1956, to form Old Kent Bank & Trust.

Lake boats [of the] Chicago-Milwaukee-Benton Harbor-South Haven Steamship Line, operating former Goodrich routes [and offering] daily lake boat excursions [plus] vacation and tourist travel. [Chicago?, 1933]. 1 sheet folded to [4] p. Illus. CU-SB, MiD-D, MiShM, OFH, WM.

MICHIGAN-WISCONSIN TRANSPORTATION COMPANY, LUDINGTON MI

Incorporated 16 May 1983, to operate what had been the Chessie System Lake Michigan ferries. Commenced ferry operations on 1 July 1983. Discontinued the Ludington-Kewaunee run on 16 November 1990. Still active as of 1990.

Lake Michigan carferry service, January 1, 1984-December 31, 1984. [Cleveland?, 1984]. 1 sheet folded to [6] p. Illus., maps. CaOKMM, MiD-D, MiGr, MiMtpC, MiShM, OBgU, WM, WManiM.

Lake Michigan carferry service, Milwaukee-Ludington, June 15, 1984-September 3, 1984. [Cleveland?, 1984]. 1 sheet folded to [6] p. Illus., maps. CSmH, MiD-D, MiGr, OBgU, WManiM.

Lake Michigan carferry service, Ludington - Kewaunee, January 2, 1985-June 13, 1986. [Ludington: Quick Print, 1984]. 1 sheet folded to [6] p. Maps. CaOKMM, MiD-D, MiGr,, MiLuRH, MiMtpC, OBgU, WM, WManiM.

Lake Michigan carferry service, schedule & fares [for period] June 14, 1986-June 12, 1987. [Ludington: Quick Print, 1986]. 1 sheet folded to [6] p. Illus., map. CaOKMM, MiD-D, WM, WManiM.

Lake Michigan carferry service, schedule & fares [for period] June 12, 1987-June 9, 1988. [Ludington: Quick Print, 1987]. 1 sheet folded to [6] p. CaOKMM, MiD-D, WM, WmaniM.

Lake Michigan carferry service, schedule & fares [for period] June 10, 1988-June 8, 1989. [Ludington: Quick Print, 1988]. 1 sheet folded to [6] p. CaOKMM, MiD-D, WM.

Lake Michigan carferry service, year-'round service between Ludington, Michigan and Kewaunee, Wisconsin, schedule & fares in effect June 9, 1989-June 7, 1990. [Ludington: Quick Print, 1989]. 1 sheet folded to [6] p. Illus., map. MiD-D.

Car ferry year-'round service, schedule and fares in effect June 8, 1990-June 6, 1991. [Ludington: Quick Print, 1990]. 1 sheet folded to [6] p. Illus. MiD-D, MiMtpC, MiShM, OBgU.

MIDWEST CRUISES, INCORPORATED, INDIANAPOLIS, IN

Incorporated 26 August 1958. Dissolved on 18 April 1989.

Great Lakes and St. Lawrence Seaway cruises, T[win] S[crew] S[hip] Orion, 1974 7 day cruises. [N.p., 1973]. 1 sheet folded to [16] p. Illus., map. MiD-D, MiMtpC, MiShM, OBgU, WManiM.

Great Lakes and St. Lawrence Seaway cruises. [N.p., 1975]. 1 sheet folded to [16] p. Illus., map. MiD-D, MiMtpC, MiShM, MnDuC, OBgU, WManiM.

Great Lakes, Saguenay, and St. Lawrence Seaway cruises. [N.p., 1977]. 1 sheet folded to [16] p. Illus., map. CSmH, MdBUS, MiD-D, MnDuC, OBgU, WM.

MILLER BOAT LINE, INCORPORATED, PUT-IN-BAY, OH

Established in 1947. Incorporated on 6 February 1978. Still active in 1990.

Passenger and auto ferry [to] Put in Bay [sic] from Catawba Point. [Sandusky, OH: Commercial Printing, 1948]. 1 sheet folded to [6] p. Illus., map. OBgU.

Passenger and auto ferry [to] Put in Bay [sic] and Middle Bass [Island] from Catawba Point. [Sandusky, OH: Commercial Printing, 1949]. 1 sheet folded to [6] p. Illus., map. MiD-D, OBgU.

Passenger and auto ferry [to] Put in Bay [sic] and Middle Bass [Island] from Catawba Point. [Sandusky, OH: Commercial Printing, 1950]. 1 sheet folded to [6] p. Illus., map. MiD-D.

Passenger and auto ferry [to] Put in Bay [sic] and Middle Bass [Island] from Catawba Point. [Sandusky, OH: Commercial Printing, 1951]. 1 sheet folded to [6] p. Illus., map. OFH.

Passenger and auto ferry [to] Put in Bay [sic] and Middle Bass [Island] from Catawba Point. [Sandusky, OH: Commercial Printing, 1954]. 1 sheet folded to [6] p. Illus., map. OBgU.

Passenger and auto ferry [to] Put in Bay [sic] and Middle Bass [Island] from Catawba Point. [Sandusky, OH: Commercial Printing, 1956]. 1 sheet folded to [6] p. Illus., map. OBgU.

Passenger and auto ferry [to] Put in Bay [sic] and Middle Bass [Island] from Catawba Point. [Sandusky, OH: Commercial Printing, 1957]. 1 sheet folded to [6] p. Illus., map. MiD-D, OBgU.

Passenger and auto ferry [to] Put in Bay [sic] and Middle Bass [Island] from Catawba Point. [Sandusky, OH: Commercial Printing, 1960]. 1 sheet folded to [6] p. Illus., map. OBgU, OFH.

Passenger and auto ferry [to] Put in Bay [sic] and Middle Bass [Island] from Catawba Point. [Sandusky, OH: Commercial Printing, 1961]. 1 sheet folded to [6] p. Illus., map. MiD-D, OFH.

Passenger and auto ferry [to] Put in Bay [sic] and Middle Bass [Island] from Catawba Point. [Sandusky, OH: Commercial Printing, 1962]. 1 sheet folded to [6] p. Illus., map. MiD-D, OBgU.

Passenger and auto ferry [to] Put in Bay [sic] and Middle Bass [Island] from Catawba Point. [Sandusky, OH: Commercial Printing, 1963]. 1 sheet folded to [6] p. Illus., map. OBgU.

Passenger and auto ferry [to] Put in Bay [sic] and Middle Bass [Island] from Catawba Point. [Sandusky, OH: Commercial Printing, 1964]. 1 sheet folded to [6] p. Illus., map. OBgU.

Passenger and auto ferry spring and summer schedules [to] Put in Bay [sic] and Middle Bass [Island] from Catawba Point. [Sandusky, OH: Commercial Printing, 1966]. 1 sheet folded to [6] p. Illus., map. OBgU, OFH.

Passenger and auto ferry summer schedules [to] Put in Bay [sic] and Middle Bass [Island] from Catawba Point. [Sandusky, OH: Commercial Printing, 1968]. 1 sheet folded to [6] p. Illus., map. OBgU.

Passenger and auto ferry spring and summer schedules [to] Put in Bay [sic] from Catawba Point. [Sandusky, OH: Commercial Printing, 1973]. 1 sheet folded to [6] p. Illus., map. OBgU, OFH.

Passenger and auto ferry spring and summer schedules [to] Put in Bay [sic] from Catawba Point. [Sandusky, OH: Commercial Printing, 1974]. 1 sheet folded to [6] p. Illus., map. OBgU.

Passenger and auto ferry spring and summer schedules [to] Put in Bay [sic] from Catawba Point. [Sandusky, OH: Commercial Printing, 1975]. 1 sheet folded to [6] p. Illus., map. OBgU.

"Short route" auto-passenger ferry to South Bass Island and Put-in-Bay via Miller Boat Line. Findlay, OH: Blosser Color-Ads, [1976]. 1 sheet folded to [6] p. Illus., map. OBgU.

Put-in-Bay on scenic, historic, relaxing South Bass Island, travel via Miller Boat Line. Put-in-Bay, OH: Kelly Faris, [1978]. 1 sheet folded to [4] p. Illus., map. OBgU.

Miller Boat Line to scenic, historic, relaxing South Bass Island, Put-in-Bay, Ohio. Put-in-Bay, OH: Kelly Faris, [1981]. 1 sheet folded to [4] p. Illus., map. OBgU.

Miller Boat Line to scenic, historic, relaxing South Bass Island, Put-in-Bay, Ohio. Put-in-Bay, OH: Kelly Faris, [1982]. 1 sheet folded to [4] p. Illus., map. OBgU.

Miller Boat Line to scenic, historic, relaxing South Bass Island, Put-in-Bay, Ohio. Put-in-Bay, OH: Kelly Faris, [1983]. 1 sheet folded to [4] p. Illus., map. OBgU.

Miller Boat Line to scenic, historic, relaxing South Bass Island, Put-in-Bay, Ohio. Put-in-Bay, OH: Kelly Faris, [1984]. 1 sheet folded to [4] p. Illus., map. OBgU.

Miller Boat Line to scenic, historic, relaxing South Bass Island, Put-in-Bay, Ohio. Put-in-Bay, OH: Kelly Faris, [1985]. 1 sheet folded to [4] p. Illus., map. OBgU.

Miller Boat Line to scenic, historic, relaxing South Bass Island, Put-in-Bay, Ohio. Put-in-Bay, OH: Kelly Faris, [1986]. 1 sheet folded to [4] p. Illus., map. OBgU.

Miller Boat Line 1987 ferry service to South Bass Island (Put-in-Bay, OH) from Catawba Point. Toledo: Mercury Printing Co., [1987]. 1 sheet folded to [6] p. Illus., maps. OBgU.

Miller Boat Line 1988 ferry service to and from South Bass Island (Put-in-Bay, Ohio) and Catawba Point. Toledo: Mercury Printing Co., [1988]. 1 sheet folded to [4] p. Illus. OBgU.

Miller Boat Line 1989 ferry to Put-in-Bay [and] South Bass Island, Ohio. [Toledo: Industrial Printing, 1989]. 1 sheet folded to [6] p. Illus., maps. OBgU.

Miller Boat Line ferry to Put-in-Bay [and] South Bass Island, Ohio. [Elyria, OH: Wilmot Printing, 1990]. 1 sheet folded to [6] p. Illus., maps. MiD-D, MiMtpC, MiShM, OBgU.

MINNEAPOLIS, ST. PAUL & BUFFALO STEAMSHIP COMPANY, BUFFALO, NY
Incorporated on 13 January 1892. Controlled by the Soo Line Railway. Became a part of the Mutual Transit Company around 1907.

General and confidential instructions to masters. Buffalo: Adams & White, 1893. 12 p. Cover title: M. St. P. & B. S.S. Co. instructions to masters. N.

MINNEAPOLIS, ST. PAUL & SAULT STE. MARIE RAILWAY COMPANY, MINNEAPOLIS, MN
Organized on 11 June 1888. Controlled by the Canadian Pacific Railway Company. Reorganized as the Minneapolis, St. Paul & Sault Ste. Marie Railroad Company on 1 September 1944.

Lake trips, 1912. [N.p., 1912]. 38 [i.e. 20] p. Illus., map. WM.

MINNESOTA-ATLANTIC TRANSIT COMPANY, BUFFALO, NY
Established in 1923 as a subsidiary of the McDougall Terminal Warehouse Company. Popularly known as the Poker Fleet. Acquired by the Terminals & Transportation Corporation of America on 13 May 1927. Merged with the Great Lakes Transit Corporation on 31 December 1941.

Memorandum of rail and lake rates as compared with all rail rates from eastern points to Duluth, Minneapolis and St. Paul, Minn., effective March 20, '36. [N.p., 1936]. 42 p. MnDuU.

Memorandum of rail and lake rates as compared with all rail rates from eastern points to Duluth, Minneapolis and St. Paul, Minn., effective March 20, '39. [N.p., 1939]. 46, [2] p. MnDuU.

MISENER TRANSPORTATION, LIMITED, ST. CATHARINES, ONT

Established in 1978 as successor to Scott Misener Steamships, Limited. On 15 March 1984, it became the Misener Shipping Agency, Incorporated, a firm still active in 1990.

The Spearpole. — Vol. 1, no. 1 (Fall 1978)-present. — St. Catharines, ONT, 1978-present. Illus. Quarterly 1978-1987, triannually 1988-present. CaOKMM, CaOStC, MiD-D, MnDuC, OBgU.

In commemoration of the naming of M[otor] V[essel] "Selkirk Settler" [and] the launch of M[otor] V[essel] "Canada Marquis." [N.p., 1983]. [8] p. Illus. CaOKMM.

Momentum. — Vol. 1, no. 1 (Spring 1983)-vol. 2, no. 3 (Winter 1984). — Toronto, 1983-1984. Illus. Triannually [not quarterly as stated]. OBgU.

Misener. Serving Canadians since 1916. [Toronto?, 1984?]. [12] p. Illus. CaOKMM.

MONTREAL & LAKE ERIE STEAMSHIP COMPANY, LIMITED, MONTREAL, QUE

Popularly known as the Jacques Line. Acquired by the Canada Steamship Lines in 1913.

Merchants' Montreal Line, [the] Thousand Island route direct steamers. Montreal: Desbarats Printing Company, [1900?]. 15, [1] p. Illus., map. WM.

Merchants' Montreal Line, [the] Thousand Island route, season 1905. [Montreal?, 1905]. 1 sheet folded to [8] p. Illus., map. CaOOA.

Merchants' Montreal Line, [the] Thousand Island route direct steamer. [Montreal?, 1907]. [12] p. Illus., map. CaOOA.

Merchants' Montreal Line, [the] Thousand Island route direct steamer. [Montreal?, 1908]. [12] p. Illus., map. CaOOA.

Merchants' Montreal Line, [the] Thousand Island direct steamers. Montreal: Desbarats Printing Company, [1911?]. [16] p. Illus., map. CaOOA.

Merchants' Montreal Line, [the] Thousand Island route direct steamers. [Montreal?, 1912?]. [20] p. Illus., map. MSaP.

MONTREAL & ROCHESTER TRANSIT COMPANY, PICTON, ONT

Probably established about 1890 by Arthur W. Hepburn. Familiarly known as the "Bay of Quinte Line." Became the Montreal, Rochester & Quebec Transit Company around 1900.

Steamer "Alexandria" [to] Rochester, Bay of Quinte, Thousand Islands, St. Lawrence Rapids and Montreal, calling at all intermediate points, 1893. [N.p., 1893]. 1 sheet folded to [6] p. Illus. CaOOA.

Steamer "Alexandria" [to] Rochester, N.Y., Bay of Quinte, Thousand Islands, St. Lawrence Rapids, and Montreal, calling at all intermediate ports, 1899. [N.p., 1899]. 1 sheet folded to [6] p. Illus. CaOOA, NR.

MONTREAL, ROCHESTER & QUEBEC TRANSIT COMPANY, PICTON, ONT

Apparently created around 1900 as successor to the Montreal & Rochester Transit Company. In 1905 it became the Ontario & Quebec Navigation Company, Limited.

Steamer Alexandria [serving] Buffalo, Olcott Beach, Rochester, Thousand Islands, Montreal, St. Lawrence Rapids, Quebec, Bay of Quinte, [and] calling at all intermediate ports, 1902. [N.p., 1902]. 1 sheet folded to [12] p. Illus., map. CaOOA.

Steamer Alexandria [serving] Buffalo, Olcott Beach, Rochester, Thousand Islands, Montreal, St. Lawrence Rapids, Quebec, Bay of Quinte, [and] calling at all intermediate points, 1904. [N.p., 1904]. 1 sheet folded to [12] p. Illus., map. CaOOA.

MUSKEGON RAILWAY & NAVIGATION COMPANY, DETROIT, MI

Incorporated 22 May 1918. Merged with the Grand Trunk Western Railroad Company on 23 August 1955. Dissolved 3 December 1956.

Agreement between [the] Muskegon Railway & Navigation Company, the Pennsylvania Railroad Company, and [the] Grand Trunk Western Railroad Company [of] October 28, 1931, providing for mutual trackage and operating rights in Muskegon, Michigan, and vicinity. Philadelphia: Press of Allen, Lane & Scott, [1931]. 6 p. MiU-H.

NATIONAL GYPSUM COMPANY, HURON CEMENT DIVISION, ALPENA, MI

The Huron Portland Cement Company was created on 26 January 1907. Its transportation division (Huron Transportation Company) began operating in November of 1916, and subsequent additions formed the "Green Fleet." In May of 1959 the Huron Portland Cement Company was acquired by National Gypsum. Still active in 1990.

Agreement between [the] Huron Portland Cement Company and [the] Seafarers' International Union of North America, Great Lakes District, affiliated with the American Federation of Labor, effective April 1, 1955. [Detroit?, 1955]. 37, [1] p. MiD-B.

Welcome aboard! Huron Cement salutes Michigan week! Open house [for the] motor vessel Paul H[enson] Townsend, Civic Center, Detroit, Michigan, May 21-23, 1962! [N.p., 1962]. [8] p. Illus., map. MiD-D.

Christening log [of the] J[oseph] A[lexander] W[ilson] Iglehart, July 7, 1965. [N.p., 1965]. [12] p. Illus. MiD-D.

Welcome aboard [for passengers sailing with the fleet]. [N.p., 1967?]. [8] p. Illus., map. MiD-D.

Rededication and blessing of [the] St[eame]r E[mory] M[oran] Ford, July 31, 1980. [N.p., 1980]. [8] p. Illus. CaOKMM, MiD-D, MnDuC, OBgU.

St[eame]r E[mory] M[oran] Ford, 1898-1980. [N.p., 1980]. [12] p. Illus. CaOKMM, MiD-D, OBgU.

NATIONAL STEEL CORPORATION, CLEVELAND, OH

Established on 7 November 1929, as a Delaware Corporation. Served as a holding company and operator of the M.A. Hanna Company fleet. On 13 September 1983, it became a part of National Intergroup, Incorporated.

M[otor] V[essel] George A[rthur] Stinson christening ceremony, August 21, 1978, Detroit, Michigan. [N.p., 1978]. [8] p. Illus. OBgU.

NESSEN TRANSPORTATION COMPANY, MANISTEE, MI

Established on 24 April 1912. Dissolved on 30 August 1937.

Nessen Line daily between Milwaukee, Ludington and Manistee. Chicago: Poole Bros., [1912?]. 1 sheet folded to [4] p. Illus. MiD-D.

NEUMAN BOAT LINE, INCORPORATED, SANDUSKY, OH

Established in 1907. Incorporated on 25 May 1948. Still active in 1990.

Come to Kelleys Island in Lake Erie...to fish, swim, sail, hunt, to rest and be happy. [Sandusky, OH, 1944]. 1 sheet folded to [6] p. Illus., map. WM.

The Neuman route, a vacation paradise. [Sandusky, OH, 1949]. 1 sheet folded to [4] p. Illus., map. OBgU.

The Neuman route, boat rides on beautiful Lake Erie. [Sandusky, OH, 1951]. 1 sheet folded to [4] p. Illus., map. MdBUS.

Kelleys Island, Put-in-Bay [and] Middle Bass [Island] schedules. [Sandusky, OH, 1956]. 1 sheet folded to [6] p. Illus., map. MiD-D, OSandF.

Kelleys Island, Put-in-Bay [and] Middle Bass [Island] schedules. [Sandusky, OH, 1957]. 1 sheet folded to [6] p. Illus., map. OBgU.

Kelleys Island, Put-in-Bay [and] Middle Bass [Island] schedules. [Sandusky, OH, 1958]. 1 sheet folded to [6] p. Illus., map. MiD-D, OBgU.

Take an exciting lake cruise, visit the delightful and historic islands of Lake Erie, Kelleys Island, Put-in-Bay, [and] Middle Bass [Island on] the Neuman route. [Sandusky, OH, 1958]. 1 sheet folded to [6] p. Illus., map. OFH.

Take an exciting lake cruise, visit the delightful and historic islands of Lake Erie, Kelleys Island, Put-in-Bay, [and] Middle Bass [Island on] the Neuman route. [Sandusky, OH, 1959?]. 1 sheet folded to [6] p. Illus. OSandF.

Cruises on Lake Erie, visit delightful and picturesque Kelleys Island. [Sandusky, OH, 1960]. 1 sheet folded to [6] p. Illus., map. MiD-D.

Cruises on Lake Erie, visit delightful and picturesque Kelleys Island. [Sandusky, OH, 1961]. 1 sheet folded to [6] p. Illus., map. OBgU.

Cruises on Lake Erie, visit delightful and picturesque Kelleys Island. [Sandusky, OH, 1962]. 1 sheet folded to [6] p. Illus., map. MiD-D.

Cruises on Lake Erie, visit delightful and picturesque Kelleys Island. [Sandusky, OH, 1965]. 1 sheet folded to [6] p. Illus., map. MiD-D, OBgU, OFH.

Cruises on Lake Erie, visit delightful and picturesque Kelleys Island. [Sandusky, OH, 1966]. 1 sheet folded to [6] p. Illus., map. MiD-D, MiShM, OBgU.

Cruises on Lake Erie, visit delightful and picturesque Kelleys Island. [Sandusky, OH, 1967]. 1 sheet folded to [6] p. Illus., map. OBgU.

Cruises on Lake Erie, visit delightful and picturesque Kelleys Island. [Sandusky, OH, 1968]. 1 sheet folded to [6] p. Illus., map. MdBUS, OBgU, OFH.

Cruises on Lake Erie, visit delightful and picturesque Kelleys Island. [Sandusky, OH, 1969]. 1 sheet folded to [6] p. Illus., map. OBgU.

Kelleys Island...so near and yet so far! [Sandusky, OH, 1970]. 1 sheet folded to [6] p. Illus., map. OFH.

Kelleys Island...so near and yet so far! [Sandusky, OH, 1971]. 1 sheet folded to [6] p. Illus., map. OBgU, OFH.

Kelleys Island. [Sandusky, OH, 1973]. 1 sheet folded to [4] p. OBgU.

Kelleys Island...so near and yet so far! [Sandusky, OH, 1973]. 1 sheet folded to [6] p. Illus., map. OFH.

Kelleys Island. [Sandusky, OH, 1974]. 1 sheet folded to [4] p. OBgU.

Kelleys Island...so near and yet so far! [Sandusky, OH, 1974]. 1 sheet folded to [6] p. Illus., map. OBgU.

Kelleys Island. [Sandusky, OH, 1975]. 1 sheet folded to [4] p. OBgU.

Kelleys Island...so near and yet so far! [Sandusky, OH, 1975]. 1 sheet folded to [6] p. Illus., map. OBgU.

Sail to Kelleys Island, peaceful, restful, natural for the naturalist, camping, fishing, picnicing, swimming, [and] hiking. [Sandusky, OH, 1976]. 1 sheet folded to [12] p. Illus., map. OBgU.

Passenger-auto ferry to Kelleys Island, peaceful, restful, natural [for] camping, fishing, picnicing, swimming, [and] hiking. [Sandusky, OH, 1978]. 1 sheet folded to [12] p. Illus., map. OBgU.

Passenger-auto ferry to Kelleys Island, peaceful, restful, natural [for] camping, fishing, picnicing, swimming, [and] hiking. [Sandusky, OH, 1979]. 1 sheet folded to [12] p. Illus., map. OBgU.

Passenger-auto ferry to Kelleys Island. [Sandusky, OH, 1980]. 1 sheet folded to [12] p. Illus., map. MdBUS.

Cruises to Kelleys Island, passenger [and] auto ferry. [Sandusky, OH, 1981]. 1 sheet folded to [12] p. Map. OBgU, OV.

Cruises to Kelleys Island, passenger [and] auto ferry. [Sandusky, OH, 1982]. 1 sheet folded to [12] p. Illus., map. OBgU.

Cruises to Kelleys Island, passenger [and] auto ferry. [Sandusky, OH, 1983]. 1 sheet folded to [12] p. Illus., map. OBgU.

Cruises to Kelleys Island, passenger [and] auto ferry. [Sandusky, OH, 1984]. 1 sheet folded to [8] p. Map. OBgU.

Kelleys Island passenger [and] auto ferry. [Sandusky, OH, 1984]. 1 sheet folded to [12] p. Illus., map. OBgU.

Lake Erie cruises aboard the 70' M[otor] V[essel] Challenger, 1984. [Sandusky, OH, 1984]. 1 sheet folded to [8] p. Illus. OBgU.

Kelleys Island passenger [and] auto ferry. [Sandusky, OH, 1985]. 1 sheet folded to [6] p. OBgU.

Kelleys Island ferry, auto and passenger, 1986. [Sandusky, OH, 1986]. 1 sheet folded to [6] p. Illus. OBgU.

Lake Erie cruises aboard the 70' M[otor] V[essel] Challenger, Port of Sandusky, 1988. [Sandusky, OH, 1988]. 1 sheet folded to [8] p. Illus. OSandF.

Kelleys Island ferry, auto and passenger, [the] shortest route to Kelleys Island, 1990. [Sandusky, OH, 1990]. 1 sheet folded to [6] p. Illus. MiD-D.

Lake Erie cruises aboard the 70' M[otor] V[essel] Challenger, Port of Sandusky, 1990. [Sandusky, OH, 1990]. 1 sheet folded to [8] p. Illus. MiD-D.

NEW YORK CENTRAL RAILROAD
NEW YORK, NY

Organized 22 December 1914. Merged with the Pennsylvania Railroad Company on 1 February 1968, to form the Pennsylvania New York Central Transportation Company.

Cruise to Georgian Bay, Manitoulin Island, Parry Sound & Killarney all-expense from New York state points. [N.p., 1939]. 1 sheet folded to [8] p. Illus., map. CaOOA.

NIAGARA NAVIGATION COMPANY, LIMITED, TORONTO, ONT

Organized in April of 1877 and filed papers on 2 July 1878. Popularly known as the Niagara River Line. Became part of the Richelieu & Ontario Line on 1 June 1912. Dissolved on 15 April 1957.

The Niagara River and Toronto via the palatial steamers of the Niagara River Line. [Buffalo?], c1895. 32 p. Illus., map. ViNeM.

The Niagara River Line via the Niagara River and Lake Ontario to & from Toronto. [Buffalo, 1899]. 1 sheet folded to [6] p. Illus., map. MSaP, OBgU.

Niagara River Line steamers [connecting] Buffalo, Niagara Falls, Lewiston, Queenston, Niagara-on-the-Lake, and Toronto via the lower Niagara River and Lake Ontario. Buffalo: M[atthews]-N[orthrup] Co., [1901]. 1 sheet folded to [6] p. Illus., map. CaOOA, OBgU.

Niagara River Line & Toronto. Toronto: Toronto Lith[ographing] Co., Ltd., c1903. 32 p. Illus., maps. CaOTAr, MSaP.

Niagara River Line & Toronto. Toronto: Toronto Lith[ographing] Co., Ltd., c1903. 32 p. Illus., maps. Second edition. CaOOA.

Time card [for the] Niagara River Line to and from Toronto via the lower Niagara River and Lake Ontario in effect June 15th, 1903. [Toronto?, 1903]. 1 sheet folded to [6] p. Illus., map. CaOOA.

Niagara River Line & Toronto. Toronto: Toronto Lith Co., [1904?]. 32 p. Illus., map. MiD-D.

Niagara River Line steamers. [Toronto?, 1904]. 1 sheet folded to [6] p. Illus., map. ViNeM.

Niagara River Line steamers [connecting] Buffalo, Niagara Falls, Lewiston, Queenston, Niagara-on-the-Lake, and Toronto via the lower Niagara River and Lake Ontario. [Toronto?, 1905]. 1 sheet folded to [6] p. Illus., map. CaOOA.

The Niagara - Toronto route. Toronto: W[illiam] R. Phillips & Co., [1905]. 48 p. Illus., map. CaOTAr, MiManiHi.

Niagara Navigation Co., Limited, connecting Buffalo, Niagara Falls [and] Toronto. [Toronto?, 1906]. 1 sheet folded to [6] p. Illus., map. CaOOA, CaOTAr.

The Niagara Navigation Company, Limited, directors' report and financial statement [for the] year ending 30th November, 1906. [Toronto?, 1906?]. [8] p. (last three pages are blank). NNC.

Niagara-Toronto route via the lower Niagara River and Lake Ontario. Toronto: Imrie Printing Co., [1906]. 44 p. Illus., map. CaOOA, CaOTAr, MSaP, ViNeM.

The Niagara-Toronto route via the lower Niagara River and Lake Ontario. [Toronto?, 1907]. 48 p. Illus., map. CaOTAr.

Niagara Navigation Company, Limited, connecting Niagara Falls [and] Toronto, season 1908. [Toronto?, 1908]. 1 sheet folded to [12] p. Illus., map. CaOTAr.

The Niagara-Toronto route. [Toronto?, 1908]. 48 p. Illus., map. CaOTPB.

Niagara Navigation Company, Limited, connecting Buffalo, Niagara Falls, [and] Toronto, season 1909. [Toronto?, 1909]. 1 sheet folded to [12] p. Illus., map. CaOOA, MSaP, MiManiHi.

Niagara Navigation Company, Limited, connecting Buffalo, Niagara Falls [and] Toronto. [Toronto?, 1910]. 32 p. Illus., map. ViNeM.

Buffalo, Niagara Falls, Toronto route. Toronto: W[illiam] A. Morison Litho Co., [1911]. 32 p. Illus., map. CaOOA, CaOStCB.

Niagara Navigation Company, Limited, connecting Buffalo, Niagara Falls [and] Toronto, season 1911. [Toronto?, 1911]. 1 sheet folded to [12] p. Illus., map. MSaP.

The Niagara Navigation Company, Limited, directors' report and financial statement [for the] year ending 30th November, 1910. [Toronto?, 1911?]. [8] p. (last 3 pages are blank). NNC.

Directors' report and financial statement [for the] year ending 30th November, 1911. [Toronto?, 1912?]. [8] p. (last 3 pages are blank). CtY, NNC.

Niagara Navigation Company, Limited, [connecting] Buffalo, Niagara Falls [and] Toronto, 1912. [Toronto?, 1912]. 1 sheet folded to [14] p. Illus., map. ViNeM.

Official guide book [of the] Niagara Navigation Company [plus the] Thousand Island & St. Lawrence River steamboat companies. Rochester: John P. Smith Printing Co., [1913]. 64 p. Illus., map. Cover title: Richelieu & Ontario lines [to] Buffalo, Niagara Falls [and] Toronto. CaOOA.

NIAGARA, ST. CATHARINES & TORONTO NAVIGATION COMPANY, LIMITED, ST. CATHARINES, ONT

The Niagara, St. Catharines & Toronto Railway was organized on 1 September 1899. In 1901 it acquired control of the Niagara, St. Catharines & Toronto Navigation Company, Limited, a firm that was incorporated on 30 April 1874. These two firms were absorbed by the Canadian Northern Railway Company around 1907. In January of 1923 the Canadian Northern became part of the Canadian National Railways system. CN discontinued its Lake Ontario operations in 1950, and the Niagara, St. Catharines & Toronto Navigation Company ceased to exist on 11 June 1956.

The garden of Canada [served by the] Niagara, St. Catharines and Toronto R[ailwa]y, Toronto to Buffalo. Toronto: Mail Job Print, [1900?]. 1 sheet folded to [16] p. Illus., map. MdBUS.

The garden of Canada [served by the] Niagara, St. Catharines and Toronto Navigation Co. [connecting] Toronto, St. Catharines, Niagara Falls, [and] Buffalo. Buffalo: Matthews-Northrup Works, [1901?]. 1 sheet folded to [16] p. Illus., map. OBgU, ViNeM.

The Niagara-St. Catharines Line [connecting] Toronto, Port Dalhousie, St. Catharines, Niagara Falls, Buffalo, Merritton, Thorold, Welland, [and] Port Colborne. [Buffalo, 1913]. 1 sheet folded to [16] p. Illus., map. Issued June, 1913. MSaP.

The Niagara-St. Catharines Line [operating] steamers "Dalhousie City" [and] "Garden City" [from] Toronto to Port Dalhousie. [Toronto?, 1914]. [8] p. Illus., map. Issued April, 1914. ViNeM.

Niagara-St. Catharines Line [suggests a] picnic at Port Dalhousie, Queen Victoria Park, Niagara Falls, Ont., [or] Montebello Park, St. Catharines, a happy two-hour sail will take you there. [Toronto, 1922]. 1 sheet folded to [4] p. Illus., map. CaOOA.

Niagara, St. Catharines [and] Toronto Line. [N.p., 1924?]. 1 sheet folded to [12] p. Illus., map. CaOOA.

Niagara, St. Catharines [and] Toronto Line. [N.p., 1926?]. 1 sheet folded to [12] p. Illus., map. CaOOA.

Toronto tours, delightful sightseeing trips from Niagara Falls across Lake Ontario to Toronto, "Queen City of

Canada." [Toronto?, 1927]. 1 sheet folded to [6] p. Illus. CaOOA.

Niagara, St. Catharines [and] Toronto line. [Toronto?, 1928?]. 1 sheet folded to [12] p. Illus., map. MdBUS.

A scenic trip to Canada [and] Niagara Falls across Lake Ontario to Toronto. [N.p., 1929?]. 1 sheet folded to [12] p. Illus., map. MiD-D.

Summer time table, 1929. [Toronto?, 1929]. 3, [1] p. Illus. CaOOA.

A scenic trip to Canada [and] Niagara Falls across Lake Ontario to Toronto. [N.p., 1930]. 1 sheet folded to [16] p. Illus., map. MiD-D.

Across the lake to Port Dalhousie and Niagara Falls. [N.p., 1931?]. 1 sheet folded to [16] p. Illus., map. CaOOA.

A scenic trip to Canada [and] Niagara Falls across Lake Ontario to Toronto. [N.p., 1932]. 1 sheet folded to [16] p. Illus., map. MiD-D.

Toronto tours from Niagara Falls, three hours sightseeing by electric car and steamer. [N.p., 1932]. 1 sheet folded to [6] p. Illus. MSaP.

Summer timetable [of the] Canadian National steamers in connection with [the] Niagara, St. Catharines & Toronto Railway (season 1933). St. Catharines: St. Catharines Standard, 1933. 1 sheet folded to [6] p. Illus., map. CaOOA.

Visit Canada, take a trip from Buffalo and Niagara Falls to Toronto [on] Canadian National steamers. [N.p., 1934?]. 1 sheet folded to [8] p. Illus., map. MiD-D, ViNeM.

Visit Canada, take a trip from Buffalo and Niagara Falls to Toronto [on] Canadian National steamers. [N.p., 1935]. 1 sheet folded to [8] p. Illus., map. OBgU, OFH.

Visit Canada, take a trip from Buffalo and Niagara Falls to Toronto. [N.p., 1936]. 1 sheet folded to [8] p. Illus., map. MSaP, MiShM, ViNeM.

Canadian National steamers (Niagara Falls route) summer schedule, 1948. [N.p., 1948]. 1 sheet folded to [4] p. CU-SB.

NICHOLSON ERIE-DOVER FERRY LINE, ERIE, OH

Established on 20 June 1929. Dissolved on 31 August 1935.

The short cut between the States and Toronto, Muskoka Lakes, Georgian Bay, [and] Michigan resorts. [N.p., 1930?]. 1 sheet folded to [8] p. Illus., map. MiD-D, OBgU.

The short cut [between] Erie, Pennsylvania, United States and Port Dover, Hamilton, Toronto, and all northern Ontario points. Hamilton: Robert Duncan & Co., [1931?]. 1 sheet folded to [8] p. Illus., maps. ViNeM.

NICHOLSON-UNIVERSAL STEAMSHIP COMPANY, DETROIT, MI

Incorporated 18 August 1924, from a merger of the Nicholson Transit Company with the Universal Carloading and Distributing Company. Acquired by the United States Freight Company on 15 May 1925, and then by the Overlakes Freight Corporation on 15 March 1932. Ceased operations at the beginning of World War II. Acquired by the Troy H. Browning Steamship Company in February of 1949. The enterprise was dissolved on 1 December 1953, with the property transferred to the Lake Fleet Division of Republic Steel Corporation.

Nicholson saves money on miles. [N.p., 1925?]. [16] p. Illus., map. MiD-D.

NIPIGON TRANSPORT, LIMITED, CALGARY, ALB

Formed on 11 August 1961, by the Hanna Mining Company. It was sold to the Algoma Central Railway on 27 March 1986.

Christening ceremony performed at Collingwood, Ontario, by Mrs. R[obert] F[erdinand] Anderson [on] Tuesday, April 28, 1981, [of the] M[otor] V[essel] "Lake Wabush." [N.p., 1981]. [4] p. Illus. On cover: Collship. CaOKMM.

NORTH SHORE NAVIGATION COMPANY OF ONTARIO, LIMITED., COLLINGWOOD, ONT

Established on 22 February 1890. Popularly known as the Black Line. Merged on 15 March 1899 with the Great Northern Transit Company to form the Northern Navigation Company of Ontario.

From hot pavements to breezy decks of Georgian Bay steamers [of the] Georgian Bay Royal Mail Line. [Chicago, 1890?]. 1 sheet folded to [10] p. Illus., map. CaOOA.

Route to the World's Fair, season 1893. Toronto: Mail Job Print, [1893]. 1 sheet folded to [14] p. Illus., map. CaOONL.

Pocket time table of the North Shore Navigation Co. of Ontario, Ltd., [the] Georgian Bay Royal Mail Line to Sault S[ainte] Marie, Mackinac, Parry Sound & French River, season 1894. Collingwood, ONT: Enterprise Print, [1894]. 1 sheet folded to [8] p. Illus. CaOOA.

The tourist's favorite routes via the North Shore Navigation Company of Ontario, Ltd. Collingwood, ONT: Bulletin Print, [1894]. 1 sheet folded to 16 [i.e. 20] p. Illus., map. MiU-T.

NORTH-WEST TRANSPORTATION COMPANY, LIMITED, SARNIA, ONT

Established on 5 March 1877. Popularly known as the Beatty Line. In 1900 it merged with the Northern Navigation Company of Ontario.

Lake Superior Royal Mail Line running regularly between Detroit, Windsor, Courtright, Sarnia, Goderich, Kincardine, Southampton, and all ports on Lakes Huron and Superior, season 1880. Toronto: Globe Printing Co., [1880]. 1 sheet folded to [12] p. Illus., map. CaOKQ.

The favorite lake route between the North-west and Pacific Coast and all points in Canada and the eastern states. Toronto: Mail Job Print, [1896?]. 1 sheet folded to [16] p. Illus., map. CaOOA.

Beatty's Sarnia Line, the highest class Canadian passenger steamers on the lakes. Toronto: Mail Job Print, [1897?]. 1 sheet folded to [4] p. CaOOA.

North-West Transportation Co., Ltd., running between Windsor, Sarnia, Sault S[ain]te Marie, Fort William, Port Arthur, and Duluth, season of 1898. Sarnia: Sarnia Canadian Print, [1898]. [12] p. Illus., map. CaOOA.

North-West Transportation Co., Ltd., running between Windsor, Sarnia, Sault S[ain]te Marie, Fort William, Port Arthur, and Duluth, season of 1900. Sarnia: Sarnia Canadian Print, [1900]. [12] p. Illus., map. CaOOA.

NORTH-WEST TRANSPORTATION, NAVIGATION & RAILWAY COMPANY, TORONTO, ONT

Established in 1858. Reorganized in March of 1859 as the North West Transit Company, and its charter expired in 1860.

The North-West Transportation, Navigation, and Railway Company: its objects. By Allan MacDonell. Printed by order of the board [of directors]. Toronto: Lovell and Gibson, 1858. 55, [1] p. CaACG, CaBViPA, CaOONL, CtY.

Prospectus of the North-West Transportation, Navigation, and Railway Company. Toronto: Globe Book and Job Office, 1858. 12 p. CaACG, CaOONL, MnHi.

NORTHERN MICHIGAN TRANSPORTA-TION COMPANY, CHICAGO, IL

Acquired the Seymour Transportation Company in 1895. Popularly known as the Northern Michigan Line. Became the Michigan Transit Company on 2 May 1918, when it merged with the Merchants Transit Company. Ceased operations in 1931.

Time table, summer schedule, season 1901. [Chicago?, 1901]. 1 sheet folded to [4] p. Illus. MiLuRH.

Summer tours on the Great Lakes. Chicago: Poole Bros., [1903]. 30 [i.e. 16] p. Illus., map. MiD-D, OBgU.

Trust deed dated Oct. 1, 1903, Northern Michigan Transportation Company to Royal Trust Company and H[arry] E. Ambler, trustees. Chicago: Gunthorp-Warren Printing Co., [1903]. 24 p. NNC.

Summer tours on the Great Lakes. Chicago: Poole Bros., [1905]. 30 [i.e. 16] p. Illus., map. Mi, MiD-D.

Summer tours on the Great Lakes, season 1906. Chicago: Poole Bros., [1906]. 30 [i.e. 16] p. Illus., map. OBgU.

Northern Michigan Transportation Co. and Manitou Steamship Company joint summer schedules, season 1907. Chicago: Poole Bros., [1907]. 1 sheet folded to [4] p. Illus. CSmH, OBgU.

Summer tours on the Great Lakes, season 1908. Chicago: Poole Bros., [1908]. 22 [i.e. 12] p. Illus., map. MiManiHi.

Northern Michigan Line, 1910. Chicago: Poole Bros., [1910]. 15, [1] p. Illus., map. MiU-H, OBgU, WM.

Northern Michigan Line, 1911. Chicago: Poole Bros., [1911]. 15, [1] p. Illus., map. MSaP, ViNeM.

Northern Michigan Line, 1912. Chicago: Poole Bros., [1912]. 19, [1] p. Illus., map. MSaP, OBgU, WM.

Northern Michigan Line, 1913. Chicago: Poole Bros., [1913]. 19, [1] p. Illus., map. MiD-D, WM.

Northern Michigan Line, 1915. Chicago: Poole Bros., [1915]. 19, [1] p. Illus., map. OBgU.

Summer tours via the Great Lakes, one way and round trip fares from Chicago or Milwaukee, season 1916. Chicago: W[illiam] F[ranklin] Hall Printing Co., [1916]. 24 p. WMCHi.

Northern Michigan Line. Chicago: Poole Bros., [1917]. 45 [i.e. 16] p. Illus., map. MiD-D.

NORTHERN NAVIGATION COMPANY, LIMITED, SARNIA, ONT

Created in March of 1910 as the successor to the Northern Navigation Company of Ontario. Acquired by the Richelieu & Ontario Navigation Company on 26 June 1911. Became the semi-independent Northern Navigation Division of Canada Steamship Lines on 4 December 1913. Originally called the "Grand Trunk Route," it was familiarly known as the Canadian National Route from 1923, when the Grand Trunk System was merged into the Canadian National Railways. It continued to operate until the end of the 1949 season. Dissolved as a corporation in August of 1983.

Northern Navigation Co., Limited, [the] Grand Trunk Route, a fresh water sea voyage, that Georgian Bay trip among the 30,000 islands, season 1910. Chicago: Poole Bros., [1910]. 46 [i.e. 24] p. Illus., map. CaOTPB, MiU-H.

Northern Navigation Company, Limited, directors' report and financial statement [for the] year ending December 31st, 1910. [N.p., 1911]. [8] p. IU.

Spring schedules, 1911. Sarnia: Sarnia Port Print, [1911]. 1 sheet folded to [4] p. CaOOA.

Northern Navigation Company, Limited, directors' report and financial statement [for the] year ending December 31st, 1911. [N.p., 1912]. 8 p. IU.

Lake Superior and Georgian Bay and 30,000 Islands. [N.p., 1912]. 46 [i.e. 24] p. Illus., map. Issued July 6, 1912. CaOTPB, WM.

Rules and regulations for officers and crews, 1912. Port Huron: Riverside Printing Co., [1912]. 77, [1] p. CaOKQAR.

Book of tours, 1913. [N.p., 1913]. 82 p. Maps. IU.

Buffalo, Niagara Falls, Toronto [and] Hamilton, 1913. Chicago: Poole Bros., 1913. 14 [i.e. 8] p. Illus., map. MSaP.

Lake Superior and Georgian Bay and 30,000 Islands. [N.p., 1913]. 46 [i.e. 24] p. Illus., map. Issued May, 1913. WM.

Northern Navigation Company, Limited, directors' report and financial statement [for the] year ending December 31st, 1912. [N.p., 1913]. 7, [1] p. IU.

Lake Superior, Georgian Bay and the 30,000 Islands. [N.p., 1914?]. 1 sheet folded to [8] p. Map. ViNeM.

Lake Superior, Georgian Bay and the 30,000 Islands, a fresh water voyage. Detroit: Campbell-Ewald Co., [1914]. 46 [i.e. 24] p. Illus., map. MSaP, MiD-D, OClWHi.

Lake Superior, Georgian Bay, and the 30,000 Islands. Detroit: Campbell-Ewald Co., [1915]. 36 [i.e. 20] p. Illus., map. CaOOA, Mi.

Lake Superior, Georgian Bay and Lake Huron Great Lakes cruises. Detroit: Campbell, Ewald Advertiser's Service, 1916. 44 [i.e. 24] p. Illus., map. MiShM, OBgU, WM.

The Northern Navigator. — Vol. 1, no. 1 (1916)-vol. 13, no. 7 (1928). — Daily newsletter while on cruise. Illus., map. Edition varies with each ship. Continued by: C.S.L. Chart [of the] Northern Navigation Divison. CaOOA, MiD-D, OBgU.

"That Georgian Bay and 30,000 Islands trip." [Detroit?, 1917?]. 1 sheet folded to [8] p. Illus., map. MiD-B.

Rules and regulations for officers and crews, revised 1917. Sarnia: Canadian Printing Co., [1917]. 52 p. CaOKQAR.

Lake Superior, Georgian Bay and Lake Huron. Detroit: The Stubbs Co., [1918]. 30 [i.e. 16] p. Illus., map. May edition. CaOOA, MiD-B, MiD-D.

Day trips from Detroit to Wallaceburg [and] to Chatham. [N.p., 1919]. 1 sheet folded to [12] p. Illus., map. MiD-B, OBgU.

Great Lakes cruises. [N.p., 1919]. 15 [i.e. 8] p. Illus., map. CaOOA, MSaP, WM.

Great Lakes cruises. Toronto: Southam Press, [1920]. 24 p. Illus., map. CaOOA, MiPhM, OBgU.

Lake Superior to the sea, an inland water voyage on the Great Lakes and far-famed St. Lawrence and Saguenay Rivers. By Garnault Agassiz. Montreal: Ronalds Press & Advertising Agency, [1920]. 96 p. Illus. CaQMMRB.

Schedules, 1920. [N.p., 1920]. 1 sheet folded to [12] p. Illus. OBgU.

Souvenir song book. [N.p., 1920?]. 43, [1] p. Words only. Pagination varies with each edition. CaOKQ, MiD-D, MiMtpC, MoKU.

Great Lakes cruises. Montreal: Ronalds Press and Advertising Agency, 1921. 16, [4] p. Illus., maps. CSmH, MiD-D, OBgU.

Great Lakes cruises. Chicago: Poole Bros., [1922]. 19 [i.e. 10] p. Illus., map. CaOOA, MiD-D, WM.

Great Lakes cruises. Chicago: Poole Bros., [1922]. 19, [1] p. Illus., map. CaQMMRB.

Great Lakes cruises. Montreal: Ronalds Press and Advertising Agency, [1923]. 19, [1] p. Illus., map. CaOOA, CSmH.

Great Lakes cruises [by the] Northern Navigation Company, Limited, [the] Canadian National route owned by Canada Steamship Lines. Detroit: John Bornman & Son, [1923]. 19, [1] p. Illus., map. ViNeM.

Canadian National route travelling East or West, the Great Lakes cruise provides a rest, 1924. Chicago: Poole Bros., [1924]. 23 [i.e. 12] p. Illus., map. CSmH, MiD-D, WM.

Travelling East or West, the Great Lakes cruise provides a rest. Chicago: Poole Bros., [1925]. 23, [1] p. Illus., map. CSmH, MiD-D.

Travelling East or West, the Great Lakes cruise provides a rest. Chicago: Poole Bros., [1926]. 23, [1] p. Illus., map. CSmH.

Travelling East or West, the Great Lakes cruise provides a rest. Chicago: Poole Bros., [1927]. 23, [1] p. Illus., map. CSmH, ViNeM.

C.S.L. Chart [of the] Northern Navigation Division. — Vol. 14, no. 1 (1928)-vol. 17, no. 7 (1933?). — Montreal?, 1928-1933? Illus. Issued daily on cruises, with a special edition for each of the three ships. Continues: The Northern Navigator. CaOKMM, OBgU.

Northern Navigation Co., Limited, owned and operated by Canada Steamship Lines, Ltd. Chicago: Poole Bros., [1928]. 23, [1] p. Illus., map. ViNeM.

Souvenir song book. Sarnia: Frontier Printing Co., [1928?]. [2], 48, [2] p. Words only. CaQMMRB.

Northern Navigation Division [of the] Canada Steamship Lines, Ltd. [promotional and time tables]. [Chicago, 1929]. 23, [1] p. Illus., map. At bottom: In the locks at the "Soo." CaOKMM, MiD-D, ViNeM.

Northern Navigation Division of the Canada Steamship Lines, Limited, season 1930. [Chicago?, 1930]. 46 [i.e. 24] p. Illus., map. MiD-D, OBgU.

Northern Navigation Division of the Canada Steamship Lines, Limited, season 1931. [Chicago: Poole Bros., 1931]. 46 [i.e. 24] p. Illus., map. At bottom: In the locks at the "Soo." MiD-D, OBgU.

Northern Navigation Division of the Canada Steamship Lines, Limited, season 1932. Chicago: Poole Bros., [1932]. 38 [i.e. 20] p. Illus., map. At bottom: In the locks at the "Soo." MiD-D, ViNeM.

Northern Navigation Division of the Canada Steamship Lines, Limited, season 1933. [Chicago?, 1933]. 38 [i.e. 20] p. Illus., map. At bottom: In the locks at the "Soo." MiD-D, MiShM, OBgU, ViNeM.

Vacation trips on the tideless seas of North America by the inland liners of the Canada Steamship Lines Northern Navigation Division. New York: Ronalds Resale Agency, c1934. 20 p. Illus., map. MiD-D.

Cruise the Great Lakes on the water highway between East and West, ideal for one way travel [or] for vacation cruises [by the Northern Navigation Division]. Chicago: Poole Bros., 1935. 1 sheet folded to [16] p. Illus., map. March issue. MdBUS, ViNeM.

All-expense cruises on the Great Lakes, 1936. Chicago: Poole Bros., 1936. 1 sheet folded to [10] p. Illus., map. Folder J. ViNeM.

Cruise the Great Lakes on the water highway between East and West, ideal for one way travel [or] for vacation cruises [with the Northern Navigation Division]. Chicago: Poole Bros., 1936. [12] p. Illus., map. March issue. Folder B. CU-SB, MdBUS, MiD-D, ViNeM.

Cruising America's great inland seas on the water highway between East and West, ideal for one way travel [or] for vacation cruises [with the Northern Navigation Division]. Chicago: Poole Bros., 1937. [16] p. Illus., map. Folder B. CSFMM, OFH, ViNeM.

Time tables [for] Windsor-Detroit-Sarnia and Sault S[ain]te Marie, Port Arthur-Fort William, also to and from Duluth, 1937. [Montreal?, 1937]. 1 sheet folded to [6] p. Issued April, 1937. Folder M. OBgU.

Cruising America's great inland seas on the water highway between East and West, ideal for vacation cruises or one way travel [with the] Northern Navigation Division. [Chicago?, 1938]. [16] p. Illus., map. Folder B. CU-SB, OBgU, ViNeM.

Cruising America's great inland seas on the water highway between East and West, ideal for vacation cruises or one way travel [with the] Northern Navigation Division, season 1939. [Chicago?, 1939]. [16] p. Illus., map. Folder B. CSmH, CU-SB, MiD-D, WM.

Great Lakes cruises from Duluth to Port Arthur, Sault S[ain]te Marie, Sarnia, Windsor, Detroit, and New York World's Fair. [Chicago?, 1939]. 1 sheet folded to [6] p. Illus. MnDuLS.

Cruising America's great inland seas on the water highway between East and West, ideal for vacation cruises or one way travel [with the] Northern Navigation Division, season 1940. [Chicago?, 1940]. [16] p. Illus., map. Folder B. CSmH, CU-SB, MdBUS, MiD-D, MnDuLS.

Cruise the Great Lakes for a glorious economical vacation [with the Northern Navigation Division]. [Chicago: Poole Bros., 1941]. 1 sheet folded to [8] p. Illus., map. April issue. CU-SB, MdBUS, MiD-D.

The glorious Great Lakes, cruise America's legendary East-West water highway [on the] Northern Navigation Division. [Chicago?], 1941. [16] p. Illus., map. April issue. [Folder B]. PPPMM, ViNeM.

The glorious Great Lakes, cruise America's legendary East-West water highway [on the] Northern Navigation Division. [Montreal?], 1941. [8] p. Illus., map. May issue. Folder B-1. ViNeM.

Northern Navigation Division time tables, 1941. [Montreal?, 1941]. 1 sheet folded to [6] p. Folder M. CU-SB.

Cruise the Great Lakes for a glorious economical vacation [with the Northern Navigation Division]. [Chicago: Poole Bros., 1942]. 1 sheet folded to [8] p. Illus., map. May edition. CU-SB.

The glorious Great Lakes, cruise America's legendary East-West water highway [on the] Northern Navigation Division. [Chicago?, 1942]. [16] p. Illus., map. April issue. CSmH, CU-SB, MdBUS, MiD-D.

Happiness [is a] Lake Superior rail-water cruise tour. [Chicago]: Carl Gorr Prtg., 1942. 1 sheet folded to [8] p. Illus. ViNeM.

Special June cruise [on the] S.S. Noronic. [Chicago?, 1942]. 1 sheet folded to [4] p. Illus. CU-SB.

The glorious Great Lakes, cruise America's legendary East-West water highway [on the] Northern Navigation Division. [Chicago?], 1943. [16] p. Illus., map. April issue. CU-SB, MiD-D, ViNeM.

Northern Navigation Division time tables, 1943. [Montreal?, 1943]. 1 sheet folded to [6] p. Folder M. CU-SB.

The glorious Great Lakes, season 1944 [for the] Northern Navigation Division. [Chicago?], 1944. [16] p. Illus., map. April edition. CU-SB, MdBUS, MiD-D, OFH, ViNeM.

Northern Navigation Division time tables, 1945. [Montreal?, 1945]. 1 sheet folded to [6] p. Folder M. CSmH.

Fascinating trips on the breezy Great Lakes aboard [the] largest [and] finest lake liners, season 1945. [Chicago?], 1945. [2], 12, [2] p. Illus., map. April issue. [Folder B]. CSmH, CU-SB, CaBVaMM, CaOPsM, MSaP, MdBUS, MiD-D, MiShM, OBgU, ViNeM.

Fascinating trips on the breezy Great Lakes aboard [the] largest [and] finest lake liners, season 1945. [Montreal?, 1945]. [12] p. Illus., map. May issue. Folder B1. CaOMM.

Fascinating trips on the breezy Great Lakes aboard [the] largest [and] finest lake liners, season 1946. [Chicago?, 1946]. [2], 12, [2] p. Illus., map. April issue. CSmH, MdBUS, MiD-D, OBgU.

Fascinating trips on the breezy Great Lakes aboard [the] largest [and] finest lake liners, season 1946. [Chicago?, 1946]. [12] p. Illus., map. May issue. MiD-D, OBgU.

Canada Steamship Lines [Northern Navigation Division] presents the Detroit-Duluth cruise, season 1947. [Chicago?, 1947]. [28] p. Illus., maps. Cover title: Over the deep. April issue. Folder B. MiD-D, OBgU, OV.

Canada Steamship Lines [Northern Navigation Division] presents the Detroit-Duluth cruise, season 1948. [Chicago?, 1948]. [28] p. Illus., maps. Cover title: Over the deep. April issue. Folder B. CSmH, CaOONL, MnDuC.

Canada Steamship Lines [Northern Navigation Division] presents the Detroit-Duluth cruise, season 1949. [Chicago?, 1949]. [2], 12, [2] p. Illus., maps. Cover title: Over the deep. CU-SB.

Canada Steamship Lines [Northern Navigation Division] presents the Detroit-Duluth cruise, season 1949. [Chicago?, 1949]. [28] p. Illus., maps. Cover title: Over the deep. May issue. Folder B. CSmH, CaOOA, MiD-D.

Isle Royale 7-day, all-expense vacation from Duluth every Tuesday June 21 to August 30, 1949. [Chicago?, 1949]. 1 sheet folded to [4] p. Illus. MnDuU.

Northern Navigation Division time tables, 1949. [Montreal?, 1949]. 1 sheet folded to [6] p. February edition. Folder M. MiD-D.

NORTHERN NAVIGATION COMPANY OF ONTARIO, LIMITED, COLLINGWOOD, ONT

Created on 16 March 1899 by the merger of the North Shore Navigation Company and the Great Northern Transit Company. In 1900 the firm absorbed the North-West Transportation Company. Associated with the Grand Trunk Railway system. Name changed to Northern Navigation Company, Limited, on 5 March 1910.

Great Lake route between all Georgian Bay ports and Mackinac Island, season 1900. Toronto: Toronto Litho Co., [1900]. 39 [i.e. 20] p. Illus., map. CaOOA.

Among the 30,000 Islands of Georgian Bay, Grand Trunk Railway system and the Northern Navigation Co. of Ont., Limited, [the] picturesque Pan-American route to Buffalo. Battle Creek: Gage Printing Co., [1901]. 16 [i.e. 8] p. Folded map. Issued March, 1901, eleventh edition. MiD-D.

To Georgian Bay and Mackinac via Northern Navigation Co. of Ontario, Limited, 1901. [N.p., 1901]. 31, [1] p. Illus. Folded maps. MiD-B.

Sarnia & Lake Superior Division [of] the Northern Navigation Co. of Ontario, Limited, owners of and operating the North-West Transportation Company, Limited, the direct lake route to and from the Canadian and American West via Sarnia, Sault S[ain]te Marie, Port Arthur, Fort William, and Duluth, season 1902. Toronto: Mail Job Print, [1902]. 38 [i.e. 20] p. Illus., maps. MSaP, MiD-D.

30,000 Islands, Georgian Bay, Mackinac Is[land] and Lake Superior. Battle Creek: Gage Printing Co., [1902?]. 30 [i.e. 20] p. Illus., folding map. Page size varies. MSaP.

To Georgian Bay and Mackinac via Northern Navigation Co. of Ontario, Limited, 1902. Toronto: Mail Job Print, [1902]. 39 [i.e. 20] p. Illus., maps. CaOOA, OBgU.

Among the 30,000 Islands of Georgian Bay [via the] Grand Trunk Railway System and the Northern Navigation Co. of Ontario, Limited, 1903. Montreal: Gazette Printing Co., [1903]. 16 [i.e. 8] p. Illus. Fifteenth edition. OBgU.

Lakes Superior and Huron [on the route of the old North-West Transportation Company, Limited], 1903. [N.p., 1903]. 38 [i.e. 20] p. Illus., maps. CaOOA.

To Georgian Bay and Mackinac via Collingwood, Meaford, Owen Sound, Killarney, Sault S[ain]te Marie [and] Mackinac, 1903. [N.p., 1903]. 39 [i.e. 20] p. Illus., map. MSaP.

Lake Superior Division (formerly N[orth]W[est] T[rans-portation] Co.), Georgian Bay and Mackinac Division, [and the] Penetanguishene and Parry Sound Division 1904 summer service. [Chicago, 1904]. 30 [i.e. 16] p. Illus., map. CaOOA, CaOTPB, MSaP.

Thirty Thousand Islands, Georgian Bay, Mackinac and Lake Superior. Battle Creek: Gage Printing Co., [1904?]. 30 [i.e. 20] p. Illus., folded map. Page size varies. MiD-D.

30,000 Islands, Georgian Bay, Mackinac Island, and Lake Superior. Battle Creek: Gage Printing Co., [1904?]. [12] p. Illus., map. MSaP, Mi.

Lake Superior Division (formerly N[orth]W[est] T[transportation] Co.), Georgian Bay and Mackinac Division, [and the] Penetanguishene and Parry Sound Division, season 1905. [Chicago: Poole Bros., 1905]. 30 [i.e. 16] p. Illus., map. CaOOA, DLC.

Lake Superior Division (formerly N[orth]W[est] T[transportation] Co.), Georgian Bay and Mackinac Division, [and the] Penetanguishene and Parry Sound Division, season 1906. Chicago: Poole Bros., [1906]. 30 [i.e. 16] p. Illus., map. MSaP, ViNeM.

Mortgage deed of trust [of the] Northern Navigation Company of Ontario, Limited, to the Toronto General Trusts Corporation, to secure an issue of 5% ten-year gold bonds amounting to $500,000.00, dated 25th September, 1908. [Toronto?, 1908]. 20, [2] p. CaOTAr.

30,000 Islands, Georgian Bay, Mackinac Island and Lake Superior. Chicago: Poole Bros., [1908]. 12 p. Illus., map. MiD-D.

A fresh water sea voyage via Northern Navigation Company Grand Trunk route to Sault S[ain]te Marie, Port Arthur, Fort William, Duluth, and Northwest and Pacific Coast, summer 1909. [N.p., 1909]. [12] p. Illus., map. WManiM.

Lake Superior and Georgian Bay. [Chicago, 1909]? 38 [i.e. 20] p. Illus., map. MiU-H.

The Northern Navigation Company of Ontario, Limited, directors' report and financial statement [for the] year ending December 31st, 1908. [N.p., 1909]. 8 p. IU.

The Northern Navigation Company of Ontario, Limited, directors' report and financial statement [for the] year ending December 31st, 1909. [N.p., 1910]. 8 p. IU.

NORTHERN STEAMSHIP COMPANY, BUFFALO, NY

Incorporated 12 June 1888, and owned by the Great Northern Railway. Commenced passenger service in 1894. In 1916 it became part of the Great Lakes Transit Corporation.

The great northern country, being the chronicles of the Happy Travellers Club in their pilgrimage across the American continent as traversed by the Great Northern Railway line and Northern Steamship Co. from Buffalo to the Pacific Coast. [St. Paul?, 1894?]. 169, [21] p. Illus., map. CU-BANC, MH, RPB, WaT.

The itinerary. Buffalo: Matthews-Northrup Co., [1894]. 52, [2] p. Illus., map. CSmH.

Northern Steamship Co. exclusively passenger steel steamships North West and North Land, season of 1894.

Buffalo: Matthews-Northrup Co., [1894]. 16 p. Cover title: Description of the new, exclusively passenger steamships "North West" and "North Land." OClWHi.

Northern Steamship Company [connecting] Buffalo, Duluth, and the Pacific Coast, 1895. Chicago: Rand, McNally & Co., [1895]. 1 sheet folded to 20 [i.e. 40] p. Illus., maps. July edition. CSmH, NBuHi.

The Northern Steamship Co.'s exclusively passenger steamships North West and North Land operating on the Great Lakes. [Cleveland: Britton Printing Co., 1895]. 92 p. Illus. CLU, MiD-B, MnHi, NN, OBgU, WM.

A summer cruise on inland seas via the Great Lakes to the far West. [Chicago: Poole Bros., 1896]. 37, [3] p. Illus., maps. OBgU.

East and West via the Great Lakes. Chicago: Poole Bros., c1896. 1 sheet folded to [12] p. Illus., maps. CSmH.

The great northern country, being the chronicles of the Happy Travellers Club in their pilgrimage across the American continent as traversed by the Great Northern Railway line and Northern Steamship Co. from Buffalo to the Pacific Coast. Edited and illustrated by R.S. Howe [and] published under the auspices of the passenger departments of the Great Northern Railway and Northern Steamship Co. [N.p., 1896?]. 217, [1] p. Illus., maps. MnHi.

The itinerary [of] Great Lakes tours, an accurate compilation of rates and general information of interest to all tourists. Chicago: Poole Bros., [1896]. 64 p. Illus., map. MnHi, NBuHi.

A summer cruise on inland seas via the Great Lakes to the far West, a description of the trip, the steamships, and the points of interest. Chicago: Poole Bros., [1896]. 37, [3] p. Illus., maps. MdBUS, MnHi, OBgU.

East and West via the Great Lakes. Chicago: Poole Bros., [1897]. 1 sheet folded to [24] p. Illus., maps. MSaP.

In all the world no trip like this. Buffalo: Gies & Co., [1897?]. [32] p. Illus., map. MiD-B, MiU-C.

The itinerary [of] Great Lakes tours, a compilation of rates and general information of interest to all tourists. Chicago: Poole Bros., [1897]. 54 p. Illus., map. Mi.

In all the world no trip like this. Buffalo: Gies & Co., [1898]. 1 sheet folded to 24 p. Illus., maps. Effective June 25th, 1898. MiD-B, MiD-D.

In all the world no trip like this. Buffalo: Gies & Co., [1898]. [32] p. Illus., map. CSmH, CtMyMHi, DSI, DeU, Mi, MiMtpC.

In all the world no trip like this. [N.p., 1899]. 1 sheet folded to [4] p. Illus. NBuHi.

In all the world no trip like this, 1899. Buffalo: Matthews-Northrup Co., [1899]. 1 sheet folded to 28 [i.e. 32] p.

Illus., map. May 1 edition. MSaP, MiD-D, MiMtpC, ViNeM.

In all the world no trip like this, 1899. Buffalo: Matthews-Northrup Co., [1899]. 1 sheet folded to 28 [i.e. 32] p. Illus., maps. July edition. CtY, NBuHi.

The North West Cyclone. — Vol. 1, no. 1 (1894?)-vol. 17?, no. 5 (1910?). — Published on board S.S. North West, 1894?-1910?. Illus. Irregular. Cataloging based on September, 1899 edition. NBuHi.

In all the world no trip like this, 1900. Chicago: Poole Bros., [1900]. 32 [i.e. 16] p. Illus., map. June edition. CaOOA, MiD-D.

In all the world no trip like this, 1900. Chicago: Poole Bros., [1900]. 32 [i.e. 16] p. Illus., map. July edition. MSaP, MiD-D.

In all the world no trip like this, 1901. Chicago: Poole Bros., [1901]. 30 [i.e. 16] p. Illus., map. June edition. CaOOA, CtY, MiD-D, WMCHi.

In all the world no trip like this, 1901. Chicago: Poole Bros., [1901]. 30 [i.e. 16] p. Illus., map. July edition. MSaP.

East and West via the Great Lakes, season 1902. Chicago: Poole Bros., [1902]. 30 [i.e. 16] p. Illus., map. MdBUS.

The great northern country, illustrating and describing the country, industries and scenery along the lines of the Great Northern Railway and Northern Steamship Company. St. Paul: Great Northern Railway, 1903. [160] p. Illus., map. WaU.

In all the world no trip like this. Buffalo: Matthews-Northrup Works, [1903]. 30 [i.e. 16] p. Illus., map. MiD-D.

In all the world no trip like this. Chicago: Poole Bros., [1904]. 30 [i.e. 16] p. Illus., map. CaOOA, MSaP, MiD-B, OBgU.

In all the world no trip like this, to see the World's Fair, St. Louis, 1904. Chicago: Poole Bros., [1904]. 30 [i.e. 16] p. Illus., map. OBgU.

In all the world no trip like this, to see the World's Fair, St. Louis, 1904. Chicago: Poole Bros., [1904]. 30 [i.e. 16]. p. Illus., map. July edition. MSaP.

East and West via the Great Lakes, in all the world no trip like this. Chicago: Poole Bros., [1905]. 30 [i.e. 16] p. Illus., map. June edition. ViNeM.

East and West via the Great Lakes, in all the world no trip like this, 1906. Chicago: Poole Bros., [1906]. 30 [i.e. 16] p. Illus., map. July edition. MSaP, Mi.

East and West via the Great Lakes, in all the world no trip like this, 1907. [Chicago: Poole Bros., 1907]. 30 [i.e. 16] p. Illus., map. June edition. MSaP.

The Great Lakes of America, in all the world no trip like this, 1908. Chicago: Poole Bros., 1908. 30 [i.e. 16] p. Illus., map. June edition. MiD-D, NBuHi, ViNeM.

In all the world no trip like this. Chicago: Poole Bros., [1909]. [20] p. Illus., map. June edition. CSmH, CaOOA, MSaP, MiD-D.

In all the world no trip like this. Chicago: Poole Bros., [1910]. 38 [i.e. 20] p. Illus., map. June edition. DLC, MSaP.

In all the world no trip like this. St. Paul: Pioneer Company, 1911. 38 [i.e. 20] p. Illus., maps. Cover title: Buffalo, Duluth, Chicago. MiD-D.

Buffalo - Chicago, 1912. [N.p., 1912]. 21 [i.e. 12] p. Illus., map. CSmH.

In all the world no trip like this. Chicago: Poole Bros., [1913]. 30 [i.e. 16] p. Illus., map. MiD-D.

Northern Steamship Company [and] Great Northern Railway [service to] Buffalo-Cleveland-Detroit-Mackinac Island-Harbor Springs-Milwaukee-Chicago, in all the world no trip like this, season 1915. Chicago: Poole Bros., [1915]. 30 [i.e. 16] p. Illus., map. MSaP, MiD-D, ViNeM.

Northern Steamship Company [and] Great Northern Railway [service to] Buffalo-Cleveland-Detroit-Mackinac Island-Harbor Springs-Milwaukee-Chicago, in all the world no trip like this, season 1916. Chicago: Poole Bros., [1916]. 30 [i.e. 16] p. Illus., map. CSmH, MiD-D, ViNeM.

NORTHERN TRANSIT COMPANY, CLEVELAND, OH

Organized in March of 1876 as successor to the Northern Transportation Company. Ceased to exist around 1900.

The scenic route of America, sailing through [the] Detroit River, Lake Erie, Welland Canal [and] Niagara Falls by daylight, [plus] Lake Ontario and a daylight ride through the Thousand Islands and the Rapids of the St. Lawrence River to Montreal. [N.p., 1899]. [12] p. Illus., map. CaOOA.

NORTHERN TRANSPORTATION COMPANY, OGDENSBURG, NY

Incorporated on 12 March 1855, as a subsidiary of the Central Vermont Railway. Ceased operations in January of 1876 and reorganized as the Northern Transit Company.

Act of incorporation, organization and by-laws of the Northern Transportation Company, organized March 12, 1855. Cleveland: Harris, Fairbanks & Co., 1855. 20 p. OClWHi.

OCEANIC SUN LINE SPECIAL SHIPPING COMPANY, INCORPORATED, ATHENS

Established in 1957, apparently as a Greek firm. Still active in 1990 as the Sun Line Cruises Company, New York NY.

Great Lakes and St. Lawrence Seaway cruises [on the] M[otor] S[hip] Stella Maris, 1974 7 day cruises. [N.p., 1974]. 1 sheet folded to [16] p. Illus., map. CSmH, MiD-D, MiShM, OBgU, WM, WManiM.

OGLEBAY, NORTON & COMPANY, CLEVELAND, OH

Established in 1890. Incorporated on 15 March 1932. On 17 October 1957 the firm was reorganized as the Oglebay Norton Company, at which time it merged with the Columbia Transportation Company and eight other associated businesses.

Raw materials for the metallurgical, ceramic, and chemical industries [carried by] lake transportation. [Cleveland?, 1947]. 79, [1] p. Illus. OClWHi.

Raw materials for the metallurgical, ceramic, and chemical industries [carried by] lake transportation. [Cleveland?, 1952]. 78, [2] p. Illus. OBgU.

OGLEBAY NORTON COMPANY, CLEVELAND, OH

Created on 17 October 1957, as successor to Oglebay, Norton & Company. Still active in 1990.

Contract between Columbia Transportation Division, Oglebay Norton Company, and the Lake Sailors Union, Independent, November 22, 1959, amended May 6, 1960, ratified May 27, 1960. [Cleveland, 1960]. 44 p. OBgU.

Telephone directory, Columbia Transportation Division, Oglebay Norton Company, 1960. [Cleveland?, 1960]. 41, [3] p. OV.

Safety rules for employees, Columbia Transportation Division, Oglebay Norton Company, 1972. [Cleveland?, 1972?]. 28 p. OBgU.

Shipmate. — Vol. 1, no. 1 (Summer 1978)-present. — Cleveland, 1978-present. Illus. Semiannual. MiD-D, MnDuC, OBgU, OV, WManiM

Agreement between Columbia Transportation Division, Oglebay Norton Company, and District 2, Marine Engineers Beneficial Association, Associated Maritime Officers, AFL-CIO, covering licensed officers and stewards, August 1, 1977. [Cleveland?, 1977]. 88 p. OBgU.

Supplemental unemployment benefit plan between Columbia Transportation Division, Oglebay Norton Company, and United Steelworkers of America and its

Local 5000, effective August 1, 1977. [Cleveland?, 1977]. 16 p. OBgU.

Program of insurance benefits for unlicensed seamen and their dependents of Columbia Transportation Division, Oglebay Norton Company, pursuant to agreement with United Steelworkers of America, as amended effective August 1, 1979. [Cleveland?, 1979]. 66 p. OBgU.

ONTARIO. ONTARIO NORTHLAND TRANSPORTATION COMMISSION, NORTH BAY, ONT

Established in 1902. Acquired the operations of the Owen Sound Transportation Company on 31 March 1974. Still active in 1990.

Go marine, the government of Ontario's roadways over the waterways [describing] an improved service between the Bruce Peninsula and Manitoulin Island. [Toronto?, 1974]. 1 sheet folded to [6] p. Illus., maps. CaOKMM.

M[otor] S[hip] Chi-Cheemaun [christening]. [N.p., 1974]. [8] p. Illus. CaOColM.

Be my guest aboard the Chi-Cheemaun & Nindawayma [by taking the] crossing challenge. [N.p., 1990]. 24 p. Illus., maps. MiD-D.

Be my guest [on the] M[otor] S[hip] Chi-Cheemaun [and] M[otor] S[hip] Nindawayma. [N.p., 1990]. 1 sheet folded to [6] p. Illus., map. MiD-D.

ONTARIO & OHIO NAVIGATION COMPANY, LIMITED, CLEVELAND, OH

Established around 1910. Ceased to exist around 1921 and route apparently taken over by the Western Reserve Navigation Company.

The short way [across Lake Erie]. Cleveland: Eisele Ptg. Co., [1910]. 1 sheet folded to [6] p. Illus., map. CaOOA.

ONTARIO & QUEBEC NAVIGATION COMPANY, LIMITED, PICTON, ONT

Incorporated on 8 March 1905, as successor to the Montreal, Rochester & Quebec Transit Company. Acquired by the Richelieu & Ontario Navigation Company in 1913. Dissolved on 21 October 1963.

The Montreal, Rochester and Quebec Line, [with the] steamer Alexandria [serving] Buffalo, Olcott Beach, Rochester, Thousand Is[lands], Montreal, St. Lawrence Rapids, Quebec [and] Bay of Quinte. [N.p., 1906?]. 1 sheet folded to [16] p. Illus., map. CaOOA.

The Montreal, Rochester and Quebec Line, [with the] steamer Alexandria [serving] Buffalo, Olcott Beach, Rochester, Thousand Is[lands], Montreal, St. Lawrence

Rapids, Quebec [and] Bay of Quinte. [N.p., 1907]. 1 sheet folded to [16] p. Illus., map. CaOOA.

The Montreal, Rochester and Quebec Line, [with the] steamer Alexandria [serving] Buffalo, Rochester, Thousand Islands, Montreal, St. Lawrence Rapids, Quebec [and] Bay of Quinte. [N.p., 1908]. 1 sheet folded to [16] p. Illus., map. CaOOA.

The Montreal, Rochester and Quebec Line, [with the] steamer Alexandria [serving] Buffalo, Rochester, Thousand Islands, Montreal, St. Lawrence Rapids, Quebec [and] Bay of Quinte. [N.p., 1910]. 1 sheet folded to [16] p. Illus., map. CaOOA.

St. Lawrence River Line [to] Toronto, Rochester, Bay of Quinte, St. Lawrence River rapids, Montreal, [and] Quebec. [Montreal: Southam, Ltd., 1911]. [12] p. Illus., map. CaOOA, NR.

St. Lawrence River Line [to] Rochester, Bay of Quinte, St. Lawrence River rapids, Montreal, [and] Quebec. Montreal: Southam, Limited, [1912?]. [12] p. Illus., map. MSaP.

ONTARIO & ST. LAWRENCE STEAMBOAT COMPANY, OSWEGO, NY

Apparently established in 1852. Comprised of the United States Mail Line (U.S.?) and the American Express Line (Canadian?). Possibly sold to the Royal Mail Line in 1868.

Great northern and eastern steamboat and rail road route, the cheapest, most expeditious and only direct route from Buffalo and Niagara Falls to Montreal, Saratoga Springs, White Mountains and Boston via [the] American line of steamers on Lake Ontario and River St. Lawrence..., 1852. Buffalo: Wightman, [1852]. [2] p. Map. NBuHi.

The Ontario and St. Lawrence Steamboat Company's hand-book for travelers to Niagara Falls, Montreal and Quebec, and through Lake Champlain to Saratoga Springs. Buffalo: Jewett, Thomas & Co., Geo. H. Derby and Co., 1852. [2], 158 p. Illus., folded map. Across top of title page: The great northern route, American Lines. Cover title: Niagara Falls, Montreal, Quebec, Saratoga, &c. CU-BANC, CaBVaU, CaOKQ, CaOOA, DLC, ICHi, MH, MH-BA, MHi, MoSHi, NBu, NN, NNH, NRU, NcD, NjP, OCl, OClWHi, OFH, OO.

The Ontario and St. Lawrence Steamboat Company's hand-book for travelers to Niagara Falls, Montreal and Quebec, and through Lake Champlain to Saratoga Springs. Buffalo: Jewett, Thomas & Co., Geo. H. Derby and Co., 1852. [2], 152 p. Illus., map. At head of title: The great northern route, American Lines. Cover title: Niagara Falls, Montreal, Quebec, Saratoga, &c. CaBVaU, CaOH, CaOKQ, CaOLU, CaOTPB, CaQMBN, MHi, MWA, MiD-B, MiU-C, NN, NRU, PHi.

The Ontario and St. Lawrence Steamboat Company's hand-book for travelers to Niagara Falls, Montreal and Quebec, and through Lake Champlain to Saratoga Springs. Buffalo: Jewett, Thomas & Co.; Rochester: D[ellon] M. Dewey, 1853, c1852. 174 p. Illus., map. Across top of title page: The great northern route, American Lines. CSt, CaOOA, CaOOP, CaOStCB, CaOTPB, DLC, DeU, MH, MHi, MWA, MiD-B, NBuHi, NRU, OCl, PP.

The Ontario and St. Lawrence Steamboat Company's hand-book for travelers to Niagara Falls, Montreal and Quebec, and through Lake Champlain to Saratoga Springs. Buffalo: Jewett, Thomas & Co.; Rochester: D[ellon] M. Dewey, 1854, c1852. 175, [1] p. Illus., folded map. Across top of title page: The great northern route, American Lines. Cover title: Niagara Falls, Montreal, Quebec, Saratoga, &c. CaOONL, CtY, MH, MWA, NBuHi.

Hand-book descriptive of the route to Ogdensburgh [sic], Montreal, Quebec, etc., via Lake Ontario and River St. Lawrence, etc. Niagara Falls: W[illiam] E. Tunis, 1856. 10 p. Map. MH.

ONTARIO CAR FERRY COMPANY, LIMITED, TORONTO, ONT

Incorporated on 30 November 1905. Owned jointly by the Grand Trunk Railway Company (later the Canadian National) and the Buffalo, Rochester & Pittsburg Railway Company (later the Baltimore & Ohio). Commenced service on 19 November 1907, but did not carry passengers until 1909. Ceased operations on 30 April 1950. Dissolved on 9 November 1954.

Summer schedule [for the] S.S. Ontario No. 1 between Rochester and Cobourg, 1910. [N.p., 1910]. 1 sheet folded to [4] p. Illus. CaOOA.

Summer schedule [of the] Buffalo, Roshester and Pittsburgh R[ailwa]y and [the] Ontario Car Ferry Company [operating] steamships Ontario No. 1 and No. 2 between Rochester, N.Y., and Cobourg, Ont. [N.p., 1924]. 1 sheet folded to [4] p. Illus. CaOOA.

Summer schedule [of the] Buffalo, Rochester and Pittsburgh R[ailwa]y and Ontario Car Ferry Company between Rochester, N.Y., and Cobourg, Ont. [N.p., 1928]. 1 sheet folded to [8] p. Illus. CaOKMM.

Rochester, N.Y., and Cobourg, Ont., steamship route, 1931 summer schedule. [Rochester?, 1931]. 1 sheet folded to [8] p. Illus., map. MiD-D.

Rochester [to] Cobourg steamship route, 1932 summer schedule. [Rochester?, 1932]. 1 sheet folded to [8] p. Illus., map. MiD-D, OBgU.

A steamer trip on Lake Ontario between Cobourg and Rochester. [N.p., 1939]. 1 sheet folded to [8] p. Illus., map. CaOTPB.

A steamer trip on Lake Ontario between Cobourg and Rochester. [N.p., 1940]. 1 sheet folded to [8] p. Illus., map. MdBUS.

A steamer trip on Lake Ontario between Cobourg and Rochester. [N.p., 1942]. 1 sheet folded to [8] p. Illus., map. NR.

A steamer trip on Lake Ontario between Cobourg and Rochester. [N.p.], 1944. 1 sheet folded to [6] p. Illus., map. May edition. CU-SB, OFH.

A steamer trip on Lake Ontario between Cobourg and Rochester. [N.p.], 1945. 1 sheet folded to [6] p. Illus., map. April edition. CSmH.

A steamer trip on Lake Ontario between Cobourg and Rochester. [N.p.], 1947. 1 sheet folded to [6] p. Illus., map. April edition. CSmH, CaOOA.

A steamer trip on Lake Ontario between Cobourg and Rochester. [N.p.], 1948. 1 sheet folded to [6] p. April edition. CU-SB.

ORANJE LINE, ROTTERDAM, HOL

Established on 16 July 1937, as the Seatransport Company, Limited. Initiated Great Lakes service in 1938. Operated under the British flag in World War II. After the War the firm was represented in the United States by Overseas Shipping, Incorporated, of Chicago and, later, by Great Lakes Overseas, Incorporated. Ceased to exist on 31 December 1970.

Great Lakes-St. Lawrence Seaway cruises, 1961. [N.p., 1961]. 1 sheet folded to [12] p. Illus., map. CSmH, MiD-D, ViNeM.

Great Lakes-St. Lawrence Seaway cruises, 1962. [The Netherlands, 1962]. 1 sheet folded to [10] p. Illus., map. CSmH, MiD-B, OBgU.

OWEN SOUND TRANSPORTATION COM-PANY, LIMITED, OWEN SOUND, ONT

Incorporated 10 March 1921. Joined with the Dominion Transportation Company in a pooling agreement in 1936, and took over complete management of the firm in 1937. Purchased on 31 March 1974, by the government of Ontario and operated thereafter by the Ontario Northland Transportation Commission.

5 days in historic waters [like] Georgian Bay, Manitoulin Island, [and] Mackinac Island [on the] S.S. Manitoulin. [N.p., 1927]. [8] p. Illus., map. CaOOA, MSaP, MiD-B.

Georgian Bay, Manitoulin, Mackinac Island, [and] Sault S[ain]te Marie [on] schedule [with the] S.S. Manitoulin, [offering] Mackinac and week-end excursions and spring and fall sailings. [N.p., 1927]. 1 sheet folded to [4] p. CaOOA.

5 days in historic waters [like] Georgian Bay, Manitoulin Island, [and] Mackinac Island. [N.p., 1928]. [8] p. Illus., map. CaOOA.

The famous Mackinac cruise via Georgian Bay and Manitoulin Island. [N.p., 1929]. [8] p. Illus., map. CaOOA.

The famous Mackinac cruise via Georgian Bay and Manitoulin Island [on the] S.S. Manitoulin. [N.p., 1930?]. [8] p. Illus., map. MiD-B, MiD-D.

The famous Mackinac cruise via Georgian Bay and Manitoulin Island [on the] S.S. Manitoulin. [N.p., 1931?]. 1 sheet folded to [12] p. Illus., map. WM.

Mackinac, Georgian Bay, and Manitoulin Island services. [N.p., 1931]. [8] p. Illus., map. MiD-D.

Low cost lake cruise vacation through picturesque Georgian Bay, Lake Huron and North Channel. [N.p., 1932]. [8] p. Illus., map. MiD-D.

Mackinac, Georgian Bay, [and] Manitoulin Island [on the] S.S. "Manitoulin." [N.p., 1933]. 1 sheet folded to [12] p. Illus., map. MiD-D, WM.

Motorist's short-cut to Manitoulin Island and north shore, save 150 mile motor drive via Tobermory. [N.p., 1933]. 1 sheet folded to [4] p. Illus., maps. MiD-D.

The famous Mackinac cruise via Georgian Bay and Manitoulin Island [on the] S.S. Manitoulin. [N.p., 1935?]. [8] p. Illus., map. MiD-D, WM.

Come! Cruise with us to Manitoulin, the north shore, North Channel ports, Sault Ste. Marie, Michipicoten [and] Mackinac Island. [N.p., 1936?]. 1 sheet folded to [16] p. Illus., map. WM.

Local freight tariff no. J1[-J16? providing] local class and commodity rates between Owen Sound and Killarney, Manitoulin Island ports, North Channel ports, and Sault S[ain]te. Marie, Ont. [N.p., 1936?-1959?]. 4 p. Irregular, but often annually. CaOOwM.

Local passenger tariff no. J1[-J16?] between Owen Sound and Sault Ste. Marie and intermediate ports, and between Owen Sound and Providence Bay and intermediate ports, and between Owen Sound and Meaford and Collingwood. [N.p., 1936-1956?]. 1 sheet folded to [4] p. Irregular, but often annually. Title varies. Published jointly with the Dominion Transportation Company until 1949. CaOOwM, MiD-D.

Sailing schedule, 1936 season. [N.p., 1936]. 1 sheet folded to [8] p. Illus. Published jointly with the Dominion Transportation Company. MiD-D.

Sailing schedule, 1937 season. [N.p., 1937]. 1 sheet folded to [8] p. Illus. Published jointly with the Dominion Transportation Company. MiD-D.

The shortest route to Manitoulin and the north shore, Tobermory to South Bay Mouth [sic] ferry service. [N.p., 1937]. 1 sheet folded to [8] p. Illus., maps. ViNeM.

The shortest route to Manitoulin and the north shore, Tobermory to South Bay Mouth [sic] ferry service. [N.p., 1939]. 1 sheet folded to [8] p. Illus., map. MiD-D.

1000 mile Great Lakes cruise, summer 1939. [N.p., 1939]. 1 sheet folded to [12] p. Illus., map. Published jointly with the Dominion Transportation Company. OBgU.

Great Lakes cruise 1000 miles, 5 or 6 days, summer 1940. [N.p., 1940]. 1 sheet folded to [12] p. Illus., map. Published jointly with the Dominion Transportation Company. CaOONL, MiD-D.

The national emergency demands you "keep fit" [with a] 5 day, 1000 mile cruise on Georgian Bay, St. Mary's River [and] Whitefish Bay. [N.p., 1941]. 1 sheet folded to [12] p. Illus., map. Published jointly with the Dominion Transportation Company. MiD-D.

The shortest route to Manitoulin & north shore, [the] Tobermory-South Bay Mouth [sic] ferry. [N.p., 1942]. 1 sheet folded to [8] p. Illus., maps. MiD-D.

Cruise 1000 miles on Georgian Bay, St. Mary's River [and] Whitefish Bay. [N.p., 1943]. 1 sheet folded to [12] p. Illus., map. Published jointly with the Dominion Transportation Company. MiD-D, OFH.

Summary of sailings, 1943. [N.p., 1943]. [2] p. Published jointly with the Dominion Transportation Company. MiD-D.

Cruise 1000 miles on Georgian Bay, St. Mary's River [and] Whitefish Bay. [N.p., 1944]. 1 sheet folded to [12] p. Illus., map. Published jointly with the Dominion Transportation Company. MiD-D, OFH.

The shortest route to Manitoulin & north shore [on the] Tobermory-South Bay Mouth [sic] ferry. [N.p., 1944]. 1 sheet folded to [4] p. Illus., map. MiD-D, OFH.

Cruise 1000 miles on Georgian Bay, St. Mary's River [and] Whitefish Bay. [N.p., 1945]. 1 sheet folded to [12] p. Illus., map. Published jointly with the Dominion Transportation Company. MiD-D, OFH.

Summary of sailings, 1945. [N.p., 1945]. 2 p. Published jointly with the Dominion Transportation Company. MiD-D.

Tobermory-South Bay Mouth [sic] ferry, the shortest route to Manitoulin Island and north shore. [N.p., 1945]. 1 sheet folded to [4] p. Illus., map. MiD-D.

Cruise 1000 miles on Georgian Bay, St. Mary's River [and] Whitefish Bay. [N.p., 1946]. 1 sheet folded to [12] p. Illus., map. Published jointly with the Dominion Transportation Company. MiD-D, OFH.

Notes & News. — Vol. 1, no. 1 (1946?) - vol. ?, no. ? (1950)? — [Owen Sound, 1946-1950]? Daily during cruises. Near-print. Continued by: Bulletin. MiD-D.

Tobermory - South Bay Mouth [sic] ferry, the shortest route to Manitoulin Island and north shore. [N.p., 1946]. 1 sheet folded to [4] p. Illus., map. MiD-D, OFH.

Cruise 1000 miles on Georgian Bay, St. Mary's River [and] Whitefish Bay. [N.p., 1947]. 1 sheet folded to [12] p. Illus., map. Published jointly with the Dominion Transportation Company. MiD-D, MiShM.

New auto ferry [to] Tobermory - South Bay Mouth [sic] [on] the all steel-modern-fireproof S.S. Norisle, the shortest route to Manitoulin Island and north shore. [N.p., 1947]. 1 sheet folded to [4] p. Illus., map. MiD-D.

Summary of sailings, 1947. [N.p., 1947]. 2 p. Published jointly with the Dominion Transportation Company. MiD-D.

Cruise 1000 miles on Georgian Bay, St. Mary's River [and] Whitefish Bay. [N.p., 1948]. 1 sheet folded to [12] p. Illus., map. Published jointly with the Dominion Transportation Company. MiD-D.

New auto ferry [to] Tobermory - South Bay Mouth [sic] [on] the all steel-modern-fireproof S.S. Norisle, the shortest route to Manitoulin Island and north shore. [N.p., 1948]. 1 sheet folded to [4] p. Illus., map. OFH.

Summary of sailings, 1948. [N.p., 1948]. [2] p. Published jointly with the Dominion Transportation Company. MiD-D.

Cruise 1000 miles on Georgian Bay, St. Mary's River [and] Whitefish Bay. [N.p., 1949]. 1 sheet folded to [12] p. Illus., map. MiD-D.

New auto ferry [to] Tobermory - South Bay Mouth [sic] [on] the all steel-modern-fireproof S.S. Norisle, the shortest route to Manitoulin Island and north shore. [N.p., 1949]. 1 sheet folded to [4] p. Illus., map. MiD-D.

Cruise 1000 miles on Georgian Bay, St. Mary's River [and] Whitefish Bay. [N.p., 1950]. 1 sheet folded to [12] p. Illus., map. MiD-D.

Summary of sailings, 1950. [N.p., 1950]. [2] p. MiD-D.

Bulletin. — Vol. 1, no. 1 (1951?)-vol. ?, no. ? (1962?). - Owen Sound, 1951?-1962?. Near-print. Issued daily on cruises. Continues: Notes & News. CaOKMM.

Cruise on Georgian Bay, St. Mary's River [and] Whitefish Bay. [N.p., 1951]. 1 sheet folded to [12] p. Illus., map. MdBUS, MiD-D, OBgU, WM.

The shortest route to Manitoulin Island, Sault S[ain]te Marie and North Shore [by] auto ferry [is] the all steel-modern-fireproof S.S. Norisle. [N.p., 1951]. 1 sheet folded to [4] p. Illus., map. MdBUS, MiD-D.

Summary of sailings, 1951. [N.p., 1951]. [2] p. MiD-D.

Cruise through vistas of sky-blue water, its [sic] different, delightful, and so inexpensive. [N.p., 1952?]. 1 sheet folded to [12] p. Illus., map. CaOKMM, MiD-D, MiShM, OBgU, OFH.

The shortest route to Manitoulin Island, Sault S[ain]te Marie and north shore [via] auto ferry [is] the all steel-modern-fireproof S.S. Norisle. [N.p., 1952]. 1 sheet folded to [4] p. Illus., map. MiD-D.

Summary of sailings, 1952. [N.p., 1952]. 2 p. MiD-D.

Summary of sailings, 1954. [N.p., 1954]. 2 p. MiD-D.

The shortest route to Manitoulin Island, Sault S[ain]te Marie and north shore auto ferry. [N.p., 1955]. 1 sheet folded to [4] p. Illus. map. OFH.

Summary of sailings, 1955. [N.p., 1955]. [2] p. MiD-D.

Cruise through vistas of sky-blue water, its [sic] different, delightful, and so inexpensive. [N.p., 1956]. 1 sheet folded to [12] p. Illus., map. MiD-D.

The shortest route to Manitoulin Island, Sault S[ain]te Marie and north shore [via] auto ferry [is] the all steel-modern-fireproof S.S. Norisle. [N.p., 1956]. 1 sheet folded to [4] p. Illus., map. MiD-D.

Summary of sailings, 1956. [N.p., 1956]. [2] p. MiD-D.

Land of the sky-blue water. [N.p., 1957?]. 18 p. Folded map inside cover. CaOOwCG.

The shortest route to Manitoulin Island, north shore uranium area, and Sault S[ain]te Marie. [N.p., 1957]. 1 sheet folded to [4] p. Illus., map. OBgU.

Cruise through vistas of sky-blue water, its [sic] different, delightful, and so inexpensive. [N.p., 1958?]. 1 sheet folded to [12] p. Illus., map. CaOKMM, MiD-D.

The shortest route to Manitoulin Island, north shore uranium area, and Sault S[ain]te Marie. [N.p., 1958]. 1 sheet folded to [4] p. Illus., map. MiD-D.

Summary of sailings, 1958. [N.p., 1958]. [2] p. MiD-D.

The shortest route to Manitoulin Island, north shore uranium area, and Sault S[ain]te Marie. [N.p., 1959]. 1 sheet folded to [4] p. Illus., map. CaOKMM, MiD-D.

Circular quoting commodity rates, including pick-up and/or delivery service between stations in Ontario and Quebec (as listed herein) and ports of call on Georgian Bay and Lake Huron, including Sault S[ain]te Marie, Ont., (as listed herein). [N.p., 1961]. 12 p. [i.e. leaves]. Effective July 31st, 1961. Near-print. CaOOwM.

Cruise through vistas of sky-blue water, its [sic] different, delightful, and so inexpensive. [N.p., 1961]. 1 sheet folded to [12] p. Illus., map. MiD-D.

The shortest route to Manitoulin Island, Sault S[ain]te Marie & Lake Superior highway. [N.p., 1961]. 1 sheet folded to [4] p. Illus., map. MiD-D.

The short route to Manitoulin Island, Sault S[ain]te Marie & Lake Superior highway. [N.p., 1962]. 1 sheet folded to [4] p. CaOKMM, MiBayHi, MiD-D.

Ferry service to Manitoulin Island, Tobermory-South Bay Mouth [sic]-Blind River-Meldrum Bay [with] 2 large ships [making] up to 5 trips daily. [Owen Sound, ONT: Richardson, Bond & Wright, 1964]. 1 sheet folded to [8] p. Illus., map. CaOOwCG.

Ferry service to Manitoulin Island, Tobermory-South Bay Mouth [sic]-Blind River-Meldrum Bay [with] 2 large ships [making] up to 5 trips daily. [Owen Sound, ONT: Richardson, Bond & Wright, 1965]. 1 sheet folded to [8] p. Illus., map. CaOOwCG, MdBUS, MiD-D, MiShM, OFH, WM.

Ferry service to Manitoulin Island, Tobermory-South Bay Mouth [sic]-Blind River-Meldrum Bay [with] 2 large ships [making] up to 5 trips daily. [Owen Sound, ONT: Richardson, Bond & Wright, 1966]. 1 sheet folded to [8] p. Illus., map. MiD-D.

Ferry service to Manitoulin Island, Tobermory-South Bay Mouth [sic]-Blind River-Meldrum Bay [with] 2 large ships [making] up to 5 trips daily. [Owen Sound, ONT: Richardson, Bond & Wright, 1967]. 1 sheet folded to [8] p. Illus., map. CaOOwCG, CaOOwM.

Ferry service to Manitoulin Island, Tobermory [and] South Bay Mouth [sic]-Blind River-Meldrum Bay [with] 2 large ships [making] up to 5 trips daily. [Owen Sound, ONT: Richardson, Bond & Wright, 1968]. 1 sheet folded to [8] p. Illus., map. CaOOwCG, MiD-D, MiMtpC, MiShM, OBgU.

Ferry service to Manitoulin Island, Tobermory-South Bay Mouth [sic] [with] 2 large ships [making] up to 5 trips daily, 1970. [Owen Sound, ONT: Richardson, Bond & Wright, 1970]. 1 sheet folded to [4] p. Illus. CaOOwM.

Ferry service to Manitoulin Island, Tobermory-South Bay Mouth [sic] [with] 2 large ships [making] up to 5 trips daily, 1971. [Owen Sound, ONT: Richardson, Bond & Wright, 1971]. 1 sheet folded to [4] p. Illus. OBgU.

Ferry service to Manitoulin Island, Tobermory-South Bay Mouth [sic] [with] 2 large ships [making] up to 5 trips daily, 1972. [Owen Sound, ONT: Richardson, Bond & Wright, 1972]. 1 sheet folded to [4] p. Illus. MiD-D.

Ferry service to Manitoulin Island, Tobermory-South Bay Mouth [sic] [with] 2 large ships [making] up to 5 trips daily, 1973. [Owen Sound, ONT: Richardson, Bond & Wright, 1973]. 1 sheet folded to [4] p. Illus. CaOKMM, CaOOwCG, CaOOwM, OBgU.

Temporary schedule, Tobermory-South Baymouth ferry service, 1974. [Owen Sound, ONT: Richardson, Bond &

Wright, 1974]. 1 sheet folded to [6] p. Illus. CaOOwCG, MiD-D, MiShM, OBgU, WM.

A way north, [the] M[otor] S[hip] Chi-Cheemaun [serving] Tobermory [and] South Baymouth, 1975 rates and schedule. [N.p., 1975]. 1 sheet folded to [8] p. Map. CaOKMM, MiD-D, OBgU.

Tobermory-South Bay Mouth [sic] ferry service [by the] M[otor] S[hip] "Chi-Cheemaun," 1976. [N.p., 1976]. 1 sheet folded to [6] p. Illus., map. MdBUS, MiD-D, MiShM, OBgU.

Tobermory-South Bay Mouth [sic] ferry service [by the] M[otor] S[hip] "Chi-Cheemaun," 1977. [N.p., 1977]. 1 sheet folded to [6] p. Illus., map. OBgU.

Tobermory-South Bay Mouth [sic] ferry service [by the] M[otor] S[hip] "Chi-Cheemaun," 1978. [N.p., 1978]. 1 sheet folded to [6] p. Map. MiD-D, MiMtpC, MiShM, OBgU, WM.

Traverse, Tobermory, South Bay Mouth [sic] ferry service [by the] M[otor] S[hip] Chi-Cheemaun, 1979. [N.p., 1979]. 1 sheet folded to [8] p. Illus., map. OBgU, WM.

Chi-Cheemaun challenge. [N.p., 1980]. 24 p. Illus., map. CaOOwCG, MdBUS.

Traverse, Tobermory-South Bay Mouth [sic] ferry service [by the] M[otor] S[hip] Chi-Cheemaun, 1980. [N.p., 1980]. 1 sheet folded to [8] p. Map. MdBUS, MiD-D, WM.

Traverse, Tobermory, South Bay Mouth [sic] ferry service [by the] M[otor] S[hip] Chi-Cheemaun, 1981. [N.p., 1981]. 1 sheet folded to [8] p. Illus., map. CaOOwM, OBgU.

Traverse, Tobermory, South Bay Mouth [sic] ferry service [by the] M[otor] S[hip] Chi-Cheemaun, 1982. [N.p., 1982]. 1 sheet folded to [8] p. Illus., map. CaOOwM, OBgU.

Traverse, Tobermory, South Bay Mouth [sic] ferry service, 1983. [N.p., 1983]. 1 sheet folded to [8] p. Illus., map. MiD-D, WM.

Traverse, Tobermory, South Bay Mouth [sic] ferry service [by the] M[otor] S[hip] Chi-Cheemaun, 1984. [N.p., 1984]. 1 sheet folded to [8] p. Illus., map. CSmH, MiD-D, WM.

Traverse ferry service to Tobermory & South Bay Mouth [sic] [by the] M[otor] S[hip] Chi-Cheemaun, 1985. [N.p., 1985]. 1 sheet folded to [10] p. Illus., map. CaOOwM, MiD-D, MiShM, OBgU.

Traverse ferry service to Tobermory & South Bay Mouth [sic] [by the] M[otor] S[hip] Chi-Cheemaun, 1986. [Weston, ONT: Southam Murray, 1986]. 1 sheet folded to [6] p. Illus., map. MiD-D, OBgU.

Traverse ferry service to Tobermory & South Bay Mouth [sic] [by the] M[otor] S[hip] Chi-Cheemaun, 1987. [Meaford, ONT: Grey Bruce Advertising, 1987]. 1 sheet folded to [6] p. Illus., map. CaOOwM, MiD-D.

Traverse ferry service to Tobermory & South Bay Mouth [sic] [by the] M[otor] S[hip] Chi-Cheemaun, 1988. [Toronto: Maher Printing, 1988]. 1 sheet folded to [6] p. Illus., map. MiD-D, OBgU.

Traverse ferry service to Tobermory & South Bay Mouth [sic] [by the] M[otor] S[hip] Chi-Cheemaun, 1989. [Toronto: Maher Printing, 1989]. 1 sheet folded to [6] p. Illus., map. MiD-D, MiShM.

Scheduled ferry service between Tobermory & South Baymouth, be my guest [in] 1990 [on the] M[otor] S[hip] Chi-Cheemaun [and] M[otor] S[hip] Nindawayma. [North Bay, ONT: Journal Printing, 1990]. 1 sheet folded to [6] p. Text in French and English. MiD-D, OBgU.

PARKER BOAT LINE, INCORPORATED, PUT-IN-BAY, OH

Incorporated on 13 December 1961. Dissolved on 2 February 1989.

Take a "mini-cruise" to Put-in-Bay on South Bass Island. Kenton, OH: Blosser Color Ads, [1971]. 1 sheet folded to [6] p. Illus., map. OFH.

Take a "mini-cruise" to Put-in-Bay on South Bass Island. Kenton, OH: Blosser Color Ads, [1973]. 1 sheet folded to [6] p. Illus., map. OBgU, OFH.

Scenic mini-cruise to Put-in-Bay and the Bass Islands. Kenton, OH: Blosser Color Ads, [1974]. 1 sheet folded to [6] p. Illus., map. OBgU.

Take the Parker mini-cruise to Put-in-Bay on South Bass Island. [N.p., 1984]. 1 sheet folded to [4] p. Illus. MiD-D, OBgU.

Enjoy the panoramic view to Put-in-Bay. [N.p., 1985]. 1 sheet folded to [6] p. Illus., map. OBgU.

PATERSON STEAMSHIPS, LIMITED, THUNDER BAY, ONT

Established on 10 February 1926. Became Paterson (Norman McLeod) & Sons, Limited, on 31 July 1950.

The Paterson News. — Vol. 1, no. 1 (October 1944)-vol. 2, no. 6 (March 1946). — Winnipeg, 1944-1946. Illus. Monthly. Re-established as vol. 1, no. 1 in June of 1985 under same title, and then publication suspended. OBgU.

PELEE ISLAND TRANSPORTATION SERVICES, PELEE ISLAND, ONT

Apparently established in 1960 as successor to the Pelee Shipping Company, Limited. Still active in 1990.

See Canada [on] daily excursions [by the] M[otor] V[essel] Pelee Islander, passenger and auto ferry. [N.p., 1979]. 1 sheet folded to [4] p. Map. MdBUS.

Cruise to Canada or [the] United States [on the] M[otor] V[essel] Pelee Islander, passenger and auto ferry. [N.p., 1980?]. 1 sheet folded to [6] p. Map. MdBUS, OBgU.

Cruise to Canada or [the] United States [on the] M[otor] V[essel] Pelee Islander, passenger and auto ferry. [N.p., 1981]. 1 sheet folded to [6] p. Map. OBgU.

Cruise to Canada or [the] United States [on the] M[otor] V[essel] Pelee Islander, passenger and auto ferry. [N.p., 1982]. 1 sheet folded to [6] p. Map. OBgU.

Cruise to Canada or [the] United States [on the] M[otor] V[essel] Pelee Islander [or] M.V. Upper Canada. [N.p., 1984]. 1 sheet folded to [6] p. Map. MiD-D, OBgU.

Cruise to Canada or [the] United States [on the] M[otor] V[essel] Pelee Islander [or] M.V. Upper Canada. [N.p., 1985]. 1 sheet folded to [6] p. Map. OBgU.

Cruise to Canada or [the] United States [on the] M[otor] V[essel] Pelee Islander [or] M.V. Upper Canada, daily crossings between Sandusky, Ohio, Pelee Island, Kingsville, or Leamington. [N.p., 1990]. 1 sheet folded to [6] p. Map. MiD-D.

PELEE SHIPPING COMPANY, LIMITED, ST. THOMAS, ONT

Commenced operations in May of 1941. Incorporated on 10 July 1944. Dissolved on 10 January 1979, and apparently succeeded by Pelee Island Transportation Services.

Take a restful short cut across Lake Erie to Canada on the S.S. Pelee, [a] modern car ferry [with] daily trips from Sandusky, Ohio to Leamington, Ontario, via Pelee Island. [N.p., 1941]. [12] p. Illus., maps. CU-SB, OFH.

Take a restful short cut across Lake Erie to Canada on the S.S. Pelee, [a] modern car ferry [with] daily trips from Sandusky, Ohio, to Leamington, Ontario, via Pelee Island. [N.p., 1942?]. [12] p. Illus., maps. CU-SB.

Take a restful short cut across Lake Erie to Canada on the S.S. Pelee, [a] modern auto ferry [with] daily crossings from Sandusky, Ohio, to Leamington or Kingsville, Ontario, via Pelee Island. [N.p.]: Hains Studios, c1943. [12] p. Illus., map. MiD-D.

See Canada [on] daily excursions [via] a short cut across Lake Erie on the Steamer Pelee, [a] modern passenger and auto ferry. [N.p.]: Hains Studios, c1944. 1 sheet folded to [10] p. Illus., map. CU-SB, MdBUS, MiD-D, OBgU, OFH.

See Canada [on] daily excursions [via] a short cut across Lake Erie on the Steamer Pelee, [a] modern passenger and auto ferry. [N.p.], 1945. 1 sheet folded to [12] p. Illus., map. CU-SB.

See Canada [on] daily excursions [via] a short cut across Lake Erie on the Steamer Pelee, [a] modern passenger and auto ferry. [N.p., 1946]. 1 sheet folded to [12] p. Illus., map. CU-SB, MdBUS, MiD-D, OBgU, OFH.

See Canada [on] daily excursions [via] a short cut across Lake Erie on the Steamer Pelee, [a] modern passenger and auto ferry. [N.p., 1947]. 1 sheet folded to [12] p. Illus., map. MdBUS, OBgU, OFH.

See Canada [on] daily excursions [via] a short cut across Lake Erie on the Steamer Pelee, [a] modern passenger and auto ferry. [N.p., 1948]. 1 sheet folded to [12] p. Illus., map. CU-SB, MiD-D, OBgU, OFH.

See Canada [on] daily excursions [via] a short cut across Lake Erie on the Steamer Pelee, [a] modern passenger and auto ferry. [N.p.], 1949. 1 sheet folded to [8] p. Illus., map. CU-SB, OBgU.

See Canada [on] daily excursions [via] a short cut across Lake Erie on the Steamer Pelee, [a] modern passenger and auto ferry. [N.p., 1950]. 1 sheet folded to [8] p. Illus., map. MiD-D, MiShM.

See Canada [on] daily excursions [via] a short cut across Lake Erie on the Steamer Pelee, [a] modern passenger and auto ferry. [N.p., 1951]. 1 sheet folded to [8] p. Illus., map. MdBUS, MiD-D, OBgU.

See Canada [on] daily excursions [via] a short cut across Lake Erie on the Steamer Pelee, [a] modern passenger and auto ferry. [N.p., 1953]. 1 sheet folded to [4] p. Illus., map. OFH.

See Canada [on] daily excursions [via] a short cut across Lake Erie on the Steamer Pelee, [a] modern passenger and auto ferry. [N.p., 1954]. 1 sheet folded to [4] p. Illus., map. OFH.

See Canada [on] daily excursions [via] a short cut across Lake Erie on the Steamer Pelee, [a] modern passenger and auto ferry. [N.p., 1956]. 1 sheet folded to [4] p. Illus., map. OBgU.

See Canada [on] daily excursions [via] a short cut across Lake Erie on the Steamer Pelee, [a] modern passenger and auto ferry. [N.p., 1957]. 1 sheet folded to [4] p. Illus., map. MiD-D, OBgU.

See Canada [on] daily excursions [via] a short cut across Lake Erie on the Steamer Pelee, [a] modern passenger and auto ferry. [N.p., 1958]. 1 sheet folded to [4] p. Illus., map. MiD-D, OFH.

Spring and fall schedule. [N.p., 1959]. 1 sheet folded to [4] p. MiD-D.

PENINSULA & NORTHERN NAVIGATION COMPANY, MILWAUKEE, WI

Incorporated on 7 July 1923, as a New York firm. Began service in June of 1924, ostensibly as a business controlled by Canadians. Sources disagree as to whether the firm ceased operations in 1928 or 1929.

Short cut route across Lake Michigan between Milwaukee and Grand Haven. Chicago: Poole Bros., [1924]. 1 sheet folded to [6] p. Illus., map. MiD-D.

The short cut route across Lake Michigan [to] Milwaukee-Grand Haven-Muskegon. [N.p., 1925?]. 1 sheet folded to [12] p. Illus., map. WM.

Between Milwaukee, Grand Haven and Muskegon, the short cut route. [N.p., 1926?]. 1 sheet folded to [12] p. Illus., map. MiD-D, OBgU.

The short cut route between Milwaukee, Grand Haven and Muskegon. [N.p., 1927?]. 1 sheet folded to [12] p. Illus., map. WM, WMCHi.

Short cut route across Lake Michigan between Milwaukee and Grand Haven. Chicago: Poole Bros., [1928?]. 1 sheet folded to [12] p. Illus, map. CaOOA, WM, WMCHi.

The short cut route across Lake Michigan between Milwaukee, Grand Haven and Muskegon. [N.p., 1929?]. 1 sheet folded to [16] p. Illus., map. WM, WMCHi.

PENNSYLVANIA RAILROAD COMPANY, PHILADELPHIA, PA

Incorporated on 13 April 1846. Merged with the New York Central Railroad Company on 1 February 1968, to form the Pennsylvania New York Central Transportation Company.

Brief on behalf of the Pennsylvania Railroad Company before the Interstate Commerce Commission (Finance Docket No. 9109) [being] application of the Pennsylvania Railroad Company...in connection with the proposed operation jointly with the Grand Trunk Western Railroad Company of car ferries between Muskegon, Michigan, and Milwaukee, Wisconsin, etc. Philadelphia: Allen, Lane & Scott, [1932]. iv, 89, [1] p. MiU-H.

Reply on behalf of the Pennsylvania Railroad Company to the exceptions filed by the intervenor, the Wisconsin & Michigan Transportation Company, before the Interstate Commerce Commision (Finance Docket No. 9109) [being] application of the Pennsylvania Railroad Company...in connection with the proposed operation jointly with the Grand Trunk Western Rilroad Company car ferries between Muskegon, Michigan, and Milwuakee, Wisconsin, etc. Philadelphia: Allen, Lane & Scott, [1932]. ii, 50 p. MiU-H

PERE MARQUETTE RAILROAD COMPANY, MARINE DEPARTMENT, DETROIT, MI

Organized on 1 November 1899. Surrendered property to the Pere Marquette Railway Company on 9 April 1917.

Pere Marquette line steamers and Pere Marquette System short line to Michigan resorts, Canada, and the East, season 1912. Milwaukee: Evening Wisconsin Co., [1912]. 11, [1] p. Illus., map. WM.

Pere Marquette line steamers and railroad connections, [the] short line to Michigan resorts, Canada and the East, season 1914. Milwaukee: Evening Wisconsin Co., [1914]. 11, [1] p. Illus, map. WMCHi.

PERE MARQUETTE RAILWAY COMPANY, DETROIT, MI

Incorporated 12 March 1917. Acquired by the Chesapeake & Ohio Railway Company on 6 June 1947. Many of its schedules were issued in cooperation with the American Automobile Association.

Pere Marquette line steamers and railroad connections, [the] short line to Michigan resorts, Canada and the East, season 1917. Milwaukee: Evening Wisconsin Co., [1917]. 1 sheet folded to [10] p. Illus., map. ViNeM.

Pere Marquette line steamers and railroad connections, [the] short line to Michigan resorts, Canada and the East, season 1919. Milwaukee: Wisconsin Printing Co., [1919]. 1 sheet folded to [10] p. Illus., map. WM.

Pere Marquette line steamers and railroad connections, [the] short line to Michigan resorts, Canada and the East, season 1921. Milwaukee: Wisconsin Printing Co., [1921]. 1 sheet folded to [10] p. Illus., map. MiD-D.

Pere Marquette line steamers across Lake Michigan, [the] short line between Wisconsin & Michigan summer resorts, season 1922. Milwaukee: Wisconsin Printing Co., [1922]. 1 sheet folded to [20] p. Illus., map. ViNeM, WM.

Pere Marquette line steamers across Lake Michigan, [the] short line between Wisconsin & Michigan summer resorts, season 1923. Milwaukee: Wisconsin Printing Co., 1923. 1 sheet folded to [12] p. Illus., map. WM.

Pere Marquette line steamers across Lake Michigan, [the] short line between Wisconsin & Michigan summer resorts, season 1924. Milwaukee: Wisconsin Printing Co., [1924]. 1 sheet folded to [12] p. Illus., map. MiD-D, WM.

Pere Marquette line steamers, season of 1925. [N.p.], c1925. 1 sheet folded to [12] p. Illus, maps. CSmH, WM.

Pere Marquette line steamers, season of 1926. [N.p.], c1926. 1 sheet folded to [12] p. Illus., maps. OBgU, WM.

Pere Marquette line steamers, the shortest line (by 65 miles) between Wisconsin and Michigan summer resorts. [N.p., 1927]. 1 sheet folded to [12] p. Illus., map. WM.

Pere Marquette line steamers, the shortest line (by 65 miles) between Wisconsin and Michigan summer resorts. [N.p., 1928]. 1 sheet folded to [12] p. Illus., map. WM.

Pere Marquette auto route across Lake Michigan between Ludington, Mich., Manitowoc, Wis. and Milwaukee Wis. [N.p., 1929]. 1 sheet folded to [12] p. Illus., maps. MiD-D, WM.

Pere Marquette line steamers, the shortest line (by 65 miles) between Wisconsin and Michigan summer resorts. [N.p., 1929]. 1 sheet folded to [12] p. Illus., map. WM.

Ferry across Lake Michigan, Pere Marquette auto ferries. [N.p., 1930?]. 1 sheet folded to [12] p. Illus., maps. MiD-D.

Pere Marquette line steamers across Lake Michigan, 1930 schedule and rates, summer schedule in effect June 1 to Sept. 5. [N.p., 1930]. 1 sheet folded to [4] p. Illus. WM.

Pere Marquette line steamers "across Lake Michigan," season 1931. [N.p., 1931]. 1 sheet folded to [12] p. Illus., maps. MiManiHi, ViNeM.

Ferry across Lake Michigan, Pere Marquette auto ferries. [N.p., 1932]. 1 sheet folded to [12] p. Illus., maps. ViCFC.

Pere Marquette line steamers, season 1932. [N.p., 1932]. 1 sheet folded to [12] p. Illus., maps. MiD-D, ViNeM, WM, WMCHi.

Across Lake Michigan [to] Milwaukee-Grand Haven-Muskegon. [N.p., 1933]. 1 sheet folded to [12] p. Illus., map. MiD-D, OBgU.

Pere Marquette line steamers, the line that carries the U.S. mail. [N.p., 1933]. 1 sheet folded to [4] p. WM.

Across Lake Michigan [to] Milwaukee-Muskegon-Chicago-Ludington, 1934. [N.p., 1934]. 1 sheet folded to [12] p. Illus., map. MiD-D, OFH, ViCFC.

Auto ferry across Lake Michigan, Pere Marquette Railway auto ferries. [N.p.], 1934. 1 sheet folded to [6] p. Illus., map. November edition. ViCFC.

Ferry across Lake Michigan, 1934. [N.p., 1934]. 1 sheet folded to [12] p. Illus., maps. CU-SB, ViCFC, WM.

Auto ferries across Lake Michigan, 1935. [N.p., 1935]. 1 sheet folded to [12] p. Illus., maps. MiD-D, ViCFC, ViNeM, WM.

Auto ferries across Lake Michigan, Pere Marquette Railway auto ferries. [N.p.], 1935. 1 sheet folded to [4] p. Illus., map. ViCFC.

Auto ferry across Lake Michigan, Pere Marquette auto ferries. [N.p.], 1936. 1 sheet folded to [6] p. Illus., map. ViCFC.

Pere Marquette Railway auto ferries across Lake Michigan, 1936. [N.p., 1936]. 1 sheet folded to [12] p. Illus., maps. CU-SB, MSaP, MiD-D, ViCFC, ViNeM, WM.

Pere Marquette Railway auto ferries across Lake Michigan, 1937. [N.p., 1937]. 1 sheet folded to [24] p. Illus., maps. CSmH, CU-SB, MiD-D, MiShM, OBgU, ViCFC, ViNeM, WM.

Pere Marquette Railway auto ferries bridging Lake Michigan, 1938. [N.p., 1938]. 1 sheet folded to [24] p. Illus., maps. Effective April 1st, 1938. CU-SB, MiD-D, ViCFC, ViNeM, WM.

Pere Marquette Railway auto ferries bridging Lake Michigan, 1938. [Cleveland: A[rthur] S. Gilman, 1938]. 1 sheet folded to [6] p. Illus., map. Effective September 1, 1938. ViCFC.

Pere Marquette Railway auto ferries bridging Lake Michigan between Ludington, Mich., and Milwaukee, Manitowoc [and] Kewaunee, 1939. [Cleveland?, 1939]. 1 sheet folded to [24] p. Illus., maps. Effective April 15, 1939. CSmH, MSaP, MiD-D, MiShM, OBgU, OFH, ViCFC, ViNeM, WM.

Pere Marquette Railway auto ferries bridging Lake Michigan between Ludington, Mich., and Milwaukee, Manitowoc [and] Kewaunee. [Cleveland?, 1939]. 1 sheet folded to [6] p. Illus., map. Effective April 15, 1939. ViCFC.

Pere Marquette Railway auto ferries bridging Lake Michigan between Ludington, Mich., and Milwaukee, Manitowoc [and] Kewaunee. [Cleveland?, 1939]. 1 sheet folded to [6] p. Illus., map. Effective October 1, 1939. ViCFC.

Driving to the Fair? Take the direct short route to New York from Duluth, St. Paul, Minneapolis, and the Northwest [on the] Pere Marquette Railway auto ferries bridging Lake Michigan. [Cleveland: Horwood Printing Co., 1940]. 1 sheet folded to [6] p. Illus., map. MiD-D, ViCFC, WMCHi.

Out of the future comes the most modern, beautiful ship on the Lakes, the S.S. "City of Midland." [Cleveland?, 1940?]. [8] p. (one folded). Illus. MiLuRH, OBgU, WManiM.

Pere Marquette Railway auto ferries bridging Lake Michigan, 1940. [Cleveland?, 1940]. 1 sheet folded to [24] p. Illus., maps. Effective April 1, 1940. CSmH, MdBUS, MiD-D, OBgU, ViCFC, ViNeM.

Pere Marquette Railway auto ferries bridging Lake Michigan between Ludington, Mich., and Milwuakee, Manitowoc [and] Kewaunee. [Cleveland: A[rthur] S. Gilman Co., 1940]. 1 sheet folded to [6] p. Illus. Effective October 10, 1940. ViCFC.

Pere Marquette Railway auto ferries bridging Lake Michigan between Ludington, Mich., and Milwaukee, Manitowoc [and] Kewaunee. [Cleveland: A[rthur] S. Gilman Co., 1940]. 1 sheet folded to [6] p. Illus. Effective October 25, 1940. ViCFC.

Auto ferries schedules and rates. [Cleveland: T[homas] M. Reese Adv[ertising] Co., 1941]. 1 sheet folded to [4] p. Illus. Effective June 1, 1941. ViCFC, WManiM.

Pere Marquette Railway auto ferries bridging Lake Michigan, 1941. [Cleveland?, 1941]. 1 sheet folded to [24] p. Illus., maps. Effective May 1, 1941. CSmH, CU-SB, MdBUS, MiD-D, MiShM, OBgU, OFH, WManiM.

Pere Marquette Railway auto ferries bridging Lake Michigan between Ludington, Mich., and Milwaukee, Manitowoc [and] Kewaunee. [Cleveland: Ben Franklin Press, 1941]. 1 sheet folded to [6] p. Illus. Effective May 1, 1941. CSmH, MiD-D, ViCFC.

Pere Marquette Railway auto ferries bridging Lake Michigan between Ludington, Mich., and Milwaukee, Manitowoc [and] Kewaunee. [Cleveland?, 1941]. 1 sheet folded to [6] p. Illus. Effective October 26, 1941. WM.

Schedules and rates [for the] Pere Marquette Railway auto ferries. [Cleveland?, 1941]. 1 sheet folded to [4] p. Illus. Effective June 1, 1941. CSmH.

Schedules and rates [for the] Pere Marquette Railway auto ferries. [Cleveland, 1941]. 1 sheet folded to [4] p. Illus. Effective July 15, 1941. ViCFC.

Schedules and fares [of the] Pere Marquette Railway auto ferries. [Cleveland: T[homas] M. Reese Adv[ertising] Co., 1941]. 1 sheet folded to [4] p. Illus. Effective November 20, 1941. ViCFC.

Pere Marquette Railway auto ferries bridging Lake Michigan, 1942. [Cleveland?, 1942]. 1 sheet folded to [24] p. Illus., maps. Effective May 15, 1942. CSmH, CU-SB, ViCFC, ViNeM, WM.

Schedules and fares [of the] Pere Marquette Railway auto ferries. [Cleveland: T[homas] M. Reese Printing Co., 1942]. 1 sheet folded to [6] p. Illus., map. Effective March 5, 1942. ViCFC.

Schedules and fares [of the] Pere Marquette Railway auto ferries. [Cleveland], 1942. 1 sheet folded to [6] p. Illus., map. Effective June 28, 1942. ViCFC, WM, WMCHi, WManiM.

Pere Marquette Railway auto ferries, the short route in and out of Michigan and the Northwest, 1943. [Cleveland?, 1943]. 1 sheet folded to [6] p. Illus., maps. Effective April 15, 1943. CU-SB, MiD-D, OFH, ViCFC, WM.

Pere Marquette Railway auto ferries, the short route in and out of Michigan and the Northwest, 1943. [Cleveland?, 1943]. 1 sheet folded to [6] p. Illus., maps. Effective October 31, 1943. ViCFC, WMCHi.

Pere Marquette Railway auto ferries, the short route in and out of Michigan and the Northwest, 1944. [Cleveland?, 1944]. 1 sheet folded to [6] p. Illus., maps. Effective May 15, 1944. CU-SB, MiD-D, OBgU, OFH, ViCFC, WMCHi.

Pere Marquette auto ferries, the short route in and out of Michigan and the Northwest. [Cleveland?, 1945]. 1 sheet folded to [6] p. Maps. Effective May 15, 1945. CU-SB, MiD-D, OBgU, WM.

Pere Marquette auto ferries, the short route in and out of Michigan and the Northwest, 1946. [Cleveland?, 1946]. 1 sheet folded to [6] p. Illus., maps. Effective April 1, 1946. CSmH, CU-SB, MdBUS, MiD-D, MiGr, MnDuC, OFH, ViNeM, WM.

Pere Marquette auto ferries, the short route in and out of Michigan and the Northwest. [Cleveland?, 1947]. 1 sheet folded to [6] p. Maps. Effective March 1, 1947. MiD-D, MiShM, OBgU, WM.

Pere Marquette auto ferries, the short route in and out of Michigan and the Northwest. [Cleveland?, 1947]. 1 sheet folded to [6] p. Maps. Effective July 1, 1947. MiD-D, MiShM.

Pere Marquette auto ferries, the short route in and out of Michigan and the Northwest. [Cleveland?, 1947]. 1 sheet folded to [6] p. Maps. Effective September 14, 1947. MiD-D, WManiM.

PICKANDS MATHER & COMPANY, CLEVELAND, OH
Incorporated as a Delaware firm on 30 March 1973. Still active as of 1990.

M[otor] V[essel] James R[ex] Barker. [Cleveland?, 1976]. 7, [1] p. Illus. MiD-D, OBgU, OClWHi, WManiM.

M[otor] V[essel] William J[ohn] DeLancey. [Cleveland?, 1981?]. [8] p. Illus. OBgU, WManiM.

PICTURED ROCKS CRUISES, INCORPORATED, MUNISING, MI
Incorporated 17 March 1972. Still active as of 1990.

Pictured Rocks boat cruises. [N.p., 1990]. 1 sheet folded to [4] p. Illus., map. MiD-D, MiMtpC, MiShM, OBgU.

PITTSBURGH STEAMSHIP COMPANY, CLEVELAND, OH.
Incorporated on 10 November 1899. Popularly known as the Steel Trust Fleet after 1901, when it became part of the U.S. Steel combine. License surrendered on 31 December 1949.

Seventh Annual Convention of the Pittsburgh [sic] Steamship Co.'s Masters and Officers held at Cleveland, Ohio, January 23, 24, 25, 1911. [Cleveland?, 1911]. 148 p. OBgU.

Third Annual Convention of the Pittsburgh [sic] Steamship Co.'s Engineers and Officers held at Cleveland, Ohio, January 26, 27, 28, 1911. [Cleveland?, 1911]. 118 p. OBgU.

Tenth Annual Convention of the Pittsburgh [sic] Steamship Co.'s Masters and Officers held at Cleveland, Ohio, March 23rd, 24th and 25th, 1914, and Sixth Annual Convention of the Pittsburgh [sic] Steamship Co.'s Engineers and Officers held at Cleveland, March 24th, 1914. [Cleveland?, 1914]. 93, [3] p. MiD-D.

PLAUNT TRANSPORTATION COMPANY, INCORPORATED, CHEBOYGAN, MI
Incorporated on 25 October 1977. Still active in 1990.

1990 [schedule of service from Cheboygan to Bois Blanc Island]. [Cheboygan MI: Tribune Printing, 1990]. 1 sheet folded to [6] p. Illus. Note: Statement indicates that the brochure was revised in April of 1989, but firm says printing occurred in 1990. MiD-D.

POSEIDON LINES, HAMBURG, GER
Established around 1950 as Poseidon Schiffahrt AG. Still active in 1990 with suffix GmbH.

Great Lakes, St. Lawrence to Continent. [N.p.], 1959. 1 sheet folded to [4] p. Map. April edition. MnDuU.

PORT HURON & DULUTH STEAMSHIP COMPANY, PORT HURON, MI
Incorporated 21 March 1901. Name changed to Northwestern Steamship Company on 1 July 1916.

Vacation trips on freight steamers. [N.p.], 1910]. 16 p. Illus., map. MiD-B.

Vacation trips on freight steamers [of the] Port Huron-Duluth Steamship Co. Port Huron, MI: Riverside Printing Co., [1911]. 16 p. Illus., map. MiD-D.

A vacation trip on a freight steamer, finest fresh water cruise in the world, Port Huron to Duluth and return. Port Huron, MI: Riverside Printing Company, [1912]. 20 p. Illus., map. Cover title: Vacation trips on freight steamers. MiD-B, MiPhM.

Vacation trips on freight steamers. [Port Huron?, 1916]. [12] p. Illus., map. Cover is a half page. ViNeM.

PORT HURON & SARNIA FERRY COMPANY, PORT HURON, MI
Incorporated 13 January 1891. Dissolved on 7 January 1937, the year construction started on a bridge to connect the two cities mentioned in the firm's name.

The vacationette trip, a most pleasant way to spend a day. Port Huron, MI: Herald Printing Co., [1914?]. [24] p. MiPhM.

PORT HURON & WASHBURN LINE, PORT HURON, MI
Apparently established in the early 1890s. Ceased to exist about 1901.

Steamer "Colorado" general average statement [of] eastbound [incident when she] stranded May 21st, 1893. Buffalo: Press of Hartman & DeCoursey, [1893]. 11, [1] p. N.

PUT-IN-BAY BOAT LINE COMPANY, PUT-IN-BAY, OH
Incorporated 7 December 1987. Still active as of 1990.

Come aboard the jet express to Put-in-Bay, the fastest way to Put-in-Bay from downtown Port Clinton. [N.p., 1990]. 1 sheet folded to [8] p. Illus., maps. MiD-D.

PYKE SALVAGE & NAVIGATION COMPANY, LIMITED, KINGSTON, ONT
Incorporated on 28 July 1944. Dissolved on 24 March 1965.

Salvage equipment & tariff. [Kingston?, 1960]. 20 p. Illus. CaOTHCA.

RED STAR NAVIGATION COMPANY, TOLEDO, OH.
Incorporated on 14 February 1925. Ceased to exist on 1 January 1931.

Toledo, Put-in-Bay, Cedar Point route through connections with C[leveland] & B[uffalo] Line to Cleveland, Buffalo [and] Niagara Falls, season 1926. [Toledo, 1926]. 1 sheet folded to [8] p. Illus., map. MiD-D.

REPUBLIC STEEL CORPORATION, LAKE FLEET DIVISION, CLEVELAND, OH
Created on 1 December 1953, as successor to the Nicholson Universal Steamship Company. On 19 December 1984, it became part of the LTV Steel Company, Incorporated.

Agreement between Lake Fleet Division of Republic Steel Corporation and [the] United Steelworkers of America, August 3, 1956. [Cleveland, 1957]. 58 p. At bottom of cover: Letter of understanding June 10, 1957. OBgU.

Agreement between Lake Fleet Division of Republic Steel Corporation and [the] United Steelworkers of America, January 16, 1960. [Cleveland, 1960]. 60 p. OBgU.

Agreement between Lake Fleet Division of Republic Steel Corporation and [the] United Steelworkers of America, September 1, 1965. [Cleveland, 1965]. [4], 96 p. OBgU.

Agreement between Lake Fleet Division, Republic Steel Corporation, and District 2, Marine Engineers Beneficial Association, A[merican] F[ederation] [of] L[abor]-C[ongress] [of] I[ndustrial] O[rganizations], covering licensed engineers, September 1, 1965. [Cleveland?, 1965]. [4], 58, [18] p. OBgU.

Agreement between Republic Steel Corporation and Associated Maritime Officers, A[merican] F[ederation] [of] L[abor]-C[ongress] [of] I[ndustrial] O[rganizations], covering licensed mates, September 1, 1965. [Cleveland?, 1965]. [4], 52, [20] p. OBgU.

Agreement for chief cooks (stewards) between Lake Fleet Division, Republic Steel Corporation, and Associated Maritime Officers, A[merican] F[ederation] [of] L[abor]-C[ongress] [of] I[ndustrial] O[rganizations], September 1, 1965. [Cleveland?, 1965]. [4], 44, [20] p. OBgU.

Glad to have you aboard. [Cleveland], 1965. 11, [1] p. Illus., map. OBgU.

Safety is smart seamanship. [Cleveland?, 1966]. 27, [1] p. Illus. OBgU.

Agreement between [the] Lake Fleet Division of Republic Steel Corporation and [the] United Steelworkers of America, August 1, 1968. [Cleveland, 1968]. [4], 108 p. OBgU.

RICHELIEU & ONTARIO NAVIGATION COMPANY, MONTREAL, QUE

Organized 8 April 1875, through a merger of the Canadian Navigation Company of Ontario and La Compagnie du Richelieu. In 1886 it acquired the St. Lawrence River Steam Navigation Company, then in June of 1911 it gained control of the Northern Navigation Company, Limited. Acquired the Thousand Island Steamboat Company and the Niagara Navigation Company on 1 June 1912. Reorganized on 12 April 1913, as the Richelieu & Ontario Navigation Company, Limited. Acquired by the Canada Steamship Lines on 1 June 1914.

Grand Trunk Railway of Canada and Richelieu & Ontario Navigation Company tariff of excursion tours & rates from Niagara Falls to Philadelphia, May to November, 1876. [N.p., 1876]. 45, [1] p. CSmH.

Handbook of Canadian excursion tours via Grand Trunk Railway and Richelieu & Ontario Navigation Co., rates of fare for season of 1880. Boston: Rand, Avery & Co., [1880]. 24 p. Illus., map. CaOKQ

List of shareholders of the Richelieu & Ontario Navigation Company [as of] 9th February, 1880. Montreal: Beauchemin & Valois, [1880]. 12 p. CaQMBN, CaQMMRB.

Beauties of the St. Lawrence, the tourist's ideal trip via the Richelieu & Ontario Navigation Company's steamers. By J[oseph] K[earney] Foran. [Montreal?, 1881?]. 24 p. Illus. CaQMBN.

Handbook of Canadian excursion tours via Grand Trunk Railway and Richelieu & Ontario Navigation Co., rates of fare for season of 1881. Boston: Rand, Avery & Co., [1881]. 32 p. Illus., map. CaOKQ.

Handbook of Canadian excursion tours via Grand Trunk Railway and Richelieu & Ontario Navigation Co., rates of fare for season of 1882. Boston: Rand, Avery & Co., [1882]. 29, [3] p. Illus., map. CaOKQ.

List of shareholders of the Richelieu & Ontario Navigation Company [as of] 20th January, 1883. Montreal: Beauchemin & Valois, [1883]. 10 p. CaQMMRB.

Eighth season of the popular excursions via the Grand Trunk Railway and Richelieu & Ontario Navigation Company's steamers from Detroit to the White Mountains and the sea shore on June 26th, July 10th, and July 24th, 1884. Detroit: E[mil] Schober, [1884]. 26 p. Illus. CaOTPB.

Rapport des directeurs de la Cie de Nav. du Richelieu & d'Ontario a l'assemblee generale annuelle tenue le 19 Fevrier 1884 dans les Bureaux de la compagnie, 1884. Montreal: Beauchemin & Valois, 1884. 7, [1] p. CaQMBN.

Excursion routes and rates from Buffalo and Niagara Falls to the Thousand Islands, Rapids of the St. Lawrence, Montreal, Quebec, the Saguenay, White Mountains, Halifax, Lake Champlain, Lake George, Portland, Saratoga, Boston, and New-York via Grand Trunk R'y and Richelieu & Ontario Nav. Co.'s steamers. Buffalo: Matthews, Northrup & Co., [1885]. 38 p. Illus., folded map. MB.

Palatial steamers between Niagara Falls, Toronto, Kingston, Montreal & Quebec. Boston: Rand, Avery Supply Co., [1885?]. 1 sheet folded to [24] p. Illus., map. ViNeM.

Palatial steamers between Niagara Falls, Toronto, Kingston, Montreal, Quebec, Murray Bay, Riviere du Loup, Tadousac [sic] and Ha! Ha! Bay. Boston: Rand, Avery Supply Co., [1886?]. 1 sheet folded to [36] p. Illus., maps. CaOOA.

Report of the directors and list of shareholders of the Richelieu and Ontario Navigation Co. [as of] 1st February, 1886. [Montreal, 1886]. 11, [1] p. CaOONL.

New official guide and summer excursion book, 1887. Montreal: C[harles] O[dilon] Beauchemin & Fils, [1887]. 88 p. Illus., folded maps. Cover title: Summer excursions and official time tables, 1887. Text in French and English. CaOONL, PP, WHi.

Palatial steamers between Niagara Falls, Toronto, Kingston, Montreal, Quebec, Murray Bay, Riviere du Loup, Tadousac [sic] and Ha! Ha! Bay, through the 1000 Islands and rapids of the St. Lawrence and the far-famed Saguenay River. Boston: Rand, Avery Supply Co., [1887]. 1 sheet folded to [36] p. Illus., maps. MiD-D.

Through the 1000 Islands and rapids of the St. Lawrence and the far-famed Saguenay River. Boston: Rand, Avery Supply Co., [1887]. 1 sheet folded to [36] p. Illus., maps. CaOKQ, CaOONL, WHi.

Palatial steamers between Niagara Falls, Toronto, Kingston, Montreal, Quebec, Murray Bay, Riviere du Loup, Tadousac [sic] and Ha! Ha! Bay. Boston: American Printing & Engraving Company, [1890]. 1 sheet folded to [36] p. Illus., maps. MSaP.

The Richelieu and Ontario Navigation Co.'s summer tours and time tables for season of 1891. Montreal: Waters Bros. & Co., [1891]. 152 p. Illus., folded map. CaOKQ.

Time table for summer arrangments, 1891. [Boston: Rand, Avery & Co., 1891]. 1 sheet folded to [10] p. Maps. CaOKQ.

Glimpses of nature's beauty, a guide to the routes and connections of the Richelieu and Ontario Navigation Company. Montreal: John Lovell & Son, [1893]. 128 p. Illus., folded maps. CaOONL, ViNeM, WHi.

Souvenir [of] Canada's cities, lakes and rivers, World's Columbian Exposition, 1893. [Montreal]: Desbarats & Co., c1893. 24 p. Illus. CaOKQ, CaOONL, CaOTPB.

Through the 1000 Islands and rapids of the St. Lawrence and the far-famed Saguenay River. Boston: American Printing & Engraving Co., [1893]. 1 sheet folded to [36] p. Illus., maps. CaOTPB.

Palatial steamers between Buffalo, Niagara Falls, Toronto, Kingston, Montreal, Quebec, Murray Bay, Riviere du Loup, Tadousac [sic] and Ha! Ha! Bay. Boston: American Printing and Engraving Company, [1894]. [12] p. Illus., maps. MSaP, NBuHi, OBgU.

America's scenic line from Buffalo, Niagara Falls and Toronto, passing through the charming scenery of the Thousand Islands and the world-renowned rapids of the St. Lawrence to Montreal, Quebec, and the Saguenay, calling at all intermediate ports shown on time schedule within, season of 1895-6. [N.p., 1895]. 1 sheet folded to [4] p. Illus., folded map. CaOOA, MiD-D.

The beauty spots of Canada, descriptive of that delightful trip down the River St. Lawrence and up the world-famed Saguenay. Official guide, 1895. Montreal: Desbarats & Co., c1895. 156 p. Illus., folded map. CaOHM, CaOKQ, CaOONG, CaOONL, CaOTPB, CaQMBN, CaQMCCA, CaSSU, DLC, NBuU, NN, WHi, WLacU.

Palatial steamers between Buffalo, Niagara Falls, Toronto, Kingston, Montreal, Quebec, Murray Bay, Riviere du Loup, Tadousac [sic], Ha! Ha! Bay, Chicoutimi and Roberval. Boston: American Printing and Engraving Co., [1895]. 1 sheet folded to [32] p. Illus., map. WM.

From Niagara to the sea, descriptive of that delightful trip down the River St. Lawrence and up the world-famed Saguenay. Official guide, 1896. Montreal: Desbarats & Co., c1896. 138 p. Illus. CaOONL, CaOTPB, CaQQS, CaSSU.

From Niagara to the sea, descriptive of that delightful trip down the River St. Lawrence and up the world-famed Saguenay. Montreal: Desbarats & Co., 1896. 176 p. Illus. CaOTPB, MiD-D.

Palatial steamers between Buffalo, Niagara Falls, Toronto, Kingston, Montreal, Quebec, Murray Bay, Riviere du Loup, Tadousac [sic], Ha! Ha! Bay, Chicoutimi and Roberval. Boston: American Printing and Engraving Company, [1896]. 1 sheet folded to [32] p. Illus., map. CaOKQAR, MdBUS, ViNeM.

From Niagara to the sea, descriptive of that delightful trip down the River St. Lawrence and up the world-famed Saguenay. Official guide, 1897. Montreal: Desbarats & Co., c1897. 164 p. Illus., folded map. CaOH, CaOONL, CaQQS.

Palatial steamers between Buffalo, Niagara Falls, Toronto, Kingston, Montreal, Quebec, Murray Bay, Riviere du Loup, Tadousac [sic], Ha! Ha! Bay, Chicoutimi, and Roberval. [Montreal?, 1897]. 1 sheet folded to [32] p. Illus., map. MiD-D, OBgU.

From Niagara to the sea, descriptive of that delightful trip down the River St. Lawrence and up the world-famed Saguenay. Official guide, 1898. Montreal: Desbarats & Co., c1898. 172 p. Illus., folded map. CaBVaU, CaOONL, CaOPeT, CaQMBM, CaQMBN, CaQMCCA, CaQQS, MiD-B, OBgU.

Palatial steamers between Buffalo, Niagara Falls, Toronto, Kingston, Montreal, Quebec, Murray Bay, Riviere du Loup, Tadousac [sic], Ha! Ha! Bay, Chicoutimi, and Roberval, 1898. [Buffalo?, 1898]. 1 sheet folded to [32] p. Illus., map. CaOOA.

America's scenic line, Niagara to the sea, the finest inland water trip in the world [serving] Buffalo, Niagara Falls, and Toronto. [N.p., 1899]. 1 sheet folded to [4] p. Illus. Corrected to August 20th, 1899. CaOOA.

Consolidation of the act of incorporation of 1857 with the amendments thereof up to 1899 of the Richelieu & Ontario Navigation Co. Montreal: C[harles] O[dilon] Beauchemin & Son, 1899. 24 p. CaOKQAR.

From Niagara to the sea, the finest inland water trip in the world. Official guide, 1899. Montreal: Desbarats & Co., [1899], c1898. 176 p. Illus. CaOKQ, CaOONL, CaOStCB, CaQMBM, CaQMBN, CaQMMRB, CaQQS, ICHi, MiD-B, MiD-D, OBgU.

Palatial steamers between Buffalo, Niagara Falls, Toronto, Kingston, Montreal, Quebec, Murray Bay, Riviere du Loup, Tadousac [sic], Ha! Ha! Bay, Chicoutimi and Roberval, 1899. [Boston?, 1899]. 1 sheet folded to 11 [i.e. 36] p. Illus., map. CaOOA, MSaP, MiD-D.

The Canadian National Exhibition [in] Toronto is the greatest, grandest, and most complete annual exhibition on the continent of America. [Toronto?, 1900?]. 1 sheet folded to [4] p. CaOOA.

From Niagara to the sea, the finest inland water trip in the world. Official guide, 1900. Montreal: Desbarats & Co., [1900]. 176 p. Illus., maps. CaOOA, NBu, NN, WHi.

From Niagara to the sea via Toronto, Rochester, 1000 Islands, Rapids, Montreal, Quebec, and Saguenay.

Buffalo: Matthews-Northrup Co., [1900]. 1 sheet folded to [8] p. Illus., map. Issued July 9, 1900. CaOOA, MSaP.

From Niagara to the sea via Toronto, Rochester, 1000 Islands, Rapids, Montreal, Quebec, and Saguenay. Buffalo: Matthews-Northrup Co., [1900]. [16] p. Illus., maps. CaOTPB, CtY, MSaP, NBuHi, ViNeM.

From Niagara to the sea! Buffalo: Matthews-Northrup Co., [1901]. [16] p. Illus., maps. Folder A. CaOKQAR, CaOOA, MSaP, ViNeM.

From Niagara to the sea! Buffalo: Matthews-Northrup Works, [1901]. 1 sheet folded to [8] p. Illus., map. Folder B. CaOOA, MSaP.

From Niagara to the sea, the finest inland water trip in the world. Official guide, 1901. Montreal: Desbarats & Co., [1901]. 144 p. Illus., folded map. CaOOA, CaOONL, CaOStCB, CaQQS, MSaP, MiD-D.

Niagara to the sea, 1902. Buffalo: Matthews-Northrup Works, [1902]. [12] p. Illus., maps. Folder A. CaOOA.

From Niagara to the sea, the finest inland water trip in the world. Official guide, 1902. Montreal: Desbarats & Co., [1902]. 146 p. Illus., folded map. CaOOA, CaOOU, CaOWA, CaQMBN, CaQQS, OBgU, OKentU, VtU, WHi.

The R & O Tourist. — Vol. 1, no. 1 (June 1902)-vol. 13?, no. ? (1914?). — Montreal, 1902-1914?. Illus. Monthly. Cataloging based on June, 1902 issue. CaOONL.

Niagara to the sea, 1903. [Buffalo?, 1903]. [12] p. Illus., maps. Folder A. CaOOA.

Niagara to the sea! [Buffalo?, 1903]. [12] p. Illus., maps. Folder A1. CaOONL, ViNeM.

From Niagara to the sea, the finest inland water trip in the world. Official guide, 1903. [Montreal?, 1903]. 144 p. Illus., map. CaNSHPL, CaOStCB, NN, ViNeM.

From Niagara to the sea, the finest inland water trip in the world. Official guide, 1904. [Montreal?, 1904]. 144 p. Illus., folded map. CaOStCB, CaQQS, MB, OBgU, WHi.

Niagara to the sea!, 1904. [Buffalo: Matthews-Northrup Co., 1904]. [12] p. Illus., maps. Folder A. CaOOA, MSaP, WM.

Niagara to the sea. Philadelphia: Edgell Press, [1905]. 18 [i.e. 12] p. Illus., map. CaOKQAR, CaOOA, MSaP, ViNeM.

From Niagara to the sea, the finest inland water trip in the world. Official guide, 1905. [Toronto: Toronto Litho[graphing] Co., 1905]. 146 p. Illus. CSmH, CaOONL, CaOTPB, CaQMBM, CaQMBN, DLC, MH, MiD-D, OBgU, OKentU.

Niagara to the sea via Toronto, Rochester, 1000 Islands, Rapids, Montreal, Quebec and Saguenay. Toronto: Mail Job Print, [1905]. 1 sheet folded to [6] p. Illus., map. Folder C. Issued April 26, 1905. CaOOA, MSaP.

Niagara to the sea via Toronto, Rochester, 1000 Islands, Rapids, Montreal, Quebec, and Saguenay. Rochester, NY: Vredenburg & Co., [1905]. 1 sheet folded to [6] p. Illus., map. CaOOA, ViNeM.

Richelieu & Ontario Navigation Company annual report, 1904. [N.p., 1905]. [4] p. CtY, NNC.

From Niagara to the sea, the finest inland water trip in the world. Official guide, 1906. Montreal: Desbarats & Co., [1906]. 148 p. Illus., map. CaOStCB, NN, OBgU.

Hotels & steamers of Canada [serving] Lake Ontario, Thousand Islands, rapids of the St. Lawrence, Niagara, Hamilton, Toronto, Charlotte, Bay of Quinte, Kingston, Clayton, Alexandria Bay [plus] hotels Manoir Richelieu [and] Tadousac [sic]. Montreal: Gazette Printing Co., [1906]. [20] p. Illus., maps. CaQMCCA, MB, MSaP, MiD-D, ViNeM.

Niagara to the sea. Chicago: Poole Bros., [1906]. 22 [i.e. 12] p. Illus., map. CaOOA, MdBUS, WM.

Richelieu & Ontario Navigation Company annual report, 1905. [N.p., 1906]. [4] p. MH-BA, NNC.

From Niagara to the sea, the finest inland water trip in the world. Official guide, 1907. Montreal: Desbarats & Co., [1907]. 146 p. Illus., folded map. CaOONL, CaOStCB, CaQQS, CaSSU, MSaP, MiD-D, OBgU.

Hotels and steamers of Canada [serving] Lake Ontario, Thousand Islands, rapids of the St. Lawrence, Niagara, Hamilton, Toronto, Charlotte, Bay of Quinte, Kingston, Clayton, Alexandria Bay [plus] hotels Manoir Richelieu and Tadousac [sic]. Montreal: Gazette Printing Co., [1907?]. [16] p. Illus., maps. Optional title: Through Canada by water. CaQMCCA, MSaP.

Niagara to the sea. Chicago: Poole Bros., [1907]. 22 [i.e. 12] p. Illus., map. OBgU, ViNeM.

Richelieu & Ontario Navigation Company annual report, 1906. [N.p., 1907]. [4] p. CtY, MH-BA, NNC.

The all water route, Niagara to the sea via Toronto, Rochester, 1000 Islands, Rapids, Montreal, Quebec, Murray Bay, Tadousac [sic], and Saguenay, 1907. [Chicago: Poole Bros., 1907]. 1 sheet folded to 12 [i.e. 16] p. Illus., map. July edition. NBuHi.

The all water route, Niagara to the sea via Toronto, Rochester, 1000 Islands, Rapids, Montreal, Quebec, Murray Bay, Tadousac [sic], and Saguenay, 1907. [Chicago: Poole Bros., 1907]. 1 sheet folded to 12 [i.e. 16] p. Illus., map. September edition. MiD-D.

From Niagara to the sea, the finest inland water trip in the world. Official guide, 1908. Montreal: Desbarats & Co., [1908]. 144 p. Illus., folded map. CaOONL, CaQQS, CaSSU, MSaP, MWA, NR, OBgU.

Niagara to the sea [via] Thousand Islands, Rapids, Montreal, Quebec [and] Saguenay River. Chicago: Poole

Bros., 1908. 22 [i.e. 12] p. Illus., map. June issue. OBgU, ViNeM.

Richelieu & Ontario Navigation Company annual report, 1907. [N.p., 1908]. [4] p. MH-BA, NNC.

Day & night between Niagara and the sea. [Chicago?, 1909?]. 1 sheet folded to [4] p. Illus., folded map. CaOOA.

Niagara to the sea, the finest inland water trip in the world. Official guide, 1909. Montreal: Desbarats & Co., [1909]. 144 p. Illus., folded map. CaOTP, CaOTPB, CaQMBM, CaQMBN, CaQMMRB, CtY, MiD-D, NN, NPlaU.

Niagara to the sea [via] Thousand Islands, Rapids, Montreal, Quebec, [and] Saguenay River. [Chicago?, 1909]. 22 [i.e. 12] p. Illus., map. May edition. CaOOA.

Niagara to the sea [via] Thousand Islands, Rapids, Montreal, Quebec [and] Saguenay River. Chicago: Poole Bros., [1909]. 22 [i.e. 12] p. Illus., map. August edition. ViNeM.

Richelieu & Ontario Navigation Company annual report, 1908. [N.p., 1909]. [4] p. MH-BA, NNC.

Souvenir of [the] St. Lawrence and Saguenay Rivers. Chicago: Poole Bros., [1909?]. [24] p. Illus., map. Cover title: Scenic selections "From Niagara to the sea." ViNeM.

Steamers and hotels on the St. Lawrence and Saguenay rivers operated by the Richelieu & Ontario Navigation Co. Chicago: Poole Bros., [1909?]. [24] p. Illus., map. Cover title: Scenic selections "From Niagara to the sea." CaOStCB, ViNeM.

New water route between Niagara Falls and 1000 Islands. Chicago: Poole Bros., [1910]. [8] p. Illus., map. CaOOA, MdBUS, ViNeM.

Niagara to the sea, the finest inland water trip in the world. Official guide, 1910. Rochester, NY: John P. Smith Printing Co., [1910]. 144 p. Illus., folded map. CaOStCB, CaQMBM, CaQMBN.

Niagara to the sea [via] Thousand Islands, Rapids, Montreal, Quebec, [and] Saguenay River. Chicago: Poole Bros., [1910]. 30 [i.e. 16] p. Illus., maps. MiU-H, OFH, ViNeM.

Sixty-fourth annual report of the Richelieu & Ontario Navigation Co. for the year ending December 31st, 1909. [Montreal?, 1910]. 15, [1] p. Illus., map. Cover title: Richelieu & Ontario Navigation Company annual report, 1909. CtY, IU, MH-BA.

Niagara to the sea, the finest inland water trip in the world. Official guide, 1911. Rochester, NY: John P. Smith Printing Co., [1911]. 144 p. Illus., folded map. CSmH, MSaP, OBgU, WHi.

Niagara to the sea [via] Thousand Islands, Rapids, Montreal, Quebec, [and] Saguenay River. [N.p., 1911]. [12] p. Illus., maps. CaOTPB, PPPMM.

Niagara to the sea [via] Thousand Islands, Rapids, Montreal, Quebec, [and] Saguenay River. Chicago: Poole Bros., [1911]. 30 [i.e. 16] p. Illus., maps. CaOOA, MiManiHi, ViNeM.

Sixty-fifth annual report of the Richelieu & Ontario Navigation Co. for the year ending December 31st, 1910. [Montreal?, 1911]. 11, [5] p. Illus., map. Cover title: Richelieu & Ontario Navigation Company annual report, 1910. CtY, IU, MH-BA, NNC.

Lower St. Lawrence summer resort hotels,...conveniently accessible by steamers of [the] Richelieu & Ontario Navigation Co. Montreal: Desbarats Printing Co., [1912]. 15, [1] p. Illus. Cover title: R & O hotels [along] the lower St. Lawrence and the Saguenay. CaOKQ.

Niagara to the sea, the finest inland water trip in the world. Official guide, 1912. Rochester, NY: John P. Smith Printing Co., [1912]. 144 p. Illus. OBgU.

Niagara to the sea [via] Thousand Islands, Rapids, Montreal, Quebec, [and] Saguenay River. Chicago: Poole Bros., [1912]. 30 [i.e. 16] p. Illus., maps. Folder A. CaOKMM, CaOOA, CaOONL, WM.

Niagara to the sea [via] Thousand Islands, Rapids, Montreal, Quebec, [and] Saguenay River. [Chicago?, 1912]. [12] p. Illus., map. CaOOA, MiD-D, ViNeM.

Sixty-sixth annual report of the Richelieu & Ontario Navigation Co. for the year ending December 31st, 1911. [Montreal?, 1912]. 11, [5] p. Illus. Cover title: Richelieu & Ontario Navigation Company annual report, 1911. CaOKQAR, CtY, IU, MH-BA, NNC.

Niagara to the sea. Official guide, 1913. Rochester, NY: John P. Smith Printing Company, [1913]. 144 p. Illus., folded map. Cover title: R & O hotels. CSmH, CaOTPB, CtY, MB, NN.

Niagara to the sea [via] Thousand Islands, Rapids, Montreal, Quebec, [and] Saguenay River. [Chicago: Poole Bros., 1913]. [12] p. Illus., map. MSaP.

Niagara to the sea [via] Thousand Islands, Rapids, Montreal, Quebec, [and] Saguenay River. Chicago: Poole Bros., [1913]. 38 [i.e. 20] p. Illus., maps. CaOOA, MSaP, MiD-D.

Sixty-seventh annual report of the Richelieu & Ontario Navigation Co. for the year ending December 31st, 1912. [Montreal?, 1913]. 15, [5] p. Illus., folded map. Cover title: Richelieu & Ontario Navigation Company annual report, 1912. CaOKQAR, IU, MH-BA, NNC.

The Thousand Islands of the St. Lawrence River. [N.p., 1913]. 1 sheet folded to [12] p. Illus., map. MiD-D.

SAGINAW TRANSPORTATION COMPANY, SAGINAW, MI

Incorporated on 26 May 1881. Dissolved on 26 September 1901.

The new Saginaw Line [serving] Niagara Falls, Buffalo, Cleveland, Detroit, Port Huron, Goderich, Ont., Bay City, East Saginaw and intermediate points [with the] steamer "Lora," season 1890. [Saginaw?, 1890]. 1 sheet folded to [4] p. ViNeM.

Something new, a week's trip on the Great Lakes through the world-famed Thousand Islands of the celebrated St. Lawrence to Ogdensburg, N.Y., via the palatial steamer Lora. Detroit: Wilton Smith Co., [1891?]. 1 sheet folded to [4] p. Illus. CaOOA.

SAINT JOSEPH-CHICAGO STEAMSHIP COMPANY, ST. JOSEPH, MI

Incorporated on 29 May 1913. The company's chances of survival were dashed when the ship it owned, the Eastland, turned over in the Chicago harbor on 24 July 1915. Automatically dissolved on 31 August 1923.

St. Joseph-Chicago Steamship Company to all Michigan and Indiana, [the] "St. Joe Line" daily excursions. St. Joseph, MI: Review Press, [1914?]. 1 sheet folded to [4] p. MiD-D.

SANDUSKY & ISLANDS STEAMBOAT COMPANY, SANDUSKY, OH

Incorporated on 3 July 1882. Dissolved on 20 June 1944.

Steamer Chippewa, double daily service between Sandusky, Lakeside, Put-in-Bay, Kelleys Island, [and] Middle Bass, 1938. [Sandusky, 1938]. 1 sheet folded to [4] p. Illus. OSandF.

Modern steel steamer City of Hancock summer schedule, July 1st to Labor Day daily between Sandusky, Lakeside, Kelleys Island, Middle Bass and Put-in-Bay. [N.p., 1939]. 1 sheet folded to [4] p. Illus. CU-SB, MiD-D, OFH.

SCOTT MISENER STEAMSHIPS, LIMITED, ST. CATHARINES, ONT

Established on 31 December 1958, as successor to Colonial Steamships, Limited. Became Misener Transportation, Limited, in 1978.

Christening of the M[otor] V[essel] "Ralph Misener" [on] Saturday, June 1st, 1968, at 11:00 A.M. [N.p., 1968]. [4] p. Illus. Includes one-page program insert. CaOKMM, CaOPoCM.

SEAWAY EXCURSION LINES, INCORPORATED, TOLEDO, OH

Incorporated on 1 May 1958, and commenced service on 30 May 1958. Ended service on 30 July 1958, when ship was hit by swing bridge in Toledo. Went into receivership on 21 August 1958, and ship sold at auction on 13 October 1958. Charter cancelled on 30 November 1960. Succeeded by Toledo Excursion Lines.

Bob-lo, where most picnics go! [N.p., 1958]. 1 sheet folded to [4] p. Illus. MiD-D, MiShM, ViNeM.

S.S. Canadiana cruises & charters daily sailing to Bob-lo. [N.p., 1958]. 1 sheet folded to [4] p. MiD-D, MiManiHi, OBgU, ViNeM.

SEAWAY LINES, LIMITED, WINDSOR, ONT

Incorporated on 22 January 1934. Associated with the Detroit & Georgian Bay Navigation Company, Limited. Removed from active corporate status on 31 October 1947.

A new Georgian Bay cruise to places off the beaten track. [N.p., 1934]. 1 sheet folded to [16] p. Illus., map. MiD-D.

Georgian Bay [and] Great Lakes cruises [to] Midland, Little Current, Killarney, Tobermory, Kincardine, Goderich, Sarnia, Windsor [and] Toledo. [N.p., 1934]. 1 sheet folded to [8] p. Illus. WM.

All-expense cruises to the fjords of the inland seas, Manitoulin Island, Mackinac and the Soo via Georgian Bay and the North Channel. [N.p., 1935]. 1 sheet folded to [16] p. Illus., map. MSaP.

Cruise to the fjords of the inland seas [along the] North Channel and Georgian Bay. [N.p., 1935]. 1 sheet folded to [16] p. Illus., map. MdBUS, MiD-D.

North Channel Georgian Bay cruise. [N.p., 1935]. [12] p. Illus., map. MiD-B, MiD-D, WM.

Through the scenic Inside Passage from Georgian Bay to Mackinac, the ideal summer cruise for 1935. [N.p., 1935]. 1 sheet folded to [16] p. Illus., map. MiD-D.

All-expense cruises to the fjords of the inland seas, Manitoulin Island, Mackinac, and the Soo via Georgian Bay and the North Channel. [N.p., 1936]. 1 sheet folded to [8] p. Illus., map. MSaP, MiD-B, ViNeM.

North Channel Georgian Bay cruise. [Detroit?, 1936]. 1 sheet folded to [16] p. Illus., map. CU-SB, MiD-D, MiShM.

Cruise to the fjords of the inland seas, cruise to North Channel, Georgian Bay. [N.p., 1937]. [8] p. Illus., maps. MiD-D, OBgU.

Georgian Bay, the 30,000 Islands, Mackinac and the "Soo." [N.p., 1937]. 1 sheet folded to [16] p. Illus., maps. CU-SB.

Special circle cruise of Georgian Bay. [Detroit?, 1937]. 1 sheet folded to [4] p. Illus. MiD-D.

A cruise to Georgian Bay and the North Channel on the Seaway Lines, Ltd. [N.p., 1938]. 1 sheet folded to [8] p. Illus., map. MiD-D.

Fiords of the inland seas and Georgian Bay on the Seaway Lines. [N.p., 1938]. 1 sheet folded to [8] p. Illus., map. CSmH, CU-SB, MSaP, MiD-D, ViNeM.

11-day vacation all expense to Georgian Bay. [N.p., 1939]. 1 sheet folded to [8] p. Illus., map. MiD-D.

14-day vacation cruise all-expense from Detroit [or] a 7-day cruise to Georgian Bay. [N.p., 1939?]. 1 sheet folded to [4] p. Illus. ViNeM.

All-expense cruises to the fjords of the inland seas. [N.p., 1940]. 1 sheet folded to [8] p. Illus., map. Issued May, 1940. MdBUS, MiD-D, ViNeM.

Complete circle cruise of Georgian Bay [through] Paul Henry Travel Service. [Detroit?, 1940?]. 1 sheet folded to [6] p. Illus., map. MiD-D.

Cruise to the fjords of the inland seas. [N.p., 1940]. 1 sheet folded to [16] p. Illus., map. MiD-D, OBgU, WM.

14-day vacation all expense to North Channel of Georgian Bay. [N.p., 1940]. 1 sheet folded to [8] p. Illus., map. WM.

Special cruise over Labor Day to the heart of Georgian Bay and the North Channel. [N.p., 1940]. 1 sheet folded to [4] p. Illus. WM.

Complete circle cruise of Georgian Bay [through] Paul Henry Travel Service. [Detroit?, 1941?]. 1 sheet folded to [8] p. Illus., map. MiD-D.

Cruise to the fjords of the inland seas. [N.p., 1941]. 1 sheet folded to [16] p. Illus., map. June edition. CU-SB, MdBUS, MiD-D, OBgU, OFH, ViNeM.

The most scenic cruise on the Great Lakes. [N.p., 1941]. 1 sheet folded to [8] p. Illus., map. CU-SB.

Special cruise over Labor Day. [N.p., 1941]. 1 sheet folded to [4] p. Illus. MdBUS.

3rd Annual Graphic Arts Cruise to the Thousand Islands. [N.p., 1941]. 1 sheet folded to [8] p. Illus., map. MdBUS, ViNeM.

SHEPLER'S, INCORPORATED, MACKINAC CITY, MI
Incorporated 7 May 1986. Still active as of 1990.

Shepler's Mackinac Island ferry 1986 schedule. [N.p., 1986]. 1 sheet folded to [4] p. Illus., map. MiD-D, OBgU.

Mackinac Island ferry schedules, 1987. [N.p., 1987]. 1 sheet folded to [6] p. Map. WM.

Shepler's Mackinac Island ferry 18 minute hydroplane ride. [N.p., 1988]. 1 sheet folded to [6] p. Illus., map. MiD-D, MiShM.

Shepler's Mackinac Island ferry 1989 schedule. [N.p., 1989]. 1 sheet folded to [6] p. Illus., map. MiD-D, Mi-MISPC.

Shepler's Mackinac Island 1990 ferry schedule. [N.p., 1990]. 1 sheet folded to [6] p. Illus., map. MiD-D, MiMtpC, MiShM, OBgU.

SHERWOOD MARINE, INCORPORATED, TORONTO, ONT
Incorporated on 1 October 1975. Dissolved on 26 March 1984.

Toronto - Niagara boat cruises [on the] Cayuga II. [Toronto?, 1976?]. 1 sheet folded to [6] p. Illus. CaOOA.

SIVERTSON BROTHERS FISHERIES, DULUTH, MN. SEE ALSO: GRAND PORTAGE
Organized in 1941. On 30 April 1973, it became Sivertson Fisheries, Incorporated.

Cruise to beautiful Isle Royale National Park. [N.p., 1969]. 1 sheet folded to [8] p. Illus. maps. MnHi.

SOO RIVER COMPANY, THOROLD, ONT
Established around March of 1975 and managed by Westdale Shipping, Limited. Went into receivership on 6 August 1982.

The Soo River Company [code book]. [St. Catharines, ONT: Lincoln Graphics, 1980]. [2], 10 p. WM.

STAR-COLE LINE, DETROIT, MI
Established around July of 1888 by a merger of the Star Line and the Cole Line. Ceased to exist about 1917.

Pleasure route of the Star-Cole Line steamers to the famous St. Clair Flats, Star Island, Grande Pointe, Oak Grove, the Oakland, & Port Huron. Detroit: O[rin] S. Gulley, Bornman & Co., 1890. 64 p. Illus., map. Cover title: Star-Cole Lines steamers, Detroit and Port Huron. MiD-B, MiD-D, MiU-T.

Summer days on the route of the Star-Cole and Red Star lines steamers to the famous St. Clair Flats, Star Island, Grande Pointe, Oak Grove, The Oakland, and Port Huron. Detroit: Gulley, Bornman & Co., [1891?]. 72 p. Illus., maps. Cover title: Summer days on the Detroit and St. Clair rivers. OBgU.

Summer days on the route of the Star-Cole and Red Star lines' steamers to the famous St. Clair Flats, Star Island,

Grande Pointe, Oak Grove, The Oakland, and Port Huron. Detroit: O[rin] S. Gulley, Bornman & Co., [1892]. 72 p. Illus., maps. Cover title: Summer days of the Detroit & St. Clair rivers. MiD-B.

Summer days on the route of the Star-Cole line's steamers to the famous St. Clair Flats, Maple Leaf, Grande Pointe, Oak Grove, The Oakland, and Port Huron. Detroit: John Bornman & Son, [1893]. 52 p. Illus., maps. Cover title: Summer days on the Detroit and St. Clair rivers. MiD-B.

Summer days on the route of the Star-Cole and Red Star lines' steamers to the famous St. Clair Flats, Star Island, The Oakland, Maple Leaf, Oak Grove, and Port Huron. Detroit: Peninsular Printing and Publishing Co., 1894. 63, [1] p. Illus., maps. Cover title: Summer days on the Detroit & St. Clair rivers. MiD-D.

Summer days on the route of Star-Cole and Red Star lines' steamers to the famous St. Clair Flats, Star Island, the new Riverside, Joe Bedore's, The Oakland, [and] Port Huron. Detroit: J[ohn] Bornman & Son, 1895. 87, [1] p. Illus., maps. Cover title: Summer days on the Detroit and St. Clair rivers. MiD-B, MiD-D.

Lake Ontario and St. Lawrence River day line summer time table to the far-famed Thousand Islands. [Detroit?, 1897]. 1 sheet folded to [8] p. Illus. CaOOA.

Summer days on the route of Star-Cole Red and White Star lines' steamers, 1897. Detroit: James H. Stone & Co., [1897]. 85, [11] p. Illus., maps. Mi.

Lake Ontario and St. Lawrence River day line summer time table to the far-famed Thousand Islands. [Detroit?, 1898]. 1 sheet folded to [8] p. Illus. CaOOA.

Summer days on the route of Star-Cole Red and White Star lines' steamers, 1898. Detroit: Thos. Smith Press, [1898]. 89, [7] p. Illus., map. Cover title: Summer days on the Detroit and St. Clair rivers. MSaP, MI, MiD-D.

Lake Ontario and St. Lawrence River day line summer time table to the far famed Thousand Islands. [N.p., 1899]. 1 sheet folded to [8] p. Illus. CaOOA, MiD-D.

Summer days on the route of Star-Cole Red and White Star lines' steamers, 1899. Detroit: Thos. Smith Press, [1899]. 89, [7] p. Illus., map. Cover title: Summer days on the Detroit and St. Clair rivers. MSaP, MiD-B, WM.

Lake Ontario and St. Lawrence River day line to the far famed Thousand Islands. [N.p., 1904]. 1 sheet folded to [12] p. Illus., map. MSaP.

Thousand Islands, Lake Ontario and St. Lawrence River by day light [plus] summer vacation trips [to] Niagara Falls, Buffalo, Rochester, Sodus Point, Oswego, and the far famed 1000 Island resorts. [N.p., 1907]. 1 sheet folded to [16] p. Illus., map. MSaP.

Lake tours [on] the Georgian Bay route sailing between Cleveland, Toledo, Detroit, and the Soo via the famous North Channel and 30,000 Islands of Georgian Bay. [N.p., 1909]. [20] p. Illus., map. OBgU.

Star Cole Line steamers lake tours, the Georgian Bay route, sailing between Cleveland, Toledo, Detroit, and the Soo via the famous North Channel and 30,000 Islands of Georgian Bay. [N.p., 1910]. [20] p. Illus., map. MiU-H.

Star Cole line steamers lake tours, the Georgian Bay route, sailing between Cleveland, Toledo, Detroit, and the Soo via the famous North Channel and 30,000 Islands of Georgian Bay. [N.p., 1912]. 22 [i.e. 12] p. Illus., map. WM.

Lake tours [on] the Georgian Bay route sailing between Cleveland, Toledo, Detroit, and the Soo via the North Channel and 30,000 Islands of Georgian Bay. [N.p., 1914]. 1 sheet folded to 9, [1] p. Illus., map. MiD-B.

STAR LINE MACKINAC ISLAND PASSENGER SERVICE, INCORPORATED, ST. IGNACE, MI
Incorporated 2 August 1977. Still active as of 1990.

Mackinac Island ferry from St. Ignace. [Eau Claire, WI: Johnson Litho, 1986]. 1 sheet folded to [4] p. Illus., map. WM.

Mackinac Island ferry from St. Ignace, [an] 18 minute hydroplane ride. [Eau Claire, WI: Johnson Litho, 1987]. 1 sheet folded to [4] p. Illus., map. MiD-D, MiMtpC.

Mackinac Island ferry 1988 schedule [from] St. Ignace and Mackinaw City. [Eau Claire, WI: Johnson Litho, 1988]. 1 sheet folded to [6] p. Illus., maps. MiD-D.

Mackinac Island ferry [from] St. Ignace and Mackinaw City, 1989 schedule. [Eau Claire, WI: Johnson Litho, 1989]. 1 sheet folded to [6] p. Illus., maps. MiD-D, Mi-MISPC.

Mackinac Island ferry 1990 schedule [from] St. Ignace and Mackinaw City. [Eau Claire, WI: Johnson Litho, 1990]. 1 sheet folded to [6] p. Illus., maps. MiD-D, MiMtpC, MiShM.

STRAITS TRANSIT, INCORPORATED, MACKINAW CITY, MI
Incorporated 25 March 1959, by former state ferry employees. Taken over by the Arnold Transit Company in April of 1977.

Schedule [for the] Mackinac Island Ferry Company. Cheboygan, MI: Observer, [1959?]. 1 sheet folded to [4] p. Illus. MnDuC.

Schedule [for the] Mackinac Island Ferry Company. Cheboygan, MI: Observer, [1960?]. 1 sheet folded to [4] p. Illus. MiD-D, MnDuC.

Mackinac Island Ferry Company schedule. Cheboygan, MI: Observer Print, [1961?]. 1 sheet folded to [4] p. Illus. MiD-D, MiManiHi, OBgU.

Mackinac Island Ferry Company schedule. Cheboygan, MI: Observer Print, [1964?]. 1 sheet folded to [4] p. Illus. MiD-D.

Mackinac Island ferries schedule. Cheboygan, MI: Cheboygan Observer, [1969]. 1 sheet folded to [4] p. Illus. MiMtpC, Mi-MISPC.

Mackinac Island ferries schedule. Cheboygan, MI: Observer, [1970]. 1 sheet folded to [4] p. Illus. MiD-D.

Mackinac Island ferries schedule. Cheboygan, MI: Cheboygan Observer, [1971]. 1 sheet folded to [4] p. Illus., map. OBgU, OFH.

Mackinac Island ferries schedule. [N.p., 1972]. 1 sheet folded to [4] p. Illus., map. CSmH.

Mackinac Island ferries schedule. [N.p., 1973]. 1 sheet folded to [4] p. Illus., map. MiD-D, OBgU.

Mackinac Island ferries schedule. [N.p., 1974]. 1 sheet folded to [4] p. Illus., map. OBgU.

Mackinac Island ferries schedule. [N.p., 1975]. 1 sheet folded to [4] p. Illus., map. OBgU.

Mackinac Island ferries schedule. Petoskey, MI: Little Traverse Printing, [1976]. 1 sheet folded to [4] p. Illus., map. MiD-D.

TASHMOO TRANSIT COMPANY, DETROIT, MI

Incorporated 21 May 1931 as a sort of successor to the White Star Navigation Company. Ceased operations in 1936. Dissolved in 1940.

Detroit to St. Clair Flats, Tashmoo Park, Algonac, Sarnia Ont., [and] Port Huron, Mich., 1933. [N.p., 1933]. 1 sheet folded to [4] p. Illus., map. WM.

Detroit to St. Clair Flats, Tashmoo Park, Algonac, Sarnia Ont., [and] Port Huron, Mich., 1934. [N.p., 1934]. 1 sheet folded to [4] p. Illus., map. WM.

Detroit to St. Clair Flats, Tashmoo Park, Algonac, Sarnia Ont., [and] Port Huron, Mich., 1935. [N.p., 1935]. 1 sheet folded to [8] p. Illus., map. CU-SB, MiD-D.

Detroit to St. Clair Flats, Tashmoo Park, Algonac, Sarnia Ont., [and] Port Huron, Mich., 1936. [N.p., 1936]. 1 sheet folded to [8] p. Illus., map. CU-SB, MiD-D, OBgU, OFH, WM.

30,000 ISLAND NAVIGATION COMPANY, MIDLAND, ONT

Organized in 1949. Though the firm's termination date is unknown, it had a short existence.

Take the boat at Midland, Ontario. Midland, ONT: Midland Press, [1950]. 1 sheet folded to [6] p. Illus., map. MiD-D.

THOUSAND ISLAND STEAMBOAT COMPANY, LIMITED, CLAYTON, NY

Incorporated on 26 May 1881. Acquired by the Richelieu & Ontario Navigation Company on 1 June 1912. Charter expired on 15 May 1914.

1000 Islands route down the St. Lawrence via [the] Rome, Watertown & Ogdensburg Railroad and [the] New American Line, season 1884. New York: Leve & Alden Printing Co., [1884]. 1 sheet folded to [12] p. Illus., maps. CaOOA.

The Thousand Island Steamboat Company (Limited) [and] the St. Lawrence River Steamboat Company (Limited) in connection with [the] Rome, Watertown and Ogdensburg Railway. [N.p., 1888]. 1 sheet folded to [8] p. CaOOA.

The Thousand Island Steamboat Co., Limited, [and] the St. Lawrence River Steamboat Co., Limited, in connection with [the] Rome, Watertown and Ogdensburg Railway. Boston: R[and] A[very] Supply Co., [1889?]. 1 sheet folded to [8] p. Illus. CaOOA.

Complete time-table, 1892, [of the] Thousand Island and St. Lawrence River steamboat companies (limited) in connection with [the] Rome, Watertown and Ogdensburg R.R. [N.p., 1892]. 1 sheet folded to [8] p. Illus. CaOOA.

Thousand Island Steamboat Co., Limited, [and] St. Lawrence River Steamboat Co., Limited, operated in connection with the R[ome], W[atertown] & O[gdensburg] Railroad, season of 1892. [N.p., 1892]. 19, [1] p. Illus., maps. CaOOA.

Complete time table, 1893, [of the] Thousand Island and St. Lawrence River steamboat companies, limited, in connection with [the] Rome, Watertown and Ogdensburg R.R. [N.p., 1893]. 1 sheet folded to [8] p. Illus. CaOOA.

Thousand Island Steamboat Co., Limited, [and] St. Lawrence River Steamboat Co., Limited, operated in connection with the R[ome], W[atertown] & O[gdensburg] Railroad, season of 1893. [N.p., 1893]. 19, [1] p. Illus., maps. CaOOA.

Complete time table, 1894, [of the] Thousand Island and St. Lawrence River steamboat companies, limited, in connection with [the] Rome, Watertown and Ogdensburg R.R. [N.p., 1894]. 1 sheet folded to [8] p. Illus. CaOOA.

Thousand Island Steamboat Co., Limited, [and] St. Lawrence River Steamboat Co., Limited, operated in connection with the R[ome], W[atertown] & O[gdensburg] Railroad, season of 1894. [N.p., 1894]. 19, [1] p. Illus., maps. CaOOA, ViNeM.

Complete time table, 1895, [of the] Thousand Island and St. Lawrence River steamboat companies, limited, in connection with [the] Rome, Watertown and Ogdensburg R.R. [N.p., 1895]. 1 sheet folded to [8] p. Illus. CaOOA.

Thousand Island Steamboat Co., Limited, [and] St. Lawrence River Steamboat Co., Limited, operated in connection with the R[ome], W[atertown] & O[gdensburg] Railroad, season of 1895. [N.p., 1895]. 23, [1] p. Illus., maps. CaOOA.

Complete time table, 1896, [of the] Thousand Island and St. Lawrence River steamboat companies, limited, in connection with [the] Rome, Watertown and Ogdensburg R.R. [N.p., 1896]. 1 sheet folded to [8] p. Illus. CaOOA.

Thousand Island Steamboat Co., Limited, [and] St. Lawrence River Steamboat Co., Limited, operated in connection with the R[ome], W[atertown] & O[gdensburg] Railroad, season of 1896. [N.p., 1896]. 26, [2] p. Illus., maps inserted at center and end. CaOOA.

Complete time table, 1897, [of the] Thousand Island and St. Lawrence River steamboat companies, limited, in connection with [the] Rome, Watertown and Ogdensburg R.R. [N.p., 1897]. 1 sheet folded to [8] p. Illus. CaOOA.

Thousand Island and St. Lawrence River steamboat companies, limited, in connection with [the] Rome, Watertown and Ogdensburg R.R. [N.p., 1897]. 1 sheet folded to [10] p. Illus. MiD-D.

Thousand Island Steamboat Co., Limited, [and] St. Lawrence River Steamboat Co., Limited, operated in connection with the R[ome], W[atertown] & O[gdensburg] Railroad, season 1897. [N.p., 1897]. 35, [1] p. Illus., map. CaOOA.

The Thousand Island and St. Lawrence River steamboat companies, limited, [operating the] American Line to Montreal [and] the Folger System in connection with the New York Central & Hudson River R.R. [N.p., 1898]. 1 sheet folded to [10] p. Illus. CaOOA.

The Thousand Island and St. Lawrence River steamboat companies, limited, [operating the] American Line to Montreal [and] the Folger System in connection with the New York Central & Hudson River R.R. Niagara Falls, NY: Gazette Press, [1898]. 1 sheet folded to [16] p. Illus., maps. ViNeM.

The Thousand Island and St. Lawrence River steamboat companies, limited, [operating the] American Line to Montreal [and] the Folger System in connection with [the] Rome, Watertown, and Ogdensburg Division of the New York Central & Hudson River R.R. Niagara Falls, NY: Gazette Press, [1898]. 1 sheet folded to [12] p. Illus., maps. CaOOA.

The Thousand Island and St. Lawrence River steamboat companies, limited, [operating] the Folger System in connection with the New York Central & Hudson River

R.R. Grand Rapids, MI: James Bayne Co., [1898?]. 1 sheet folded to [10] p. Illus. CaOOA.

The Thousand Island and St. Lawrence River steamboat companies, limited, [operating] the Folger System in connection with the New York Central & Hudson River R.R. Grand Rapids, MI: James Bayne Co., [1899]. 33, [3] p. Illus., maps. CaOOA, OBgU.

The Thousand Island and St. Lawrence River steamboat companies, limited, [operating] the Folger System in connection with the New York Central & Hudson River R.R. [Grand Rapids, MI: James Bayne Co., 1899]. 1 sheet folded to [8] p. Illus. CaOOA.

The Thousand Island and St. Lawrence River steamboat companies, limited, [operating] the Folger System in connection with the New York Central & Hudson River R.R. [Grand Rapids, MI: James Bayne Co., 1900]. 1 sheet folded to [8] p. Illus. CaOOA.

The Thousand Island and St. Lawrence River steamboat companies, limited, [operating] the Folger System in connection with the New York Central & Hudson River R.R. Grand Rapids, MI: James Bayne Co., [1900]. 35, [1] p. Illus., maps. CaOOA, MiD-D.

The Thousand Island and St. Lawrence River steamboat companies, limited, [operating] the Folger System in connection with the New York Central & Hudson River R.R. [Grand Rapids, MI: James Bayne Co., 1901]. 1 sheet folded to [8] p. Illus. CaOOA.

The Thousand Island and St. Lawrence River steamboat companies, limited, [operating] the Folger System in connection with the New York Central & Hudson River R.R. Grand Rapids, MI: James Bayne Co., [1901]. 47, [1] p. Illus., maps. CaOOA, ViNeM.

The Thousand Island and St. Lawrence River steamboat companies, limited, [operating] the Folger System in connection with the New York Central & Hudson River R.R. [Grand Rapids, MI: James Bayne Co., 1902]. 1 sheet folded to [8] p. Illus. CaOOA.

The Thousand Island and St. Lawrence River steamboat companies, limited, [operating] the Folger System in connection with the New York Central & Hudson River R.R. Clayton, NY: Thousand Islands Publishing Co., [1902]. 55, [1] p. Illus., maps. CaOOA.

The Thousand Island and St. Lawrence River steamboat companies, limited, [operating] the Folger System in connection with the New York Central & Hudson River R.R. [N.p., 1903]. 1 sheet folded to [8] p. Illus. CaOOA.

The Thousand Island and St. Lawrence River steamboat companies, limited, [operating] the Folger System in connection with the New York Central & Hudson River R.R. Clayton, NY: T[housand] I[slands] Pub[lishing] Co., [1904]. 1 sheet folded to [8] p. Illus. To take effect June 19, 1904. ViNeM.

The Thousand Island and St. Lawrence River steamboat companies, limited, [operating] the Folger System in connection with the New York Central & Hudson River R.R. [N.p., 1905]. 1 sheet folded to [8] p. Illus. CaOOA.

The Thousand Island and St. Lawrence River steamboat . companies, limited, [operating] the Folger System in connection with the New York Central & Hudson River R.R. [N.p., 1905]. 58, [2] p. Illus., maps. CaOOA, MiD-D.

The Thousand Island and St. Lawrence River steamboat companies, limited, [operating] the Folger System in connection with the New York Central & Hudson River R.R. [N.p., 1906]. 1 sheet folded to [8] p. Illus. CaOOA.

The Thousand Island and St. Lawrence River steamboat companies, limited, [operating] the Folger System in connection with the New York Central & Hudson River R.R. [N.p., 1906]. 75, [1] p. Illus., maps. CaOOA.

The Thousand Island and St. Lawrence River steamboat companies, limited, [operating] the Folger System in connection with the New York Central & Hudson River R.R. [N.p., 1907]. 1 sheet folded to [8] p. Illus. CaOOA.

The Thousand Island and St. Lawrence River steamboat companies, limited, [operating] the Folger System in connection with the New York Central & Hudson River R.R. [N.p., 1908]. 83, [1] p. Illus., folded map. CaOOA.

The Thousand Island and St. Lawrence River steamboat companies, limited, [operating] the Folger System in connection with the New York Central & Hudson River R.R. [N.p., 1909]. 1 sheet folded to [8] p. Illus. CaOOA.

The Thousand Island and St. Lawrence River steamboat companies, limited, [operating] the Folger System in connection with the New York Central & Hudson River R.R. [N.p., 1909]. 91, [1] p. Illus., folded map. OBgU.

The Thousand Island and St. Lawrence River steamboat companies, limited, [operating] the Folger System in connection with the New York Central & Hudson River R.R. [N.p., 1910]. 1 sheet folded to [8] p. Illus. CaOOA.

The Thousand Island and St. Lawrence River steamboat companies, limited, in connection with the New York Central Lines. [N.p., 1911]. 95, [1] p. Illus., folded map. CaOOA.

The Thousand Island and St. Lawrence River steamboat companies, limited, in connection with the New York Central Lines. Grand Rapids, MI: James Bayne Co., [1912]. 102 p. Illus., folded map. CaOOA.

The Thousand Islands of the St. Lawrence River, attractive trips for the tourist by the steamers of the Thousand Island Steamboat Co. [N.p., 1912]. 1 sheet folded to [12] p. Illus., map. CU-SB, CaOOA.

The Thousand Islands of the St. Lawrence River, sight seeing trips among the islands by steamers of the Thousand Island Steamboat Company. [N.p., 1913]. 1 sheet folded to [12] p. Illus., map. MiD-D.

TOLEDO EXCURSION LINES, INCORPORATED, TOLEDO, OH
Incorporated on 17 October 1958 as successor to Seaway Excursion Lines, Inc. Commenced service on 30 May 1959, and ship sold at auction on 13 June 1960. Charter cancelled on 31 August 1962.

Welcome aboard the Canadiana for a pleasure-packed trip. [N.p., 1959]. 1 sheet folded to [4] p. Illus., map. MiD-D.

TRAVERSE BAY TRANSPORTATION COMPANY, TRAVERSE CITY, MI
Incorporated 14 May 1907. Dissolved 14 March 1918.

Beautiful Grand Traverse Bay resorts reached by [the] Traverse Bay Transportation Co. new steamer "Chequamegon," 1908. Traverse City, MI: Eagle Press, [1908]. [16] p. Illus., map. MiManiHi.

UNION STEAMBOAT COMPANY, BUFFALO, NY
Organized 3 February 1869. Merged with the Erie Railroad Company on 30 June 1896. Became part of the Great Lakes Transit Corporation on 22 March 1916.

For Lake Superior! The Union Steamboat Company and [the] Atlantic, Duluth and Pacific Line from Buffalo, Erie, Cleveland, Detroit and Sarnia to Sault S[ain]te Marie, Marquette, Houghton, Bayfield and Duluth. [Buffalo, 1871]. 1 sheet folded to [4] p. MiD-D.

For Lake Superior! The Union Steamboat Company and Atlantic, Duluth and Pacific Lake Company from Buffalo, Erie, Cleveland, Detroit, and Sarnia to Sault S[ain]te Marie, Marquette, Houghton, Bayfield and Duluth connecting with the Lake Superior and Mississippi Rail Road to St. Paul, Minneapolis, and all points in Minnesota, northern Wisconsin and Iowa and the Northern Pacific Railroad to the Red River of the North and the wonderful country beyond, 1872. [Buffalo, 1872]. [4] p. CU-BANC.

The Union Steamboat Company, plaintiffs, against the Green Bay & Minnesota Railway Co., defendant, [in the] United States Circuit Court, Western District of Wisconsin, June term, 1878, [being] plaintiff's brief on motion for new trial. Madison, WI: David Atwood, [1878]. 16 p. MnHi.

The Union Steamboat Co.'s through freight line via the Great Lakes and the New York, Lake Erie & Western R.R. and connections, east-bound tariff from Chicago, Milwaukee and Green Bay, no. 1, April 25, 1880. Chicago: J[udson] M.W. Jones Stationery and Printing Co., [1880]. 32 p. N.

Telegraphic code of the Union Steamboat Co. Buffalo: Baker, Jones & Co., 1882. 146 p. NBu.

UNITED STATES AND DOMINION TRANS-PORTATION COMPANY, CHICAGO, IL
Commenced operations about 1898. Associated with Booth Fisheries. Apparently ceased to exist in 1928 and succeeded by the United States & Dominion Transportation Company, Limited.

The only line making a daylight circuit of beautiful Isle Royale [and connecting] Duluth, Port Arthur, Isle Royale, Bayfield, Ashland [and] Apostle Islands. Chicago: Henry O. Shepard Co., [1898?]. 7, [1] p. Illus., map. ViNeM.

The only line making a daylight circuit of beautiful Isle Royale [and connecting] Duluth, Isle Royale, Ft. William, Port Arthur, Cornucopia, [and] Grand Marais. [Chicago, 1899]? 1 sheet folded to [8] p. Illus., map. MnHi.

The only line making a daylight circuit of beautiful Isle Royale [and connecting] Duluth, Isle Royale, Ft. William, Port Arthur, Cornucopia, [and] Grand Marais. Chicago: Poole Bros., [1900?]. 7, [1] p. Illus., map. MnDuC.

"Booth's Line" [serving] Lake Superior, Georgian Bay [and] Lake Winnipeg. Chicago: Poole Bros., [1901]. 1 sheet folded to [14] p. Illus., map. CaOOA.

"Booth's Line" to the land of the Ojibways. Chicago: Jacobs & Holmes, [1904]. [16] p. Illus., map. Note: Claims to be time- table for 1904-1905. CaOOA.

Land of the Ojibways, America's most delightful vacation ground. [Chicago?, 1906]. [16] p. Illus., map. MSaP.

Lake Superior [via] Duluth, Isle Royale, Sault S[ain]te Marie, Michipicoten [and] Georgian Bay [on] the North-Western Line and the steel steamers of the "Booth Line." Chicago: Poole Bros., 1909. 10, [2] p. Illus., map. MiD-D.

Lake Superior, Duluth, Isle Royale, Sault S[ain]te Marie, Michipicoten, [and] Georgian Bay. Chicago: Poole Bros., [1912]. 10, [2] p. Illus., map. WM.

UNITED STATES & DOMINION TRANSPORTATION COMPANY., LIMITED., OWEN SOUND, ONT
Created on 21 May 1929, apparently as successor to the United States and Dominion Transportation Company. Changed name to the Dominion Transportation Company, Limited, on 19 March 1934.

Georgian Bay, North Channel, Lake Superior, and Lake Huron south shore ports, 1930. [N.p., 1930]. [12] p. Illus., map. MiD-D.

Georgian Bay, North Channel, Lake Superior and Lake Huron south shore ports. [N.p., 1931]. [12] p. Illus., map. MiD-B.

Georgian Bay, North Channel, and Lake Superior, "the vacationists' paradise," season 1933. Toronto: Lloyds Maps, [1933]. 1 sheet folded to [10] p. Illus., map. WM.

Georgian Bay, North Channel, and Lake Superior, "the vacationists' paradise," season 1934. Toronto: Lloyds Maps, [1934]. 1 sheet folded to [10] p. Illus., map. MiD-D, WM.

UNITED STATES STEEL CORPORATION, PITTSBURGH STEAMSHIP DIVISION, CLEVELAND, OH
The Pittsburgh Steamship Company was formed on 10 November 1899. In February of 1901 it became a subsidiary of United States Steel. On 1 July 1951 it was made a division of USS, remaining so until 1 July 1967. The USS Great Lakes Fleet was still active in 1990.

U.S. Steel News, Pittsburgh Steamship Company number. [N.p.], c1937. 32, [2] p. Illus., map. Appeared as vol. 2, no. 9, September, 1937. MnDuC, WManiM.

Minutes [of] annual meeting, March 28-29, 1950. [N.p., 1950]. 3, 2, 108 leaves. MnDuC.

The Great Lakes..., the main artery in the lifeline of American industry, by Donald C[onway] Potts, President. [N.p., 1953]. 16 p. MSaP, OClWHi, WMCHi.

Pittsburgh Sidelights. — Vol. 1, no. 1 (May 1953?)-vol. 22, no. 1? (May-June 1974?). — Cleveland, 1953-1974. Illus. Monthly (1953-Oct. 1958), bimonthly (Nov. 1958-1974). Beginning with vol. 9, no. 1 (May-June 1961) the cover reads USS Sidelights. Continued by: Sidelights. MnDuC, OBgU, OV.

Annual meeting [of] masters and chief engineers, March 22-23, 1955. [N.p., 1955]. [4], 218, 5, 2 leaves. Illus. Cover title: Minutes of annual meeting, 1955. MnDuC.

Annual meeting [of] masters and chief engineers, March 26-28, 1956. [N.p., 1956]. [2], 236, 4, 2 leaves. Illus. Cover title: Minutes of annual meeting, 1956. MnDuC.

Stand By. — Vol. 1, no. 1 (June 1958)-vol. 6, no. 3 (Autumn 1963). — Cleveland?, 1958-1963. Monthly during the navigation season, irregular at other times. Published as a safety newsletter. OBgU.

Accident prevention program manual. [N.p., 1960]. 190, [22] leaves. Illus. MnDuI.

Agreement between [the] Pittsburgh Steamship Division [of the] United States Steel Corporation and [the] Great Lakes District Local 101, February 27, 1960. [Cleveland, 1960]. 64 p. OBgU.

Annual meeting of masters and chief engineers, March 22 and 23, 1960. [N.p., 1960]. [2], 126 leaves. Cover title: Minutes of annual meeting, 1960. MnDuC.

Agreement between [the] Pittsburgh Steamship Division [of the] United States Steel Corporation and District 2 [of the] Marine Engineers Beneficial Association, AFL-CIO, July 26, 1962. [Cleveland, 1962]. 56 p. OBgU.

Hull manual for masters and mates, Great Lakes fleet. [N.p.], c1963. 178, [4] p. Illus. MnDuI, OBgU.

Minimum requirements for an effective safety program. [N.p., 1964]. [50] p., [11] leaves. MnDuC, MnDuI.

Lake Shipping [Division] operating manual [for the] Great Lakes fleet. [N.p., 1966]. [314] p., [23] leaves. Illus. Title from cover of 3-ring notebook. MiD-D.

Agreement between United States Steel Corporation and [the] United Steelworkers of America covering unlicensed seamen, iron ore and steel products vessels [of the] Great Lakes fleet, August 1, 1968. [N.p., 1968]. 72 p. WManiM.

General safety and vessel conduct rules and regulations. [N.p., 1971]. 53, [1] p. Illus. MnDuI, OBgU.

Hull manual for masters and mates. [N.p.], c1972. [4], 184 p. Illus. MnDuC, OBgU.

M[otor] V[essel] Roger Blough. [Pittsburgh]: USS Visual Services, [1972]. [14] p. plus foldout diagram. Illus., map. MiD-D, MnDuC.

Great Lakes fleet. [N.p., 1973?]. [20] p. Illus. MnDuC, OBgU.

Agreement between United States Steel Corporation and District 2, Marine Engineers Beneficial Association, A[merican] F[ederation] [of] L[abor]-C[ongress] [of] I[ndustrial] O[rganizations], covering licensed engineers [of the] former Pittsburgh fleet, August 1, 1974. [N.p., 1974]. 67, [1] p. MnDuI.

Agreement between United States Steel Corporation and masters, mates and pilots, Great Lakes and Rivers District, covering licensed mates [on] iron ore and steel products vessels, Great Lakes fleet, August 1, 1974. [N.p., 1974]. 62 p. MnDuI.

Agreement between [the] United States Steel Corporation and [the] United Steelworkers of America covering unlicensed seamen [on the] iron ore and steel products vessels, Great Lakes fleet, August 1, 1974. [N.p., 1974]. 83, [1] p. OBgU.

Sidelights. — Vol. 1, no. 1 (July 1, 1974)-vol. 6, no. 3 (September/October 1979). — Cleveland, 1974-1979. Irregular during shipping season. Continues in part journal of same name from the Pittsburgh Steamship Division. OBgU.

Program of insurance benefits for employees of United States Steel Corporation and subsidiary companies pursuant to agreement with United Steelworkers of America, unlicensed seamen, as amended, effective August 1, 1975. [N.p., 1975]. 80 p. MnDuI.

UNIVERSAL STEAMSHIP COMPANY, CHICAGO, IL

Incorporated 28 March 1923 as a Delaware business. Charter withdrawn on 14 August 1928.

Universal Steamship Company, libellant-appellant, vs. American Steamship Company, claimant, as owner of the steamer Louis R[ogers] Davidson, et al., respondents-appellees, [being] brief for Universal Steamship Company, appellant, in the United States Circuit Court of Appeals for the Seventh District, no. 3790. Cleveland: Gates Legal Publishing Co., [1926]. [4], 40 p. OBgU.

UPPER LAKES SHIPPING, LIMITED, TORONTO, ONT

Founded in March of 1931 as Northland Steamships, Limited. On 16 August 1932, it became known as the Upper Lakes & St. Lawrence Transportation Company, Limited. Became Upper Lakes Shipping, Limited, on 29 December 1958. On 31 December 1983, the firm transferred its head office to Calgary, Alberta, and adopted the name ULS International, Incorporated. On 31 December 1988, the name of the business was changed to ULS Corporation.

Ship-shore News. — Vol. 1, no. 1 (April 1959)-present. — Toronto and Ashawa, ONT, 1959-present. Illus. Irregular. Title was Ship-shore Digest from vol. 16, no. 7 (October 1977) through vol. 20, no. 11 (November/December 1981). CaOONL, CaOStC, MiD-D, MnDuC, OV.

Christening and commissioning of the S.S. Red Wing of Upper Lakes Shipping, Ltd., Saturday, July 23rd, 1960. [N.p., 1960]. [8] p. Illus. MSaP, MiD-D, NBuHi.

Representative press reports on the Great Lakes Shipping Inquiry, October, 1962. [Hamilton, 1962]. 14 p. CaOKQ.

Representative newspaper editorials on the Norris Report into the "Disruption of shipping on the Great Lakes." [Toronto?, 1963]. [18] p. Illus. CaOKQ.

Ships of the fleet. [Toronto, 1973]. 24 p. Illus., map. CaOONL, MnDuC, OBgU, WHi.

Christening of the M[otor] V[essel] Canadian Olympic. [N.p., 1976]. [4] p. Illus. CaOPoCM.

M[otor] V[essel] Canadian Pioneer [christening]. [N.p., 1981]. [4] p. Illus. CaOKMM, CaOPoCM, OBgU.

ULS [history and promotional]. [Toronto?, 1983?]. [24] p. (2 folded). Illus., map. CaOPoCM, MiD-D, MnDuC, OBgU.

ULS self-unloading ships. [N.p., 1984?]. 1 sheet folded to [16] p. Illus. CaOKMM.

VOIGHT'S MARINE SERVICE, LIMITED, ELLISON BAY, WI

Established on 1 January 1971. Still active in 1990.

Enjoy beautiful scenery and clean clear air on a cruise aboard the "Yankee Clipper" to Washington Island. [N.p., 1979]. 1 sheet folded to [6] p. Illus., map. MiManiHi.

"Yankee Clipper" to Washington Island leaving from Gills Rock. [Sturgeon Bay, WI: Bayprint, 1986]. 1 sheet folded to [6] p. Illus., map. MiD-D.

"The waterful experience" aboard the Island Clipper and the Yankee Clipper to Washington Island and beyond..., departs from Gills Rock. [Green Bay: Quigley Printing, 1988]. 1 sheet folded to [8] p. Illus., maps. MiD-D.

"The waterful experience" aboard the Island Clipper and the Yankee Clipper to Washington Island and beyond..., departs from Gills Rock. [Green Bay: Quigley Printing, 1989]. 1 sheet folded to [8] p. Illus., maps. MiD-D.

WALKERVILLE & DETROIT FERRY COMPANY, DETROIT, MI

Incorporated 13 July 1888. Dissolved 19 August 1946.

Direct to Canada's main highways. [N.p., 1930?]. 1 sheet folded to [8] p. Illus., map. MiD-B.

WARD'S LAKE SUPERIOR LINE, DETROIT, MI

The Ward Line was founded by Samuel Ward. It was inherited by Eber Brock Ward on 24 February 1854. Excursions to Lake Superior were made possible by the opening of the "Soo" Canal on 18 June 1855.

Grand pleasure excursion to Lake Superior [on] the new and superb steamer Planet! [Detroit, 1855]. [4] p. Illus. Note: 3 pages are blank. MiD-B.

WASAC WATERWAYS, INCORPORATED, CLEVELAND, OH

Incorporated on 9 March 1962. Charter cancelled on 20 May 1965.

S.S. Erie Queen, a luxurious yacht-style ship designed especially for private charter parties and day and evening cruises for social, business meeting, and convention groups up to 500 capacity. [N.p., 1962]. 1 sheet folded to [4] p. Illus. OFH, ViNeM, WM.

S.S. Erie Queen, a luxurious yacht-style ship designed especially for private charter-parties and day and evening cruises for social, business meeting, and convention groups. [N.p., 1963?]. 1 sheet folded to [6] p. Illus. MiD-B, MiD-D, MiMtpC, MiShM, WM.

WESTERN RESERVE NAVIGATION COMPANY, CLEVELAND, OH

Incorporated 21 March 1921 as apparent successor to the Ontario & Ohio Navigation Company. Discontinued on 15 February 1927, and apparently succeeded by the Cleveland & Canada Navigation Company.

Short route to Canada, the Western Reserve Navigation Co. [linking] Cleveland, Ohio, U.S.A. to Port Stanley and Erieau, Ontario, Canada. [N.p., 1923]. 1 sheet folded to [8] p. Illus., map. Effective May 18, 1923. MiD-D, OBgU.

"The short route to Canada" between Cleveland, Ohio, U.S.A. and Port Stanley, Ontario, Canada. [N.p., 1924]. 1 sheet folded to [8] p. Illus., map. Effective May 16, 1924. Time table no. 3. CaOOA.

"The short route to Canada" between Cleveland and Port Stanley. Cleveland: Doyle & Waltz, [1925]. 14 [i.e. 8] p. Illus., map. At bottom: Time table no. 4. OBgU, OFH.

"The short route to Canada" between Cleveland and Port Stanley. Cleveland: Doyle & Waltz, [1926]. 14 [i.e. 8] p. Illus., map. Time table no. 5. Note: Text says the schedule is for 1925, but the printer's mark indicates the job was done in January of 1926. MiD-D.

WESTERN TRANSIT COMPANY, BUFFALO, NY

Organized on 4 December 1883 as a subsidiary of the New York Central Railroad. Became a part of the Great Lakes Transit Corporation in the spring of 1916.

Average statement [for] steamer "Livingstone," Kellogg & Robinson, adjusters. Chicago: Libby & Sherwood Printing Co., 1894. 23, [1] p. N.

The Western Transit Co. [serving] Buffalo, Duluth and intermediate ports [as the] New York Central & Hudson River R.R. line of screw steamers, 1894. Buffalo: Matthews-Northrup Co., [1894]. 1 sheet folded to [16] p. Illus., map. MiD-D, ViNeM.

WESTERN TRANSPORTATION COMPANY, BUFFALO, NY

Organized on 31 December 1855. Reorganized on 4 December 1883 as the Western Transit Company.

Articles of association and by-laws of the Western Transportation Company together with the act under which the company is incorporated and that part of the revised statutes referred to therein, and the rules of order of the board of directors. Buffalo: Clapp, Matthews and Co., 1856. 33, [1] p. OClWHi.

WHITE STAR LINE, DETROIT, MI

Incorporated on 14 April 1896, and for three years operated in a pool agreement with the Star-Cole Line. Declared bankruptcy in 1925 and succeeded by the White Star Navigation Company. Dissolved by court order on 27 December 1940.

Detroit and St. Clair rivers by daylight, the most charming water trip in the West. [Detroit?, 1900]. 24 p. MiPhM.

Summer days on the route of the White Star Line steamers. [Detroit?, 1900]. 79, [1] p. Illus., map. Cover title: Summer days on the Detroit and St. Clair rivers. MiD-D, MiPhM.

Daylight trips on the Detroit and St. Clair rivers by the White Star Line. [Detroit]: James H. Stone & Co., [1901]. 96, [20] p. Illus., maps. OBgU, WM.

Detroit and St. Clair rivers by daylight, the most charming water trip in the West, 1901 summer time table. Detroit: John Bornman & Son, [1901]. 24 p. Illus., map. MiD-D.

Souvenir [of] Parke, Davis & Co.'s Eleventh Annual Excursion to Tashmoo Park on St[eame]r Tashmoo [on] Friday, June 14, 1901. [Detroit?, 1901]. 21, [3] p. Illus. ViNeM.

Pleasure trips on the White Star Line, the most charming water trips in the West. Detroit: John Bornman & Son, [1902]. [1], 53, [1], lxv p. Illus., map. WM.

How a White Star Line "annual" sowed the seed that brought a fine crop. By Judson Grenell. [Detroit, 1906]. lxvi, 70 p. Illus., map. Cover title: Along lake and river, Bessie Beauchamp's impressions of an alluring panorama of 250 miles. MiD-D.

Two hundred and fifty miles of scenic panorama. [Detroit?, 1906]. 128 p. Illus., map. Cover title: 250 miles of ever changing panorama. OO, WM.

A wonderful scenic panorama, a story of the health, pleasure, profit, and recreation that are combined in a trip on any of the steamers of the White Star Line. By Judson Grinnell [sic]. Detroit: John Bornman & Son, [1907]. 58, lxx p. Illus. Cover title: Along lake and river. MiD-D.

A wonderful scenic panorama, a story of the health, pleasure, profit, and recreation that are combined in a trip on any of the steamers of the White Star Line. By Judson Grenell. Detroit: American Print. Co., 1908. 58, lxx p. Illus. Cover title: A panorama never to be forgotten. MiD-B, MiD-D.

Looking for the light, a story of idle hours on the White Star Line. By Judson Grenell. Detroit: John Bornman & Son, [1910]. 64, lxiv p. Illus., map. Cover title: Idle hours on a White Star liner. WMCHi.

White Star Line. Detroit: John Bornman & Son, [1910]. 16 p. Illus., map. MiD-B.

Ideal outings [to] Toledo, Sugar Island Park, Detroit, St. Clair Flats, Tashmoo, Sarnia, Ont., [and] Port Huron. [Detroit?, 1911]. 16 p. Illus., map. OBgU.

Rest and recreation on a White Star liner. By Judson Grenell. Port Huron: Riverside Ptg. Co., [1911]. 64, lxiv p. Illus. OBgU.

Through lakes and rivers on White Star Line steamers. What can be seen on excursion trips between Detroit, Michigan, and Toledo, Ohio, and between Detroit and Port Huron, Michigan, over a scenic route unsurpassed in interest by any other water route on the American continent. By Judson Grenell. Detroit: John Bornman & Son, 1912. 64, lxvi p. Illus., map. Cover title: White Star Magazine. MiD-B.

White Star Line [serving] Toledo, Sugar Island Park, Detroit, St. Clair Flats, Tashmoo, [and] Port Huron. [Detroit?, 1912]. 16 p. Illus., map. OClWHi.

Seeing the world with the aid of the White Star Line steamers. By Judson Grenell. Detroit: John Bornman & Son, 1913. 62, lxvi p. Illus., map. Cover title: White Star Magazine, o'er the placid waters of lake and river. MiD-D, MiPhM, MiU-H.

What the sage saw while traveling on the White Star Line steamers. Detroit: Saturday Night Press, 1914. 62, lxvi p. Illus. Cover title: White Star Magazine, "o'er the placid waters of lake and river." OClWHi.

"Threads of travel," comprising pertinent paragraphs & peculiar perspectives of popular places & prominent people treating of "a trip from Toledo to Detroit to Port Huron." By Harold Blake Shumm. [Detroit?, 1915]. 60, lxviii p. Illus., map. Cover title: White Star Magazine. Mi, MiPhM.

The dreams of youth: what two young people saw while on the White Star Line steamers. Detroit: Liggett & Gagnier, 1916. 60, lxviii p. Illus., map. Cover title: White Star Magazine. MiD-D.

Toledo Ohio, Sugar Island Park, Detroit Michigan, St. Clair Flats, Tashmoo Park, Sarnia Ontario [and] Port Huron Michigan. Detroit: Liggett & Gagnier, [1916]. 30 [i.e. 16] p. Illus., map. ViNeM.

White Star Magazine. [Detroit]: Topping-Sanders Co., 1917. 58, lxx p. Illus., map. MiD-B.

White Star Magazine. Detroit: Liggett & Gagnier, [1918]. 58, lxx p. Illus., map. MiD-B, MiD-D, MiU-H.

White Star Magazine. Detroit: Liggett & Gagnier, [1919]. 56, lxxii p. Illus., map. MiD-B, MiD-D, OBgU.

Schedule of steamer and service connections [to] Toledo, Sugar Island, Detroit, St. Clair Flats, Tashmoo Park, Sarnia Ont., [and] Port Huron, Mich., 1920. [Detroit?, 1920]. 15, [1] p. Illus., map. WM.

White Star Magazine. Detroit: Liggett & Gagnier, [1920]. 56, lxxii p. Illus., map. MiD-D.

Schedule of steamer service and connections [to] Toledo, Sugar Island, Detroit, St. Clair Flats, Tashmoo Park, Sarnia Ont., [and] Port Huron, Mich., 1921. [Detroit?, 1921]. 15, [1] p. Illus., map. MiD-B, MSaP.

Schedule of steamer service and connections [to] Toledo, Sugar Island, Detroit, St. Clair Flats, Tashmoo Park, Sarnia Ont., [and] Port Huron, Mich., 1922. [Detroit?, 1922]. 15, [1] p. Illus., map. CSmH, OBgU, WM.

White Star Magazine. [Detroit?, 1922]. 54, lxxii p. Illus., map. MiD-B, MiPh, MiPhM, OO.

Schedule of steamer service and connections [to] Toledo, Sugar Island, Detroit, St. Clair Flats, Tashmoo Park, Sarnia Ont., [and] Port Huron, Mich., 1923. [Detroit?, 1923]. 15, [1] p. Illus., map. WM.

White Star Magazine. Detroit: J[oseph] S. Gagnier, [1923]. 65, lxii p. Illus., map. MiD-B, OBgU, OFH.

Schedule of steamer service and connections [to] Toledo, Sugar Island, Detroit, St. Clair Flats, Tashmoo Park, Sarnia Ont., [and] Port Huron, Mich. Detroit: Inland Press, [1924]. 15, [1] p. Illus., map. CaOOA, MiD-D, MiShM, WM.

White Star Magazine. Detroit: J[oseph] S. Gagnier, [1924]. 65, lxii p. Illus., map. Mi, MiD-B, MiD-D, OFH.

WHITE STAR NAVIGATION COMPANY, DETROIT, MI

Incorporated on 25 May 1925 as successor to the White Star Line. Ceased to operate in 1930, and automatically dissolved in 1933. Continued by the Tashmoo Transit Company.

Detroit to St. Clair Flats, Tashmoo Park, Algonac, Sarnia Ont., [and] Port Huron, Mich. [Detroit?, 1925]. [8] p. Illus., map. CSmH, MiD-D.

Detroit to St. Clair Flats, Tashmoo Park, Algonac, Sarnia Ont., [and] Port Huron, Mich. [Detroit?, 1926]. [12] p. Illus., map. CtMyMHi, MiD-B, WM.

Detroit to St. Clair Flats, Tashmoo Park, Algonac, Sarnia Ont., [and] Port Huron, Mich. [Detroit?, 1927]. [12] p. Illus., map. CSmH, MiD-B, WM.

Detroit to St. Clair Flats, Tashmoo Park, Algonac, Sarnia Ont., [and] Port Huron, Mich., 1928. [Detroit?, 1928]. [12] p. Illus., map. CaOMM, MiD-D, WM.

Detroit to St. Clair Flats, Tashmoo Park, Algonac, Sarnia Ont., [and] Port Huron, Mich., 1929. [Detroit?, 1929]. 11, [1] p. Illus., map. WM.

Detroit to St. Clair Flats, Tashmoo Park, Algonac, Sarnia Ont., [and] Port Huron, Mich., 1930. [Detroit?, 1930]. 11, [1] p. Illus., map. MiD-D, WM.

WILSON MARINE TRANSIT COMPANY, CLEVELAND, OH

Changed name from Wilson Transit Company on 19 April 1957, shortly after it acquired the Great Lakes Steamship Company. Acquired by Litton Industries in 1966 and operated as a division. Sold to the American Ship Building Company on 15 August 1972.

The Wilson Whistle. — Vol. 1, no. 1 (August 1949)-vol. ?, no. 39? (August 1960?). — Cleveland, 1949-1960? Illus. Irregular. OBgU.

Agreement between Wilson Marine Transit Company and United Steelworkers of America, January 16, 1960. [Cleveland, 1960]. 60 p. OBgU.

Agreement between Wilson Marine Transit Company and Associated Maritime Officers, A[merican] F[ederation] [of] L[abor]-C[ongress] [of] I[ndustrial] O[rganizations], covering licensed mates, September 1, 1965. [Cleveland?, 1965]. [4], 53, [17] p. OBgU.

Agreement between Wilson Marine Transit Company and District 2, Marine Engineers Beneficial Association, A[merican] F[ederation] [of] L[abor]-C[ongress] [of] I[ndustrial] O[rganizations], covering licensed engineers, September 1, 1965. [Cleveland?, 1965]. [4], 58, [18] p. OBgU.

Agreement between Wilson Marine Transit Company and United Steelworkers of America, September 1, 1965. [Cleveland, 1965]. [4], 100 p. OBgU.

Agreement for chief cooks (stewards) between Wilson Marine Transit Company and Associated Maritime Officers, A[merican] F[ederation] [of] L[abor]-C[ongress] [of] I[ndustrial] O[rganizations], a division of District 2 M[arine] E[ngineers] B[eneficial] A[ssociation], September 1, 1965. [Cleveland?, 1965]. [4], 45, [14] p. OBgU.

Wilson Marine Transit Company, 1872-1966. [Cleveland?, 1966?]. [20] p. Illus., map. MnDuC, OBgU, OV.

WISCONSIN & MICHIGAN STEAMSHIP COMPANY, MILWAUKEE, WI

Created in 1934 when the Wisconsin & Michigan Transportation Company merged with the Pere Marquette Line (not to be confused with the Pere Marquette Railroad fleet). Popularly known as the "Clipper Line." Still an active Wisconsin firm in 1990.

Across Lake Michigan [connecting] Milwaukee-Muskegon-Chicago-Ludington, 1934. [N.p., 1934]. 1 sheet folded to [12] p. Illus., map. MiD-D, OFH, ViCFC, ViNeM.

S.S. Illinois between Chicago and Muskegon. [N.p., 1934]. 1 sheet folded to [6] p. Illus., map. ViNeM, WM.

Milwaukee-Muskegon, cross Lake Michigan in cool comfort. [N.p., 1935]. 1 sheet folded to [6] p. Illus. OBgU.

Chicago special across Lake Michigan. [N.p., 1936]. 1 sheet folded to [6] p. Illus. MdBUS.

Milwaukee - Muskegon, the short cut across Lake Michigan. [N.p., 1936]. 1 sheet folded to [6] p. Illus., map. MSaP, OBgU, ViNeM.

S.S. Missouri between Chicago and Muskegon by water, 1936. [N.p., 1936]. 1 sheet folded to [4] p. Illus. ViNeM.

Milwaukee-Muskegon, the short cut across Lake Michigan [offering] low rates on automobiles, 1937. [N.p., 1937]. 1 sheet folded to [6] p. Illus., map. CSmH, OBgU.

Cruise across Lake Michigan, 1938. [N.p., 1938]. 1 sheet folded to [6] p. WM.

Milwaukee-Muskegon, the short cut across Lake Michigan. [N.p., 1938]. 1 sheet folded to [6] p. Illus. MiD-D, OBgU.

Cruise across Lake Michigan, 1939. [N.p., 1939]. 1 sheet folded to [6] p. Illus. CSmH, WM, WMCHi.

Tourist short cut across Lake Michigan, [a] short cut to either fair. [N.p., 1939]. 1 sheet folded to [8] p. Illus., map. CSmH, WM.

Tourist short cut across Lake Michigan, [a] short cut to either fair, 1940. [N.p., 1940]. 1 sheet folded to [8] p. Map. MSaP, MdBUS, MiD-D, OFH, ViNeM, WM, WMCHi.

Thrilling eleven-hour cruise across Lake Michigan and return [on the] S.S. Milwaukee Clipper [between] Milwaukee-Muskegon. [N.p., 1941]. 1 sheet folded to [8] p. Illus. MdBUS, WM, WMCHi, WManiM.

Tourists and vacationists! Highspot your vacation with a Milwaukee Clipper cruise across Lake Michigan, save 240 miles. [N.p., 1941]. 1 sheet folded to [16] p. Illus., maps. CSmH, CU-SB, MdBUS, MiD-D, MiU-H, OBgU, ViNeM, WM, WManiM.

Across Lake Michigan [on the] S.S. Milwaukee Clipper, [a] touring-vacationing short cut [between] Milwaukee-Muskegon [that] saves 240 miles. [N.p., 1942]. 1 sheet folded to [20] p. Illus. CSmH, CU-SB, MdBUS, MiD-D, OBgU, OFH, ViNeM, WM.

Fun ahoy! Come on this festive 11-hour cruise across Lake Michigan and return, Milwaukee-Muskegon. [N.p., 1942]. 1 sheet folded to [20] p. Illus. MSaP, MiD-D, WM, WMCHi, WManiM.

New S.S. Milwaukee Clipper lake cruises, 1942. [N.p., 1942]. 1 sheet folded to [8] p. Illus. MiD-D.

This year everybody's cruising! [N.p., 1942?]. 1 sheet folded to [4] p. Illus., map. MiD-D.

New S.S. Milwaukee Clipper lake cruises [to] Chicago, Milwaukee, Muskegon (tourist autos carried), 1943. [N.p., 1943]. 1 sheet folded to [8] p. Illus. CU-SB, MdBUS, MiD-D, OBgU, ViNeM, WM, WManiM.

Thrills, fun, relaxation, rest aboard the S.S. Milwaukee Clipper, season 1944. [N.p., 1944]. 1 sheet folded to [8] p. Illus., maps. CU-SB, MiD-D, OBgU, OFH, WMCHi, WManiM.

Rest up! Have fun! On the S.S. Milwaukee Clipper, season 1945. [N.p., 1945]. 1 sheet folded to [16] p. Illus. CSmH, CU-SB, MiD-D, OBgU, OFH, WM.

S.S. Milwaukee Clipper [connecting] Milwaukee-Muskegon. Relax! Have fun! On the million dollar luxury liner! 1946 season. [N.p., 1946]. 1 sheet folded to [18] p. Illus., map. CSmH, CU-SB, MdBUS, MiD-D, OFH, ViNeM, WM, WManiM.

Fun...afloat! Aboard the S.S. Milwaukee Clipper cruising between Milwaukee and Muskegon, season 1947. [N.p., 1947]. 1 sheet folded to [16] p. Illus., maps. CSmH, CU-SB, MdBUS, MiD-D, OBgU, ViNeM.

Rest, zest, fun! Cross Lake Michigan on the S.S. Milwaukee Clipper for a delightful change, sailing between Milwaukee and Muskegon, season 1948. [N.p., 1948]. 1 sheet folded to [16] p. Illus. MdBUS, MiD-D, OBgU, OFH, WManiM.

Fun, romance, relaxation! Enjoy a holiday afloat! Cross Lake Michigan on the S.S. Milwaukee Clipper. [N.p., 1949]. [8] p. Illus., maps. CSmH, CU-SB, MSaP, MdBUS, MiD-D, ViNeM, WM.

Milwaukee-Muskegon daily cross lake service [on the] S.S. Milwaukee Clipper, a restful pleasure-filled short cut across Lake Michigan. [N.p., 1950]. 1 sheet folded to [4] p. Effective September 12, 1950. MdBUS.

Motorists and vacationists cross Lake Michigan, autos carried, save 240 driving miles, 1950. [N.p., 1950]. [8] p. Illus., maps. CSmH, MdBUS, MiD-D, OBgU.

Motorists—-cruise across Lake Michigan between Milwaukee, Wisconsin [and] Muskegon, Michigan, 1951. [N.p., 1951]. [8] p. Illus., maps. CSmH, MdBUS, MiD-D, OV, ViNeM, WManiM.

Motorists [and] vacationists short cut across Lake Michigan, save 240 driving miles [between] Milwaukee, Wis. [and] Muskegon, Mich., 1952. [N.p., 1952]. [8] p. Illus., maps. CSmH, MdBUS, MiD-B, MiD-D, OBgU, ViNeM, WM.

Passenger-auto ferry across Lake Michigan, short cut [that will] save 240 driving miles, 1953. [N.p., 1953]. [8] p. Illus., maps. CSmH, MiD-D, OBgU, WM.

Auto-tourist route across Lake Michigan, save 240 driving miles, 1954. [N.p., 1954]. [8] p. Illus., maps. CSmH, MdBUS, MiMtpC, ViNeM, WM.

Auto-tourist route across Lake Michigan, save 240 driving miles, 1955. [N.p., 1955]. [8] p. Illus., maps. MdBUS, NBuHi, ViNeM, WM.

Auto-tourist route across Lake Michigan, save 240 driving miles, 1956. [N.p., 1956]. [8] p. Illus., maps. CSmH, MSaP, MdBUS, MiD-D, MiShM, OBgU, ViNeM, WM.

Auto-tourist route across Lake Michigan, save 240 driving miles, 1957. [N.p., 1957]. [8] p. Illus., maps. CSmH, CaOKMM, MdBUS, MiShM, OBgU, OFH, ViNeM, WM, WManiM.

Auto-tourist short cut across Lake Michigan, save 240 driving miles, 1958. [N.p., 1958]. [8] p. Illus., maps. CSmH, MiD-D, MiMtpC, MiShM, OBgU, WM.

Auto-tourist short cut across Lake Michigan [connecting] Milwaukee, Wis. [and] Muskegon, Mich., save 240 driving miles, 1959. [N.p., 1959]. 1 sheet folded to [12] p. Illus., maps. CSmH, CaOKMM, MiD-D, OBgU, WM.

Auto-tourist short cut across Lake Michigan [connecting] Milwaukee, Wis. [and] Muskegon, Mich., save 240 driving miles, 1960. [N.p., 1960]. 1 sheet folded to [12] p. Illus., maps. MiD-D, OBgU, WM, WManiM.

Milwaukee, Wisconsin-Muskegon, Michigan daily cross lake service [on the] S.S. Milwaukee Clipper, 1960. 1 sheet folded to [4] p. Illus. OFH.

Auto tourist short-cut across Lake Michigan, sailings [between] Milwaukee, Wis. [and] Muskegon, Mich., save 240 driving miles, 1961. [N.p., 1961]. 1 sheet folded to [12] p. Illus., maps. CSmH, MiD-D, MiShM, WM, WManiM.

Auto tourist short-cut [between] Milwaukee, Wis. [and] Muskegon, Mich., across Lake Michigan sailings morning, afternoon [and] night, save 240 driving miles, 1962. [N.p., 1962]. 1 sheet folded to [12] p. Illus., maps. MiD-D, MiShM, MnDuC, OBgU, ViNeM, WM, WManiM.

Auto tourist short-cut across Lake Michigan, sailings morning, afternoon [and] night [between] Milwaukee, Wis. [and] Muskegon, Mich., save 240 driving miles, 1963. [N.p., 1963]. 1 sheet folded to [12] p. Illus., maps. CSmH, CaOKMM, MdBUS, MiShM, OBgU, ViNeM, WM, WManiM.

Auto tourist short-cut across Lake Michigan sailing morning, afternoon [and] night [between] Milwaukee, Wis. [and] Muskegon, Mich., save 275 driving miles, 1964. [N.p., 1964]. 1 sheet folded to [12] p. Illus., map. CSmH, MdBUS, MiD-D, MiMtpC, MiShM, MnDuC, OBgU, WM, WManiM.

Auto tourist short-cut across Lake Michigan [with] sailings [connecting] Milwaukee, Wis. [and] Muskegon, Mich., 1965. [N.p., 1965]. 1 sheet folded to [12] p. Illus., maps. MiD-D, MiMtpC, MiShM, OBgU, ViNeM, WManiM.

Auto-tourist short-cut [between] Milwaukee, Wis. [and] Muskegon, Mich., save 275 driving miles, 1966. [N.p., 1966]. 1 sheet folded to [12] p. Illus., maps. MdBUS, MiD-D, OBgU, WManiM.

Auto tourist short-cut across Lake Michigan, sailings [between] Milwaukee, Wis. [and] Muskegon, Mich., save 275 driving miles, 1967. [N.p., 1967]. 1 sheet folded to [12] p. Illus., maps. MdBUS, MiD-D, MiMtpC, MiShM, OBgU, WManiM.

Auto tourist short-cut [between] Milwaukee, Wis. [and] Muskegon, Mich., save 275 driving miles, 1968. [N.p., 1968]. 1 sheet folded to [12] p. Illus., maps. MiD-D, MiMtpC, MiShM, MnDuC, OBgU, OFH, WM, WManiM.

S.S. Milwaukee Clipper 1968 Milwaukee, Wisconsin-Muskegon, Michigan, daily cross lake service, a restful pleasure-filled short cut across Lake Michigan. [N.p., 1968]. 1 sheet folded to [4] p. Illus. MiD-D, OBgU.

Across Lake Michigan auto ferry service [between] Milwaukee [and] Muskegon, save 275 driving miles, 1969 season. [N.p., 1969]. 1 sheet folded to [12] p. Illus., maps. MiD-D, MiShM, MnDuC, OBgU, OFH, ViNeM, WM, WManiM.

Across Lake Michigan auto ferry service [between] Milwaukee Muskegon, save 275 driving miles, 1970 season. [N.p., 1970]. 1 sheet folded to [12] p. Illus., maps. CSmH, MdBUS, MiD-D, MiManiHi, MnDuC, OBgU, OFH, ViNeM, WM, WManiM.

S.S. Milwaukee Clipper 1970 Milwaukee, Wisconsin-Muskegon, Michigan, daily cross lake service, a restful pleasure-filled short cut across Lake Michigan. [N.p., 1970]. 1 sheet folded to [4] p. Illus. MiD-D, OBgU, ViNeM.

WISCONSIN & MICHIGAN TRANSPORTATION COMPANY, MILWAUKEE, WI

Succeeded the Crosby Transportation Company when incorporated on 27 February 1925. Familiarly called the Milwaukee-Grand Haven-Muskegon Line. In 1934 it merged with the Michigan Salt Transportation Company (popularly known as the Pere Marquette Line steamers) to form the Wisconsin & Michigan Steamship Company.

The Crosby route, the Milwaukee-Muskegon route, season 1925. Chicago: Poole Bros., [1925]. 1 sheet folded to [8] p. Illus. WM.

Across Lake Michigan [connecting] Milwaukee-Grand Haven-Muskegon, 1926. Chicago: Poole Bros., [1926]. 1 sheet folded to [8] p. Illus. OBgU, WM.

Winter schedule across Lake Michigan [connecting] Milwaukee-Grand Haven-Muskegon. Chicago: Poole Bros., 1926. 1 sheet folded to [4] p. WM.

Across Lake Michigan [connecting] Milwaukee-Grand Haven-Muskegon, 1927. Chicago: Poole Bros., [1927]. 1 sheet folded to [8] p. Illus. WM.

Across Lake Michigan [connecting] Milwaukee-Grand Haven-Muskegon, 1928. Chicago: Poole Bros., [1928]. 1 sheet folded to [8] p. Illus. WM.

Across Lake Michigan [connecting] Milwaukee-Grand Haven-Muskegon, 1929. Chicago: Poole Bros., [1929]. 1 sheet folded to [8] p. Illus. WM.

Across Lake Michigan [connecting] Milwaukee-Grand Haven-Muskegon, 1930. Chicago: Poole Bros., [1930]. 1 sheet folded to [8] p. Illus. May 1st edition. ViNeM.

Across Lake Michigan [connecting] Milwaukee-Grand Haven-Muskegon, 1931. Chicago: Poole Bros., [1931]. 1 sheet folded to [12] p. Illus., map. MiD-D, OBgU, ViNeM.

Across Lake Michigan [connecting] Milwaukee-Grand Haven-Muskegon, 1932. Chicago: Poole Bros., [1932]. 1 sheet folded to [12] p. Illus., map. MdBUS, WM, WManiM.

Brief, abstract and argument of intervaner [sic] [for the] Wisconsin & Michigan Transportation Company before the Interstate Commerce Commission. [N.p., 1932]. [6], 102 p. MiU-H.

Across Lake Michigan [connecting] Milwaukee-Grand Haven-Muskegon, 1933. [N.p., 1933]. 1 sheet folded to [12] p. Illus., map. MiD-D, MiShM, OBgU.

WISCONSIN CENTRAL RAILWAY COMPANY, MILWAUKEE, WI

Chartered on 27 December 1897. On 19 February 1954 it was reorganized as the Wisconsin Central Railroad Company.

The bridging of Lake Michigan. Chicago: Henry O. Shepard Co., [1898?]. 30, [2] p. Illus., map. OBgU.

YANKCANUCK STEAMSHIPS, LIMITED, SAULT STE. MARIE, ONT

Incorporated on 7 April 1951, as successor to the Yankcanuck Transportation Company, Limited. Ceased to exist about 1973.

M[otor] V[essel] Yankcanuck, christened and commissioned April 27, 1963,...at Collingwood, Ontario. [N.p., 1963]. [12] p. Illus. On cover: Collship. MiD-D.

APPENDIX 1
MAPS OF GREAT LAKES SHIPPING PORTS

LAKE SUPERIOR
LAKE MICHIGAN
LAKE HURON and GEORGIAN BAY
LAKE ERIE and LAKE ONTARIO
The ST. LAWRENCE RIVER

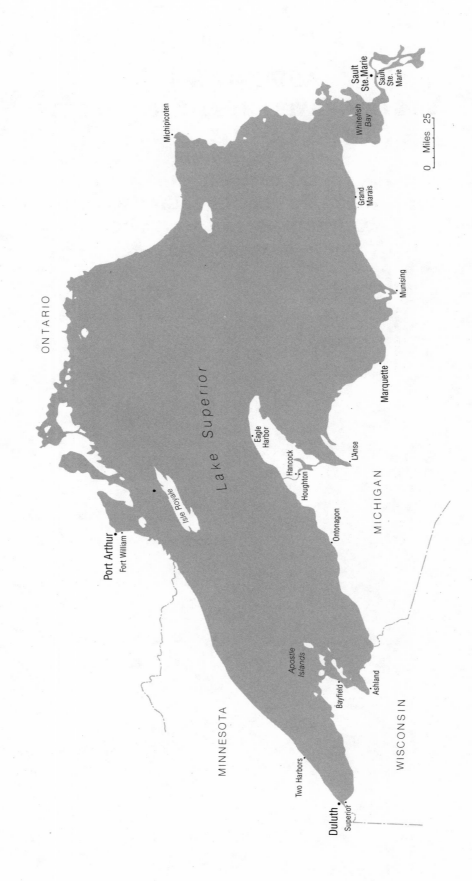

Figure 2. Lake Superior

Figure 3. Lake Michigan

Figure 4. Lake Huron and
Georgian Bay

134

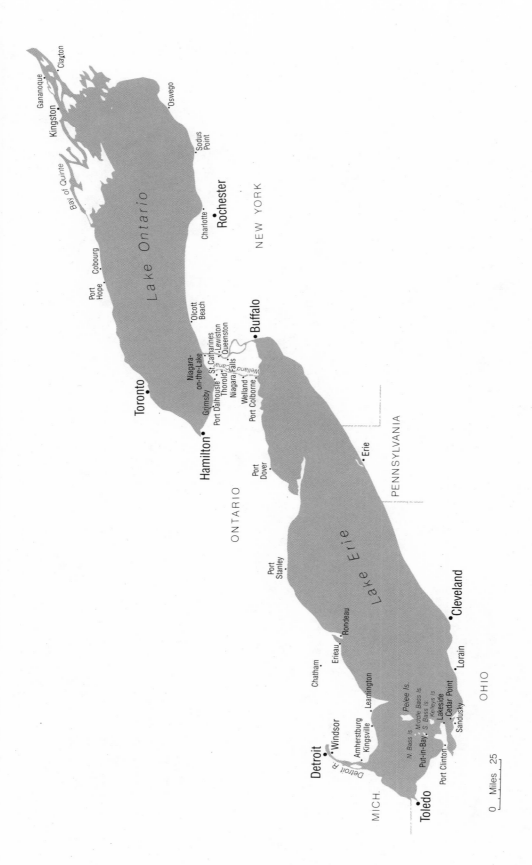

Figure 5. Lake Erie and Lake Ontario

135

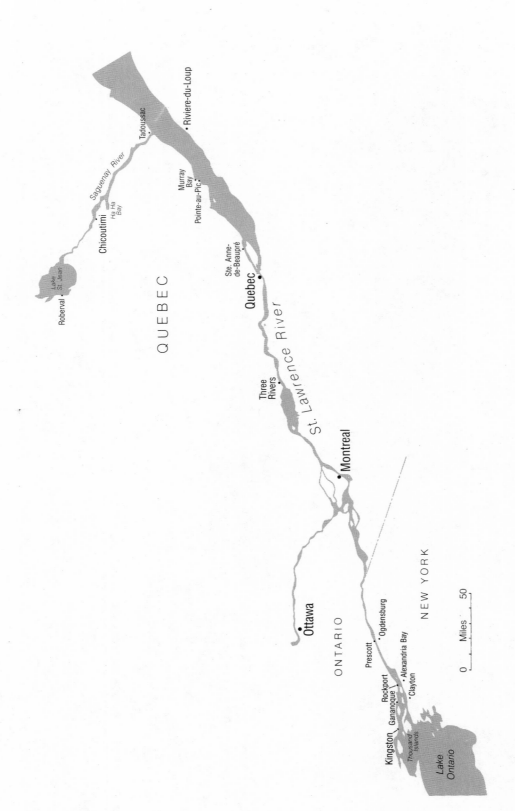

Figure 6. The St. Lawrence River

136

APPENDIX 2

Table 2a. **Ship Passengers at Selected Ports/U.S. Commissioner of Navigation.** A majority of the items listed in this work were produced by or for navigation firms that were in the business of carrying passengers on the Great Lakes. Literally millions of people were annually served by this industry, as revealed in the following sample statistics collected by the United States Commissioner of Navigation and published in his annual reports (Supt. Docs. C11.1). The figures below state the total number of passengers counted on a sampling basis for the year ending June 30.

YEAR	CHICAGO	CLEVELAND	DETROIT	DULUTH	ROCHESTER
1915	211,262	98,058	503,554	21,379	16,013
1916	239,695	330,420	923,077	41,557	3,030
1917	315,058	578,494	979,161	59,614	0
1918	432,479	816,910	816,962	41,289	11,398
1919	358,892	548,863	4,871,104	34,542	15,132
1920	583,885	747,718	1,436,753	39,894	13,984
1921	626,393	841,759	1,375,653	65,655	15,278
1922	683,582	732,861	869,017	50,746	7,870
1923	682,397	752,357	975,280	26,371	10,027
1924	650,920	645,892	841,816	15,561	6,135
1925	561,013	587,658	1,248,087	51,845	14,835
1926	672,888	689,557	1,138,040	1,906	8,538
1927	542,625	612,075	1,103,854	22,699	4,540
1928	434,755	526,704	1,045,224	17,087	11,124
1929	449,986	532,994	1,195,426	18,001	14,152
1930	476,102	449,676	1,050,382	19,247	5,072
1931	315,588	655,574	862,674	14,780	4,483
1932	286,999	373,129	692,582	16,658	11,150
1933	271,357	335,309	466,729	17,729	6,114
1934	588,172	282,604	342,532	23,405	10,858
1935	325,641	356,687	431,374	28,976	17,377
1936	267,753	428,000	546,419	27,146	10,520

Table 2b. **Ship Passengers at Selected Ports/U.S. Army Corps of Engineers.** The United States Army Corps of Engineers also kept statistics on the number of passengers frequenting ships at various ports on the Great Lakes (Supt. Docs. D103.1/2 and W7.1). Some samples of these figures, given for a calendar year, are as follows:

YEAR	BUFFALO	MILWAUKEE	MUSKEGON	SOO CANAL	TOLEDO
1913	1,401,706	150,000	69,774	77,194	424,479
1914	1,330,368	250,000	71,449	59,801	195,522
1915	1,927,035	120,000	62,317	56,336	236,895

continued on next page

Table 2b continued

YEAR	BUFFALO	MILWAUKEE	MUSKEGON	SOO CANAL	TOLEDO
1916	1,588,615	225,000	75,324	54,922	297,145
1917	1,389,420	231,900	62,283	38,339	324,176
1918	1,484,977	198,717	64,489	34,990	211,335
1919	1,894,662	130,342	90,893	56,992	395,009
1920	1,738,111	162,460	95,870	68,451	132,144
1921	1,586,761	148,942	76,207	66,621	178,830
1922	1,557,552	180,038	79,005	59,043	215,948
1923	2,712,179	200,837	86,551	56,384	181,708
1924	2,586,492	262,389	64,760	53,776	222,604
1925	1,999,060	307,342	84,596	56,956	245,582
1926	1,367,021	281,215	59,338	52,704	107,358
1927	1,068,467	220,809	64,659	55,115	109,665
1928	1,526,616	240,332	62,690	56,053	134,896
1929	1,259,589	279,215	68,070	54,415	124,625
1930	1,075,531	225,958	50,955	45,303	174,246
1931	1,663,462	56,629	49,803	33,606	134,937
1932	2,199,751	67,677	40,442	20,241	35,528
1933	1,868,763	218,216	32,909	20,943	49,138
1934	1,784,849	167,518	34,538	33,636	63,456
1935	1,507,606	184,690	47,049	32,937	70,444
1936	1,661,201	287,062	61,188	40,785	80,832
1937	1,954,386	324,540	30,121	47,253	83,456
1938	2,081,545	275,194	21,140	41,552	89,764
1939	1,991,625	300,155	24,140	40,501	98,384
1940	1,550,810	213,887	22,712	53,129	103,163
1941	1,436,040	289,704	86,160	89,824	108,596
1942	1,126,836	208,340	83,798	42,845	167,558
1943	1,193,121	216,062	58,675	40,292	116,378
1944	941,718	258,234	75,147	47,666	115,356
1945	1,087,982	268,449	65,372	46,004	46,533
1946	1,086,814	330,348	149,443	87,871	90,410
1947	1,070,793	225,610	142,991	90,500	531
1948	911,305	210,193	130,897	112,101	43,866
1949	898,853	196,961	121,681	113,009	60,076
1950	706,854	179,562	114,401	63,366	36,178
1951	448,353	181,736	117,401	87,403	28,512
1952	469,639	188,112	159,818	99,858	27,188
1953	482,958	229,387	145,193	110,076	22,974
1954	422,665	204,449	127,467	119,803	25,186
1955	420,905	228,997	141,573	182,534	23,724
1956	293,803	219,266	138,309	123,208	44,810
1957	11,278	194,959	117,630	178,826	24,022
1958	13,715	186,283	109,136	269,772	109,158
1959	14,955	223,017	121,616	369,504	172,213
1960	12,546	196,321	109,567	324,056	25,365
1961	12,586	186,526	113,276	289,166	21,373
1962	8,990	185,595	113,205	275,617	27,507
1963	21,509	201,561	96,712	271,773	22,176

continued on next page

Table 2b continued

YEAR	BUFFALO	MILWAUKEE	MUSKEGON	SOO CANAL	TOLEDO
1964	30,994	216,603	103,704	268,856	18,986
1965	31,265	208,837	98,556	308,589	16,580
1966	35,116	211,084	107,035	350,233	23,910
1967	33,153	195,474	95,415	333,901	19,968
1968	32,411	212,878	101,034	338,117	21,314
1969	30,206	190,484	101,096	333,478	18,955
1970	22,695	230,602	111,594	202,234	15,617
1971	19,617	166,562	742	207,971	16,074
1972	0	134,059	0	195,679	11,180
1973	0	144,142	0	191,191	22,904
1974	2	150,931	0	180,775	15,699
1975	0	106,260	0	192,561	16,036
1976	24	115,442	0	193,700	26,192
1977	0	116,455	0	183,100	0
1978	0	113,381	0	188,319	10,820
1979	0	101,606	0	156,490	10,820
1980	0	97,681	0	153,611	22,800
1981	0	72,494	0	174,755	19,900
1982	0	88,184	0	153,820	17,700
1983	0	109,294	0	171,767	19,680
1984	0	167,428	0	171,418	197,282
1985	0	101,652	0	176,008	210,562
1986	0	73,478	0	175,316	238,058
1987	0	Unknown	0	277,335	Unknown
1988	0	101,382	0	343,344	74,624
1989	0	44,900	0	318,097	22,490
1990	0	Unknown	0	277,503	Unknown

Table 2c. **Ship Passengers at Selected Ports/U.S. Department of Commerce.** For a short period of time the Steamboat Inspection Service, of the U.S. Department of Commerce, gathered information on the number of passengers using water transportation at selected Great Lakes ports. Some of these statistics, extracted from the agency's annual reports (Supt. Docs. T38.1), are shown below for years ending June 30.

YEAR	CHICAGO	DETROIT	GD. HAVEN	MARQUETTE	PT. HURON
1914	1,260,713	10,368,258	71,520	61,850	782,157
1915	1,259,206	9,739,637	313,436	71,117	635,275
1916	639,495	10,899,526	280,925	52,899	714,693
1917	1,020,098	10,624,473	415,360	65,274	996,059
1918	703,240	10,751,202	402,525	36,480	561,708
1919	601,614	10,151,391	320,424	16,262	401,529
1920	866,077	13,218,336	413,595	15,416	513,900

Table 2d. **Ship Passengers at Selected Ports/U.S. Shipping Board.** Many foreign travellers used Great Lakes cruise ships for the purpose of visiting the United States. The extent of this international tourism was, for a time, monitored by the Research Bureau of the United States Shipping Board in its annual Report No. 157 (Supt. Docs. C27.9/12). The following examples from this compilation are for the calendar year, and show passengers arriving and departing.

YEAR	CLEVELAND	DETROIT	DULUTH	ROCHESTER	SANDUSKY
1929	18,446	2,493	7,272	79,026	3,085
1930	17,892	3,162	6,221	73,104	3,526
1931	15,419	1,365	4,970	50,571	4,482
1932	13,641	1,144	2,766	34,305	3,460
1933	8,529	1,242	1,933	38,488	4,666
1934	12,010	3,025	1,640	55,019	1,809
1935	13,744	2,020	1,904	52,012	1,797
1936	17,796	2,359	2,952	58,298	2,139
1937	613	2,461	4,513	58,924	1,984

Table 3a. **Ship Passengers on the Great Lakes/U.S. Army Corps of Engineers.** The preceding passenger statistics provide evidence of the number of people using Great Lakes ship transportation at various ports. An idea of the total passenger load on America's inland seas can be found in Transportation Series No. 1 (Transportation on the Great Lakes), issued by the U.S. Army Corps of Engineers in 1926 and 1937 (Supt. Docs. W7.23).

1910 - 5,515,263	1918 - 3,956,501	1928 - 26,461,393
1911 - 5,502,443	1919 - 6,069,416	1929 - 28,017,811
1912 - 4,765,548	1920 - 4,920,076	1930 - 20,575,472
1913 - 6,021,677	1921 - 5,198,411	1931 - 13,619,312
1914 - 7,349,009	1922 - 5,267,078	1932 - 11,800,692
1915 - 4,638,320	1923 - 6,515,143	1933 - 11,905,570
1916 - 6,245,200	1926 - 28,840,459	1934 - 11,038,844
1917 - 4,771,778	1927 - 28,128,626	1935 - 10,781,770

Table 3b. **Ship Passengers on the Great Lakes/*Marine Review*, February 1930.** The figures cited above include only those passengers using ports in the United States, so all Canadian traffic on the Great Lakes is unaccounted for. Furthermore, the statistics prior to 1926 exclude passengers at some ports along Great Lakes' connecting waters, like Sault Sainte Marie and Detroit. Consequently, a better picture of Great Lakes passenger service in the 1920's and before can be seen in the more comprehensive table below. The figures for the first three years come from the United States Bureau of the Census, while the numbers for the most recent six years appear in the Marine Review for February of 1930 (volume 60, number 2). The scope of this transporttion business can be better appreciated when one considers that in 1922 the total population of the United States was 110,000,000. This means that in some years, at least on a per capita statistical basis, nearly one out of every four people living in the U.S. travelled commercially on the Great Lakes.

1880 - 1,356,010	1923 - 23,076,974	1926 - 28,123,747
1889 - 2,235,993	1924 - 23,104,442	1927 - 27,161,024
1906 - 14,079,121	1925 - 25,643,576	1928 - 24,104,992

Table 4. **Ship Passengers by Carrier/Interstate Commerce Commission.** The distribution of passengers among the various Great Lakes carriers can be seen in the following sample statistics. The figures, covering the calendar year, come from File No. 48-C-5 (Supt. Docs. IC1wat.10) and Statement No. Q-650 (Supt. Docs. IC1wat.11) of the Interstate Commerce Commission.

YEAR	CD&GB LINE	C&B LINE	D&C LINE	N. NAV. CO.	W&M SS CO.
1936	20,249	293,397	234,578	17,855	74,545
1937	25,737	280,471	206,579	20,738	61,593
1938	18,621	235,373	204,612	18,498	39,253
1939	17,717	38,469	330,143	14,051	51,052
1940	35,182	15,341	351,934	17,955	49,519
1941	27,684	37,808	409,566	22,872	91,892
1942	32,056	Unknown	418,684	21,372	78,170
1943	23,834	244,051	440,584	25,206	79,307
1944	44,913	258,601	377,578	29,598	88,146
1945	25,357	253,435	310,339	25,533	88,260
1946	24,035	365,953	306,513	22,202	144,427
1947	19,680	208,093	181,529	27,126	140,158
1948	15,134	204,708	179,412	33,717	118,091
1949	14,388	164,541	362,655	34,383	118,772
1950	15,493	141,044	190,493	Defunct	113,542
1951	24,878	Defunct	Defunct	Defunct	115,263
1952	23,431	Defunct	Defunct	Defunct	158,950
1953	23,801	Defunct	Defunct	Defunct	144,240
1954	24,037	Defunct	Defunct	Defunct	137,692
1955	22,214	Defunct	Defunct	Defunct	140,956
1956	20,902	Defunct	Defunct	Defunct	128,926
1957	18,861	Defunct	Defunct	Defunct	116,357
1958	18,866	Defunct	Defunct	Defunct	108,385
1959	18,702	Defunct	Defunct	Defunct	120,482
1960	17,979	Defunct	Defunct	Defunct	109,413
1961	16,057	Defunct	Defunct	Defunct	114,225
1962	13,896	Defunct	Defunct	Defunct	116,681
1963	12,499	Defunct	Defunct	Defunct	100,592
1964	13,745	Defunct	Defunct	Defunct	102,642
1965	13,724	Defunct	Defunct	Defunct	93,706
1966	14,203	Defunct	Defunct	Defunct	103,005
1967	11,848	Defunct	Defunct	Defunct	85,118
1968	Defunct	Defunct	Defunct	Defunct	88,538
1969	Defunct	Defunct	Defunct	Defunct	95,675
1970	Defunct	Defunct	Defunct	Defunct	104,025

Table 5. **Iron Ore Shipments from Selected Ports.** Although most of the citations in this book relate to items produced by passenger lines, a substantial number of pieces were generated by companies involved in the transport of iron ore. The scope of these operations can be seen in the following figures, which represent the gross tons of iron ore carried by vessels from each port. The statistics thru 1897 come from U.S. House Document 277, Fifty-fifth Congress, Second Session. The numbers from 1898 to 1906 are taken from publications of the Lake Superior Iron Ore Association, and the remainder are extracted from the annual reports of the Lake Carriers' Association.

YEAR	ESCANABA	MARQUETTE	2 HARBORS	SUPERIOR	DULUTH, MN.
1884	1,356,587	918,489	None	None	None
1885	1,219,777	750,047	225,484	None	None
1886	1,538,821	853,396	304,396	None	None
1887	2,072,708	803,411	390,467	None	None
1888	2,202,965	844,694	450,475	None	None
1889	3,003,632	1,376,335	819,639	None	None
1890	3,714,662	1,307,395	826,063	None	None
1891	3,058,590	1,056,027	890,299	None	None
1892	4,010,085	1,026,338	1,165,076	4,245	None
1893	2,048,981	1,086,934	903,329	80,273	440,592
1894	1,644,776	1,424,850	1,373,253	Unknown	1,369,252
1895	2,860,172	1,079,485	2,118,156	117,884	1,598,783
1896	2,321,928	1,578,600	1,813,992	167,245	1,988,932
1897	2,302,121	1,945,519	2,651,465	531,825	2,376,064
1898	2,802,000	2,246,000	2,666,000	550,000	2,631,000
1899	3,720,000	2,734,00	3,833,000	879,000	3,510,000
1900	3,437,000	2,662,000	4,007,000	1,523,000	3,889,000
1901	4,023,000	2,354,000	5,010,000	2,321,000	3,438,000
1902	5,413,704	2,595,010	5,605,185	4,180,568	5,598,408
1903	4,277,561	2,007,346	5,120,656	3,978,579	5,356,473
1904	3,644,267	1,907,301	4,566,542	4,169,990	4,649,611
1905	5,307,938	2,977,828	7,779,850	5,118,385	8,807,559
1906	5,851,050	2,791,033	8,180,125	6,083,057	11,220,218
1907	5,761,988	3,013,826	8,188,906	7,440,386	13,445,977
1908	3,351,502	1,487,487	5,702,237	3,564,030	8,808,168
1909	5,747,991	2,909,458	9,181,131	6,540,505	13,470,503
1910	4,959,869	3,248,929	8,271,165	8,437,261	13,609,155
1911	4,278,445	2,200,380	6,367,537	9,920,490	6,934,269
1912	5,234,655	3,296,761	9,370,969	14,240,714	9,370,969
1913	5,399,444	3,137,617	10,075,718	13,788,343	12,331,126
1914	3,664,451	1,755,726	5,610,262	11,309,748	6,318,291
1915	5,649,289	3,099,589	8,642,942	8,342,793	15,437,419
1916	7,457,444	3,858,092	10,735,853	12,787,046	21,837,949
1917	7,156,854	3,207,145	9,990,901	13,978,741	20,567,419
1918	6,774,969	3,457,054	8,723,472	14,068,341	20,567,288
1919	4,963,358	2,132,935	6,424,545	10,919,965	16,821,209
1920	7,361,070	3,415,108	9,278,464	14,812,398	15,479,334
1921	1,806,656	786,946	3,286,338	4,991,278	9,164,803
1922	4,592,354	1,976,220	5,952,437	11,234,195	13,044,771
1923	5,607,411	2,789,285	6,418,464	17,820,476	20,163,619

continued on next page

Table 5 continued

YEAR	ESCANABA	MARQUETTE	2 HARBORS	SUPERIOR	DULUTH, MN.
1924	4,244,669	2,516,548	4,817,494	13,355,214	12,882,082
1925	5,644,278	3,487,968	6,016,096	14,560,477	17,707,978
1926	6,599,597	3,417,462	6,266,272	16,476,264	18,638,395
1927	5,865,224	3,238,855	5,703,159	14,627,936	15,432,188
1928	5,487,556	3,410,902	5,733,501	15,413,694	17,454,063
1929	6,348,573	4,448,388	6,601,735	19,623,139	20,562,705
1930	4,096,813	2,961,670	6,308,245	14,153,553	14,001,327
1931	1,608,044	1,622,524	3,324,937	6,737,063	7,267,023
1932	329,870	314,767	410,714	791,212	1,047,997
1933	1,647,980	2,622,584	3,277,941	5,835,101	5,839,523
1934	1,543,737	2,207,566	3,199,695	6,996,206	6,015,630
1935	1,823,655	2,963,603	3,234,171	10,276,176	6,995,979
1936	2,392,958	4,284,377	5,546,040	16,236,502	11,738,528
1937	3,147,977	5,101,700	9,743,476	22,222,116	16,731,688
1938	1,077,809	1,333,038	3,833,114	6,823,488	3,920,961
1939	2,531,260	4,458,894	8,663,503	14,925,013	9,081,476
1940	3,423,334	5,486,289	10,705,000	21,502,083	16,267,848
1941	4,513,079	5,658,672	15,011,066	27,745,737	20,498,781
1942	6,255,360	4,859,005	18,812,328	31,528,615	23,968,309
1943	6,330,565	3,798,609	19,275,591	27,732,942	21,373,773
1944	5,778,300	3,730,262	19,331,761	25,939,951	20,332,214
1945	4,684,168	3,890,974	17,625,890	24,654,056	20,036,365
1946	3,052,648	2,548,968	13,925,588	19,145,431	15,695,759
1947	4,141,643	4,744,651	16,964,098	25,802,412	19,364,852
1948	4,760,529	4,091,428	18,747,287	29,727,358	19,116,644
1949	3,816,109	3,903,219	14,763,497	25,298,709	15,751,829
1950	5,007,221	4,085,570	17,089,983	26,425,022	18,768,161
1951	6,542,335	4,771,928	19,730,558	31,570,513	21,600,540
1952	5,506,431	4,066,247	15,626,220	28,455,673	16,495,624
1953	6,163,352	5,135,796	21,122,847	35,076,168	22,928,898
1954	3,967,417	3,449,489	12,864,988	22,169,692	12,728,854
1955	5,952,327	5,596,865	17,150,987	33,976,275	17,394,459
1956	5,215,035	4,847,058	14,367,742	29,122,611	12,775,877
1957	5,907,580	4,620,332	17,148,596	27,403,865	17,445,241
1958	3,286,799	3,354,316	10,540,536	15,797,373	7,775,436
1959	3,074,915	3,163,325	8,167,657	12,310,520	7,413,562
1960	6,591,989	4,484,287	13,785,457	18,521,376	10,877,355
1961	5,129,576	3,910,540	10,806,256	15,625,655	4,208,287
1962	4,771,782	4,185,685	11,771,209	14,890,702	3,781,242
1963	5,057,085	5,691,211	None	15,320,993	13,293,142
1964	6,497,380	6,955,761	None	15,460,387	14,678,455
1965	6,064,785	6,312,177	None	16,163,992	15,764,680
1966	6,603,091	7,125,892	2,793,813	15,620,068	15,822,344
1967	6,565,770	7,249,008	2,352,819	11,872,700	14,098,255
1968	6,223,762	6,333,226	2,565,876	12,354,340	14,229,187
1969	6,899,568	7,016,874	4,945,307	14,873,615	15,838,402
1970	8,943,169	4,089,648	5,031,694	12,476,512	16,505,458

continued on next page

Table 5 continued

YEAR	ESCANABA	MARQUETTE	2 HARBORS	SUPERIOR	DULUTH, MN.
1971	8,359,311	3,415,514	4,405,363	10,999,674	14,222,073
1972	9,356,779	3,062,382	6,129,029	10,172,524	14,865,838
1973	8,747,280	3,433,596	7,740,025	11,939,941	17,940,892
1974	8,883,445	3,026,497	10,379,348	10,149,765	17,887,464
1975	8,949,124	4,387,198	8,224,871	6,423,462	14,329,239
1976	10,228,125	5,544,176	7,977,458	6,145,348	14,049,747
1977	7,890,410	4,030,295	3,201,459	7,701,180	10,687,104
1978	11,434,204	6,002,561	9,477,247	12,533,603	13,567,770
1979	11,815,965	5,331,816	11,123,739	13,674,527	15,039,093
1980	9,724,537	5,721,059	10,009,828	10,146,136	13,262,856
1981	8,743,140	5,341,676	9,995,569	10,668,741	13,070,900
1982	5,319,304	1,934,053	4,478,167	7,957,838	5,982,175
1983	7,416,487	3,509,393	8,336,322	8,667,947	6,559,590
1984	8,618,846	4,457,341	6,804,947	11,149,768	7,763,650
1985	7,384,643	5,071,106	8,719,429	8,506,371	6,132,547
1986	7,378,399	3,573,564	6,155,788	8,988,170	5,034,790
1987	5,907,451	7,062,259	7,121,685	11,313,051	7,595,375
1988	6,554,565	7,927,044	10,808,214	11,996,794	6,918,963
1989	5,651,258	8,972,764	9,352,595	10,877,547	7,291,267
1990	4,908,609	4,925,893	11,483,533	11,052,629	7,605,933

Table 6. **Bulk Cargoes Carried on the Great Lakes/Lake Carriers' Association.** The preceding statistics give a partial picture of the cargoes carried by boat on the Great Lakes. A better picture of the contributions made by the inland freshwater fleets can be seen in the following figures. These numbers represent the tons of each commodity handled by bulk-freight vessels on a yearly basis. The information comes from the annual reports of the Lake Carriers' Association.

YEAR	IRON	COAL	GRAIN	STONE
1900	18,570,315	8,907,663	5,591,208	Unknown
1901	20,157,522	9,819,615	4,667,820	Unknown
1902	27,039,169	9,196,039	4,893,812	Unknown
1903	23,649,550	13,351,291	5,732,468	Unknown
1904	21,226,591	12,370,023	4,186,824	Unknown
1905	33,476,904	14,401,199	6,112,859	Unknown
1906	37,513,589	17,273,718	6,863,068	Unknown
1907	41,290,709	21,486,927	7,010,937	Unknown
1908	25,427,094	19,288,098	6,024,493	Unknown
1909	41,683,599	18,617,396	6,651,245	Unknown
1910	42,618,758	26,478,068	5,803,514	Unknown
1911	32,130,411	25,700,104	6,959,465	Unknown
1912	47,435,771	24,673,210	9,372,252	Unknown
1913	49,070,478	33,362,379	11,697,160	Unknown
1914	32,021,897	27,281,228	9,793,850	Unknown
1915	46,318,804	26,220,000	11,098,815	3,854,106

continued on next page

Table 6 continued

YEAR	IRON	COAL	GRAIN	STONE
1916	64,734,198	28,440,483	10,555,975	5,553,927
1917	62,498,901	31,192,613	7,161,716	6,748,801
1918	61,156,732	32,102,022	6,548,680	7,161,716
1919	47,177,395	26,424,068	6,091,703	6,407,285
1920	58,527,226	26,409,710	6,736,348	7,821,980
1921	22,300,726	26,660,652	12,470,405	3,925,705
1922	42,613,184	19,868,925	14,267,020	7,592,137
1923	59,036,704	33,137,028	11,850,446	9,920,422
1924	42,623,572	25,860,515	15,222,787	9,225,624
1925	54,081,298	28,048,538	13,320,346	11,351,948
1926	58,537,855	31,011,290	12,087,316	12,628,244
1927	51,107,136	34,794,291	14,692,536	14,033,376
1928	53,980,874	34,823,002	16,372,098	15,677,551
1929	65,204,600	39,254,578	10,021,099	16,269,612
1930	46,582,982	38,072,060	9,851,299	12,432,628
1931	23,467,786	31,176,359	9,479,640	7,208,946
1932	3,567,985	24,857,369	8,890,409	3,928,840
1933	21,623,898	31,776,654	8,713,127	6,664,629
1934	22,249,600	35,476,575	7,951,145	7,392,218
1935	28,362,368	35,289,135	6,750,261	9,082,155
1936	44,822,023	44,699,443	7,433,967	12,080,672
1937	62,598,836	44,318,765	5,829,399	14,429,379
1938	19,263,011	34,623,287	10,679,125	8,240,768
1939	45,072,724	40,368,121	11,172,079	12,208,205
1940	63,712,982	49,319,604	9,644,950	14,893,316
1941	80,116,360	53,535,365	11,387,480	17,633,448
1942	92,076,781	52,533,792	8,501,586	18,570,048
1943	84,404,852	51,969,459	11,810,116	17,339,675
1944	81,170,538	60,163,330	16,228,880	16,856,279
1945	75,714,750	55,246,197	18,717,773	16,318,193
1946	59,356,716	53,726,531	10,197,850	17,551,555
1947	77,898,087	58,059,884	11,409,228	20,891,130
1948	82,937,192	60,563,530	9,876,880	22,282,425
1949	69,556,269	40,929,565	12,542,565	20,322,136
1950	78,205,592	57,640,222	9,327,450	23,395,011
1951	89,092,012	50,945,656	13,150,144	25,871,319
1952	74,910,798	46,284,192	15,214,778	23,277,942
1953	95,844,449	51,034,713	14,317,229	26,999,207
1954	60,793,697	46,367,167	11,866,241	24,975,440
1955	89,169,973	53,378,385	10,787,786	29,722,293
1956	80,195,929	57,374,685	14,319,650	30,753,412
1957	87,278,815	56,779,772	11,234,810	30,439,375
1958	54,787,479	44,949,995	12,625,829	22,496,239
1959	51,450,731	47,228,449	13,609,452	26,159,660
1960	73,073,053	46,701,235	14,134,959	27,179,458
1961	60,897,367	43,969,565	16,607,745	25,418,364
1962	63,085,330	46,184,285	15,918,950	24,730,834

continued on next page

Table 6 continued.

YEAR	IRON	COAL	GRAIN	STONE
1963	67,298,000	51,642,796	18,777,164	28,547,128
1964	78,115,327	52,142,742	21,637,255	30,771,477
1965	78,627,591	54,574,092	21,875,439	30,819,351
1966	85,273,676	55,585,464	25,013,943	34,021,957
1967	80,605,929	52,890,668	17,616,863	31,716,614
1968	83,631,049	48,861,866	16,325,298	33,093,501
1969	86,307,605	46,924,447	16,594,713	36,083,477
1970	87,018,233	49,683,710	23,820,347	38,477,439
1971	78,162,234	43,341,847	25,239,080	33,998,558
1972	81,158,094	43,235,484	26,692,466	37,345,901
1973	94,545,275	39,604,341	26,536,921	42,888,052
1974	87,577,977	34,989,243	19,589,153	43,096,337
1975	79,966,250	39,192,505	24,511,214	37,681,469
1976	86,618,697	37,493,151	23,487,552	38,203,609
1977	67,050,071	38,984,388	25,992,734	37,219,714
1978	88,914,634	37,766,570	32,090,391	39,754,445
1979	92,053,933	45,833,297	28,881,619	36,976,066
1980	72,967,359	41,306,125	31,509,534	28,011,339
1981	74,904,645	39,096,577	28,235,436	24,586,743
1982	38,512,574	36,759,518	28,283,271	15,076,245
1983	52,085,008	36,578,742	28,846,648	18,418,662
1984	57,264,830	43,134,292	28,152,658	23,156,860
1985	52,171,226	36,334,525	20,055,902	24,992,777
1986	45,550,944	36,266,922	20,155,541	27,225,922
1987	55,091,699	37,731,742	22,338,366	33,163,539
1988	60,987,672	40,521,133	19,101,760	35,501,484
1989	59,562,540	39,469,501	15,007,810	35,075,213
1990	61,497,446	37,993,533	15,840,535	33,746,820

Table 7. **Package Freight Carried on the Great Lakes/*Marine Review*, February 1930.** Cargo-carrying vessels on the Great Lakes played an important role in the movement of package freight. This type of load was generally individual pieces of merchandise, rather than bulk shipments. These goods were transported from and to selected ports in the following quantities, as listed in short tons by the *Marine Review* of February 1930 (vol. 60, no. 2).

DATE	BUFFALO	DULUTH	CHICAGO	DETROIT	CLEVELAND	MILWAUKEE
1924	922,373	902,441	751,187	207,144	157,550	535,230
1925	826,511	896,282	604,952	238,004	225,636	525,531
1926	499,834	885,447	533,490	227,322	146,916	481,166
1927	841,184	881,876	767,250	243,592	154,533	505,023
1928	972,497	854,663	765,815	260,214	196,979	696,657

Table 8.   **Ships Operating on the Great Lakes/U.S. Bureau of Marine Inspection and Navigation.**
The number of U.S. documented vessels operating on the Great Lakes, and their gross tonage, has varied substantially over time. This fact is evidenced by the following figures, which were mainly compiled by the United States Bureau of Marine Inspection and Navigation (Supt. Docs. C11.10; C25.10; C25.15; T17.10). It should be noted that gas vessels and steam vessels were lumped together for statistical purposes until 1915. Dates shown are for the year ending June 30 until 1941, at which time the figures are for January 1 of the year given.

YEAR	SAILSHIPS	STEAMSHIPS	ALL SHIPS	TOTAL TONS
1868	1,855	624	5,365	695,604
1869	1,752	636	4,875	661,366
1870	1,699	642	5,349	684,704
1871	1,662	682	5,513	712,027
1872	1,654	708	5,337	724,493
1873	1,663	802	5,576	788,412
1874	1,696	876	5,600	842,381
1875	1,710	891	5,496	837,892
1876	1,643	921	3,193	613,211
1877	1,604	923	3,191	610,160
1878	1,546	918	3,166	604,656
1879	1,473	896	3,087	597,376
1880	1,459	931	3,127	605,102
1881	1,417	988	3,207	663,383
1882	1,412	1,101	3,379	711,269
1883	1,373	1,149	3,403	723,911
1884	1,333	1,165	3,380	733,069
1885	1,322	1,175	3,379	749,948
1886	1,235	1,280	3,405	762,560
1887	1,286	1,225	3,144	683,721
1888	1,277	1,342	3,290	874,102
1889	1,285	1,455	3,412	972,271
1890	1,272	1,527	3,510	1,063,063
1891	1,243	1,592	3,600	1,154,870
1892	1,226	1,631	3,657	1,183,582
1893	1,205	1,731	3,761	1,261,067
1894	1,139	1,731	3,341	1,227,400
1895	1,100	1,755	3,342	1,241,459
1896	1,044	1,792	3,333	1,324,067
1897	993	1,775	3,230	1,410,103
1898	960	1,764	3,256	1,437,500
1899	874	1,732	3,162	1,446,348
1900	832	1,739	3,167	1,565,587
1901	784	1,778	3,253	1,706,294
1902	726	1,795	3,172	1,816,511
1903	676	1,796	3,110	1,902,698
1904	623	1,820	3,075	2,019,208
1905	583	1,820	3,011	2,062,147
1906	519	1,844	3,052	2,234,432
1907	466	1,873	3,103	2,439,741

continued on next page

Table 8 continued.

YEAR	SAILSHIPS	STEAMSHIPS	ALL SHIPS	TOTAL TONS
1908	429	1,942	3,172	2,729,169
1909	389	1,982	3,199	2,782,481
1910	362	2,107	3,273	2,895,102
1911	324	2,174	3,286	2,943,523
1912	303	2,269	3,367	2,949,924
1913	272	2,333	3,447	2,939,786
1914	241	2,339	3,406	2,882,922
1915	220	1,615	3,161	2,818,009
1916	191	1,590	3,051	2,760,815
1917	165	1,508	3,001	2,779,087
1918	133	1,508	2,939	2,797,503
1919	125	1,541	3,043	3,023,762
1920	108	1,586	3,091	3,138,690
1921	95	1,432	2,942	2,839,514
1922	86	1,353	2,745	2,723,857
1923	83	1,351	2,719	2,758,401
1924	75	1,320	2,693	2,791,204
1925	70	1,311	2,677	2,853,019
1926	65	1,273	2,626	2,844,473
1927	58	1,224	2,560	2,805,350
1928	52	1,192	2,537	2,773,341
1929	51	1,159	2,513	2,771,287
1930	45	1,115	2,450	2,758,321
1931	40	1,090	2,441	2,766,545
1932	36	904	2,272	1,856,563
1933	34	849	2,209	1,813,570
1934	32	821	2,206	1,802,305
1935	29	790	2,195	1,773,054
1936	30	763	2,200	1,766,674
1937	26	722	2,159	1,712,900
1938	21	692	2,340	1,786,995
1939	15	661	2,108	1,711,965
1940	12	623	2,059	1,669,389
1941	10	586	2,023	1,640,790
1942	10	558	2,005	1,624,377
1943	9	481	1,758	1,620,292
1944	9	500	1,628	1,792,538
1945	7	540	1,819	2,061,456
1946	5	546	1,880	2,182,866
1947	3	515	1,904	2,091,170
1948	3	494	1,920	2,079,447
1949	3	486	1,964	2,076,267
1950	3	408	2,026	1,628,267
1951	3	387	2,043	1,565,096
1952	1	359	2,027	1,556,034
1953	1	354	2,027	1,624,423
1954	0	348	2,015	1,616,132
1955	0	331	2,005	1,590,291
1956	2	311	2,000	1,557,995

continued on next page

Table 8 continued.

YEAR	SAILSHIPS	STEAMSHIPS	ALL SHIPS	TOTAL TONS
1957	1	299	1,962	1,569,387
1958	1	299	1,981	1,637,694
1959	1	279	1,970	1,627,293
1960	1	268	1,950	1,728,215
1961	1	300	2,020	2,120,738
1962	1	279	1,971	2,056,276
1963	1	256	1,962	1,931,503
1964	1	241	1,973	1,857,502
1965	0	236	1,951	1,877,931

BIBLIOGRAPHY

Every public repository known to have a collection of Great Lakes navigation literature has been visited or contacted in the course of preparing this compilation. This is not to say, however, that all institutions with materials of this nature are included in this work.

Some possible collections of shipping literature were unable at the time of this study to determine if they had materials published by the Great Lakes shipping industry. Examples of these institutions are the Northwest Michigan Maritime Museum (Frankfort, MI), Western Lake Erie Historical Society (Toledo), Fairport Harbor Historical Society (Ohio), Marine Collection at Lake Superior State University (Sault Ste. Marie, MI), Huronia Museum (Midland, ONT), and the Marine Transportation Unit of the Canadian National Museum of Science (Ottawa).

Other institutions—like the Smithsonian, the Great Lakes Historical Society (Vermilion, OH), and the Marine Museum of Upper Canada (Toronto)—had many unprocessed and uncataloged materials in their holdings at the time of my visit. As additional staff and circumstances allow, these backlogs may be made available to researchers and thus yield more corporate maritime transportation literature.

Two Montreal business libraries and archives, which probably have Great Lakes navigation paper, are not included in this work. Both the Canadian National and the Canadian Pacific operated fleets on America's freshwater inland seas. It is logical to assume, therefore, that the historical collections of these firms contain materials germane to this compilation. However, such repositories are not included in this book because, strictly speaking, they are not in the public domain.

I mention these omissions from this book so that users, not discovering what they seek herein, will know that they may someday find what they are looking for in the holdings of these various institutions. There are, of course, some major collections that are held by individuals, but they fall outside the scope of this union list. Hopefully, in years to come, some of these privately owned collections will be donated to public repositories so that all interested researchers will have access to them.

A number of sources were consulted in the course of preparing the capsule histories that follow the name of each firm included in this text. Those works that provided most of the data used in these sketches are as follows:

Ashdown, Dana. *Railway Steamships of Ontario.* Erin, ONT: Boston Mills Press, 1988.

Beeson, Harvey C. *Beeson's Marine Directory.* Chicago, IL, 1888-1921.

Elliot, James. *Red Stacks Over the Horizon.* Grand Rapids, MI: Eerdmans Publishing Company, 1967.

Freshwater Press, etc. *Great Lakes Red Book.* Cleveland, OH, 1904-1990.

Great Lakes Historical Society. *Inland Seas.* Vermilion, OH, 1945-1990.

Great Lakes Maritime Institute. *Telescope* [Magazine]. Detroit, MI, 1952-1990.

Great Lakes Publishing Company. *Great Lakes News.* Cleveland, OH, 1915-1948.

Greenwood, John. *Greenwood's Guide to Great Lakes Shipping.* Cleveland, OH: Freshwater Press, 1961-1990.

———. *Namesakes, 1900-1909.* Cleveland, OH: Freshwater Press, 1987.

———. *Namesakes, 1910-1919.* Cleveland, OH: Freshwater Press, 1986.

———. *Namesakes, 1920-1929.* Cleveland, OH: Freshwater Press, 1984.

———. *Namesakes, 1930-1955.* Cleveland, OH: Freshwater Press, 1978.

———. *Namesakes, 1956-1980.* Cleveland, OH: Freshwater Press, 1981.

———. *Namesakes II.* Cleveland, OH: Freshwater Press, 1973.

———. *Namesakes of the Lakes.* Cleveland: Freshwater Press, 1970.

Hilton, George. *The Great Lakes Car Ferries.* Berkeley, CA: Howell-North, 1962.

Lake Carriers' Association. *The Bulletin.* Cleveland, OH, 1911-1986.

Mansfield, John. *History of the Great Lakes.* Chicago, IL: J.H. Beers & Company, 1899.

Marine Historical Society of Detroit. *Detroit Marine Historian*. Detroit MI, 1947-1990.

Marine Publishing Company. *Great Lakes Journal*. Grand Haven, MI, 1931-1942.

Moody, John. *Moody's Industrial Manual*. New York, NY, 1954-1990.

———. *Moody's Manual of Investments: American and Foreign*. New York, NY, 1909-1954.

———. *Moody's Manual of Railroads*. New York, NY, 1900-1924.

———. *Moody's Transportation Manual*. New York, NY, 1954-1990.

Penton Publishing Company, etc. *Marine Review*. Cleveland, OH, 1890-1935.

Poor, Henry. *Poor's [Industrials and Railroads]*. New York, NY, 1925-1941.

———. *Poor's Manual of Industrials*. New York, NY, 1910-1918.

———. *Poor's Manual of Railroads*. New York, NY, 1868-1924.

Steamship Historical Society of America. *Steamboat Bill*. Baltimore, MD, 1940-1990.

Thompson, Mark. *Steamboats & Sailors of the Great Lakes*. Detroit, MI: Wayne State University Press, 1991.

Van der Linden, Peter. *Great Lakes Ships We Remember*. Cleveland, OH: Freshwater Press, 1979.

———. Great Lakes Ships we Remember II. Cleveland, OH: Freshwater Press, 1984.

Wright, Richard. *Freshwater Whales: A History of the American Ship Building Company*. Kent, OH: Kent State University Press, 1969.

INDEX

G

Gage Printing Company (Battle Creek, MI), 98, 99

Gagnier, Joseph S. (Detroit, MI), 126

Gananoque, ONT, 83

Garden City (SS, 1892-1936), 93

Gardner Printing Company (Cleveland, OH), 52

Garside and Mackie (Warrington, ENG), 36

Gartland Steamship Company (Chicago, IL), 69

Gates Legal Publishing Company (Cleveland, OH), 123

Gault, John C. (SS, 1881-1907), 82

Gazette Press (Niagara Falls, NY), 120

Gazette Print (Green Bay, WI), 78

Gazette Printing Company (Montreal, QUE), 31, 98, 114

Gazette Publishing Company (Green Bay, WI), 78

General Electric Company (Schenectady, NY), 54

General Printing Company (Chicago, IL), 40

General Printing Company (Pontiac, MI), 47

Georgian Bay, ONT, 11, 18, 42, 45, 46, 47, 48, 49, 50, 61, 62, 63, 65, 66, 67, 69, 70, 71, 81, 92, 94, 95, 96, 98, 99, 103, 104, 105, 116, 117, 118, 122, 134

Georgian Bay Line. See Chicago, Duluth & Georgian Bay Transit Company

Georgian Bay Navigation Company, Limited (Detroit, MI), 69

Georgian Bay Royal Mail Line (Collingwood, ONT), 94

Georgian Bay Tourist & Steamships, Limited (Penetang, ONT), 69, 70

Georgian Bay Tourist Company of Midland, Limited (Midland, ONT), 70

Gies & Company (Buffalo, NY), 52, 53, 99

Giles Litho[graphy] & Liberty Printing Company (New York, NY), 64

Gills Rock, WI, 124

Gilman, Arthur S. (Cleveland, OH), 109

Girard Trust Company (Philadelphia, PA), 68

Globe Book and Job Office (Toronto, ONT), 95

Globe Printing Company (Toronto, ONT), 95

Godenrath, Percy Francis (1875-1944), 23, 24, 25, 26

Goderich, ONT, 63, 95, 116

Goodrich Transit Company (Chicago, IL), 70-72, 88

Goodrich Transportation Company (Chicago, IL), 72

Gorr (Carl) Printing Company (Chicago, IL), 55, 97

Graham & Morton Transportation Company (Benton Harbor, MI), 72, 73

Grain, 144-146

Grand Central Art Galleries (New York, NY), 27

Grand Haven, MI, 39, 57, 70, 71, 108, 109, 128, 129, 139

Grand Hotel (Mackinac Island, MI), 41, 42, 62

Grand Marais, MI, 122

Grand Pointe (St. Clair Flats, MI), 117, 118

Grand Portage-Isle Royale Transportation Line, Incorporated (Duluth, MN), 73

Grand Rapids, MI, 39

Grand Rapids Chamber of Commerce (Grand Rapids, MI), 50

Grand Traverse Bay, MI, 121

Grand Trunk Milwaukee Car Ferry Company (Detroit, MI), 73, 74

Grand Trunk-Pennsylvania Transportation Company, 74

Grand Trunk Railway Company (Montreal, QUE), 34, 57, 65, 73, 76, 77, 83, 95, 98, 99, 112

Grand Trunk Western Railroad Company (Detroit, MI), 57, 73, 74, 90, 108

Graphic Arts Cruise, 44

Great Lakes Association of Marine Operators (Cleveland, OH), 48, 49

Great Lakes Cruise Bureau (Chicago, IL), 74

Great Lakes Litho Company (Cleveland, OH), 54

Great Lakes Steamship Company, Incorporated (Cleveland, OH), 74-75

Great Lakes Towing Company (Cleveland, OH), 75

Great Lakes Transit Company (Chicago, IL), 75

Great Lakes Transit Corporation (Buffalo, NY), 75-76

Great Northern Railway Company (St. Paul, MN), 99, 100

Great Northern Transit Company, Limited (Collingwood, ONT), 76-77

Great Western Railroad (Montreal, QUE), 65

Greater Buffalo (SS, 1923-1942), 60

Greater Detroit (SS, 1923-1957), 59, 60

Green Bay, WI, 49, 70, 71, 72, 78, 121

Green Bay & Minnesota Railway Company (Green Bay, WI), 121

Green Bay Transportation Company (Green Bay, WI), 77

Greene, Edward B[elden] (SS, 1952-1985), 55

Greenfield Village (Dearborn, MI), 42, 62, 63

Grenell, Judson (1847-1930), 125

Grey-Bruce Advertising (Meaford, ONT), 106

Grimsby, ONT, 21

Grinnell, Judson (1847-1930), 125

Grummond's Mackinac Line (Detroit, MI), 77

Guardian Savings & Trust Company (Cleveland, OH), 79

Gulley (Orin S.), Bornman & Company (Detroit, MI), 64, 65, 117, 118

Gulley Printing House (Detroit, MI), 64

Gunthorp-Warren Printing Company (Chicago, IL), 51, 95

Note: The ships listed in this index are Motor Vessels (MV), Motorships (MS), Steamships (SS), or Twin Screw Ships (TSS). The dates after the names of various vessels indicate the time period when the boat existed under that designation. If the ship was still afloat under its cited signature in 1990, then the word "date" (as in "to date") is given as the ending year. The dates after the names of individuals are their birth and death years, respectively.

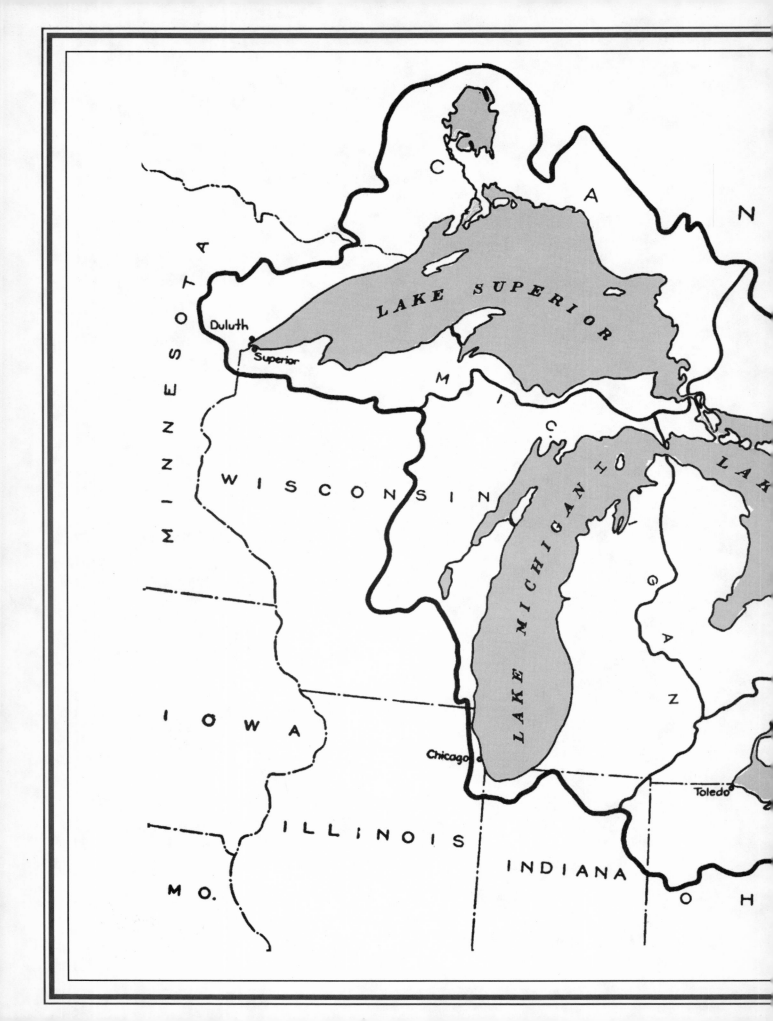